PASCAL

THE HARVARD CLASSICS
EDITED BY CHARLES W ELIOT LLD

BLAISE PASCAL

THOUGHTS
TRANSLATED BY W F TROTTER

LETTERS
TRANSLATED BY M L BOOTH

MINOR WORKS
TRANSLATED BY O W WIGHT

WITH INTRODUCTIONS AND NOTES

VOLUME 48

P F COLLIER & SON COMPANY
NEW YORK

Designed, Printed, and Bound at
The Collier Press, New York

CONTENTS

THOUGHTS

MINOR WORKS

NOTE

Passages erased by Pascal are enclosed in square brackets, thus [ ]. *Words,* added or corrected by the editor of the text, are similarly denoted. The translation is from the text of Brunschvicg.

INTRODUCTORY NOTE

BLAISE PASCAL *was born at Clermont in Auvergne on June 19, 1623, the son of the president of the Court of Aids of Clermont. He was a precocious child, and soon showed amazing mathematical talent. His early training was scientific rather than literary or theological, and scientific interests predominated during the first period of his activity. He corresponded with the most distinguished scholars of the time, and made important contributions to pure and applied mathematics and to physics.*

Meantime, an accident had brought the Pascal family into contact with Jansenist doctrine, and Blaise became an ardent convert. Jansenism, which took its name from Jansenius, the bishop of Ypres, had its headquarters in the Cistercian Abbey of Port-Royal, and was one of the most rigorous and lofty developments of post-Reformation Catholicism. In doctrine it somewhat resembled Calvinism in its insistence on Grace and Predestination at the expense of the freedom of the will, and in its cultivation of a thoroughgoing logical method of apologetics. In practise it represented an austere and even ascetic morality, and it did much to raise the ethical and intellectual level of seventeenth century France.

Jansenism was attacked as heretical, especially by the Jesuits; and the civil power ultimately took measures to crush the movement, disbanding the nuns of Port-Royal, and by its persecutions affording to many of the Jansenists opportunities for the display of a heroic obstinacy. In this struggle Pascal took an important part by the publication, under the pseudonym of "Louis de Montalte," of a series of eighteen letters, attacking the morality of the Jesuits and defending Jansenism against the charge of heresy. In spite of the fact that the party for which he fought was defeated, in these "Provincial Letters," as they are usually called, Pascal inflicted a blow on the Society of Jesus from which that order has never entirely recovered.

Pascal now formed the plan of writing an "Apology for the Christian Religion," and during the rest of his life he was collecting materials and making notes for this work. But he had long been feeble in health; in the ardor of his religious devotion he had undergone incredible hardships; and on August 19, 1662, he died in his fortieth year.

It was from the notes for his contemplated " Apology" that the Port-Royalists compiled and edited the book known as his "Pensées" or "Thoughts." The early texts were much tampered with, and the material has been frequently rearranged; but now at last it is possible to read these fragmentary jottings as they came from the hand of their author. In spite of their incompleteness and frequent incoherence, the " Thoughts" have long held a high place among the great religious classics. Much of the theological argument implied in these utterances has little appeal to the modern mind, but the acuteness of the observation of human life, the subtlety of the reasoning, the combination of precision and fervid imagination in the expression, make this a book to which the discerning mind can return again and again for insight and inspiration.

PASCAL'S THOUGHTS

SECTION I

Thoughts on Mind and on Style

I

THE difference between the mathematical and the intuitive mind.—In the one the principles are palpable, but removed from ordinary use; so that for want of habit it is difficult to turn one's mind in that direction: but if one turns it thither ever so little, one sees the principles fully, and one must have a quite inaccurate mind who reasons wrongly from principles so plain that it is almost impossible they should escape notice.

But in the intuitive mind the principles are found in common use, and are before the eyes of everybody. One has only to look, and no effort is necessary; it is only a question of good eyesight, but it must be good, for the principles are so subtle and so numerous, that it is almost impossible but that some escape notice. Now the omission of one principle leads to error; thus one must have very clear sight to see all the principles, and in the next place an accurate mind not to draw false deductions from known principles.

All mathematicians would then be intuitive if they had clear sight, for they do not reason incorrectly from principles known to them; and intuitive minds would be mathematical if they could turn their eyes to the principles of mathematics to which they are unused.

The reason, therefore, that some intuitive minds are not mathematical is that they cannot at all turn their attention to the principles of mathematics. But the reason that mathematicians are not intuitive is that they do not see what is before them, and that, accustomed to the exact and plain principles of mathematics, and not reasoning till they have well inspected and arranged their principles, they are lost in matters of intuition where the principles do not allow of such arrangement. They are scarcely seen; they are felt rather than seen; there is the greatest difficulty in making them felt by those who do not of themselves perceive them. These principles are so fine and so numerous that a very delicate and very clear sense is needed to perceive them, and to judge rightly and justly when they are perceived, without for the most part being able to demonstrate them in order as in mathematics; because the principles are not known to us in the same way, and because it would be an endless matter to undertake it. We must see the matter at once, at one glance, and not by a process of reasoning, at least to a certain degree. And thus it is rare that mathematicians are intuitive, and that men of intuition are mathematicians, because mathematicians wish to treat matters of intuition mathematically, and make themselves ridiculous, wishing to begin with definitions and then with axioms, which is not the way to proceed in this kind of reasoning. Not that the mind does not do so, but it does it tacitly, naturally, and without technical rules; for the expression of it is beyond all men, and only a few can feel it.

Intuitive minds, on the contrary, being thus accustomed to judge at a single glance, are so astonished when they are presented with propositions of which they understand nothing, and the way to which is through definitions and axioms so sterile, and which they are not accustomed to see thus in detail, that they are repelled and disheartened.

But dull minds are never either intuitive or mathematical.

Mathematicians who are only mathematicians have exact minds, provided all things are explained to them by means of definitions and axioms; otherwise they are inaccurate and insufferable, for they are only right when the principles are quite clear.

And men of intuition who are only intuitive cannot have the patience to reach to first principles of things speculative and conceptual, which they have never seen in the world, and which are altogether out of the common.

2

There are different kinds of right understanding; some have right understanding in a certain order of things, and not in others, where they go astray. Some draw conclusions well from a few premises, and this displays an acute judgment.

Others draw conclusions well where there are many premises.

For example, the former easily learn hydrostatics, where the premises are few, but the conclusions are so fine that only the greatest acuteness can reach them.

And in spite of that these persons would perhaps not be great mathematicians, because mathematics contain a great number of premises, and there is perhaps a kind of intellect that can search with ease a few premises to the bottom: and cannot in the least penetrate those matters in which there are many premises.

There are then two kinds of intellect: the one able to penetrate acutely and deeply into the conclusions of given premises, and this is the precise intellect; the other able to comprehend a great number of premises without confusing them, and this is the mathematical intellect. The one has force and exactness, the other comprehension. Now the one quality can exist without the other; the intellect can be strong and narrow, and can also be comprehensive and weak.

3

Those who are accustomed to judge by feeling do not understand the process of reasoning, for they would understand at first sight, and are not used to seek for principles. And others, on the contrary, who are accustomed to reason from principles, do not at all understand matters of feeling, seeking principles, and being unable to see at a glance.

4

Mathematics, Intuition.—True eloquence makes light of eloquence, true morality makes light of morality; that is to say, the morality of the judgment, which has no rules, makes light of the morality of the intellect.

For it is to judgment that perception belongs, as science belongs to intellect. Intuition is the part of judgment, mathematics of intellect.

To make light of philosophy is to be a true philosopher.

5

Those who judge of a work by rule are in regard to others as those who have a watch are in regard to others. One says, "It is two hours ago;" the other says, "It is only three-quarters of an hour." I look at my watch, and say to the one, "You are weary," and to the other, "Time gallops with you;" for it is only an hour and a half ago, and I laugh at those who tell me that time goes slowly with me, and that I judge by imagination. They do not know that I judge by my watch.

6

Just as we harm the understanding, we harm the feelings also.

The understanding and the feelings are moulded by intercourse; the understanding and feelings are corrupted by intercourse. Thus good or bad society improves or corrupts them. It is, then, all-important to know how to choose in order to improve and not to corrupt them; and we cannot make this choice, if they be not already improved and not corrupted. Thus a circle is formed, and those are fortunate who escape it.

7

The greater intellect one has, the more originality one finds in men. Ordinary persons find no difference between men.

8

There are many people who listen to a sermon in the same way as they listen to vespers.

9

When we wish to correct with advantage, and to show another that he errs, we must notice from what side he views the matter, for on that side it is usually true, and admit that truth to him, but reveal to him the side on which it is false. He is satisfied with that, for he sees that he was not mistaken, and that he only failed to see all sides. Now, no one is offended at not seeing everything; but one does not like to be mistaken, and that perhaps arises from the fact that man naturally cannot see everything, and that naturally he cannot err in the side he looks at, since the perceptions of our senses are always true.

10

People are generally better persuaded by the reasons which they have themselves discovered than by those which have come into the mind of others.

11

All great amusements are dangerous to the Christian life; but among all those which the world has invented there is none more to be feared than the theatre. It is a representation of the passions so natural and so delicate that it excites them and gives birth to them in our hearts, and, above all, to that of love, principally when it is represented as very chaste and virtuous. For the more innocent it appears to innocent souls, the more they are likely to be touched by it. Its violence pleases our self-love, which immediately forms a desire to produce the same effects which are seen so well represented; and, at the same time, we make ourselves a conscience founded on the propriety of the feelings which we see there, by which the fear of pure souls is removed, since they imagine that it

cannot hurt their purity to love with a love which seems
to them so reasonable.

So we depart from the theatre with our hearts so filled
with all the beauty and tenderness of love, the soul and the
mind so persuaded of its innocence, that we are quite
ready to receive its first impressions, or rather to seek an
opportunity of awakening them in the heart of another,
in order that we may receive the same pleasures and the
same sacrifices which we have seen so well represented in
the theatre.

12

Scaramouch,[1] who only thinks of one thing.

The doctor,[1] who speaks for a quarter of an hour after
he has said everything, so full is he of the desire of
talking.

13

One likes to see the error, the passion of Cleobuline,[2]
because she is unconscious of it. She would be displeasing, if she were not deceived.

14

When a natural discourse paints a passion or an effect,
one feels within oneself the truth of what one reads, which
was there before, although one did not know it. Hence
one is inclined to love him who makes us feel it, for he has
not shown us his own riches, but ours. And thus this benefit renders him pleasing to us, besides that such community
of intellect as we have with him necessarily inclines the
heart to love.

15

Eloquence, which persuades by sweetness, not by authority; as a tyrant, not as a king.

16

Eloquence is an art of saying things in such a way—
(1) that those to whom we speak may listen to them with-

[1] Stock characters in Italian comedy.
[2] Princess of Corinth, in Mlle. de Scudéry's romance of " Artamène ou le
grand Cyrus."

out pain and with pleasure; (2) that they feel themselves interested, so that self-love leads them more willingly to reflection upon it.

It consists, then, in a correspondence which we seek to establish between the head and the heart of those to whom we speak on the one hand, and, on the other, between the thoughts and the expressions which we employ. This assumes that we have studied well the heart of man so as to know all its powers, and then to find the just proportions of the discourse which we wish to adapt to them. We must put ourselves in the place of those who are to hear us, and make trial on our own heart of the turn which we give to our discourse in order to see whether one is made for the other, and whether we can assure ourselves that the hearer will be, as it were, forced to surrender. We ought to restrict ourselves, so far as possible, to the simple and natural, and not to magnify that which is little, or belittle that which is great. It is not enough that a thing be beautiful; it must be suitable to the subject, and there must be in it nothing of excess or defect.

17

Rivers are roads which move, and which carry us whither we desire to go.

18

When we do not know the truth of a thing, it is of advantage that there should exist a common error which determines the mind of man, as, for example, the moon, to which is attributed the change of seasons, the progress of disease, &c. For the chief malady of man is restless curiosity about things which he cannot understand; and it is not so bad for him to be in error as to be curious to no purpose.

The manner in which Epictetus, Montaigne, and Salomon de Tultie[3] wrote, is the most usual, the most suggestive, the most remembered, and the oftenest quoted; because it is entirely composed of thoughts born from the common talk of life. As when we speak of the common error which

[3] The name assumed by Pascal in his " Provincial Letters."

exists among men that the moon is the cause of everything, we never fail to say that Salomon de Tultie says
that when we do not know the truth of a thing, it is of
advantage that there should exist a common error, &c.;
which is the thought above.

19

The last thing one settles in writing a book is what one
should put in first.

20

Order.—Why should I undertake to divide my virtues
into four rather than into six? Why should I rather establish virtue in four, in two, in one? Why into *Abstine
et sustine*[*] rather than into "Follow Nature," or "Conduct
your private affairs without injustice," as Plato, or anything else? But there, you will say, everything is contained
in one word. Yes, but it is useless without explanation,
and when we come to explain it, as soon as we unfold this
maxim which contains all the rest, they emerge in that
first confusion which you desired to avoid. So, when
they are all included in one, they are hidden and useless,
as in a chest, and never appear save in their natural confusion. Nature has established them all without including
one in the other.

21

Nature has made all her truths independent of one another.
Our art makes one dependent on the other. But this is
not natural. Each keeps its own place.

22

Let no one say that I have said nothing new; the arrangement of the subject is new. When we play tennis, we
both play with the same ball, but one of us places it better.
    I had as soon it said that I used words employed before.
And in the same way if the same thoughts in a different
arrangement do not form a different discourse, no more do

[*] "Abstain and endure "—a Stoic maxim.

the same words in their different arrangement form different thoughts!

23

Words differently arranged have a different meaning, and meanings differently arranged have different effects.

24

Language.—We should not turn the mind from one thing to another, except for relaxation, and that when it is necessary and the time suitable, and not otherwise. For he that relaxes out of season wearies, and he who wearies us out of season makes us languid, since we turn quite away. So much does our perverse lust like to do the contrary of what those wish to obtain from us without giving us pleasure, the coin for which we will do whatever is wanted.

25

Eloquence.—It requires the pleasant and the real; but the pleasant must itself be drawn from the true.

26

Eloquence is a painting of thought; and thus those who, after having painted it, add something more, make a picture instead of a portrait.

27

Miscellaneous. Language.—Those who make antitheses by forcing words are like those who make false windows for symmetry. Their rule is not to speak accurately, but to make apt figures of speech.

28

Symmetry is what we see at a glance; based on the fact that there is no reason for any difference, and based also on the face of man; whence it happens that symmetry is only wanted in breadth, not in height or depth.

29

When we see a natural style, we are astonished and delighted; for we expected to see an author, and we find a man. Whereas those who have good taste, and who seeing a book expect to find a man, are quite surprised to find an author. *Plus poetice quam humane locutus es.*[5] Those honour nature well, who teach that she can speak on everything, even on theology.

30

We only consult the ear because the heart is wanting. The rule is uprightness.

Beauty of omission, of judgment.

31

All the false beauties which we blame in Cicero have their admirers, and in great number.

32

There is a certain standard of grace and beauty which consists in a certain relation between our nature, such as it is, weak or strong, and the thing which pleases us.

Whatever is formed according to this standard pleases us, be it house, song, discourse, verse, prose, woman, birds, rivers, tree, rooms, dress, &c. Whatever is not made according to this standard displeases those who have good taste.

And as there is a perfect relation between a song and a house which are made after a good model because they are like this good model, though each after its kind; even so there is a perfect relation between things made after a bad model. Not that the bad model is unique, for there are many; but each bad sonnet, for example, on whatever false model it is formed, is just like a woman dressed after that model.

[5] " You have spoken more poetically than humanly."

Nothing makes us understand better the ridiculousness of a false sonnet than to consider nature and the standard, and then to imagine a woman or a house made according to that standard.

33

Poetical beauty.—As we speak of poetical beauty, so ought we to speak of mathematical beauty and medical beauty. But we do not do so; and the reason is that we know well what is the object of mathematics, and that it consists in proofs, and what is the object of medicine, and that it consists in healing. But we do not know in what grace consists, which is the object of poetry. We do not know the natural model which we ought to imitate; and through lack of this knowledge, we have coined fantastic terms, " The golden age," " The wonder of our times," " Fatal," &c., and call this jargon poetical beauty.

But whoever imagines a woman after this model, which consists in saying little things in big words, will see a pretty girl adorned with mirrors and chains, at whom he will smile; because we know better wherein consists the charm of woman than the charm of verse. But those who are ignorant would admire her in this dress, and there are many villages in which she would be taken for the queen; hence we call sonnets made after this model " Village Queens."

34

No one passes in the world as skilled in verse unless he has put up the sign of a poet, a mathematician, &c. But educated people do not want a sign, and draw little distinction between the trade of a poet and that of an embroiderer.

People of education are not called poets or mathematicians, &c.; but they are all these, and judges of all these. No one guesses what they are. When they come into society, they talk on matters about which the rest are talking. We do not observe in them one quality rather than another, save when they have to make use of it. But then we remember it, for it is characteristic of such persons that we do not say of them that they are fine speakers, when it is not a question of oratory, and that we say of them that they are fine speakers, when it is such a question.

It is therefore false praise to give a man when we say of him, on his entry, that he is a very clever poet; and it is a bad sign when a man is not asked to give his judgment on some verses.

35

We should not be able to say of a man, "He is a mathematician," or a "preacher," or "eloquent"; but that he is "a gentleman." That universal quality alone pleases me. It is a bad sign when, on seeing a person, you remember his book. I would prefer you to see no quality till you meet it and have occasion to use it, (*Ne quid nimis,*[6]) for fear some one quality prevail and designate the man. Let none think him a fine speaker, unless oratory be in question, and then let them think it.

36

Man is full of wants: he loves only those who can satisfy them all. "This one is a good mathematician," one will say. But I have nothing to do with mathematics; he would take me for a proposition. "That one is a good soldier." He would take me for a besieged town. I need then an upright man who can accommodate himself generally to all my wants.

37

Since we cannot be universal and know all that is to be known of everything, we ought to know a little about everything. For it is far better to know something about everything than to know all about one thing. This universality is the best. If we can have both, still better; but if we must choose, we ought to choose the former. And the world feels this and does so; for the world is often a good judge.

38

A poet and not an honest man.

[6] "Nothing in excess."

39

If lightning fell on low places, &c., poets, and those who can only reason about things of that kind, would lack proofs.

40

If we wished to prove the examples which we take to prove other things, we should have to take those other things to be examples; for, as we always believe the difficulty is in what we wish to prove, we find the examples clearer and a help to demonstration.

Thus when we wish to demonstrate a general theorem, we must give the rule as applied to a particular case; but if we wish to demonstrate a particular case, we must begin with the general rule. For we always find the thing obscure which we wish to prove, and that clear which we use for the proof; for, when a thing is put forward to be proved, we first fill ourselves with the imagination that it is therefore obscure, and on the contrary that what is to prove it is clear, and so we understand it easily.

41

Epigrams of Martial.—Man loves malice, but not against one-eyed men nor the unfortunate, but against the fortunate and proud. People are mistaken in thinking otherwise.

For lust is the source of all our actions, and humanity, &c. We must please those who have humane and tender feeling. That epigram about two one-eyed people is worthless, for it does not console them, and only gives a point to the author's glory. All that is only for the sake of the author is worthless. *Ambitiosa recident ornamenta.*[7]

42

To call a king " Prince " is pleasing, because it diminishes his rank.

[7] " They cut off superfluous ornament "—Horace.

43

Certain authors, speaking of their works, say, " My
book," " My commentary," " My history," &c. They resemble middle-class people who have a house of their own,
and always have " My house " on their tongue. They would
do better to say, " Our book" " Our commentary," " Our
history," &c., because there is in them usually more of other
people's than their own.

44

Do you wish people to believe good of you? Don't speak.

45

Languages are ciphers, wherein letters are not changed
into letters, but words into words, so that an unknown
language is decipherable.

46

A maker of witticisms, a bad character.

47

There are some who speak well and write badly. For
the place and the audience warm them, and draw from their
minds more than they think of without that warmth.

48

When we find words repeated in a discourse, and, in trying to correct them, discover that they are so appropriate
that we would spoil the discourse, we must leave them
alone. This is the test; and our attempt is the work of
envy, which is blind, and does not see that repetition is
not in this place a fault; for there is no general rule.

49

To mask nature and disguise her. No more king, pope,
bishop,—but *august monarch*, &c.; not Paris,—*the capital
of the kingdom*. There are places in which we ought to call

Paris, Paris, and others in which we ought to call it the capital of the kingdom.

50

The same meaning changes with the words which express it. Meanings receive their dignity from words instead of giving it to them. Examples should be sought.

51

Sceptic, for obstinate.

52

No one calls another a Cartesian but he who is not one himself, a pedant but a pedant, a provincial but a provincial; and I would wager it was the printer who put it on the title of *Letters to a Provincial*.

53

A carriage *upset* or *overturned,* according to the meaning. *To spread abroad* or *upset,* according to the meaning. (The argument by force of M. le Maître over the friar.)

54

Miscellaneous.—A form of speech, "I should have liked to apply myself to that."

55

The *aperitive* virtue of a key, the *attractive* virtue of a hook.

56

To guess: "The part that I take in your trouble." The Cardinal[8] did not want to be guessed.
"My mind is disquieted." I am disquieted is better.

57

I always feel uncomfortable under such compliments as these: "I have given you a great deal of trouble," "I am afraid I am boring you," "I fear this is too long." We either carry our audience with us, or irritate them.

[8] Cardinal Mazarin.

58

You are ungraceful: "Excuse me, pray." Without that excuse I would not have known there was anything amiss. "With reverence be it spoken . . ." The only thing bad is their excuse.

59

"To extinguish the torch of sedition;" too luxuriant. "The restlessness of his genius;" two superfluous grand words.

THE MISERY OF MAN WITHOUT GOD

60

FIRST part: Misery of man without God.
      Second part: Happiness of man with God.
    Or, First part: That nature is corrupt. Proved by
        nature itself.
Second part: That there is a Redeemer. Proved by
        Scripture.

61

Order.—I might well have taken this discourse in an order like this; to show the vanity of all conditions of men, to show the vanity of ordinary lives, and then the vanity of philosophic lives, sceptics, stoics; but the order would not have been kept. I know a little what it is, and how few people understand it. No human science can keep it. Saint Thomas did not keep it. Mathematics keep it, but they are useless on account of their depth.

62

Preface to the first part.—To speak of those who have treated of the knowledge of self; of the divisions of Charron, which sadden and weary us; of the confusion of Montaigne; that he was quite aware of his want of method, and shunned it by jumping from subject to subject; that he sought to be fashionable.

His foolish project of describing himself! And this not casually and against his maxims, since every one makes mistakes, but by his maxims themselves, and by first and chief design. For to say silly things by chance and weakness is a common misfortune; but to say them intentionally is intolerable, and to say such as that . . .

63

Montaigne.—Montaigne's faults are great. Lewd words; this is bad, notwithstanding Mademoiselle de Gournay.[1] Credulous; *people without eyes.* Ignorant; *squaring the circle, a greater world.* His opinions on suicide, on death. He suggests an indifference about salvation, *without fear and without repentance.* As his book was not written with a religious purpose, he was not bound to mention religion; but it is always our duty not to turn men from it. One can excuse his rather free and licentious opinions on some relations of life (730, 231); but one cannot excuse his thoroughly pagan views on death, for a man must renounce piety altogether, if he does not at least wish to die like a Christian. Now, through the whole of his book his only conception of death is a cowardly and effeminate one.

64

It is not in Montaigne, but in myself, that I find all that I see in him.

65

What good there is in Montaigne can only have been acquired with difficulty. The evil that is in him, I mean apart from his morality, could have been corrected in a moment, if he had been informed that he made too much of trifles and spoke too much of himself.

66

One must know oneself. If this does not serve to discover truth, it at least serves as a rule of life, and there is nothing better.

67

The vanity of the sciences.—Physical science will not console me for the ignorance of morality in the time of affliction. But the science of ethics will always console me for the ignorance of the physical sciences.

[1] Montaigne's adopted daughter, who defends him in a Preface which she added to his Essays.

68

Men are never taught to be gentlemen, and are taught everything else; and they never plume themselves so much on the rest of their knowledge as on knowing how to be gentlemen. They only plume themselves on knowing the one thing they do not know.

69

The infinites, the mean.—When we read too fast or too slowly, we understand nothing.

70

Nature . . . —[Nature has set us so well in the centre, that if we change one side of the balance, we change the other also. *I act. Τά ζῶα τρέχει.*[2] This makes me believe that the springs in our brain are so adjusted that he who touches one touches also its contrary.]

71

Too much and too little wine. Give him none, he cannot find truth; give him too much, the same.

72

Man's disproportion.—[This is where our innate knowledge leads us. If it be not true, there is no truth in man; and if it be true, he finds therein great cause for humiliation, being compelled to abase himself in one way or another. And since he cannot exist without this knowledge, I wish that, before entering on deeper researches into nature, he would consider her both seriously and at leisure, that he would reflect upon himself also, and knowing what proportion there is . . . .] Let man then contemplate the whole of nature in her full and grand majesty, and turn his vision from the low objects which surround him. Let him gaze on that brilliant light, set like an eternal lamp to illumine

[2] " Animals run."

the universe; let the earth appear to him a point in comparison with the vast circle described by the sun; and let him
wonder at the fact that this vast circle is itself but a very
fine point in comparison with that described by the stars in
their revolution round the firmament. But if our view be
arrested there, let our imagination pass beyond; it will sooner
exhaust the power of conception than nature that of supply-
ing material for conception. The whole visible world is
only an imperceptible atom in the ample bosom of nature.
No idea approaches it. We may enlarge our conceptions
beyond all imaginable space; we only produce atoms in comparison with the reality of things. It is an infinite sphere,
the centre of which is everywhere, the circumference nowhere. In short it is the greatest sensible mark of the
almighty power of God, that imagination loses itself in that
thought.

Returning to himself, let man consider what he is in
comparison with all existence; let him regard himself as
lost in this remote corner of nature; and from the little cell
in which he finds himself lodged, I mean the universe, let
him estimate at their true value the earth, kingdoms, cities,
and himself. What is a man in the Infinite?

But to show him another prodigy equally astonishing, let
him examine the most delicate things he knows. Let a mite
be given him, with its minute body and parts incomparably
more minute, limbs with their joints, veins in the limbs,
blood in the veins, humours in the blood, drops in the
humours, vapours in the drops. Dividing these last things
again, let him exhaust his powers of conception, and let
the last object at which he can arrive be now that of our
discourse. Perhaps he will think that here is the smallest
point in nature. I will let him see therein a new abyss. I
will paint for him not only the visible universe, but all that
he can conceive of nature's immensity in the womb of this
abridged atom. Let him see therein an infinity of universes,
each of which has its firmament, its planets, its earth, in the
same proportion as in the visible world; in each earth animals, and in the last mites, in which he will find again all
that the first had, finding still in these others the same thing
without end and without cessation. Let him lose himself in

wonders as amazing in their littleness as the others in their vastness. For who will not be astounded at the fact that our body, which a little ago was imperceptible in the universe, itself imperceptible in the bosom of the whole, is now a colossus, a world, or rather a whole, in respect of the nothingness which we cannot reach? He who regards himself in this light will be afraid of himself, and observing himself sustained in the body given him by nature between those two abysses of the Infinite and Nothing, will tremble at the sight of these marvels; and I think that, as his curiosity changes into admiration, he will be more disposed to contemplate them in silence than to examine them with presumption.

For in fact what is man in nature? A Nothing in comparison with the Infinite, an All in comparison with the Nothing, a mean between nothing and everything. Since he is infinitely removed from comprehending the extremes, the end of things and their beginning are hopelessly hidden from him in an impenetrable secret; he is equally incapable of seeing the Nothing from which he was made, and the Infinite in which he is swallowed up.

What will he do then, but perceive the appearance of the middle of things, in an eternal despair of knowing either their beginning or their end. All things proceed from the Nothing, and are borne towards the Infinite. Who will follow these marvellous processes? The Author of these wonders understands them. None other can do so.

Through failure to contemplate these Infinites, men have rashly rushed into the examination of nature, as though they bore some proportion to her. It is strange that they have wished to understand the beginnings of things, and thence to arrive at the knowledge of the whole, with a presumption as infinite as their object. For surely this design cannot be formed without presumption or without a capacity infinite like nature.

If we are well-informed, we understand that, as nature has graven her image and that of her Author on all things, they almost all partake of her double infinity. Thus we see that all the sciences are infinite in the extent of their researches. For who doubts that geometry, for instance, has

an infinite infinity of problems to solve? They are also infinite in the multitude and fineness of their premises; for it
is clear that those which are put forward as ultimate are not
self-supporting, but are based on others which, again having
others for their support, do not permit of finality. But
we represent some as ultimate for reason, in the same way
as in regard to material objects we call that an indivisible
point beyond which our senses can no longer perceive anything, although by its nature it is infinitely divisible.

Of these two Infinites of science, that of greatness is the
most palpable, and hence a few persons have pretended
to know all things. "I will speak of the whole," said
Democritus.

But the infinitely little is the least obvious. Philosophers
have much oftener claimed to have reached it, and it is
here they have all stumbled. This has given rise to such
common titles as *First Principles, Principles of Philosophy,*
and the like, as ostentatious in fact, though not in appearance, as that one which blinds us, *De omni scibili.*[3]

We naturally believe ourselves far more capable of reaching the centre of things than of embracing their circumference. The visible extent of the world visibly exceeds us,
but as we exceed little things, we think ourselves more capable of knowing them. And yet we need no less capacity for
attaining the Nothing than the All. Infinite capacity is
required for both, and it seems to me that whoever shall
have understood the ultimate principles of being might also
attain to the knowledge of the Infinite. The one depends
on the other, and one leads to the other. These extremes
meet and reunite by force of distance, and find each other
in God, and in God alone.

Let us then take our compass; we are something, and we
are not everything. The nature of our existence hides from
us the knowledge of first beginnings which are born of the
Nothing; and the littleness of our being conceals from us
the sight of the Infinite.

Our intellect holds the same position in the world of
thought as our body occupies in the expanse of nature.

[3] " Concerning everything knowable "—the title under which Pico della
Mirandola announced the 900 propositions which he undertook to defend
in 1486.

Limited as we are in every way, this state which holds the mean between two extremes is present in all our impotence. Our senses perceive no extreme. Too much sound deafens us; too much light dazzles us; too great distance or proximity hinders our view. Too great length and too great brevity of discourse tend to obscurity; too much truth is paralysing; (I know some who cannot understand that to take four from nothing leaves nothing). First principles are too self-evident for us; too much pleasure disagrees with us. Too many concords are annoying in music; too many benefits irritate us; we wish to have the wherewithal to over-pay our debts. *Beneficia eo usque læta sunt dum videntur exsolvi posse; ubi multum antevenere, pro gratia odium redditur.*[4] We feel neither extreme heat nor extreme cold. Excessive qualities are prejudicial to us and not perceptible by the senses; we do not feel but suffer them. Extreme youth and extreme age hinder the mind, as also too much and too little education. In short, extremes are for us as though they were not, and we are not within their notice. They escape us, or we them.

This is our true state; this is what makes us incapable of certain knowledge and of absolute ignorance. We sail within a vast sphere, ever drifting in uncertainty, driven from end to end. When we think to attach ourselves to any point and to fasten to it, it wavers and leaves us; and if we follow it, it eludes our grasp, slips past us, and vanishes for ever. Nothing stays for us. This is our natural condition, and yet most contrary to our inclination; we burn with desire to find solid ground and an ultimate sure foundation whereon to build a tower reaching to the Infinite. But our whole groundwork cracks, and the earth opens to abysses.

Let us therefore not look for certainty and stability. Our reason is always deceived by fickle shadows; nothing can fix the finite between the two Infinites, which both enclose and fly from it.

If this be well understood, I think that we shall remain at rest, each in the state wherein nature has placed him.

[4] " Benefits are pleasant while it seems possible to requite them; when they become much greater, they produce hatred rather than gratitude."— Tacitus.

As this sphere which has fallen to us as our lot is always distant from either extreme, what matters it that man should have a little more knowledge of the universe? If he has it, he but gets a little higher. Is he not always infinitely removed from the end, and is not the duration of our life equally removed from eternity, even if it lasts ten years longer?

In comparison with these Infinites all finites are equal, and I see no reason for fixing our imagination on one more than on another. The only comparison which we make of ourselves to the finite is painful to us.

If man made himself the first object of study, he would see how incapable he is of going further. How can a part know the whole? But he may perhaps aspire to know at least the parts to which he bears some proportion. But the parts of the world are all so related and linked to one another, that I believe it impossible to know one without the other and without the whole.

Man, for instance, is related to all he knows. He needs a place wherein to abide, time through which to live, motion in order to live, elements to compose him, warmth and food to nourish him, air to breathe. He sees light; he feels bodies; in short, he is in a dependant alliance with everything. To know man, then, it is necessary to know how it happens that he needs air to live, and, to know the air, we must know how it is thus related to the life of man, etc. Flame cannot exist without air; therefore to understand the one, we must understand the other.

Since everything then is cause and effect, dependant and supporting, mediate and immediate, and all is held together by a natural though imperceptible chain, which binds together things most distant and most different, I hold it equally impossible to know the parts without knowing the whole, and to know the whole without knowing the parts in detail.

[The eternity of things in itself or in God must also astonish our brief duration. The fixed and constant immobility of nature, in comparison with the continual change which goes on within us, must have the same effect.]

And what completes our incapability of knowing things,

is the fact that they are simple, and that we are composed of two opposite natures, different in kind, soul and body. For it is impossible that our rational part should be other than spiritual; and if any one maintain that we are simply corporeal, this would far more exclude us from the knowledge of things, there being nothing so inconceivable as to say that matter knows itself. It is impossible to imagine how it should know itself.

So if we are simply material, we can know nothing at all; and if we are composed of mind and matter, we cannot know perfectly things which are simple, whether spiritual or corporeal. Hence it comes that almost all philosophers have confused ideas of things, and speak of material things in spiritual terms, and of spiritual things in material terms. For they say boldly that bodies have a tendency to fall, that they seek after their centre, that they fly from destruction, that they fear the void, that they have inclinations, sympathies, antipathies, all of which attributes pertain only to mind. And in speaking of minds, they consider them as in a place, and attribute to them movement from one place to another; and these are qualities which belong only to bodies.

Instead of receiving the ideas of these things in their purity, we colour them with our own qualities, and stamp with our composite being all the simple things which we contemplate.

Who would not think, seeing us compose all things of mind and body, but that this mixture would be quite intelligible to us? Yet it is the very thing we least understand. Man is to himself the most wonderful object in nature; for he cannot conceive what the body is, still less what the mind is, and least of all how a body should be united to a mind. This is the consummation of his difficulties, and yet it is his very being. *Modus quo corporibus adhærent spiritus comprehendi ab hominibus non potest, et hoc tamen homo est.*[5] Finally, to complete the proof of our weakness, I shall conclude with these two considerations . . .

---

[5] "The manner in which spirits are united to bodies cannot be understood by men, yet such is man."—St. Augustine.

73

[But perhaps this subject goes beyond the capacity of reason. Let us therefore examine her solutions to problems within her powers. If there be anything to which her own interest must have made her apply herself most seriously, it is the inquiry into her own sovereign good. Let us see, then, wherein these strong and clear-sighted souls have placed it, and whether they agree.

One says that the sovereign good consists in virtue, another in pleasure, another in the knowledge of nature, another in truth, *Felix qui potuit rerum cognoscere causas,*[6] another in total ignorance, another in indolence, others in disregarding appearances, another in wondering at nothing, *nihil admirari prope res una quæ possit facere et servare beatum,*[7] and the true sceptics in their indifference, doubt, and perpetual suspense, and others, wiser, think to find a better definition. We are well satisfied.

To transpose after the laws to the following title.

We must see if this fine philosophy have gained nothing certain from so long and so intent study; perhaps at least the soul will know itself. Let us hear the rulers of the world on this subject. What have they thought of her substance? 394.[8] Have they been more fortunate in locating her? 395. What have they found out about her origin, duration, and departure? 399.[8]

Is then the soul too noble a subject for their feeble lights? Let us then abase her to matter and see if she knows whereof is made the very body which she animates, and those others which she contemplates and moves at her will. What have those great dogmatists, who are ignorant of nothing, known of this matter? *Harum sententiarum,* 393.[8]

This would doubtless suffice, if reason were reasonable. She is reasonable enough to admit that she has been unable to find anything durable, but she does not yet despair of reaching it; she is as ardent as ever in this search, and is confident she has within her the necessary powers for this

---

[6] " Happy he who could understand the causes of things."—Virgil.
[7] " To wonder at nothing is almost the only thing which can make and keep a man happy."—Horace.
[8] References to Montaigne's Essays, ii. 12.

conquest. We must therefore conclude, and, after having examined her powers in their effects, observe them in themselves, and see if she has a nature and a grasp capable of laying hold of the truth.]

74

A letter *on the foolishness of human knowledge and philosophy*.
This letter before *Diversion*.
Felix qui potuit . . . *Nihil admirari.*
280 kinds of sovereign good in Montaigne.

75

Part I., 1, 2, c. 1, section 4.
[*Probability.*—it will not be difficult to put the case a stage lower, and make it appear ridiculous. To begin at the very beginning.] What is more absurd than to say that lifeless bodies have passions, fears, hatreds,—that insensible bodies, lifeless and incapable of life, have passions which presuppose at least a sensitive soul to feel them, nay more, that the object of their dread is the void? What is there in the void that could make them afraid? Nothing is more shallow and ridiculous. This is not all; it is said that they have in themselves a source of movement to shun the void. Have they arms, legs, muscles, nerves?

76

To write against those who made too profound a study of science. Descartes.

77

I cannot forgive Descartes. In all his philosophy he would have been quite willing to dispense with God. But he had to make Him give a fillip to set the world in motion; beyond this, he has no further need of God.

78

Descartes useless and uncertain.

79

[*Descartes.*—We must say summarily: "This is made by figure and motion," for it is true. But to say what these are, and to compose the machine, is ridiculous. For it is useless, uncertain, and painful. And were it true, we do not think all philosophy is worth one hour of pain.]

80

How comes it that a cripple does not offend us, but that a fool does? Because a cripple recognizes that we walk straight, whereas a fool declares that it is we who are silly; if it were not so, we should feel pity and not anger.

Epictetus asks still more strongly: "Why are we not angry if we are told that we have a headache, and why are we angry if we are told that we reason badly, or choose wrongly?" The reason is that we are quite certain that we have not a headache, or are not lame, but we are not so sure that we make a true choice. So having assurance only because we see with our whole sight, it puts us into suspense and surprise when another with his whole sight sees the opposite, and still more so when a thousand others deride our choice. For we must prefer our own lights to those of so many others, and that is bold and difficult. There is never this contradiction in the feelings towards a cripple.

81

It is natural for the mind to believe, and for the will to love; so that, for want of true objects, they must attach themselves to false.

82

Imagination.—It is that deceitful part in man, that mistress of error and falsity, the more deceptive that she is not always so; for she would be an infallible rule of truth, if she were an infallible rule of falsehood. But being most generally false, she gives no sign of her nature, impressing the same character on the true and the false.

I do not speak of fools, I speak of the wisest men; and it

is among them that the imagination has the great gift of persuasion. Reason protests in vain; it cannot set a true value on things.

This arrogant power, the enemy of reason, who likes to rule and dominate it, has established in man a second nature to show how all-powerful she is. She makes men happy and sad, healthy and sick, rich and poor; she compels reason to believe, doubt, and deny; she blunts the senses, or quickens them; she has her fools and sages; and nothing vexes us more than to see that she fills her devotees with a satisfaction far more full and entire than does reason. Those who have a lively imagination are a great deal more pleased with themselves than the wise can reasonably be. They look down upon men with haughtiness; they argue with boldness and confidence, others with fear and diffidence; and this gaiety of countenance often gives them the advantage in the opinion of the hearers, such favour have the imaginary wise in the eyes of judges of like nature. Imagination cannot make fools wise; but she can make them happy, to the envy of reason which can only make its friends miserable; the one covers them with glory, the other with shame.

What but this faculty of imagination dispenses reputation, awards respect and veneration to persons, works, laws, and the great? How insufficient are all the riches of the earth without her consent!

Would you not say that this magistrate, whose venerable age commands the respect of a whole people, is governed by pure and lofty reason, and that he judges causes according to their true nature without considering those mere trifles which only affect the imagination of the weak? See him go to sermon, full of devout zeal, strengthening his reason with the ardour of his love. He is ready to listen with exemplary respect. Let the preacher appear, and let nature have given him a hoarse voice or a comical cast of countenance, or let his barber have given him a bad shave, or let by chance his dress be more dirtied than usual, then however great the truths he announces, I wager our senator lose his gravity.

If the greatest philosopher in the world find himself upon a plank wider than actually necessary, but hanging over a precipice, his imagination will prevail, though his reason convince him of his safety. Many cannot bear the thought without a cold sweat. I will not state all its effects.

Every one knows that the sight of cats or rats, the crushing of a coal, etc., may unhinge the reason. The tone of voice affects the wisest, and changes the force of a discourse or a poem.

Love or hate alters the aspect of justice. How much greater confidence has an advocate, retained with a large fee, in the justice of his cause! How much better does his bold manner make his case appear to the judges, deceived as they are by appearances! How ludicrous is reason, blown with a breath in every direction!

I should have to enumerate almost every action of men who scarce waver save under her assaults. For reason has been obliged to yield, and the wisest reason takes as her own principles those which the imagination of man has everywhere rashly introduced. [He ⸴who would follow reason only would be deemed foolish by the generality of men. We must judge by the opinion of the majority of mankind. Because it has pleased them, we must work all day for pleasures seen to be imaginary; and after sleep has refreshed our tired reason, we must forthwith start up and rush after phantoms, and suffer the impressions of this mistress of the world. This is one of the sources of error, but it is not the only one.]

Our magistrates have known well this mystery. Their red robes, the ermine in which they wrap themselves like furry cats, the courts in which they administer justice, the *fleurs-de-lis,* and all such august apparel were necessary; if the physicians had not their cassocks and their mules, if the doctors had not their square caps and their robes four times too wide, they would never have duped the world, which cannot resist so original an appearance. If magistrates had true justice, and if physicians had the true art of healing, they would have no occasion for square caps; the majesty of these sciences would of itself be venerable enough. But having only imaginary knowledge, they must employ those silly tools that strike the imagination with which they have to deal; and thereby in fact they inspire respect. Soldiers alone are not disguised in this manner, because indeed their part is the most essential; they establish themselves by force, the others by show.

Therefore our kings seek out no disguises. They do not mask themselves in extraordinary costumes to appear such; but they are accompanied by guards and halberdiers. Those armed and red-faced puppets who have hands and power for them alone, those trumpets and drums which go before them, and those legions round about them, make the stoutest tremble. They have not dress only, they have might. A very refined reason is required to regard as an ordinary man the Grand Turk, in his superb seraglio, surrounded by forty thousand janissaries.

We cannot even see an advocate in his robe and with his cap on his head, without a favourable opinion of his ability. The imagination disposes of everything; it makes beauty, justice, and happiness, which is everything in the world. I should much like to see an Italian work, of which I only know the title, which alone is worth many books, *Della opinione regina del mondo*.[9] I approve of the book without knowing it, save the evil in it, if any. These are pretty much the effects of that deceptive faculty, which seems to have been expressly given us to lead us into necessary error. We have, however, many other sources of error.

Not only are old impressions capable of misleading us; the charms of novelty have the same power. Hence arise all the disputes of men, who taunt each other either with following the false impressions of childhood, or with running rashly after the new. Who keeps the due mean? Let him appear and prove it. There is no principle, however natural to us from infancy, which may not be made to pass for a false impression either of education or of sense.

"Because," say some, "you have believed from childhood that a box was empty when you saw nothing in it, you have believed in the possibility of a vacuum. This is an illusion of your senses, strengthened by custom, which science must correct." "Because," say others, "you have been taught at school that there is no vacuum, you have perverted your

---

[9] "On opinion, queen of the world." The book has not been certainly identified.

common sense which clearly comprehended it, and you must
correct this by returning to your first state." Which has
deceived you, your senses or your education?

We have another source of error in diseases. They spoil
the judgment and the senses; and if the more serious
produce a sensible change, I do not doubt that slighter ills
produce a proportionate impression.

Our own interest is again a marvellous instrument for
nicely putting out our eyes. The justest man in the world
is not allowed to be judge in his own cause; I know some
who, in order not to fall into this self-love, have been perfectly unjust out of opposition. The sure way of losing a
just cause has been to get it recommended to these men by
their near relatives.

Justice and truth are two such subtle points, that our
tools are too blunt to touch them accurately. If they reach
the point, they either crush it, or lean all round, more on
the false than on the true.

[Man is so happily formed that he has no . . . good of
the true, and several excellent of the false. Let us now see
how much . . . But the most powerful cause of error is
the war existing between the senses and reason.]

83

We must thus begin the chapter on the deceptive powers.
Man is only a subject full of error, natural and ineffaceable,
without grace. Nothing shows him the truth. Everything
deceives him. These two sources of truth, reason and the
senses, besides being both wanting in sincerity, deceive each
other in turn. The senses mislead the reason with false
appearances, and receive from reason in their turn the same
trickery which they apply to her; reason has her revenge.
The passions of the soul trouble the senses, and make false
impressions upon them. They rival each other in falsehood
and deception.

But besides those errors which arise accidentally and
through lack of intelligence, with these heterogeneous
faculties . . .

84

The imagination enlarges little objects so as to fill our soul with a fantastic estimate; and, with rash insolence, it belittles the great to its own measure, as when talking of God.

85

Things which have most hold on us, as the concealment of our few possessions, are often a mere nothing. It is a nothing which our imagination magnifies into a mountain. Another turn of the imagination would make us discover this without difficulty.

86

[My fancy makes me hate a croaker, and one who pants when eating. Fancy has great weight. Shall we profit by it? Shall we yield to this weight because it is natural? No, but by resisting it. . . .]

87

Quasi quidquam infelicius sit homini cui sua figmenta dominantur [10] (Plin.)

88

Children who are frightened at the face they have blackened are but children. But how shall one who is so weak in his childhood become really strong when he grows older? We only change our fancies. All that is made perfect by progress perishes also by progress. All that has been weak can never become absolutely strong. We say in vain, "He has grown, he has changed"; he is also the same.

89

Custom is our nature. He who is accustomed to the faith believes in it, can no longer fear hell, and believes in nothing else. He who is accustomed to believe that the king is terrible . . . &c. Who doubts then that our soul, being ac-

---

[10] "As if anything more unfortunate could happen to a man ruled by his own fancies."

customed to see number, space, motion, believes that and
nothing else?

90

*Quod crebro videt non miratur, etiamsi cur fiat nescit;
quod ante non viderit, id si evenerit, ostentum esse censet.*[11]
(Cic. 583.)
Næ iste magno conatu magnas nugas dixerit.[12]

91

Spongia solis.[13]—When we see the same effect always
recur, we infer a natural necessity in it, as that there will
be a to-morrow, &c.   But nature often deceives us, and does
not subject herself to her own rules.

92

What are our natural principles but principles of custom?
In children they are those which they have received from
the habits of their fathers, as hunting in animals.   A different custom will cause different natural principles.   This
is seen in experience; and if there are some natural principles ineradicable by custom, there are also some customs
opposed to nature, ineradicable by nature, or by a second
custom.   This depends on disposition.

93

Parents fear lest the natural love of their children may
fade away.   What kind of nature is that which is subject to
decay?   Custom is a second nature which destroys the
former.   But what is nature?   For is custom not natural?
I am much afraid that nature is itself only a first custom, as
custom is a second nature.

[11] " What a man sees often he does not wonder at, although he knows
not why it happens; if something occurs which he has not seen before, he
thinks it a marvel."
[12] " Verily, that man will have uttered great trifles with huge effort."—
Terence.
[13] " Spots on the sun."

94

The nature of man is wholly natural, *omne animal.*[14]
There is nothing he may not make natural; there is nothing natural he may not lose.

95

Memory, joy, are intuitions; and even mathematical propositions become intuitions, for education produces natural intuitions, and natural intuitions are erased by education.

96

When we are accustomed to use bad reasons for proving natural effects, we are not willing to receive good reasons when they are discovered. An example may be given from the circulation of the blood as a reason why the vein swells below the ligature.

97

The most important affair in life is the choice of a calling; chance decides it. Custom makes men masons, soldiers, slaters. " He is a good slater," says one, and, speaking of soldiers, remarks, " They are perfect fools." But others affirm, " There is nothing great but war, the rest of men are good-for-nothing." We choose our callings according as we hear this or that praised or despised in our childhood, for we naturally love truth and hate folly. These words move us; the only error is in their application. So great is the force of custom that out of those whom nature has only made men, are created all conditions of men. For some districts are full of masons, others of soldiers, &c. Certainly nature is not so uniform. It is custom then which does this, for it constrains nature. But sometimes nature gains the ascendency, and preserves man's instinct, in spite of all custom, good or bad.

[14] " All animal."

98

Bias leading to error. It is a deplorable thing to see all men deliberating on means alone, and not on the end. Each thinks how he will acquit himself in his condition; but as for the choice of condition, or of country, chance gives them to us.

It is a pitiable thing to see so many Turks, heretics and infidels, follow the way of their fathers for the sole reason that each has been imbued with the prejudice that it is the best. And that fixes for each man his condition of lock-smith, soldier, &c.

Hence savages care nothing for Provence.

99

There is an universal and essential difference between the actions of the will and all other actions.

The will is one of the chief factors in belief, not that it creates belief, but because things are true or false according to the aspect in which we look at them. The will, which prefers one aspect to another, turns away the mind from considering the qualities of all that it does not like to see; and thus the mind, moving in accord with the will, stops to consider the aspect which it likes, and so judges by what it sees.

100

Self-love.—The nature of self-love and of this human Ego is to love self only and consider self only. But what will man do? He cannot prevent this object that he loves from being full of faults and wants. He wants to be great, and he sees himself small. He wants to be happy, and he sees himself miserable. He wants to be perfect, and he sees himself full of imperfections. He wants to be the object of love and esteem among men, and he sees that his faults merit only their hatred and contempt. This embarrassment in which he finds himself produces in him the most un-righteous and criminal passion that can be imagined; for he conceives a mortal enmity against that truth which reproves

him, and which convinces him of his faults. He would annihilate it, but, unable to destroy it in its essence, he destroys
it as far as possible in his own knowledge and in that of
others; that is to say, he devotes all his attention to hiding
his faults both from others and from himself, and he cannot
endure either that others should point them out to him, or
that they should see them.

Truly it is an evil to be full of faults; but it is a still
greater evil to be full of them, and to be unwilling to recognise them, since that is to add the further fault of a
voluntary illusion. We do not like others to deceive us;
we do not think it fair that they should be held in higher
esteem by us than they deserve; it is not then fair that we
should deceive them, and should wish them to esteem us
more highly than we deserve.

Thus, when they discover only the imperfections and
vices which we really have, it is plain they do us no wrong,
since it is not they who cause them; they rather do us good,
since they help us to free ourselves from an evil, namely,
the ignorance of these imperfections. We ought not to
be angry at their knowing our faults and despising us; it
is but right that they should know us for what we are, and
should despise us, if we are contemptible.

Such are the feelings that would arise in a heart full of
equity and justice. What must we say then of our own
heart, when we see in it a wholly different disposition?
For is it not true that we hate truth and those who tell it us,
and that we like them to be deceived in our favour, and
prefer to be esteemed by them as being other than what we
are in fact? One proof of this makes me shudder. The
Catholic religion does not bind us to confess our sins indis-
criminately to everybody; it allows them to remain hidden
from all other men save one, to whom she bids us reveal
the innermost recesses of our heart, and show ourselves as
we are. There is only this one man in the world whom she
orders us to undeceive, and she binds him to an inviolable
secrecy, which makes this knowledge to him as if it were
not. Can we imagine anything more charitable and pleasant?
And yet the corruption of man is such that he finds even
this law harsh; and it is one of the main reasons which

have caused a great part of Europe to rebel against the Church.

How unjust and unreasonable is the heart of man, which feels it disagreeable to be obliged to do in regard to one man what in some measure it were right to do to all men! For is it right that we should deceive men?

There are different degrees in this aversion to truth; but all may perhaps be said to have it in some degree, because it is inseparable from self-love. It is this false delicacy which makes those who are under the necessity of reproving others choose so many windings and middle courses to avoid offence. They must lessen our faults, appear to excuse them, intersperse praises and evidence of love and esteem. Despite all this, the medicine does not cease to be bitter to self-love. It takes as little as it can, always with disgust, and often with a secret spite against those who administer it.

Hence it happens that if any have some interest in being loved by us, they are averse to render us a service which they know to be disagreeable. They treat us as we wish to be treated. We hate the truth, and they hide it from us. We desire flattery, and they flatter us. We like to be deceived, and they deceive us.

So each degree of good fortune which raises us in the world removes us further from truth, because we are most afraid of wounding those whose affection is most useful and whose dislike is most dangerous. A prince may be the byword of all Europe, and he alone will know nothing of it. I am not astonished; to tell the truth is useful to whom it is spoken, but disadvantageous to those who tell it, because it makes them disliked. Now those who live with princes love their own interests more than that of the prince whom they serve; and so they take care not to confer on him a benefit so as to injure themselves.

This evil is no doubt greater and more common among the higher classes; but the lower are not exempt from it, since there is always some advantage in making men love us. Human life is thus only a perpetual illusion; men deceive and flatter each other. No one speaks of us in our presence as he does of us in our absence. Human society is founded on mutual deceit; few friendships would endure if each knew what his friend said of him in his absence, although he then spoke in sincerity and without passion.

Man is then only disguise, falsehood, and hypocrisy, both in himself and in regard to others. He does not wish any one to tell him the truth; he avoids telling it to others, and all these dispositions, so removed from justice and reason, have a natural root in his heart.

101

I set it down as a fact that if all men knew what each said of the other, there would not be four friends in the world. This is apparent from the quarrels which arise from the indiscreet tales told from time to time. I say, further, all men would be . . .

102

Some vices only lay hold of us by means of others, and these, like branches, fall on removal of the trunk.

103

The example of Alexander's chastity has not made so many continent as that of his drunkenness has made intemperate. It is not shameful not to be as virtuous as he, and it seems excusable to be no more vicious. We do not believe ourselves to be exactly sharing in the vices of the vulgar, when we see that we are sharing in those of great men; and yet we do not observe that in these matters they are ordinary men. We hold on to them by the same end by which they hold on to the rabble; for, however exalted they are, they are still united at some point to the lowest of men. They are not suspended in the air, quite removed from our society. No, no; if they are greater than we, it is because their heads are higher; but their feet are as low as ours. They are all on the same level, and rest on the same earth; and by that extremity they are as low as we are, as the meanest folk, as infants, and as the beasts.

104

When our passion leads us to do something, we forget our duty; for example, we like a book and read it, when we ought to be doing something else. Now, to remind ourselves of our duty, we must set ourselves a task we dislike; we then plead that we have something else to do, and by this means remember our duty.

105

How difficult it is to submit anything to the judgment of another, without prejudicing his judgment by the manner in which we submit it! If we say, "I think it beautiful," "I think it obscure," or the like, we either entice the imagination into that view, or irritate it to the contrary. It is better to say nothing; and then the other judges according to what really is, that is to say, according as it then is, and according as the other circumstances, not of our making, have placed it. But we at least shall have added nothing, unless it be that silence also produces an effect, according to the turn and the interpretation which the other will be disposed to give it, or as he will guess it from gestures or countenance, or from the tone of the voice, if he is a physiognomist. So difficult is it not to upset a judgment from its natural place, or rather so rarely is it firm and stable!

106

By knowing each man's ruling passion, we are sure of pleasing him; and yet each has his fancies, opposed to his true good, in the very idea which he has of the good. It is a singularly puzzling fact.

107

Lustravit lampade terras.[15]—The weather and my mood have little connection. I have my foggy and my fine days within me; my prosperity or misfortune has little to do with the matter. I sometimes struggle against luck, the glory of mastering it makes me master it gaily; whereas I am sometimes surfeited in the midst of good fortune.

[15] " He has illumined the earth with a lamp."

108

Although people may have no interest in what they are saying, we must not absolutely conclude from this that they are not lying; for there are some people who lie for the mere sake of lying.

109

When we are well we wonder what we would do 'if we were ill, but when we are ill we take medicine cheerfully; the illness persuades us to do so. We have no longer the passions and desires for amusements and promenades which health gave to us, but which are incompatible with the necessities of illness. Nature gives us, then, passions and desires suitable to our present state. We are only troubled by the fears which we, and not nature, give ourselves, for they add to the state in which we are the passions of the state in which we are not.

As nature makes us always unhappy in every state, our desires picture to us a happy state; because they add to the state in which we are the pleasures of the state in which we are not. And if we attained to these pleasures, we should not be happy after all; because we should have other desires natural to this new state.

We must particularise this general proposition. . . .

110

The consciousness of the falsity of present pleasures, and the ignorance of the vanity of absent pleasures, cause inconstancy.

111

Inconstancy.—We think we are playing on ordinary organs when playing upon man. Men are organs, it is true, but, odd, changeable, variable [with pipes not arranged in proper order]. Those who only know how to play on ordinary organs will not produce harmonies on these. We must know where [the keys] are.

112

Inconstancy.—Things have different qualities, and the soul different inclinations; for nothing is simple which is presented to the soul, and the soul never presents itself simply to any object. Hence it comes that we weep and laugh at the same thing.

113

Inconstancy and oddity.—To live only by work, and to rule over the most powerful State in the world, are very opposite things. They are united in the person of the great Sultan of the Turks.

114

Variety is as abundant as all tones of the voice, all ways of walking, coughing, blowing the nose, sneezing. We distinguish vines by their fruit, and call them the Condrien, the Desargues, and such and such a stock. Is this all? Has a vine ever produced two bunches exactly the same, and has a bunch two grapes alike? &c.

I can never judge of the same thing exactly in the same way. I cannot judge of my work, while doing it. I must do as the artists, stand at a distance, but not too far. How far then? Guess.

115

Variety.—Theology is a science, but at the same time how many sciences? A man is a whole; but if we dissect him, will he be the head, the heart, the stomach, the veins, each vein, each portion of a vein, the blood, each humour in the blood?

A town, a country-place, is from afar a town and a country-place. But, as we draw near, there are houses, trees, tiles, leaves, grass, ants, limbs of ants, in infinity. All this is contained under the name of country-place.

116

Thoughts.—All is one, all is different. How many natures exist in man? How many vocations? And by what chance

does each man ordinarily choose what he has heard praised?
A well-turned heel.

117

The heel of a slipper.—" Ah! How well this is turned!
Here is a clever workman! How brave is this soldier!"
This is the source of our inclinations, and of the choice of
conditions. " How much this man drinks! How little that
one!" This makes people sober or drunk, soldiers, cowards,
&c.

118

Chief talent, that which rules the rest.

119

Nature imitates herself. A seed sown in good ground
brings forth fruit. A principle, instilled into a good mind,
brings forth fruit. Numbers imitate space, which is of a
different nature.

All is made and led by the same master, root, branches,
and fruits; principles and consequences.

120

[Nature diversifies and imitates; art imitates and diversifies.]

121

Nature always begins the same things again, the years,
the days, the hours; in like manner spaces and numbers
follow each other from beginning to end. Thus is made a
kind of infinity and eternity. Not that anything in all this
is infinite and eternal, but these finite realities are infinitely
multiplied. Thus it seems to me to be only the number
which multiplies them that is infinite.

122

Time heals griefs and quarrels, for we change and are
no longer the same persons. Neither the offender nor the
offended are any more themselves. It is like a nation which

we have provoked, but meet again after two generations.
They are still Frenchmen, but not the same.

123

He no longer loves the person whom he loved ten years
ago. I quite believe it. She is no longer the same, nor is
he. He was young, and she also; she is quite different. He
would perhaps love her yet, if she were what she was
then.

124

We view things not only from different sides, but with
different eyes; we have no wish to find them alike.

125

Contraries.—Man is naturally credulous and incredulous,
timid and rash.

126

Description of man: dependency, desire of independence,
need.

127

Condition of man: inconstancy, weariness, unrest.

128

The weariness which is felt by us in leaving pursuits to
which we are attached. A man dwells at home with pleasure;
but if he sees a woman who charms him, or if he enjoys
himself in play for five or six days, he is miserable if he
return to his former way of living. Nothing is more common than that.

129

Our nature consists in motion; complete rest is death.

130

Restlessness.—If a soldier, or labourer, complain of the
hardship of his lot, set him to do nothing.

131

Weariness.—Nothing is so insufferable to man as to be completely at rest, without passions, without business, without diversion, without study. He then feels his nothingness, his forlornness, his insufficiency, his dependence, his weakness, his emptiness. There will immediately arise from the depth of his heart weariness, gloom, sadness, fretfulness, vexation, despair.

132

Methinks Cæsar was too old to set about amusing himself with conquering the world. Such sport was good for Augustus or Alexander. They were still young men, and thus difficult to restrain. But Cæsar should have been more mature.

133

Two faces which resemble each other, make us laugh, when together, by their resemblance, though neither of them by itself makes us laugh.

134

How useless is painting, which attracts admiration by the resemblance of things, the originals of which we do not admire!

135

The struggle alone pleases us, not the victory. We love to see animals fighting, not the victor infuriated over the vanquished. We would only see the victorious end; and, as soon as it comes, we are satiated. It is the same in play and the same in the search for truth. In disputes we like to see the clash of opinions, but not at all to contemplate truth when found. To observe it with pleasure, we have to see it emerge out of strife. So in the passions, there is pleasure in seeing the collision of two contraries; but when one acquires the mastery, it becomes only brutality. We never seek things for themselves, but for the search. Likewise in plays, scenes which do not rouse the emotion of fear are worthless, so are extreme and hopeless misery, brutal lust, and extreme cruelty.

136

A mere trifle consoles us, for a mere trifle distresses us.

137

Without examining every particular pursuit, it is enough to comprehend them under diversion.

138

Men naturally slaters and of all callings, save in their own rooms.

139

Diversion.—When I have occasionally set myself to consider the different distractions of men, the pains and perils to which they expose themselves at court or in war, whence arise so many quarrels, passions, bold and often bad ventures, &c., I have discovered that all the unhappiness of men arises from one single fact, that they cannot stay quietly in their own chamber. A man who has enough to live on, if he knew how to stay with pleasure at home, would not leave it to go to sea or to besiege a town. A commission in the army would not be bought so dearly, but that it is found insufferable not to budge from the town; and men only seek conversation and entertaining games, because they cannot remain with pleasure at home.

But on further consideration, when, after finding the cause of all our ills, I have sought to discover the reason of it, I have found that there is one very real reason, namely, the natural poverty of our feeble and mortal condition, so miserable that nothing can comfort us when we think of it closely.

Whatever condition we picture to ourselves, if we muster all the good things which it is possible to possess, royalty is the finest position in the world. Yet, when we imagine a king attended with every pleasure he can feel, if he be without diversion, and be left to consider and reflect on what he is, this feeble happiness will not sustain him; he will necessarily fall into forebodings of dangers, of revolutions which may happen, and, finally, of death and inevitable disease; so that if he be without what is called diversion, he is unhappy, and more unhappy than the least of his subjects who plays and diverts himself.

Hence it comes that play and the society of women, war, and high posts, are so sought after. Not that there is in fact any happiness in them, or that men imagine true bliss to consist in money won at play, or in the hare which they hunt; we would not take these as a gift. We do not seek that easy and peaceful lot which permits us to think of our unhappy condition, nor the dangers of war, nor the labour of office, but the bustle which averts these thoughts of ours, and amuses us.

Reasons why we like the chase better than the quarry.

Hence it comes that men so much love noise and stir; hence it comes that the prison is so horrible a punishment; hence it comes that the pleasure of solitude is a thing incomprehensible. And it is in fact the greatest source of happiness in the condition of kings, that men try incessantly to divert them, and to procure for them all kinds of pleasures.

The king is surrounded by persons whose only thought is to divert the king, and to prevent his thinking of self. For he is unhappy, king though he be, if he think of himself.

This is all that men have been able to discover to make themselves happy. And those who philosophise on the matter, and who think men unreasonable for spending a whole day in chasing a hare which they would not have bought, scarce know our nature. The hare in itself would not screen us from the sight of death and calamities; but the chase which turns away our attention from these, does screen us.

The advice given to Pyrrhus to take the rest which he was about to seek with so much labour, was full of difficulties.

[To bid a man live quietly is to bid him live happily. It is to advise him to be in a state perfectly happy, in which he can think at leisure without finding therein a cause of distress. This is to misunderstand nature.

As men who naturally understand their own condition avoid nothing so much as rest, so there is nothing they leave undone in seeking turmoil. Not that they have an instinctive knowledge of true happiness. . . .

So we are wrong in blaming them. Their error does not lie in seeking excitement, if they seek it only as a diversion; the evil is that they seek it as if the possession of the objects of their quest would make them really happy. In this respect it is right to call their quest a vain one. Hence in all this both the censurers and the censured do not understand man's true nature.]

And thus, when we take the exception against them, that what they seek with such fervour cannot satisfy them, if they replied—as they should do if they considered the matter thoroughly—that they sought in it only a violent and impetuous occupation which turned their thoughts from self, and that they therefore chose an attractive object to charm and ardently attract them, they would leave their opponents without a reply. But they do not make this reply, because they do not know themselves. They do not know that it is the chase, and not the quarry, which they seek.

[Dancing: we must consider rightly where to place our feet.

—A gentleman sincerely believes that hunting is great and royal sport; but a beater is not of this opinion.]

They imagine that if they obtained such a post, they would then rest with pleasure, and are insensible of the insatiable nature of their desire. They think they are truly seeking quiet, and they are only seeking excitement.

They have a secret instinct which impels them to seek amusement and occupation abroad, and which arises from the sense of their constant unhappiness. They have another secret instinct, a remnant of the greatness of our original nature, which teaches them that happiness in reality consists only in rest, and not in stir. And of these two contrary instincts they form within themselves a confused idea, which hides itself from their view in the depths of their soul, inciting them to aim at rest through excitement, and always to fancy that the satisfaction which they have not will come to them, if, by surmounting whatever difficulties confront them, they can thereby open the door to rest.

Thus passes away all man's life. Men seek rest in a struggle against difficulties; and when they have conquered these, rest becomes insufferable. For we think either of the misfortunes we have or of those which threaten us. And even if we should see ourselves sufficiently sheltered on all sides, weariness of its own accord would not fail to arise from the depths of the heart wherein it has its natural roots, and to fill the mind with its poison.

Thus so wretched is man that he would weary even without any cause for weariness from the peculiar state of his disposition; and so frivolous is he, that, though full of a thousand reasons for weariness, the least thing, such as playing billiards or hitting a ball, is sufficient to amuse him.

But will you say what object has he in all this? The pleasure of bragging to-morrow among his friends that he has played better than another. So others sweat in their own rooms to show to the learned that they have solved a problem in Algebra, which no one had hitherto been able to solve. Many more expose themselves to extreme perils, in my opinion as foolishly, in order to boast afterwards that they have captured a town. Lastly, others wear themselves out in studying all these things, not in order to become wiser, but only in order to prove that they know them; and these are the most senseless of the band, since they are so knowingly, whereas one may suppose of the others, that if they knew it, they would no longer be foolish.

This man spends his life without weariness in playing every day for a small stake. Give him each morning the money he can win each day, on condition he does not play; you make him miserable. It will perhaps be said that he seeks the amusement of play and not the winnings. Make him then play for nothing; he will not become excited over it, and will feel bored. It is then not the amusement alone that he seeks; a languid and passionless amusement will weary him. He must get excited over it, and deceive himself by the fancy that he will be happy to win what he would not have as a gift on condition of not playing; and he must make for himself an object of passion, and excite over it his desire, his anger, his fear, to obtain his imagined end, as children are frightened at the face they have blackened.

Whence comes it that this man, who lost his only son a few months ago, or who this morning was in such trouble through being distressed by lawsuits and quarrels, now no longer thinks of them? Do not wonder; he is quite taken up in looking out for the boar which his dogs have been hunting so hotly for the last six hours. He requires nothing more. However full of sadness a man may be, he is happy for the time, if you can prevail upon him to enter into some amusement; and however happy a man may be, he will soon be discontented and wretched, if he be not diverted and occupied by some passion or pursuit which prevents weariness from overcoming him. Without amusement there is no joy; with amusement there is no sadness. And this also constitutes the happiness of persons in high position, that they have a number of people to amuse them, and have the power to keep themselves in this state.

Consider this. What is it to be superintendent, chancellor, first president, but to be in a condition wherein from early morning a large number of people come from all quarters to see them, so as not to leave them an hour in the day in which they can think of themselves? And when they are in disgrace and sent back to their country houses, where they lack neither wealth nor servants to help them on occasion, they do not fail to be wretched and desolate, because no one prevents them from thinking of themselves.

140

[How does it happen that this man, so distressed at the death of his wife and his only son, or who has some great lawsuit which annoys him, is not at this moment sad, and that he seems so free from all painful and disquieting thoughts? We need not wonder; for a ball has been served him, and he must return it to his companion. He is occupied in catching it in its fall from the roof, to win a game. How can he think of his own affairs, pray, when he has this other matter in hand? Here is a care worthy of occupying this great soul, and taking away from him every other thought of the mind. This man, born to know the universe, to judge all causes, to govern a whole state, is altogether occupied and taken up with the business of catching a hare. And if he does not lower himself to this, and wants always to be on the strain, he will be more foolish still, because he would raise himself above humanity; and after all he is only a man, that is to say capable of little and of much, of all and of nothing; he is neither angel nor brute, but man.]

141

Men spend their time in following a ball or a hare; it is the pleasure even of kings.

142

Diversion.—Is not the royal dignity sufficiently great in itself to make its possessor happy by the mere contemplation of what he is? Must he be diverted from this thought like ordinary folk? I see well that a man is made happy by diverting him from the view of his domestic sorrows so as to occupy all his thoughts with the care of dancing well. But will it be the same with a king, and will he be happier in the pursuit of these idle amusements than in the con- templation of his greatness? And what more satisfactory object could be presented to his mind? Would it not be a deprivation of his delight for him to occupy his soul with the thought of how to adjust his steps to the cadence of an air, or of how to throw a [ball] skilfully, instead of leaving it to enjoy quietly the contemplation of the majestic glory which encompasses him? Let us make the trial; let us leave a king all alone to reflect on himself quite at leisure, with- out any gratification of the senses, without any care in his mind, without society; and we will see that a king without diversion is a man full of wretchedness. So this is carefully avoided, and near the persons of kings there never fail to be a great number of people who see to it that amusement follows business, and who watch all the time of their leisure to supply them with delights and games, so that there is no blank in it. In fact kings are surrounded with persons who are wonderfully attentive in taking care that the king be not alone and in a state to think of himself, knowing well that he will be miserable, king though he be, if he meditate on self.

In all this I am not talking of Christian kings as Christians, but only as kings.

143

Diversion.—Men are intrusted from infancy with the care of their honour, their property, their friends, and even with the property and the honour of their friends. They are overwhelmed with business, with the study of languages, and with physical exercise; and they are made to understand that they cannot be happy unless their health, their honour, their fortune and that of their friends be in good condition, and that a single thing wanting will make them unhappy. Thus they are given cares and business which make them bustle about from break of day.—It is, you will exclaim, a strange way to make them happy! What more could be done to make them miserable?—Indeed! what could be done? We should only have to relieve them from all these cares; for then they would see themselves: they would reflect on what they are, whence they came, whither they go, and thus we cannot employ and divert them too much. And this is why, after having given them so much business, we advise them, if they have some time for relaxation, to employ it in amusement, in play, and to be always fully occupied.

How hollow and full of ribaldry is the heart of man!

144

I spent a long time in the study of the abstract sciences, and was disheartened by the small number of fellow-students in them. When I commenced the study of man, I saw that these abstract sciences are not suited to man, and that I was wandering further from my own state in examining them, than others in not knowing them. I pardoned their little knowledge; but I thought at least to find many companions in the study of man, and that it was the true study which is suited to him. I have been deceived; still fewer study it than geometry. It is only from want of knowing how to study this that we seek the other studies. But is it not that even here is not the knowledge which man should have, and that for the purposes of happiness it is better for him not to know himself?

145

[One thought alone occupies us; we cannot think of two things at the same time. This is lucky for us according to the world, not according to God.]

146

Man is obviously made to think. It is his whole dignity and his whole merit; and his whole duty is to think as he ought. Now, the order of thought is to begin with self, and with its Author and its end.

Now, of what does the world think? Never of this, but of dancing, playing the lute, singing, making verses, running at the ring, &c., fighting, making oneself king, without thinking what it is to be a king and what to be a man.

147

We do not content ourselves with the life we have in ourselves and in our own being; we desire to live an imaginary life in the mind of others, and for this purpose we endeavour to shine. We labour unceasingly to adorn and preserve this imaginary existence, and neglect the real. And if we possess calmness, or generosity, or truthfulness, we are eager to make it known, so as to attach these virtues to that imaginary existence. We would rather separate them from ourselves to join them to it; and we would willingly be cowards in order to acquire the reputation of being brave. A great proof of the nothingness of our being, not to be satisfied with the one without the other, and to renounce the one for the other! For he would be infamous who would not die to preserve his honour.

148

We are so presumptuous that we would wish to be known by all the world, even by people who shall come after, when we shall be no more; and we are so vain that the esteem of five or six neighbours delights and contents us.

149

We do not trouble ourselves about being esteemed in the towns through which we pass. But if we are to remain a little while there, we are so concerned. How long is necessary? A time commensurate with our vain and paltry life.

150

Vanity is so anchored in the heart of man that a soldier, a soldier's servant, a cook, a porter brags, and wishes to have his admirers. Even philosophers wish for them. Those who write against it want to have the glory of having written well; and those who read it desire the glory of having read it. I who write this have perhaps this desire, and perhaps those who will read it . . . .

151

Glory.—Admiration spoils all from infancy. Ah! How well said! Ah! How well done! How well-behaved he is! &c.

The children of Port-Royal, who do not receive this stimulus of envy and glory, fall into carelessness.

152

Pride.—Curiosity is only vanity. Most frequently we wish to know but to talk. Otherwise we would not take a sea voyage in order never to talk of it, and for the sole pleasure of seeing without hope of ever communicating it.

153

Of the desire of being esteemed by those with whom we are.—Pride takes such natural possession of us in the midst

of our woes, errors, &c. We even lose our life with joy,
provided people talk of it.

Vanity: play, hunting, visiting, false shams, a lasting
name.

154

[I have no friends] to your advantage].

155

A true friend is so great an advantage, even for the greatest lords, in order that he may speak well of them, and
back them in their absence, that they should do all to have
one. But they should choose well; for, if they spend all
their efforts in the interests of fools, it will be of no use,
however well these may speak of them; and these will not
even speak well of them if they find themselves on the
weakest side, for they have no influence; and thus they will
speak ill of them in company.

156

Ferox gens, nullam esse vitam sine armis rati.[16]—They
prefer death to peace; others prefer death to war.

Every opinion may be held preferable to life, the love of
which is so strong and so natural.

157

Contradiction: contempt for our existence, to die for
nothing, hatred of our existence.

158

Pursuits.—The charm of fame is so great, that we like
every object to which it is attached, even death.

159

Noble deeds are most estimable when hidden. When
I see some of these in history (as p. 184), they please me
greatly. But after all they have not been quite hidden, since

[16] " A fierce people, who thought life was nothing without arms."—Livy.

they have been known; and though people have done what they could to hide them, the little publication of them spoils all, for what was best in them was the wish to hide them.

160

Sneezing absorbs all the functions of the soul, as well as work does; but we do not draw therefrom the same conclusions against the greatness of man, because it is against his will. And although we bring it on ourselves, it is nevertheless against our will that we sneeze. It is not in view of the act itself; it is for another end. And thus it is not a proof of the weakness of man, and of his slavery under that action.

It is not disgraceful for man to yield to pain, and it is disgraceful to yield to pleasure. This is not because pain comes to us from without, and we ourselves seek pleasure; for it is possible to seek pain, and yield to it purposely, without this kind of baseness. Whence comes it, then, that reason thinks it honourable to succumb under stress of pain, and disgraceful to yield to the attack of pleasure? It is because pain does not tempt and attract us. It is we ourselves who choose it voluntarily, and will it to prevail over us. So that we are masters of the situation; and in this man yields to himself. But in pleasure it is man who yields to pleasure. Now only mastery and sovereignty bring glory, and only slavery brings shame.

161

Vanity.—How wonderful it is that a thing so evident as the vanity of the world is so little known, that it is a strange and surprising thing to say that it is foolish to seek greatness!

162

He who will know fully the vanity of man has only to consider the causes and effects of love. The cause is *I know not what* (Corneille), and the effects are dreadful. This

I know not what, so small an object that we cannot recognise it, agitates a whole country, princes, armies, the entire world.

Cleopatra's nose: had it been shorter, the whole aspect of the world would have been altered.

163

Vanity.—The cause and the effects of love: Cleopatra.

164

He who does not see the vanity of the world is himself very vain. Indeed who do not see it but youths who are absorbed in fame, diversion, and the thought of the future? But take away their diversion, and you will see them dried up with weariness. They feel then their nothingness without knowing it; for it is indeed to be unhappy to be in insufferable sadness as soon as we are reduced to thinking of self, and have no diversion.

165

Thoughts.—*In omnibus requiem quæsivi.*[11] If our condition were truly happy, we would not need diversion from thinking of it in order to make ourselves happy.

166

Diversion.—Death is easier to bear without thinking of it, than is the thought of death without peril.

167

The miseries of human life have established all this: as men have seen this, they have taken up diversion.

168

Diversion.—As men are not able to fight against death, misery, ignorance, they have taken it into their heads, in order to be happy, not to think of them at all.

[11] " In all things I have sought rest."

169

Despite these miseries, man wishes to be happy, and only wishes to be happy, and cannot wish not to be so. But how will he set about it? To be happy he would have to make himself immortal; but, not being able to do so, it has occurred to him to prevent himself from thinking of death.

170

Diversion.—If man were happy, he would be the more so, the less he was diverted, like the Saints and God.—Yes; but is it not to be happy to have a faculty of being amused by diversion?—No; for that comes from elsewhere and from without, and thus is dependent, and therefore subject to be disturbed by a thousand accidents, which bring inevitable griefs.

171

Misery.—The only thing which consoles us for our miseries is diversion, and yet this is the greatest of our miseries. For it is this which principally hinders us from reflecting upon ourselves, and which makes us insensibly ruin ourselves. Without this we should be in a state of weariness, and this weariness would spur us to seek a more solid means of escaping from it. But diversion amuses us, and leads us unconsciously to death.

172

We do not rest satisfied with the present. We anticipate the future as too slow in coming, as if in order to hasten its course; or we recall the past, to stop its too rapid flight. So imprudent are we that we wander in the times which are not ours, and do not think of the only one which belongs to us; and so idle are we that we dream of those times which are no more, and thoughtlessly overlook that which alone exists. For the present is generally painful to us. We conceal it from our sight, because it troubles us; and if it be delightful to us, we regret to see it pass away. We try to sustain it by the future, and think of arranging matters which are not in our power, for a time which we have no certainty of reaching.

Let each one examine his thoughts, and he will find them all occupied with the past and the future. We scarcely ever think of the present; and if we think of it, it is only to take light from it to arrange the future. The present is never our end. The past and the present are our means; the future alone is our end. So we never live, but we hope to live; and, as we are always preparing to be happy, it is inevitable we should never be so.

173

They say that eclipses foretoken misfortune, because misfortunes are common, so that, as evil happens so often, they often foretell it; whereas if they said that they predict good fortune, they would often be wrong. They attribute good fortune only to rare conjunctions of the heavens; so they seldom fail in prediction.

174

Misery.—Solomon and Job have best known and best spoken of the misery of man; the former, the most fortunate, and the latter the most unfortunate of men; the former knowing the vanity of pleasures from experience, the latter the reality of evils.

175

We know ourselves so little, that many think they are about to die when they are well, and many think they are well when they are near death, unconscious of approaching fever, or of the abscess ready to form itself.

176

Cromwell was about to ravage all Christendom; the royal family was undone, and his own for ever established, save for a little grain of sand which formed in his ureter. Rome herself was trembling under him; but this small piece of gravel having formed there, he is dead, his family cast down, all is peaceful, and the king is restored.

177

[Three hosts.] Would he who had possessed the friendship of the King of England, the King of Poland, and the Queen of Sweden, have believed he would lack a refuge and shelter in the world?

178

Macrobius: on the innocents slain by Herod.

179

When Augustus learnt that Herod's own son was amongst the infants under two years of age, whom he had caused to be slain, he said that it was better to be Herod's pig than his son.—Macrobius, *Sat.,* book ii. chap. 4.

180

The great and the humble have the same misfortunes, the same griefs, the same passions; but the one is at the top of the wheel, and the other near the centre, and so less disturbed by the same revolutions.

181

We are so unfortunate that we can only take pleasure in a thing on condition of being annoyed if it turn out ill, as a thousand things can do, and do every hour. He who should find the secret of rejoicing in the good, without troubling himself with its contrary evil, would have hit the mark. It is perpetual motion.

182

Those who have always good hope in the midst of misfortunes, and who are delighted with good luck, are suspected of being very pleased with the ill success of the affair, if they are not equally distressed by bad luck; and they are overjoyed to find these pretexts of hope, in order to show that they are concerned, and to conceal by the joy which they feign to feel that which they have at seeing the failure of the matter.

183

We run carelessly to the precipice, after we have put something before us to prevent us seeing it.

SECTION III

OF THE NECESSITY OF THE WAGER

184

A LETTER to incite to the search after God.

And then to make people seek Him among the philosophers, sceptics, and dogmatists, who disquiet him who inquires of them.

185

The conduct of God, who disposes all things kindly, is to put religion into the mind by reason, and into the heart by grace. But to will to put it into the mind and heart by force and threats is not to put religion there, but terror, *terorrem potius quam religionem.*[1]

186

Nisi terrerentur et non docerentur, improba quasi dominatio videretur (Aug. Ep. 48 or 49).[2] *Contra mendacium ad Consentium.*[3]

187

Order.—Men despise religion; they hate it, and fear it is true. To remedy this, we must begin by showing that religion is not contrary to reason; that it is venerable, to inspire respect for it; then we must make it lovable, to make good men hope it is true; finally, we must prove it is true.

Venerable, because it has perfect knowledge of man; lovable, because it promises the true good.

[1] " Terror rather than religion."
[2] " If they were not terrified and were instructed, it would seem like an unjust tyranny."
[3] " To meet a lie, appeal to the Council."

188

In every dialogue and discourse, we must be able to say to those who take offence, " Of what do you complain? "

189

To begin by pitying unbelievers; they are wretched enough by their condition. We ought only to revile them where it is beneficial; but this does them harm.

190

To pity atheists who seek, for are they not unhappy enough? To inveigh against those who make a boast of it.

191

And will this one scoff at the other? Who ought to scoff? And yet, the latter does not scoff at the other, but pities him.

192

To reproach Miton with not being troubled, since God will reproach him.

193

Quid fiet hominibus qui minima contemnunt, majora non credunt.[4]

194

. . . Let them at least learn what is the religion they attack, before attacking it. If this religion boasted of having a clear view of God, and of possessing it open and unveiled, it would be attacking it to say that we see nothing in the world which shows it with this clearness. But since, on the contrary, it says that men are in darkness and estranged from God, that He has hidden Himself from their knowledge, that this is in fact the name which He gives Himself in the Scriptures, *Deus absconditus;*[5] and finally, if it endeavours equally

[4] " What will happen to men who despise the smallest things, and do not believe the greater."
[5] " A hidden God."—Isaiah, xlv. 15.

to establish these two things: that God has set up in the
Church visible signs to make Himself known to those who
should seek Him sincerely, and that He has nevertheless so
disguised them that He will only be perceived by those
who seek Him with all their heart; what advantage can
they obtain, when, in the negligence with which they make
profession of being in search of the truth, they cry out that
nothing reveals it to them; and since that darkness in which
they are, and with which they upbraid the Church, establishes
only one of the things which she affirms, without touching
the other, and, very far from destroying, proves her doctrine?

In order to attack it, they should have protested that they
had made every effort to seek Him everywhere, and even
in that which the Church proposes for their instruction, but
without satisfaction. If they talked in this manner, they
would in truth be attacking one of her pretensions. But I
hope here to show that no reasonable person can speak thus,
and I venture even to say that no one has ever done so. We
know well enough how those who are of this mind behave.
They believe they have made great efforts for their instruction, when they have spent a few hours in reading some
book of Scripture, and have questioned some priest on the
truths of the faith. After that, they boast of having made
vain search in books and among men. But, verily, I will tell
them what I have often said, that this negligence is insufferable. We are not here concerned with the trifling interest
of some stranger, that we should treat it in this fashion; the
matter concerns ourselves and our all.

The immortality of the soul is a matter which is of so great
consequence to us, and which touches us so profoundly, that
we must have lost all feeling to be indifferent as to knowing
what it is. All our actions and thoughts must take such
different courses, according as there are or are not eternal
joys to hope for, that it is impossible to take one step with
sense and judgment, unless we regulate our course by our
view of this point which ought to be our ultimate end.

Thus our first interest and our first duty is to enlighten
ourselves on this subject, whereon depends all our conduct.
Therefore among those who do not believe, I make a vast
difference between those who strive with all their power to

inform themselves, and those who live without troubling or thinking about it.

I can have only compassion for those who sincerely bewail their doubt, who regard it as the greatest of misfortunes, and who, sparing no effort to escape it, make of this inquiry their principal and most serious occupation.

But as for those who pass their life without thinking of this ultimate end of life, and who, for this sole reason that they do not find within themselves the lights which convince them of it, neglect to seek them elsewhere, and to examine thoroughly whether this opinion is one of those which people receive with credulous simplicity, or one of those which, although obscure in themselves, have nevertheless a solid and immovable foundation, I look upon them in a manner quite different.

This carelessness in a matter which concerns themselves, their eternity, their all, moves me more to anger than pity; it astonishes and shocks me; it is to me monstrous. I do not say this out of the pious zeal of a spiritual devotion. I expect, on the contrary, that we ought to have this feeling from principles of human interest and self-love; for this we need only see what the least enlightened persons see.

We do not require great education of the mind to understand that here is no real and lasting satisfaction; that our pleasures are only vanity; that our evils are infinite; and, lastly, that death, which threatens us every moment, must infallibly place us within a few years under the dreadful necessity of being for ever either annihilated or unhappy.

There is nothing more real than this, nothing more terrible. Be as heroic as we like, that is the end which awaits the noblest life in the world. Let us reflect on this, and then say whether it is not beyond doubt that there is no good in this life but in the hope of another; that we are happy only in proportion as we draw near it; and that, as there are no more woes for those who have complete assurance of eternity, so there is no more happiness for those who have no insight into it.

Surely then it is a great evil thus to be in doubt, but it is at least an indispensable duty to seek when we are in such doubt; and thus the doubter who does not seek is altogether completely unhappy and completely wrong. And if besides this he is easy and content, profess to be so, and indeed boasts of it; if it is this state itself which is the subject of his joy and vanity, I have no words to describe so silly a creature.

How can people hold these opinions? What joy can we find in the expectation of nothing but hopeless misery? What reason for boasting that we are in impenetrable darkness? And how can it happen that the following argument occurs to a reasonable man?

"I know not who put me into the world, nor what the world is, not what I myself am. I am in terrible ignorance of everything. I know not what my body is, nor my senses, nor my soul, nor even that part of me which thinks what I say, which reflects on all and on itself, and knows itself no more than the rest. I see those frightful spaces of the universe which surround me, and I find myself tied to one corner of this vast expanse, without knowing why I am put in this place rather than in another, nor why the short time which is given me to live is assigned to me at this point rather than at another of the whole eternity which was before me or which shall come after me. I see nothing but infinites on all sides, which surround me as an atom, and as a shadow which endures only for an instant and returns no more. All I know is that I must soon die, but what I know least is this very death which I cannot escape.

"As I know not whence I come, so I know not whither I go. I know only that, in leaving this world, I fall for ever either into annihilation or into the hands of an angry God, without knowing to which of these two states I shall be for ever assigned. Such is my state, full of weakness and uncertainty. And from all this I conclude that I ought to spend all the days of my life without caring to inquire into what must happen to me. Perhaps I might find some solution to my doubts, but I will not take the trouble, nor take a step to seek it; and after treating with scorn those who are concerned with this care, I will go without foresight and without fear to try the great event, and let myself be led carelessly to death, uncertain of the eternity of my future state."

Who would desire to have for a friend a man who talks in this fashion? Who would choose him out from others to tell him of his affairs? Who would have recourse to him in affliction? And indeed to what use in life could one put him?

In truth, it is the glory of religion to have for enemies men so unreasonable: and their opposition to it is so little dangerous that it serves on the contrary to establish its truths. For the Christion faith goes mainly to establish these two facts, the corruption of nature, and redemption by Jesus Christ. Now I contend that if these men do not serve to prove the truth of the redemption by the holiness of their behaviour, they at least serve admirably to show the corruption of nature by sentiments so unnatural.

Nothing is so important to man as his own state, nothing is so formidable to him as eternity; and thus it is not natural that there should be men indifferent to the loss of their existence, and to the perils of everlasting suffering. They are quite different with regard to all other things. They are afraid of mere trifles; they foresee them; they feel them. And this same man who spends so many days and nights in rage and despair for the loss of office, or for some imaginary insult to his honour, is the very one who knows without anxiety and without emotion that he will lose all by death. It is a monstrous thing to see in the same heart and at the same time this sensibility to trifles and this strange insensibility to the greatest objects. It is an incomprehensible enchantment, and a supernatural slumber, which indicates as its cause an all-powerful force.

There must be a strange confusion in the nature of man, that he should boast of being in that state in which it seems incredible that a single individual should be. However, experience has shown me so great a number of such persons that the fact would be surprising, if we did not know that the greater part of those who trouble themselves about the matter are disingenuous, and not in fact what they say. They are people who have heard it said that it is the fashion to be thus daring. It is what they call shaking off the yoke, and they try to imitate this. But it would not be difficult to make them understand how greatly they deceive them-

selves in thus seeking esteem. This is not the way to gain
it, even I say among those men of the world who take a
healthy view of things, and who know that the only way
to succeed in this life is to make ourselves appear honourable, faithful, judicious, and capable of useful service to a
friend; because naturally men love only what may be useful to them. Now, what do we gain by hearing it said of a
man that he has now thrown off the yoke, that he does not
believe there is a God who watches our actions, that he
considers himself the sole master of his conduct, and that
he thinks he is accountable for it only to himself? Does he
think that he has thus brought us to have henceforth complete confidence in him, and to look to him for consolation,
advice, and help in every need of life? Do they profess to
have delighted us by telling us that they hold our soul to be
only a little wind and smoke, especially by telling us this in a
haughty and self-satisfied tone of voice? Is this a thing
to say gaily? Is it not, on the contrary, a thing to say sadly,
as the saddest thing in the world?

If they thought of it seriously, they would see that this
is so bad a mistake, so contrary to good sense, so opposed to
decency, and so removed in every respect from that good
breeding which they seek, that they would be more likely
to correct than to pervert those who had an inclination to
follow them. And indeed, make them give an account of
their opinions, and of the reasons which they have for
doubting religion, and they will say to you things so feeble
and so petty, that they will persuade you of the contrary.
The following is what a person one day said to such an
one very appositely, "If you continue to talk in this manner,
you will really make me religious." And he was right, for
who would not have a horror of holding opinions in which
he would have such contemptible persons as companions!

Thus those who only feign these opinions would be very
unhappy, if they restrained their natural feelings in order
to make themselves the most conceited of men. If, at the
bottom of their heart, they are troubled at not having more
light, let them not disguise the fact; this avowal will not
be shameful. The only shame is to have none. Nothing
reveals more an extreme weakness of mind than not to

know the misery of a godless man. Nothing is more indicative of a bad disposition of heart than not to desire the truth of eternal promises. Nothing is more dastardly than to act the bravado before God. Let them then leave these impieties to those who are sufficiently ill-bred to be really capable of them. Let them at least be honest men, if they cannot be Christians. Finally, let them recognise that there are two kinds of people one can call reasonable; those who serve God with all their heart because they know Him, and those who seek Him with all their heart because they do not know Him.

But as for those who live without knowing Him and without seeking Him, they judge themselves so little worthy of their own care, that they are not worthy of the care of others; and it needs all the charity of the religion which they despise, not to despise them even to the point of leaving them to their folly. But because this religion obliges us always to regard them, so long as they are in this life, as capable of the grace which can enlighten them, and to believe that they may, in a little time, be more replenished with faith than we are, and that, on the other hand, we may fall into the blindness wherein they are, we must do for them what we would they should do for us if we were in their place, and call upon them to have pity upon themselves, and to take at least some steps in the endeavour to find light. Let them give to reading this some of the hours which they otherwise employ so uselessly; whatever aversion they may bring to the task, they will perhaps gain something, and at least will not lose much. But as for those who bring to the task perfect sincerity and a real desire to meet with truth, those I hope will be satisfied and convinced of the proofs of a religion so divine, which I have here collected and in which I have followed somewhat after this order . . .

195

Before entering into the proofs of the Christian religion, I find it necessary to point out the sinfulness of those men who live in indifference to the search for truth in a matter which is so important to them, and which touches them so nearly.

Of all their errors, this doubtless is the one which most convicts them of foolishness and blindness, and in which it is easiest to confound them by the first glimmerings of common sense, and by natural feelings.

For it is not to be doubted that the duration of this life is but a moment; that the state of death is eternal, whatever may be its nature; and that thus all our actions and thoughts must take such different directions according to the state of that eternity, that it is impossible to take one step with sense and judgment, unless we regulate our course by the truth of that point which ought to be our ultimate end.

There is nothing clearer than this; and thus, according to the principles of reason, the conduct of men is wholly unreasonable, if they do not take another course.

On this point therefore we condemn those who live without thought of the ultimate end of life, who let themselves be guided by their own inclinations and their own pleasures without reflection and without concern, and, as if they could annihilate eternity by turning away their thought from it, think only of making themselves happy for the moment.

Yet this eternity exists, and death, which must open into it, and threatens them every hour, must in a little time infallibly put them under the dreadful necessity of being either annihilated or unhappy for ever, without knowing which of these eternities is for ever prepared for them.

This is a doubt of terrible consequence. They are in peril of eternal woe; and thereupon, as if the matter were not worth the trouble, they neglect to inquire whether this is one of those opinions which people receive with too credulous a facility, or one of those which, obscure in themselves, have a very firm, though hidden, foundation. Thus they know not whether there be truth or falsity in the matter, nor whether there be strength or weakness in the proofs. They have them before their eyes; they refuse to look at them; and in that ignorance they choose all that is necessary to fall into this misfortune if it exist, to await death to make trial of it, yet to be very content in this state, to make profession of it and indeed to boast of it. Can we think seriously on the importance of this subject without being horrified at conduct so extravagant?

This resting in ignorance is a monstrous thing, and they who pass their life in it must be made to feel its extravagance and stupidity, by having it shown to them, so that they may be confounded by the sight of their folly. For this is how men reason, when they choose to live in such ignorance of what they are, and without seeking enlightenment. "I know not," they say . . .

196

Men lack heart; they would not make a friend of it.

197

To be insensible to the extent of despising interesting things, and to become insensible to the point which interests us most.

198

The sensibility of man to trifles, and his insensibility to great things, indicates a strange inversion.

199

Let us imagine a number of men in chains, and all condemned to death, where some are killed each day in the sight of the others, and those who remain see their own fate in that of their fellows, and wait their turn, looking at each other sorrowfully and without hope. It is an image of the condition of men.

200

A man in a dungeon, ignorant whether his sentence be pronounced, and having only one hour to learn it, but this hour enough, if he know that it is pronounced, to obtain its repeal, would act unnaturally in spending that hour, not in ascertaining his sentence, but in playing piquet. So it is against nature that man, &c. It is making heavy the hand of God.

Thus not only the zeal of those who seek Him proves God, but also the blindness of those who seek Him not.

201

All the objections of this one and that one only go against themselves, and not against religion. All that infidels say . . .

202

[From those who are in despair at being without faith, we see that God does not enlighten them; but as to the rest, we see there is a God who makes them blind.]

203

Fascinatio nugacitatis.[6]—That passion may not harm us, let us act as if we had only eight hours to live.

204

If we ought to devote eight hours of life, we ought to devote a hundred years.

205

When I consider the short duration of my life, swallowed up in the eternity before and after, the little space which I fill, and even can see, engulfed in the infinite immensity of spaces of which I am ignorant, and which know me not, I am frightened, and am astonished at being here rather than there; for there is no reason why here rather than there, why now rather than then. Who has put me here? By whose order and direction have this place and time been alloted to me? *Memoria hospitis unius diei prætereuntis.*[7]

206

The eternal silence of these infinite spaces frightens me.

207

How many kingdoms know us not?

[6] " The bewitching of naughtiness."—Wisdom, iv. 12.
[7] " The remembrance of a guest that tarrieth but a day."—Wisdom, v. 14.

208

Why is my knowledge limited? Why my stature? Why my life to one hundred years rather than to a thousand? What reason has nature had for giving me such, and for choosing this number rather than another in the infinity of those from which there is no more reason to choose one than another, trying nothing else?

209

Art thou less a slave by being loved and favoured by thy master? Thou art indeed well off, slave. Thy master favours thee; he will soon beat thee.

210

The last act is tragic, however happy all the rest of the play is; at the last a little earth is thrown upon our head, and that is the end for ever.

211

We are fools to depend upon the society of our fellow-men. Wretched as we are, powerless as we are, they will not aid us; we shall die alone. We should therefore act as if we were alone, and in that case should we build fine houses, &c.? We should seek the truth without hesitation; and, if we refuse it, we show that we value the esteem of men more than the search for truth.

212

Instability.—It is a horrible thing to feel all that we possess slipping away.

213

Between us and heaven or hell there is only life, which is the frailest thing in the world.

214

Injustice.—That presumption should be joined to meanness is extreme injustice.

215

To fear death without danger, and not in danger, for one must be a man.

216

Sudden death alone is feared; hence confessors stay with lords.

217

An heir finds the title-deeds of his house. Will he say, "Perhaps they are forged?" and neglect to examine them?

218

Dungeon.—I approve of not examining the opinion of Copernicus; but this . . . ! It concerns all our life to know whether the soul be mortal or immortal.

219

It is certain that the mortality or immortality of the soul must make an entire difference to morality. And yet philosophers have constructed their ethics independently of this: they discuss to pass an hour.

Plato, to incline to Christianity.

220

The fallacy of philosophers who have not discussed the immortality of the soul. The fallacy of their dilemma in Montaigne.

221

Atheists ought to say what is perfectly evident; now it is not perfectly evident that the soul is material.

222

Atheists.—What reason have they for saying that we cannot rise from the dead? What is more difficult, to be born or to rise again; that what has never been should be, or that what has been should be again? Is it more difficult to come into existence than to return to it? Habit makes the one appear easy to us; want of habit makes the other impossible. A popular way of thinking!

Why cannot a virgin bear a child? Does a hen not lay eggs without a cock? What distinguishes these outwardly from others? And who has told us that the hen may not form the germ as well as the cock?

223

What have they to say against the resurrection, and against the child-bearing of the Virgin? Which is the more difficult, to produce a man or an animal, or to reproduce it? And if they had never seen any species of animals, could they have conjectured whether they were produced without connection with each other?

224

How I hate these follies of not believing in the Eucharist, &c.! If the Gospel be true, if Jesus Christ be God, what difficulty is there?

225

Atheism shows strength of mind, but only to a certain degree.

226

Infidels, who profess to follow reason, ought to be exceedingly strong in reason. What say they then? "Do we not see," say they, "that the brutes live and die like men, and Turks like Christians? They have their ceremonies, their prophets, their doctors, their saints, their monks, like us," &c. (Is this contrary to Scripture? Does it not say all this?)

If you care but little to know the truth, here is enough of it to leave you in repose. But if you desire with all your heart to know it, it is not enough; look at it in detail. This would be sufficient for a question in philosophy; but not here, where it concerns your all. And yet, after a trifling reflection of this kind, we go to amuse ourselves, &c. Let us inquire of this same religion whether it does not give a reason for this obscurity; perhaps it will teach it to us.

227

Order by dialogues.—What ought I to do? I see only darkness everywhere. Shall I believe I am nothing? Shall I believe I am God?

"All things change and succeed each other." You are mistaken; there is . . .

228

Objection of atheists: "But we have no light."

229

This is what I see and what troubles me. I look on all sides, and I see only darkness everywhere. Nature presents to me nothing which is not matter of doubt and concern. If I saw nothing there which revealed a Divinity, I would come to a negative conclusion; if I saw everywhere the signs of a Creator, I would remain peacefully in faith. But, seeing too much to deny and too little to be sure, I am in a state to be pitied; wherefore I have a hundred times wished that if a God maintains nature, she should testify to Him unequivocally, and that, if the signs she gives are deceptive, she should suppress them altogether; that she should say everything or nothing, that I might see which cause I ought to follow. Whereas in my present state, ignorant of what I am or of what I ought to do, I know neither my condition nor my duty. My heart inclines wholly to know, where is the true good, in order to follow it; nothing would be too dear to me for eternity.

I envy those whom I see living in the faith with such carelessness, and who make such a bad use of a gift of which it seems to me I would make such a different use.

230

It is incomprehensible that God should exist, and it is incomprehensible that He should not exist, that the soul should be joined to the body, and that we should have no soul; that the world should be created, and that it should not be created, &c.; that original sin should be, and that it should not be.

231

Do you believe it to be impossible that God is infinite, without parts?—Yes. I wish therefore to show you an infinite and indivisible thing. It is a point moving everywhere with an infinite velocity; for it is one in all places, and is all totality in every place.

Let this effect of nature, which previously seemed to you impossible, make you know that there may be others of which you are still ignorant. Do not draw this conclusion from your experiment, that there remains nothing for you to know; but rather that there remains an infinity for you to know.

232

Infinite movement, the point which fills everything, the moment of rest; infinite without quantity, indivisible and infinite.

233

Infinite—nothing.—Our soul is cast into a body, where it finds number, time, dimension. Thereupon it reasons, and calls this nature, necessity, and can believe nothing else.

Unity joined to infinity adds nothing to it, no more than one foot to an infinite measure. The finite is annihilated in the presence of the infinite, and becomes a pure nothing. So our spirit before God, so our justice before divine justice. There is not so great a disproportion between our justice and that of God, as between unity and infinity.

The justice of God must be vast like His compassion. Now justice to the outcast is less vast, and ought less to offend our feelings than mercy towards the elect.

We know that there is an infinite, and are ignorant of its nature. As we know it to be false that numbers are finite, it is therefore true that there is an infinity in number. But we do not know what it is. It is false that it is even, it is false that it is odd; for the addition of a unit can make no change in its nature. Yet it is a number, and every number

is odd or even (this is certainly true of every finite number).
So we may well know that there is a God without knowing
what He is. Is there not one substantial truth, seeing there
are so many things which are not the truth itself?

We know then the existence and nature of the finite, because we also are finite and have extension. We know
the existence of the infinite, and are ignorant of its nature,
because it has extension like us, but not limits like us. But
we know neither the existence nor the nature of God, because He has neither extension nor limits.

But by faith we know His existence; in glory we shall
know His nature. Now, I have already shown that we may
well know the existence of a thing, without knowing its
nature.

Let us now speak according to natural lights.

If there is a God, He is infinitely incomprehensible, since,
having neither parts nor limits, He has no affinity to us. We
are then incapable of knowing either what He is or if He
is. This being so, who will dare to undertake the decision
of the question? Not we, who have no affinity to Him.

Who then will blame Christians for not being able to give
a reason for their belief, since they profess a religion for
which they cannot give a reason? They declare, in expound-
ing it to the world, that it is a foolishness, *stultitiam;* and
then you complain that they do not prove it! If they proved
it, they would not keep their word; it is in lacking proofs,
that they are not lacking in sense. "Yes, but although this
excuses those who offer it as such, and takes away from
them the blame of putting it forward without reason, it does
not excuse those who receive it." Let us then examine
this point, and say, "God is, or He is not." But to which
side shall we incline? Reason can decide nothing here.
There is an infinite chaos which separates us. A game is
being played at the extremity of this infinite distance where
heads or tails will turn up. What will you wager? According to reason, you can do neither the one thing nor the other;
according to reason, you can defend neither of the propositions.

Do not then reprove for error those who have made a
choice; for you know nothing about it. "No, but I blame

them for having made, not this choice, but a choice; for again both he who chooses heads and he who chooses tails are equally at fault, they are both in the wrong. The true course is not to wager at all."

—Yes; but you must wager. It is not optional. You are embarked. Which will you choose then? Let us see. Since you must choose, let us see which interests you least. You have two things to lose, the true and the good; and two things to stake, your reason and your will, your knowledge and your happiness; and your nature has two things to shun, error and misery. Your reason is no more shocked in choosing one rather than the other, since you must of necessity choose. This is one point settled. But your happiness? Let us weigh the gain and the loss in wagering that God is. Let us estimate these two chances. If you gain, you gain all; if you lose, you lose nothing. Wager then without hesitation that He is.—"That is very fine. Yes, I must wager; but I may perhaps wager too much."—Let us see. Since there is an equal risk of gain and of loss, if you had only to gain two lives, instead of one, you might still wager. But if there were three lives to gain, you would have to play (since you are under the necessity of playing), and you would be imprudent, when you are forced to play, not to chance your life to gain three at a game where there is an equal risk of loss and gain. But there is an eternity of life and happiness. And this being so, if there were an infinity of chances, of which one only would be for you, you would still be right in wagering one to win two, and you would act stupidly, being obliged to play, by refusing to stake one life against three at a game in which out of an infinity of chances there is one for you, if there were an infinity of an infinitely happy life to gain. But there is here an infinity of an infinitely happy life to gain, a chance of gain against a finite number of chances of loss, and what you stake is finite. It is all divided; wherever the infinite is and there is not an infinity of chances of loss against that of gain, there is no time to hesitate, you must give all. And thus, when one is forced to play, he must renounce reason to preserve his life, rather than risk it for infinite gain, as likely to happen as the loss of nothingness.

For it is no use to say it is uncertain if we will gain, and it is certain that we risk, and that the infinite distance between the *certainty* of what is staked and the *uncertainty* of what will be gained, equals the finite good which is certainly staked against the uncertain infinite. It is not so, as every player stakes a certainty to gain an uncertainty, and yet he stakes a finite certainty to gain a finite uncertainty, without transgressing against reason. There is not an infinite distance between the certainty staked and the uncertainty of the gain; that is untrue. In truth, there is an infinity between the certainty of gain and the certainty of loss. But the uncertainty of the gain is proportioned to the certainty of the stake according to the proportion of the chances of gain and loss. Hence it comes that, if there are as many risks on one side as on the other, the course is to play even; and then the certainty of the stake is equal to the uncertainty of the gain, so far is it from fact that there is an infinite distance between them. And so our proposition is of infinite force, when there is the finite to stake in a game where there are equal risks of gain and of loss, and the infinite to gain. This is demonstrable; and if men are capable of any truths, this is one.

"I confess it, I admit it. But still is there no means of seeing the faces of the cards?"—Yes, Scripture and the rest, &c.—"Yes, but I have my hands tied and my mouth closed; I am forced to wager, and am not free. I am not released, and am so made that I cannot believe. What then would you have me do?"

True. But at least learn your inability to believe, since reason brings you to this, and yet you cannot believe. Endeavour then to convince yourself, not by increase of proofs of God, but by the abatement of your passions. You would like to attain faith, and do not know the way; you would like to cure yourself of unbelief, and ask the remedy for it. Learn of those who have been bound like you, and who now stake all their possessions. These are people who know the way which you would follow, and who are cured of an ill of which you would be cured. Follow the way by which they began; by acting as if they believe, taking the holy water, having masses said, &c. Even this will naturally make you believe, and deaden your acuteness.—" But this is what I am afraid of."—And why? What have you to lose?

But to show you that this leads you there, it is this which will lessen the passions, which are your stumbling-blocks.

The end of this discourse.—Now what harm will befall you in taking this side? You will be faithful, honest, humble, grateful, generous, a sincere friend, truthful. Certainly you will not have those poisonous pleasures, glory and luxury; but will you not have others? I will tell you that you will thereby gain in this life, and that, at each step you take on this road, you will see so great certainty of gain, so much nothingness in what you risk, that you will at last recognize that you have wagered for something certain and infinite, for which you have given nothing.

" Ah! This discourse transports me, charms me," &c.

If this discourse pleases you and seems impressive, know that it is made by a man who has knelt, both before and after it, in prayer to that Being, infinite and without parts, before whom he lays all he has, for you also to lay before Him all you have for your own good and for His glory, that so strength may be given to lowliness.

234

If we must not act save on a certainty, we ought not to act on religion, for it is not certain. But how many things we do on an uncertainty, sea voyages, battles! I say then we must do nothing at all, for nothing is certain, and that there is more certainty in religion than there is as to whether we may see to-morrow; for it is not certain that we may see to-morrow, and it is certainly possible that we may not see it. We cannot say as much about religion. It is not certain that it is; but who will venture to say that it is certainly possible that it is not? Now when we work for to-morrow, and so on an uncertainty, we act reasonably; for we ought to work for an uncertainty according to the doctrine of chance which was demonstrated above.

St. Augustine has seen that we work for an uncertainty, on sea, in battle, &c. But he has not seen the doctrine of chance which proves that we should do so. Montaigne has seen that we are shocked at a fool, and that habit is all-powerful; but he has not seen the reason of this effect.

All these persons have seen the effects, but they have not seen the causes. They are, in comparison with those who have discovered the causes, as those who have only eyes are in comparison with those who have intellect. For the effects are perceptible by sense, and the causes are visible only to the intellect. And although these effects are seen by the mind, this mind is, in comparison with the mind which sees the causes, as the bodily senses are in comparison with the intellect.

235

Rem viderunt, causam non viderunt.[a]

236

According to the doctrine of chance, you ought to put yourself to the trouble of searching for the truth; for if you die without worshipping the True Cause, you are lost.— "But," say you, "if He had wished me to worship Him, He would have left me signs of His will."—He has done so; but you neglect them. Seek them therefore; it is well worth it.

237

Chances.—We must live differently in the world, according to these different assumptions:—(1) that we could always remain in it; (2) that it is certain that we shall not remain here long, and uncertain if we shall remain here one hour. This last assumption is our condition.

238

What do you then promise me, in addition to certain troubles, but ten years of self-love (for ten years is the chance), to try hard to please without success?

239

Objection.—Those who hope for salvation are so far happy; but they have as a counterpoise the fear of hell.

[a] "They saw the thing, not the cause."

Reply.—Who has most reason to fear hell: he who is in ignorance whether there is a hell, and who is certain of damnation if there is; or he who certainly believes there is a hell, and hopes to be saved if there is?

240

"I would soon have renounced pleasure," say they, "had I faith." For my part I tell you, "You would soon have faith, if you renounced pleasure." Now, it is for you to begin. If I could, I would give you faith. I cannot do so, nor therefore test the truth of what you say. But you can well renounce pleasure, and test whether what I say is true.

241

Order.—I would have far more fear of being mistaken, and of finding that the Christian religion was true, than of not being mistaken in believing it true.

SECTION IV

OF THE MEANS OF BELIEF

242

*P*REFACE *to the second part.*—To speak of those who have treated of this matter.

I admire the boldness with which these persons undertake to speak of God. In addressing their argument to infidels, their first chapter is to prove Divinity from the works of nature. I should not be astonished at their enterprise, if they were addressing their argument to the faithful; for it is certain that those who have the living faith in their heart see at once that all existence is none other than the work of the God whom they adore. But for those in whom this light is extinguished, and in whom we purpose to rekindle it, persons destitute of faith and grace, who, seeking with all their light whatever they see in nature that can bring them to this knowledge, find only obscurity and darkness; to tell them that they have only to look at the smallest things which surround them, and they will see God openly, to give them, as a complete proof of this great and important matter, the course of the moon and planets, and to claim to have concluded the proof with such an argument, is to give them ground for believing that the proofs of our religion are very weak. And I see by reason and experience that nothing is more calculated to arouse their contempt.

It is not after this manner that Scripture speaks, which has a better knowledge of the things that are of God. It says, on the contrary, that God is a hidden God, and that, since the corruption of nature, He has left men in a darkness from which they can escape only through Jesus Christ, without whom all communion with God is cut off. *Nemo novit Patrem, nisi Filius, et cui voluerit Filius revelare.*[1]

[1] Matthew, xi. 27.

90

This is what Scripture points out to us, when it says in so many places that those who seek God find Him. It is not of that light, "like the noonday sun," that this is said. We do not say that those who seek the noonday sun, or water in the sea, shall find them; and hence the evidence of God must not be of this nature. So it tells us elsewhere: *Vere tu es Deus absconditus.*[a]

243

It is an astounding fact that no canonical writer has ever made use of nature to prove God. They all strive to make us believe in Him. David, Solomon, &c., have never said, "There is no void, therefore there is a God." They must have had more knowledge than the most learned people who came after them, and who have all made use of this argument. This is worthy of attention.

244

"Why! Do you not say yourself that the heavens and birds prove God?" No. "And does your religion not say so?" No. For although it is true in a sense for some souls to whom God gives this light, yet it is false with respect to the majority of men.

245

There are three sources of belief: reason, custom, inspiration. The Christian religion, which alone has reason, does not acknowledge as her true children those who believe without inspiration. It is not that she excludes reason and custom. On the contrary, the mind must be opened to proofs, must be confirmed by custom, and offer itself in humbleness to inspirations, which alone can produce a true and saving effect. *Ne evacuetur crux Christi.*[b]

246

Order.—After the letter "that we ought to seek God," to write the letter "on removing obstacles"; which is the discourse on "the machine," on preparing the machine, on seeking by reason.

[a] Isaiah, xlv. 15.   [b] 1 Corinthians, i. 17.

247

Order.—A letter of exhortation to a friend to induce him to seek. And he will reply, " But what is the use of seeking? Nothing is seen." Then to reply to him, " Do not despair." And he will answer that he would be glad to find some light, but that, according to this very religion, if he believed in it, it will be of no use to him, and that therefore he prefers not to seek. And to answer to that: The machine.

248

A Letter which indicates the use of proofs by the machine. —Faith is different from proof; the one is human, the other is a gift of God. *Justus ex fide vivit.*[4] It is this faith that God Himself puts into the heart, of which the proof is often the instrument, *fides ex auditu;*[5] but this faith is in the heart, and makes us not say *scio,*[6] but *credo.*[7]

249

It is superstition to put one's hope in formalities; but it is pride to be unwilling to submit to them.

250

The external must be joined to the internal to obtain anything from God, that is to say, we must kneel, pray with the lips, &c., in order that proud man, who would not submit himself to God, may be now subject to the creature. To expect help from these externals is superstition; to refuse to join them to the internal is pride.

251

Other religions, as the pagan, are more popular, for they consist in externals. But they are not for educated people. A purely intellectual religion would be more suited to the learned, but it would be of no use to the common people. The Christian religion alone is adapted to all,

---

[4] Romans, i. 17.   [5] Romans, x. 17.   [6] " I know."   [7] " I believe."

being composed of externals and internals. It raises the common people to the internal, and humbles the proud to the external; it is not perfect without the two, for the people must understand the spirit of the letter, and the learned must submit their spirit to the letter.

252

For we must not misunderstand ourselves; we are as much automatic as intellectual; and hence it comes that the instrument by which conviction is attained is not demonstration alone. How few things are demonstrated? Proofs only convince the mind. Custom is the source of our strongest and most believed proofs. It bends the automaton, which persuades the mind without its thinking about the matter. Who has demonstrated that there will be a to-morrow, and that we shall die? And what is more believed? It is then custom which persuades us of it; it is custom that makes so many men Christians; custom that makes them Turks, heathens, artisans, soldiers, &c. (Faith in baptism is more received among Christians than among Turks.) Finally, we must have recourse to it when once the mind has seen where the truth is, in order to quench our thirst, and steep ourselves in that belief, which escapes us at every hour; for always to have proofs ready is too much trouble. We must get an easier belief, which is that of custom, which, without violence, without art, without argument, makes us believe things, and inclines all our powers to this belief, so that our soul falls naturally into it. It is not enough to believe only by force of conviction, when the automaton is inclined to believe the contrary. Both our parts must be made to believe, the mind by reasons which it is sufficient to have seen once in a lifetime, and the automaton by custom, and by not allowing it to incline to the contrary. *Inclina cor meum, Deus.*[8]

The reason acts slowly, with so many examinations, and on so many principles, which must be always present, that at every hour it falls asleep, or wanders, through want of having all its principles present. Feeling does not act

[8] Psalms, cxix. 36.

thus; it acts in a moment, and is always ready to act. We must then put our faith in feeling; otherwise it will be always vacillating.

253

Two extremes: to exclude reason, to admit reason only.

254

It is not a rare thing to have to reprove the world for too much docility. It is a natural vice like credulity, and as pernicious. Superstition.

255

Piety is different from superstition.

To carry piety as far as superstition is to destroy it.

The heretics reproach us for this superstitious submission. This is to do what they reproach us for . . .

Infidelity, not to believe in the Eucharist, because it is not seen.

Superstition to believe propositions. Faith, &c.

256

I say there are few true Christians, even as regards faith. There are many who believe but from superstition. There are many who do not believe solely from wickedness. Few are between the two.

In this I do not include those who are of truly pious character, nor all those who believe from a feeling in their heart.

257

There are only three kinds of persons: those who serve God, having found Him; others who are occupied in seeking Him, not having found Him; while the remainder live without seeking Him, and without having found Him. The first are reasonable and happy, the last are foolish and unhappy; those between are unhappy and reasonable.

258

Unus quisque sibi Deum fingit.[9]
Disgust.

259

Ordinary people have the power of not thinking of that
about which they do not wish to think. " Do not meditate
on the passages about the Messiah," said the Jew to his
son. Thus our people often act. Thus are false religions
preserved, and even the true one, in regard to many persons.

But there are some who have not the power of thus
preventing thought, and who think so much the more as
they are forbidden. These undo false religions, and even
the true one, if they do not find solid arguments.

260

They hide themselves in the press, and call numbers to
their rescue. Tumult.

Authority.—So far from making it a rule to believe a
thing because you have heard it, you ought to believe nothing
without putting yourself into the position as if you had
never heard it.

It is your own assent to yourself, and the constant voice
of your own reason, and not of others, that should make
you believe.

Belief is so important! A hundred contradictions might
be true. If antiquity were the rule of belief, men of ancient
time would then be without rule. If general consent, if
men had perished?

False humility, pride.

Lift the curtain. You try in vain; if you must either
believe, or deny, or doubt. Shall we then have no rule?
We judge that animals do well what they do. Is there no
rule whereby to judge men?

To deny, to believe, and to doubt well, are to a man
what the race is to a horse.

Punishment of those who sin, error.

[9] " Each one makes a God for himself."

261

Those who do not love the truth take as a pretext that it is disputed, and that a multitude deny it. And so their error arises only from this, that they do not love either truth or charity. Thus they are without excuse.

262

Superstition and lust. Scruples, evil desires. Evil fear; fear, not such as comes from a belief in God, but such as comes from a doubt whether He exists or not. True fear comes from faith; false fear comes from doubt. True fear is joined to hope, because it is born of faith, and because men hope in the God in whom they believe. False fear is joined to despair, because men fear the God in whom they have no belief. The former fear to lose Him; the latter fear to find Him.

263

"A miracle," says one, "would strengthen my faith." He says so when he does not see one. Reasons, seen from afar, appear to limit our view; but when they are reached, we begin to see beyond. Nothing stops the nimbleness of our mind. There is no rule, say we, which has not some exceptions, no truth so general which has not some aspect in which it fails. It is sufficient that it be not absolutely universal to give us a pretext for applying the exception to the present subject, and for saying, "This is not always true; there are therefore cases where it is not so." It only remains to show that this is one of them; and that is why we are very awkward or unlucky, if we do not find one some day.

264

We do not weary of eating and sleeping every day, for hunger and sleepiness recur. Without that we should weary of them. So, without the hunger for spiritual things, we weary of them. Hunger after righteousness, the eighth beatitude.

265

Faith indeed tells what the senses do not tell, but not the contrary of what they see. It is above them, and not contrary to them.

266

How many stars have telescopes revealed to us which did not exist for our philosophers of old! We freely attack Holy Scripture on the great number of stars, saying, " There are only one thousand and twenty-eight, we know it." There is grass on the earth, we see it—from the moon we would not see it—and on the grass are leaves, and in these leaves are small animals; but after that no more.—O presumptuous man!—the compounds are composed of elements, and the elements not.—O presumptuous man! Here is a fine reflection.—We must not say that there is anything which we do not see.—We must then talk like others, but not think like them.

267

The last proceeding of reason is to recognize that there is an infinity of things which are beyond it. It is but feeble if it does not see so far as to know this. But if natural things are beyond it, what will be said of supernatural?

268

Submission.—We must know where to doubt, where to feel certain, where to submit. He who does not do so, understands not the force of reason. There are some who offend against these three rules, either by affirming everything as demonstrative, from want of knowing what demonstration is; or by doubting everything, from want of knowing where to submit; or by submitting in everything, from want of knowing where they must judge.

269

Submission is the use of reason in which consists true Christianity.

270

St. Augustine.—Reason would never submit, if it did not judge that there are some occasions on which it ought to submit. It is then right for it to submit, when it judges that it ought to submit.

271

Wisdom sends us to childhood. *Nisi efficiamini sicut parvuli.*[10]

272

There is nothing so conformable to reason as this disavowal of reason.

273

If we submit everything to reason, our religion will have no mysterious and supernatural element. If we offend the principles of reason, our religion will be absurd and ridiculous.

274

All our reasoning reduces itself to yielding to feeling.
But fancy is like, though contrary to feeling, so that we cannot distinguish between these contraries. One person says that my feeling is fancy, another that his fancy is feeling. We should have a rule. Reason offers itself; but it is pliable in every sense; and thus there is no rule.

275

Men often take their imagination for their heart; and they believe they are converted as soon as they think of being converted.

276

M. de Roannez said: "Reasons come to me afterwards, but at first a thing pleases or shocks me without my knowing the reason, and yet it shocks me for that reason which I only discover afterwards." But I believe, not that it shocked him for the reasons which were found afterwards, but that these reasons were only found because it shocks him.

[10] Matthew, xviii. 3.

277

The heart has its reasons, which reason does not know. We feel it in a thousand things. I say that the heart naturally loves the Universal Being, and also itself naturally, according as it gives itself to them; and it hardens itself against one or the other at its will. You have rejected the one, and kept the other. Is it by reason that you love yourself?

278

It is the heart which experiences God, and not the reason. This, then, is faith: God felt by the heart, not by the reason.

279

Faith is a gift of God; do not believe that we said it was a gift of reasoning. Other religions do not say this of their faith. They only gave reasoning in order to arrive at it, and yet it does not bring them to it.

280

The knowledge of God is very far from the love of Him.

281

Heart, instinct, principles.

282

We know truth, not only by the reason, but also by the heart, and it is in this last way that we know first principles; and reason, which has no part in it, tries in vain to impugn them. The sceptics, who have only this for their object, labour to no purpose. We know that we do not dream, and however impossible it is for us to prove it by reason, this inability demonstrates only the weakness of our reason, but not, as they affirm, the uncertainty of all our knowledge. For the knowledge of first principles, as space, time, motion, number, is as sure as any of those which we get from reasoning. And reason must trust these intuitions of the heart, and must base on them every argument. (We have intuitive knowledge of the tri-dimensional nature of space, and of the infinity of number, and reason then shows that there are no two square numbers one of which is double of the other. Principles are intuited, propositions are inferred, all with certainty, though in different ways.) And it is as useless and absurd for reason to demand from the heart proofs of her first principles, before admitting them, as it would be for the heart to demand from reason an intuition of all demonstrated propositions before accepting them.

This inability ought, then, to serve only to humble reason, which would judge all, but not to impugn our certainty, as if only reason were capable of instructing us. Would to God, on the contrary, that we had never need of it, and that we knew everything by instinct and intuition! But nature has refused us this boon. On the contrary, she has given us but very little knowledge of this kind; and all the rest can be acquired only by reasoning.

Therefore, those to whom God has imparted religion by intuition are very fortunate, and justly convinced. But to those who do not have it, we can give it only by reasoning, waiting for God to give them spiritual insight, without which faith is only human, and useless for salvation.

283

Order.—Against the objection that Scripture has no order.
The heart has its own order; the intellect has its own, which is by principle and demonstration. The heart has another. We do not prove that we ought to be loved by enumerating in order the causes of love; that would be ridiculous.

Jesus Christ and Saint Paul employ the rule of love, not of intellect; for they would warm, not instruct. It is the same with Saint Augustine. This order consists chiefly in digressions on each point to indicate the end, and keep it always in sight.

284

Do not wonder to see simple people believe without reasoning. God imparts to them love of Him and hatred of self. He inclines their heart to believe. Men will never believe with a saving and real faith, unless God inclines their heart; and they will believe as soon as He inclines it. And this is what David knew well, when he said: *Inclina cor meum, Deus, in* . . .[11]

285

Religion is suited to all kinds of minds. Some pay attention only to its establishment, and this religion is such that its very establishment suffices to prove its truth. Others trace it even to the apostles. The more learned go back to the beginning of the world. The angels see it better still, and from a more distant time.

286

Those who believe without having read the Testaments, do so because they have an inward disposition entirely holy, and all that they hear of our religion conforms to it. They feel that a God has made them; they desire only to love God; they desire to hate themselves only. They feel that they have no strength in themselves; that they are incapable of coming to God; and that if God does not come to them, they can have no communion with Him. And they hear our religion say that men must love God only, and hate self only; but that all being corrupt and unworthy of God, God made himself man to unite Himself to us. No more is required to persuade men who have this disposition in their heart, and who have this knowledge of their duty and of their inefficiency.

287

Those whom we see to be Christians without the knowledge of the prophecies and evidences, nevertheless judge of their religion as well as those who have that knowledge. They judge of it by the heart, as others judge of it by the intellect. God Himself inclines them to believe, and thus they are most effectively convinced.

[11] Psalms, cxix. 36.

I confess indeed that one of those Christians who believe without proofs will not perhaps be capable of convincing an infidel who will say the same of himself. But those who know the proofs of religion will prove without difficulty that such a believer is truly inspired by God, though he cannot prove it himself.

For God having said in His prophecies (which are undoubtedly prophecies), that in the reign of Jesus Christ He would spread His spirit abroad among nations, and that the youths and maidens and children of the Church would prophesy; it is certain that the Spirit of God is in these, and not in the others.

288

Instead of complaining that God has hidden Himself, you will give Him thanks for having revealed so much of Himself; and you will also give Him thanks for not having revealed Himself to haughty sages, unworthy to know so holy a God.

Two kinds of persons know Him: those who have a humble heart, and who love lowliness, whatever kind of intellect they may have, high or low; and those who have sufficient understanding to see the truth, whatever opposition they may have to it.

289

Proof.—1. The Christian religion, by its establishment, having established itself so strongly, so gently, whilst so contrary to nature.—2. The sanctity, the dignity, and the humility of a Christian soul.—3. The miracles of Holy Scripture.—4. Jesus Christ in particular.—5. The apostles in particular.—6. Moses and the prophets in particular.—7. The Jewish people.—8. The prophecies.—9. Perpetuity: no religion has perpetuity.—10. The doctrine which gives a reason for everything.—11. The sanctity of this law.—12. By the course of the world.

Surely, after considering what is life and what is religion, we should not refuse to obey the inclination to follow it, if it comes into our heart; and it is certain that there is no ground for laughing at those who follow it.

290

Proofs of religion.—Morality, Doctrine, Miracles, Prophecies, Types.

JUSTICE AND THE REASON OF EFFECTS

291

IN the letter *On Injustice* can come the ridiculousness of the law that the elder gets all. "My friend, you were born on this side of the mountain, it is therefore just that your elder brother gets everything."

"Why do you kill me?"

292

He lives on the other side of the water.

293

"Why do you kill me? What! do you not live on the other side of the water? If you lived on this side, my friend, I should be an assassin, and it would be unjust to slay you in this manner. But since you live on the other side, I am a hero, and it is just."

294

. . . On what shall man found the order of the world which he would govern? Shall it be on the caprice of each individual? What confusion! Shall it be on justice? Man is ignorant of it.

Certainly had he known it, he would not have established this maxim, the most general of all that obtain among men, that each should follow the customs of his own country. The glory of true equity would have brought all nations under subjection, and legislators would not have taken as their model the fancies and caprice of Persians and Germans instead of this unchanging justice. We should have seen it set up in all the States on earth and in all times; whereas we see neither justice nor injustice which does not change its nature with change in climate. Three degrees of latitude reverse all jurisprudence; a meridian decides the truth. Fundamental laws change after a few years of possession; right has its epochs; the entry of Saturn into the lion marks to us the origin of such and such a crime. A strange justice that is bounded by a river! Truth on this side of the Pyrenees, error on the other side.

Men admit that justice does not consist in these customs, but that it resides in natural laws, common to every country. They would certainly maintain it obstinately, if reckless chance which has distributed human laws had encountered even one which was universal; but the farce is that the caprice of men has so many vagaries that there is no such law.

Theft, incest, infanticide, patricide, have all had a place among virtuous actions. Can anything be more ridiculous than that a man should have the right to kill me because he lives on the other side of the water, and because his ruler has a quarrel with mine, though I have none with him?

Doubtless there are natural laws; but good reason once corrupted has corrupted all. *Nihil amplius nostrum est; quod nostrum dicimus, artis est.*[1] *Ex senatus consultis et plebiscitis crimina exercentur.*[2] *Ut olim vitiis, sic nunc legibus laboramus.*[3]

The result of this confusion is that one affirms the essence of justice to be the authority of the legislator; another, the interest of the sovereign; another, present custom, and this is the most sure. Nothing, according to reason alone, is just in itself; all changes with time. Custom creates the whole of equity, for the simple reason that it is accepted. It is the mystical foundation of its authority; whoever carries it back to first principles destroys it. Nothing is so faulty as those laws which correct faults. He who obeys them because they are just, obeys a justice which is imaginary, and not the essence of law; it is quite self-

[1] " We can claim nothing more; what we call ours is art's."
[2] " Decrees of the senate and of the people are responsible for crimes."
[3] " As once we suffered from vices, so now from laws."

contained, it is law and nothing more. He who will examine its motive will find it so feeble and so trifling that if he be not accustomed to contemplate the wonders of human imagination, he will marvel that one century has gained for it so much pomp and reverence. The art of opposition and of revolution is to unsettle established customs, sounding them even to their source, to point out their want of authority and justice. We must, it is said, get back to the natural and fundamental laws of the State, which an unjust custom has abolished. It is a game certain to result in the loss of all; nothing will be just on the balance. Yet people readily lend their ear to such arguments. They shake off the yoke as soon as they recognise it; and the great profit by their ruin, and by that of these curious investigators of accepted customs. But from a contrary mistake men sometimes think they can justly do everything which is not without an example. That is why the wisest of legislators said that it was often necessary to deceive men for their own good; and another, a good politician, *Cum veritatem qua liberetur ignoret, expedit qoud fallatur.*[4] We must not see the fact of usurpation; law was once introduced without reason, and has become reasonable. We must make it regarded as authoritative, eternal, and conceal its origin, if we do not wish that it should soon come to an end.

295

Mine, thine.—"This dog is mine," said those poor children; "that is my place in the sun." Here is the beginning and the image of the usurpation of all the earth.

296

When the question for consideration is whether we ought to make war, and kill so many men—condemn so many Spaniards to death—only one man is judge, and he is an interested party. There should be a third, who is disinterested.

---

[4] "When a man does not understand the truth by which he might be freed, it is expedient that he should be deceived."—St. Augustine.

297

Veri juris.[5]—We have it no more; if we had it, we should take conformity to the customs of a country as the rule of justice. It is here that, not finding justice, we have found force, &c.

298

Justice, Might.—It is right that what is just should be obeyed; it is necessary that what is strongest should be obeyed. Justice without might is helpless; might without justice is tyrannical. Justice without might is gainsaid, because there are always offenders; might without justice is condemned. We must then combine justice and might, and for this end make what is just strong, or what is strong just.

Justice is subject to dispute; might is easily recognized and is not disputed. So we cannot give might to justice, because might has gainsaid justice, and has declared that it is she herself who is just. And thus being unable to make what is just strong, we have made what is strong just.

299

The only universal rules are the laws of the country in ordinary affairs, and of the majority in others. Whence comes this? From the might which is in them. Hence it comes that kings, who have power of a different kind, do not follow the majority of their ministers.

No doubt equality of goods is just; but, being unable to cause might to obey justice, men have made it just to obey might. Unable to strengthen justice, they have justified might; so that the just and the strong should unite, and there should be peace, which is the sovereign good.

300

"When a strong man armed keepeth his goods, his goods are in peace."

[5] "Of the true law."

301

Why do we follow the majority? Is it because they have more reason? No, because they have more power.

Why do we follow ancient laws and opinions? Is it because they are more sound? No, but because they are unique, and remove from us the root of difference.

302

. . . It is the effect of might, not of custom. For those who are capable of originality are few; the greater number will only follow, and refuse glory to those inventors who seek it by their inventions. And if these are obstinate in their wish to obtain glory, and despise those who do not invent, the latter will call them ridiculous names, and would beat them with a stick. Let no one then boast of his subtility, or let him keep his complacency to himself.

303

Might is the sovereign of the world, and not opinion.— But opinion makes use of might.—It is might that makes opinion. Gentleness is beautiful in our opinion. Why? Because he who will dance on a rope will be alone, and I will gather a stronger mob of people who will say that it is unbecoming.

304

The cords which bind the respect of men to each other are in general cords of necessity; for there must be different degrees, all men wishing to rule, and not all being able to do so, but some being able.

Let us then imagine we see society in the process of formation. Men will doubtless fight till the stronger party overcomes the weaker, and a dominant party is established. But when this is once determined, the masters, who do not desire the continuation of strife, then decree that the power which is in their hands shall be transmitted as they please. Some place it in election by the people, others in hereditary succession, &c.

And this is the point where imagination begins to play its part. Till now power makes fact; now power is sustained by imagination in a certain party, in France in the nobility, in Switzerland in the burgesses, &c.

These cords which bind the respect of men to such and such an individual are therefore the cords of imagination.

305

The Swiss are offended by being called gentlemen, and prove themselves true plebeians in order to be thought worthy of great office.

306

As duchies, kingships, and magistracies are real and necessary, because might rules all, they exist everywhere and always. But since only caprice makes such and such a one a ruler, the principle is not constant, but subject to variation, &c.

307

The chancellor is grave, and clothed with ornaments, for his position is unreal. Not so the king, he has power, and has nothing to do with the imagination. Judges, physicians, &c., appeal only to the imagination.

308

The habit of seeing kings accompanied by guards, drums, officers, and all the paraphernalia which mechanically inspire respect and awe, makes their countenance, when sometimes seen alone without these accompaniments, impress respect and awe on their subjects; because we cannot separate in thought their persons from the surroundings with which we see them usually joined. And the world, which knows not that this effect is the result of habit, believes that it arises by a natural force, whence come these words, "The character of Divinity is stamped on his countenance," &c.

309

Justice.—As custom determines what is agreeable, so also does it determine justice.

310

King and tyrant.—I, too, will keep my thoughts secret.
I will take care on every journey.
Greatness of establishment, respect for establishment.
The pleasure of the great is the power to make people happy.
The property of riches is to be given liberally.
The property of each thing must be sought. The property of power is to protect.
When force attacks humbug, when a private soldier takes the square cap off a first president, and throws it out of the window.

311

The government founded on opinion and imagination reigns for some time, and this government is pleasant and voluntary; that founded on might lasts for ever. Thus opinion is the queen of the world, but might is its tyrant.

312

Justice is what is established; and thus all our established laws will necessarily be regarded as just without examination, since they are established.

313

Sound opinions of the people.—Civil wars are the greatest of evils. They are inevitable, if we wish to reward desert; for all will say they are deserving. The evil we have to fear from a fool who succeeds by right of birth, is neither so great nor so sure.

314

God has created all for Himself. He has bestowed upon Himself the power of pain and pleasure.

You can apply it to God, or to yourself. If to God, the Gospel is the rule. If to yourself, you will take the place of God. As God is surrounded by persons full of charity, who ask of Him the blessings of charity that are in His power, so . . . Recognise then and learn that you are only a king of lust, and take the ways of lust.

315

The Reason of effects.—It is wonderful that men would not have me honour a man clothed in brocade, and followed by seven or eight lackeys! Why! He will have me thrashed, if I do not salute him. This custom is a force. It is the same with a horse in fine trappings in comparison with another! Montaigne is a fool not to see what difference there is, to wonder at our finding any, and to ask the reason. "Indeed," says he, "how comes it," &c. . . .

316

Sound opinions of the people.—To be spruce is not altogether foolish, for it proves that a great number of people work for one. It shows by one's hair, that one has a valet, a perfumer, &c., by one's band, thread, lace, . . . &c. Now it is not merely superficial nor merely outward show to have many arms at command. The more arms one has, the more powerful one is. To be spruce is to show one's power.

317

Deference means, " Put yourself to inconvenience." This is apparently silly, but is quite right. For it is to say, " I would indeed put myself to inconvenience if you required it, since indeed I do so when it is of no service to you." Deference further serves to distinguish the great. Now if deference was displayed by sitting in an arm-chair, we should show deference to everybody, and so no distinction would be made; but, being put to inconvenience, we distinguish very well.

318

He has four lackeys.

319

How rightly do we distinguish men by external appearances rather than by internal qualities! Which of us two shall have precedence? Who will give place to the other? The least clever. But I am as clever as he. We should have to fight over this. He has four lackeys, and I have only one. This can be seen; we have only to count. It falls to me to yield, and I am a fool if I contest the matter. By this means we are at peace, which is the greatest of boons.

320

The most unreasonable things in the world become most reasonable, because of the unruliness of men. What is less reasonable than to choose the eldest son of a queen to rule a State? We do not choose as captain of a ship the passenger who is of the best family.

This law would be absurd and unjust; but because men are so themselves, and always will be so, it becomes reasonable and just. For whom will men choose, as the most virtuous and able? We at once come to blows, as each claims to be the most virtuous and able. Let us then attach this quality to something indisputable. This is the king's eldest son. That is clear, and there is no dispute. Reason can do no better, for civil war is the greatest of evils.

321

Children are astonished to see their comrades respected.

322

To be of noble birth is a great advantage. In eighteen years it places a man within the select circle, known and respected, as another would have merited in fifty years. It is a gain of thirty years without trouble.

323

What is the Ego?

Suppose a man puts himself at a window to see those

who pass by. If I pass by, can I say that he placed himself there to see me? No; for he does not think of me in particular. But does he who loves some one on account of beauty really love that person? No; for the small-pox, which will kill beauty without killing the person, will cause him to love her no more.

And if one loves me for my judgment, memory, he does not love *me*, for I can lose these qualities without losing myself. Where then is this Ego, if it be neither in the body nor in the soul? And how love the body or the soul, except for these qualities which do not constitute *me*, since they are perishable? For it is impossible and would be unjust to love the soul of a person in the abstract, and whatever qualities might be therein. We never then love a person, but only qualities.

Let us then jeer no more at those who are honoured on account of rank and office; for we love a person only on account of borrowed qualities.

324

The people have very sound opinions, for example:

1. In having preferred diversion and hunting to poetry. The half-learned laugh at it, and glory in being above the folly of the world; but the people are right for a reason which these do not fathom.

2. In having distinguished men by external marks, as birth or wealth. The world again exults in showing how unreasonable this is; but it is very reasonable. Savages laugh at an infant king.

3. In being offended at a blow, or in desiring glory so much. But it is very desirable on account of the other essential goods which are joined to it; and a man who has received a blow, without resenting it, is overwhelmed with taunts and indignities.

4. In working for the uncertain; in sailing on the sea; in walking over a plank.

325

Montaigne is wrong. Custom should be followed only because it is custom, and not because it is reasonable or just. But people follow it for this sole reason, that they think it just. Otherwise they would follow it no longer, although it were the custom; for they will only submit to reason or justice. Custom without this would pass for tyranny; but the sovereignty of reason and justice is no more tyrannical than that of desire. They are principles natural to man.

It would therefore be right to obey laws and customs, because they are laws; but we should know that there is neither truth nor justice to introduce into them, that we know nothing of these, and so must follow what is accepted. By this means we would never depart from them. But the people cannot accept this doctrine; and, as they believe that truth can be found, and that it exists in law and custom, they believe them, and take their antiquity as a proof of their truth, and not simply of their authority apart from truth. Thus they obey laws, but they are liable to revolt when these are proved to be valueless; and this can be shown of all, looked at from a certain aspect.

326

Injustice.—It is dangerous to tell the people that the laws are unjust; for they obey them only because they think them just. Therefore it is necessary to tell them at the same time that they must obey them because they are laws, just as they must obey superiors, not because they are just, but because they are superiors. In this way all sedition is prevented, if this can be made intelligible, and it be understood what is the proper definition of justice.

327

The world is a good judge of things, for it is in natural ignorance, which is man's true state. The sciences have two extremes which meet. The first is the pure natural ignorance in which all men find themselves at birth. The other extreme is that reached by great intellects, who, having run through all that men can know, find they know nothing, and come back again to that same ignorance from which they set out; but this is a learned ignorance which is conscious of

itself. Those between the two, who have departed from
natural ignorance and not been able to reach the other,
have some smattering of this vain knowledge, and pretend
to be wise. These trouble the world, and are bad judges
of everything. The people and the wise constitute the
world; these despise it, and are despised. They judge badly
of everything, and the world judges rightly of them.

328

The reason of effects.—Continual alternation of *pro* and
con.

We have then shown that man is foolish, by the estimation
he makes of things which are not essential; and all these
opinions are destroyed. We have next shown that all these
opinions are very sound, and that thus, since all these
vanities are well founded, the people are not so foolish as is
said. And so we have destroyed the opinion which destroyed
that of the people.

But we must now destroy this last proposition, and show
that it remains always true that the people are foolish,
though their opinions are sound; because they do not perceive the truth where it is, and, as they place it where it is
not, their opinions are always very false and very unsound.

329

The weakness of man is the reason why so many things
are considered fine, as to be good at playing the lute.

It is only an evil because of our weakness.

330

The power of kings is founded on the reason and on the
folly of the people, and specially on their folly. The greatest and most important thing in the world has weakness for
its foundation, and this foundation is wonderfully sure; for
there is nothing more sure than this, that the people will be
weak. What is based on sound reason is very ill founded,
as the estimate of wisdom.

331

We can only think of Plato and Aristotle in grand aca-
demic robes. They were honest men, like others, laughing
with their friends, and when they diverted themselves with
writing the *Laws* and the *Politics,* they did it as an amusement. That part of their life was the least philosophic and
the least serious; the most philosophic was to live simply and
quietly. If they wrote on politics, it was as if laying down
rules for a lunatic asylum; and if they presented the appearance of speaking of a great matter, it was because they
knew that the madmen, to whom they spoke, thought they
were kings and emperors. They entered into their principles
in order to make their madness as little harmful as possible.

332

Tyranny consists in the desire of universal power beyond
its scope.

There are different assemblies of the strong, the fair, the
sensible, the pious, in which each man rules at home, not
elsewhere. And sometimes they meet, and the strong and the
fair foolishly fight as to who shall be master, for their
mastery is of different kinds. They do not understand one
another, and their fault is the desire to rule everywhere.
Nothing can effect this, not even might, which is of no use
in the kingdom of the wise, and is only mistress of external
actions.

Tyranny.— . . . So these expressions are false and tyrannical: " I am fair, therefore I must be feared. I am strong,
therefore I must be loved. I am . . ."

Tyranny is the wish to have in one way what can only
be had in another. We render different duties to different
merits; the duty of love to the pleasant; the duty of fear to
the strong; the duty of belief to the learned.

We must render these duties; it is unjust to refuse them,
and unjust to ask others. And so it is false and tyrannical
to say, " He is not strong, therefore I will not esteem him;
he is not able, therefore I will not fear him."

333

Have you never seen people who, in order to complain of the little fuss you make about them, parade before you the example of great men who esteem them? In answer I reply to them, "Show me the merit whereby you have charmed these persons, and I also will esteem you."

334

The reason of effects.—Lust and force are the source of all our actions; lust causes voluntary actions, force involuntary ones.

335

The reason of effects.—It is then true to say that all the world is under a delusion; for, although the opinions of the people are sound, they are not so as conceived by them, since they think the truth to be where it is not. Truth is indeed in their opinions, but not at the point where they imagine it. [Thus] it is true that we must honour noblemen, but not because noble birth is real superiority, &c.

336

The reason of effects.—We must keep our thought secret, and judge everything by it, while talking like the people.

337

The reason of effects.—Degrees. The people honour persons of high birth. The semi-learned depise them, saying that birth is not a personal, but a chance superiority. The learned honour them, not for popular reasons, but for secret reasons. Devout persons, who have more zeal than knowledge, depise them, in spite of that consideration which makes them honoured by the learned, because they judge them by a new light which piety gives them. But perfect Christians honour them by another and higher light. So arise a succession of opinions for and against, according to the light one has.

338

True Christians nevertheless comply with folly, not because they respect folly, but the command of God, who for
the punishment of men has made them subject to these
follies. *Omnis creatura subjecta est vanitati. Liberabitur.*[e]
Thus Saint Thomas explains the passage in Saint James on
giving place to the rich, that if they do it not in the sight of
God, they depart from the command of religion.

[e] Romans, viii. 20-21.

SECTION VI

THE PHILOSOPHERS

339

I CAN well conceive a man without hands, feet, head (for it is only experience which teaches us that the head is more necessary than feet). But I cannot conceive man without thought; he would be a stone or a brute.

340

The arithmetical machine produces effects which approach nearer to thought than all the actions of animals. But it does nothing which would enable us to attribute will to it, as to the animals.

341

The account of the pike and frog of Liancourt. They do it always, and never otherwise, nor any other thing showing mind.

342

If an animal did by mind what it does by instinct, and if it spoke by mind what it speaks by instinct, in hunting, and in warning its mates that the prey is found or lost; it would indeed also speak in regard to those things which affect it closer, as example, " Gnaw me this cord which is wounding me, and which I cannot reach."

343

The beak of the parrot, which it wipes, although it is clean.

344

Instinct and reason, marks of two natures.

345

Reason commands us far more imperiously than a master; for in disobeying the one we are unfortunate, and in disobeying the other we are fools.

346

Thought constitutes the greatness of man.

347

Man is but a reed, the most feeble thing in nature, but he is a thinking reed. The entire universe need not arm itself to crush him. A vapour, a drop of water suffices to kill him. But, if the universe were to crush him, man would still be more noble than that which killed him, because he knows that he dies and the advantage which the universe has over him; the universe knows nothing of this.

All our dignity consists then in thought. By it we must elevate ourselves, and not by space and time which we cannot fill. Let us endeavour then to think well; this is the principle of morality.

348

A thinking reed.—It is not from space that I must seek my dignity, but from the government of my thought. I shall have no more if I possess worlds. By space the universe encompasses and swallows me up like an atom; by thought I comprehend the world

349

Immateriality of the soul.—Philosophers who have mastered their passions. What matter could do that?

350

The Stoics.—They conclude that what has been done once can be done always, and that since the desire of glory imparts some power to those whom it possesses, others can well do likewise. There are feverish movements which health cannot imitate.

Epictetus concludes that since there are consistent Christians, every man can easily be so.

351

Those great spiritual efforts, which the soul sometimes essays, are things on which it does not lay hold. It only leaps to them, not as upon a throne, for ever, but merely for an instant.

352

The strength of a man's virtue must not be measured by his efforts, but by his ordinary life.

353

I do not admire the excess of a virtue as of valour, except I see at the same time the excess of the opposite virtue, as in Epaminondas, who had the greatest valour and the greatest kindness. For otherwise it is not to rise, it is to fall. We do not display greatness by going to one extreme, but in touching both at once, and filling all the intervening space. But perhaps this is only a sudden movement of the soul from one to the other extreme, and in fact it is ever at one point only, as in the case of a firebrand. Be it so, but at least this indicates agility, if not expanse of soul.

354

Man's nature is not always to advance; it has its advances and retreats.

Fever has its cold and hot fits; and the cold proves as well as the hot the greatness of the fire of fever.

The discoveries of men from age to age turn out the same. The kindness and the malice of the world in general are the same. *Plerumque gratæ principibus vices.*[1]

---

[1] " Changes are usually pleasing to princes."—Horace.

355

Continuous eloquence wearies.

Princes and kings sometimes play. They are not always on their thrones. They weary there. Grandeur must be abandoned to be appreciated. Continuity in everything is unpleasant. Cold is agreeable, that we may get warm.

Nature acts by progress, *itus et reditus*. It goes and returns, then advances further, then twice as much backwards, then more forward than ever, &c.

The tide of the sea behaves in the same manner; and so apparently does the sun in its course.

356

The nourishment of the body is little by little. Fulness of nourishment and smallness of substance.

357

When we would pursue virtues to their extremes on either side, vices present themselves, which insinuate themselves insensibly there, in their insensible journey towards the infinitely little; and vices present themselves in a crowd towards the infinitely great, so that we lose ourselves in them, and no longer see virtues. We find fault with perfection itself.

358

Man is neither angel nor brute, and the unfortunate thing is that he who would act the angel acts the brute.

359

We do not sustain ourselves in virtue by our own strength, but by the balancing of two opposed vices, just as we remain upright amidst two contrary gales. Remove one of the vices, and we fall into the other.

360

What the Stoics propose is so difficult and foolish!
The Stoics lay down that all those who are not at the high

degree of wisdom are equally foolish and vicious, as those who are two inches under water.

361

The Sovereign good. Dispute about the sovereign good. —Ut sis contentus temetipso et ex te nascentibus bonis.[2] There is a contradiction, for in the end they advise suicide. Oh! What a happy life, from which we are to free ourselves as from the plague!

362

Ex senatus-consultis et plebiscitis . . . To ask like passages.

363

Ex senatus-consultis et plebiscitis scelera exercentur. Sen. 588.[3]

Nihil tam absurde dici potest quod non dicatur ab aliquo philosophorum.[4] *Divin.*

Quibusdam destinatis sententiis consecrati quæ non probant coguntur defendere.[5] Cic.

Ut omnium rerum sic litterarum quoque intemperantia laboramus.[6] Senec.

Id maxime quemque decet, quod est cujusque suum maxime.[7]

Hos natura modos primum dedit.[8]

Paucis opus est litteris ad bonam mentem.[9]

Si quando turpe non sit, tamen non est non turpe quum id ab multitudine laudetur.[10]

Mihi sic usus est, tibi ut opus est facto, fac.[11] Ter.

---

[2] " That you may be contented with yourself and the good things that spring from you."—Seneca.

[3] " Decrees of the senate and of the people are responsible for crimes."

[4] " Nothing can be said so absurd that it may not be said by some philosopher."—Cicero.

[5] " Those who are given over to certain preconceived ideas are forced to defend what they cannot prove."

[6] " In literature as in all things, we labor in excess."

[7] " That becomes any one best which is most his own."—Cicero.

[8] " Nature first gave those customs."—Virgil.

[9] " For the good mind few books are necessary."

[10] " If perchance a thing is not base, it does not escape baseness by being praised by the crowd."

[11] " That is my custom; you must do as necessity bids."

364

Rarum est enim ut satis se quisque vereatur.[12]
Tot circa unum caput tumultuantes deos.[13]
Nihil turpius quam cognitioni assertionem præcurrere.[14]
Cic.
Nec me pudet, ut istos, fateri nescire quid nesciam.[15]
Melius non incipiet.[16]

365

Thought.—All the dignity of man consists in thought. Thought is therefore by its nature a wonderful and incomparable thing. It must have strange defects to be contemptible. But it has such, so that nothing is more ridiculous. How great it is in its nature! How vile it is in its defects! But what is this thought? How foolish it is!

366

The mind of this sovereign judge of the world is not so independent that it is not liable to be disturbed by the first din about it. The noise of a cannon is not necessary to hinder its thoughts; it needs only the creaking of a weathercock or a pulley. Do not wonder if at present it does not reason well; a fly is buzzing in its ears; that is enough to render it incapable of good judgment. If you wish it to be able to reach the truth, chase away that animal which holds its reason in check and disturbs that powerful intellect which rules towns and kingdoms. Here is a comical god! *O ridicolosissimo eroe!*[17]

367

The power of flies: they win battles, hinder our soul from acting, eat our body.

---

[12] " It is a rare thing for any one to fear himself enough."
[13] " So many gods brawling around one poor man."
[14] " There is nothing more unseemly than to understand before the thing has been stated."
[15] " I am not ashamed, as your friends are, to confess that I do not know what I do not know."
[16] " He will not begin better (than he can finish)."—Seneca.
[17] " O most ridiculous hero."

368

When it is said that heat is only the motion of certain molecules, and light the *conatus recedendi* which we feel, it astonishes us. What! Is pleasure only the ballet of our spirits? We have conceived so different an idea of it! And these sensations seem so removed from those others which we say are the same as those with which we compare them! The sensation from the fire, that warmth which affects us in a manner wholly different from touch, the reception of sound and light, all this appears to us mysterious, and yet it is material like the blow of a stone. It is true that the smallness of the spirits which enter into the pores touches other nerves, but there are always some nerves touched.

369

Memory is necessary for all the operations of reason.

370

[Chance gives rise to thoughts, and chance removes them; no art can keep or acquire them.

A thought has escaped me. I wanted to write it down. I write instead, that it has escaped me.]

371

[When I was small, I hugged my book; and because it sometimes happened to me to . . . in believing I hugged it, I doubted. . . .]

372

In writing down my thought, it sometimes escapes me; but this makes me remember my weakness, that I constantly forget. This is as instructive to me as my forgotten thought; for I strive only to know my nothingness.

373

Scepticism.—I shall here write my thoughts without order, and not perhaps in unintentional confusion; that is true order, which will always indicate my object by its very disorder. I should do too much honour to my subject, if I treated it with order, since I want to show that it is incapable of it.

374

What astonishes me most is to see that all the world is not astonished at its own weakness. Men act seriously, and each follows his own mode of life, not because it is in fact good to follow since it is the custom, but as if each man knew certainly where reason and justice are. They find themselves continually deceived, and by a comical humility think it is their own fault, and not that of the art which they claim always to possess. But it is well there are so many such people in the world, who are not sceptics for the glory of scepticism, in order to show that man is quite capable of the most extravagant opinions, since he is capable of believing that he is not in a state of natural and inevitable weakness, but, on the contrary, of natural wisdom.

Nothing fortifies scepticism more than that there are some who are not sceptics; if all were so, they would be wrong.

375

[I have passed a great part of my life believing that there was justice, and in this I was not mistaken; for there is justice according as God has willed to reveal it to us. But I did not take it so, and this is where I made a mistake; for I believe that our justice was essentially just, and that I had that whereby to know and judge of it. But I have so often found my right judgment at fault, that at last I have come to distrust myself, and then others. I have seen changes in all nations and men, and thus after many changes of judgment regarding true justice, I have recognised that our nature was but in continual change, and I have not changed since; and if I changed, I would confirm my opinion.

The sceptic Arcesilaus, who became a dogmatist.]

376

This sect derives more strength from its enemies than from its friends; for the weakness of man is far more evident in those who know it not than in those who know it.

377

Discourses on humility are a source of pride in the vain, and of humility in the humble. So those on scepticism cause believers to affirm. Few men speak humbly of humility, chastely of chastity, few doubtingly of scepticism. We are only falsehood, duplicity, contradiction; we both conceal and disguise ourselves from ourselves.

378

Scepticism.—Excess, like defect of intellect, is accused of madness. Nothing is good but mediocrity. The majority has settled that, and finds fault with him who escapes it at whichever end. I will not oppose it. I quite consent to put myself there, and refuse to be at the lower end, not because it is low, but because it is an end; for I would likewise refuse to be placed at the top. To leave the mean is to abandon humanity. The greatness of the human soul consists in knowing how to preserve the mean. So far from greatness consisting in leaving it, it consists in not leaving it.

379

It is not good to have too much liberty. It is not good to have all one wants.

380

All good maxims are in the world. We only need to apply them. For instance, we do not doubt that we ought to risk our lives in defence of the public good; but for religion, no.

It is true there must be inequality among men; but if this be conceded, the door is opened not only to the highest power, but to the highest tyranny.

We must relax our minds a little; but this opens the door

to the greatest debauchery. Let us mark the limits. There are no limits in things. Laws would put them there, and the mind cannot suffer it.

381

When we are too young, we do not judge well; so, also, when we are too old. If we do not think enough, or if we think too much on any matter, we get obstinate and infatuated about it. If one considers one's work immediately after having done it, one is entirely prepossessd in its favour; by delaying too long, one can no longer enter into the spirit of it. So with pictures seen from too far or too near; there is but one exact point which is the true place wherefrom to look at them: the rest are too near, too far, too high, or too low. Perspective determines that point in the art of painting. But who shall determine it in truth and morality?

382

When all is equally agitated, nothing appears to be agitated, as in a ship. When all tend to debauchery, none appears to do so. He who stops draws attention to the excess of others, like a fixed point.

383

The licentious tell men of orderly lives that they stray from nature's path, while they themselves follow it; as people in a ship think those move who are on the shore. On all sides the language is similar. We must have a fixed point in order to judge. The harbour decides for those who are in a ship; but where shall we find a harbour in morality?

384

Contradiction is a bad sign of truth; several things which are certain are contradicted; several things which are false pass without contradiction. Contradiction is not a sign of falsity, nor the want of contradiction a sign of truth.

385

Scepticism.—Each thing here is partly true and partly false. Essential truth is not so; it is altogether pure and altogether true. This mixture dishonours and annihilates it. Nothing is purely true, and thus nothing is true, meaning by that pure truth. You will say it is true that homicide is wrong. Yes; for we know well the wrong and the false. But what will you say is good? Chastity? I say no; for the world would come to an end. Marriage? No; continence is better. Not to kill? No; for lawlessness would be horrible, and the wicked would kill all the good. To kill? No; for that destroys nature. We possess truth and goodness only in part, and mingled with falsehood and evil.

386

If we dreamt the same thing every night, it would affect us as much as the objects we see every day. And if an artisan were sure to dream every night for twelve hours' duration that he was a king, I believe he would be almost as happy as a king, who should dream every night for twelve hours on end that he was an artisan.

If we were to dream every night that we were pursued by enemies, and harassed by these painful phantoms, or that we passed every day in different occupations, as in making a voyage, we should suffer almost as much as if it were real, and should fear to sleep, as we fear to wake when we dread in fact to enter on such mishaps. And, indeed, it would cause pretty nearly the same discomforts as the reality.

But since dreams are all different, and each single one is diversified, what is seen in them affects us much less than what we see when awake, because of its continuity, which is not, however, so continuous and level as not to change too; but it changes less abruptly, except rarely, as when we travel, and then we say, "It seems to me I am dreaming." For life is a dream a little less inconstant.

387

[It may be that there are true demonstrations; but this is not certain. Thus, this proves nothing else but that it is not certain that all is uncertain, to the glory of scepticism.]

388

Good sense.—They are compelled to say, "You are not
acting in good faith; we are not asleep," &c. How I love
to see this proud reason humiliated and suppliant! For
this is not the language of a man whose right is disputed, and
who defends it with the power of armed hands. He is not
foolish enough to declare that men are not acting in good
faith, but he punishes this bad faith with force.

389

Ecclesiastes shows that man without God is in total ignorance and inevitable misery. For it is wretched to have the
wish, but not the power. Now he would be happy and
assured of some truth, and yet he can neither know, nor
desire not to know. He cannot even doubt.

390

My God! How foolish this talk is! "Would God have
made the world to damn it? Would He ask so much from
persons so weak?" &c. Scepticism is the cure for this evil,
and will take down this vanity.

391

Conversation.—Great words to religion. I deny it.
Conversation.—Scepticism helps religion.

392

Against Scepticism.—[. . . It is, then, a strange fact
that we cannot define these things without obscuring them,
while we speak of them with all assurance.] We assume that
all conceive of them in the same way; but we assume it
quite gratuitously, for we have no proof of it. I see, in
truth, that the same words are applied on the same occasions,
and that every time two men see a body change its place,
they both express their view of this same fact by the same
word, both saying that it has moved; and from this conformity of application we derive a strong conviction of a

conformity of ideas. But this is not absolutely or finally convincing, though there is enough to support a bet on the affirmative, since we know that we often draw the same conclusions from different premises.

This is enough, at least, to obscure the matter; not that it completely extinguishes the natural light which assures us of these things. The academicians would have won. But this dulls it, and troubles the dogmatists to the glory of the sceptical crowd, which consists in this doubtful ambiguity, and in a certain doubtful dimness, from which our doubts cannot take away all the clearness, nor our own natural lights chase away all the darkness.

393

It is a singular thing to consider that there are people in the world, who, having renounced all the laws of God and nature, have made laws for themselves which they strictly obey, as, for instance, the soldiers of Mahomet, robbers, heretics, &c. It is the same with logicians. It seems that their licence must be without any limits or barriers, since they have broken through so many that are so just and sacred.

394

All the principles of sceptics, stoics, atheists, &c., are true. But their conclusions are false, because the opposite principles are also true.

395

Instinct, Reason.—We have an incapacity of proof, insurmountable by all dogmatism. We have an idea of truth, invincible to all scepticism.

396

Two things instruct man about his whole nature; instinct and experience.

397

The greatness of man is great in that he knows himself to be miserable. A tree does not know itself to be miserable. It is then being miserable to know oneself to be miserable; but it is also being great to know that one is miserable.

398

All these same miseries prove man's greatness. They are the miseries of a great lord, of a deposed king.

399

We are not miserable without feeling it. A ruined house is not miserable. Man only is miserable. *Ego vir videns.*[18]

400

The greatness of man.—We have so great an idea of the soul of man that we cannot endure being despised, or not being esteemed by any soul; and all the happiness of men consists in this esteem.

401

Glory.—The brutes do not admire each other. A horse does not admire his companion. Not that there is no rivalry between them in a race, but that is of no consequence; for, when in the stable, the heaviest and most ill-formed does not give up his oats to another as men would have others do to them. Their virtue is satisfied with itself.

402

The greatness of man even in his lust, to have known how to extract from it a wonderful code, and to have drawn from it a picture of benevolence.

403

Greatness.—The reasons of effects indicate the greatness of man, in having extracted so fair an order from lust.

404

The greatest baseness of man is the pursuit of glory. But it is also the greatest mark of his excellence; for whatever possessions he may have on earth, whatever health and essential comfort, he is not satisfied if he has not the esteem of men. He values human reason so highly that, whatever

[18] " I am the man (that hath seen affliction)."—Lamentations, iii. 1.

advantages he may have on earth, he is not content if he is not also ranked highly in the judgment of man. This is the finest position in the world. Nothing can turn him from that desire, which is the most indelible quality of man's heart.

And those who most despise men, and put them on a level with the brutes, yet wish to be admired and believed by men, and contradict themselves by their own feelings; their nature, which is stronger than all, convincing them of the greatness of man more forcibly than reason convinces them of their baseness.

405

Contradiction.—Pride counterbalancing all miseries. Man either hides his miseries, or, if he disclose them, glories in knowing them.

406

Pride counterbalances and takes away all miseries. Here is a strange monster, and a very plain aberration. He is fallen from his place, and is anxiously seeking it. This is what all men do. Let us see who will have found it.

407

When malice has reason on its side, it becomes proud, and parades reason in all its splendour. When austerity or stern choice has not arrived at the true good, and must needs return to follow nature, it becomes proud by reason of this return.

408

Evil is easy, and has infinite forms; good is almost unique. But a certain kind of evil is as difficult to find as what we call good; and often on this account such particular evil gets passed off as good. An extraordinary greatness of soul is needed in order to attain to it as well as to good.

409

The greatness of man.—The greatness of man is so evident, that it is even proved by his wretchedness. For what in animals is nature we call in man wretchedness; by which we recognise that, his nature being now like that of animals, he has fallen from a better nature which once was his.

For who is unhappy at not being a king, except a deposed king? Was Paulus Emilius unhappy at being no longer consul? On the contrary, everybody thought him happy in having been consul, because the office could only be held for a time. But men thought Perseus so unhappy in being no longer king, because the condition of kingship implied his being always king, that they thought it strange that he endured life. Who is unhappy at having only one mouth? And who is not unhappy at having only one eye? Probably no man ever ventured to mourn at not having three eyes. But any one is inconsolable at having none.

410

Perseus, King of Macedon.—Paulus Emilius reproached Perseus for not killing himself.

411

Notwithstanding the sight of all our miseries, which press upon us and take us by the throat, we have an instinct which we cannot repress, and which lifts us up.

412

There is internal war in man between reason and the passions.

If he had only reason without passions . . .

If he had only passions without reason . . .

But having both, he cannot be without strife, being unable to be at peace with the one without being at war with the other. Thus he is always divided against, and opposed to himself.

413

This internal war of reason against the passions has made a division of those who would have peace into two sects. The first would renounce their passions, and become gods; the others would renounce reason, and become brute beasts. (Des Barreaux.) But neither can do so, and reason still remains, to condemn the vileness and unjustice of the passions, and to trouble the repose of those who abandon themselves to them; and the passions keep always alive in those who would renounce them.

414

Men are so necessarily mad, that not to be mad would amount to another form of madness.

415

The nature of man may be viewed in two ways: the one according to its end, and then he is great and incomparable; the other according to the multitude, just as we judge of the nature of the horse and the dog, popularly, by seeing its fleetness, *et animum arcendi;*[19] and then man is abject and vile. These are the two ways which make us judge of him differently, and which occasion such disputes among philosophers.

For one denies the assumption of the other. One says, "He is not born for this end, for all his actions are repugnant to it." The other says, "He forsakes his end, when he does these base actions."

416

For Port Royal. Greatness and wretchedness.—Wretchedness being deduced from greatness, and greatness from wretchedness, some have inferred man's wretchedness all the more because they have taken his greatness as a proof of it, and others have inferred his greatness with all the more force, because they have inferred it from his very wretchedness. All that the one party has been able to say in proof of his greatness has only served as an argument of his wretchedness to the others, because the greater our fall, the more wretched we are, and *vice versa*. The one party is brought back to the other in an endless circle, it being certain that in proportion as men possess light they discover both the greatness and the wretchedness of man. In a word, man knows that he is wretched. He is therefore wretched, because he is so; but he is really great because he knows it.

[19] " And instinct of guarding."

417

This twofold nature of man is so evident that some have thought that we had two souls. A single subject seemed to them incapable of such sudden variations from unmeasured presumption to a dreadful dejection of heart.

418

It is dangerous to make a man see too clearly his equality with the brutes without showing him his greatness. It is also dangerous to make him see his greatness too clearly, apart from his vileness. It is still more dangerous to leave him in ignorance of both. But it is very advantageous to show him both. Man must not think that he is on a level either with the brutes or with the angels, nor must he be ignorant of both sides of his nature; but he must know both.

419

I will not allow man to depend upon himself, or upon another, to the end that being without a resting place and without repose . . .

420

If he exalt himself, I humble him; if he humble himself, I exalt him; and I always contradict him, till he understands that he is an incomprehensible monster.

421

I blame equally those who choose to praise man, those who choose to blame him, and those who choose to amuse themselves; and I can only approve of those who seek with lamentation.

422

It is good to be tired and wearied by the vain search after the true good, that we may stretch out our arms to the Redeemer.

423

Contraries. *After having shown the vileness and the greatness of man.*—Let man now know his value. Let him love himself, for there is in him a nature capable of good; but let him not for this reason love the vileness which is in him. Let him despise himself, for this capacity is barren; but let him not therefore despise this natural capacity. Let him hate himself, let him love himself; he has within him the capacity of knowing the truth and of being happy, but he possesses no truth, either constant or satisfactory.

I would then lead man to the desire of finding truth; to be free from passions, and ready to follow it where he may find it, knowing how much his knowledge is obscured by the passions. I would indeed that he should hate in himself the lust which determines his will by itself, so that it may not blind him in making his choice, and may not hinder him when he has chosen.

424

All these contradictions, which seem most to keep me from the knowledge of religion, have led me most quickly to the true one.

SECTION VII

MORALITY AND DOCTRINE

425

SECOND part.—That man without faith cannot know the true good, nor justice.

All men seek happiness. This is without exception. Whatever different means they employ, they all tend to this end. The cause of some going to war, and of others avoiding it, is the same desire in both, attended with different views. The will never takes the least step but to this object. This is the motive of every action of every man, even of those who hang themselves.

And yet after such a great number of years, no one without faith has reached the point to which all continually look. All complain, princes and subjects, noblemen and commoners, old and young, strong and weak, learned and ignorant, healthy and sick, of all countries, all times, all ages, and all conditions.

A trial so long, so continuous, and so uniform, should certainly convince us of our inability to reach the good by our own efforts. But example teaches us little. No resemblance is ever so perfect that there is not some slight difference; and hence we expect that our hope will not be deceived on this occasion as before. And thus, while the present never satisfies us, experience dupes us, and from misfortune to misfortune leads us to death, their eternal crown.

What is it then that this desire and this inability proclaim to us, but that there was once in man a true happiness of which there now remain to him only the mark and empty trace, which he in vain tries to fill from all his surroundings, seeking from things absent to help he does not obtain in

138

things present? But these are all inadequate, because the infinite abyss can only be filled by an infinite and immutable object, that is to say, only by God Himself.

He only is our true good, and since we have forsaken Him, it is a strange thing that there is nothing in nature which has not been serviceable in taking His place; the stars, the heavens, earth, the elements, plants, cabbages, leeks, animals, insects, calves, serpents, fever, pestilence, war, famine, vices, adultery, incest. And since man has lost the true good, everything can appear equally good to him, even his own destruction, though so opposed to God, to reason, and to the whole course of nature.

Some seek good in authority, others in scientific research, others in pleasure. Others, who are in fact nearer the truth, have considered it necessary that the universal good, which all men desire, should not consist in any of the particular things which can only be possessed by one man, and which, when shared, afflict their possessor more by the want of the part he has not, than they please him by the possession of what he has. They have learned that the true good should be such as all can possess at once, without diminution and without envy, and which no one can lose against his will. And their reason is that this desire being natural to man, since it is necessarily in all, and that it is impossible not to have it, they infer from it . . .

426

True nature being lost, everything becomes its own nature; as the true good being lost, everything becomes its own true good.

427

Man does not know in what rank to place himself. He has plainly gone astray, and fallen from his true place without being able to find it again. He seeks it anxiously and unsuccessfully everywhere in impenetrable darkness.

428

If it is a sign of weakness to prove God by nature, do
not despise Scripture; if it is a sign of strength to have
known these contradictions, esteem Scripture.

429

The vileness of man in submitting himself to the brutes,
and in even worshipping them.

430

*For Port Royal. The beginning, after having explained
the incomprehensibility.*—The greatness and the wretchedness of man are so evident that the true religion must necessarily teach us both that there is in man some great source
of greatness, and a great source of wretchedness. It must
then give us a reason for these astonishing contradictions.

In order to make man happy, it must prove to him that
there is a God; that we ought to love Him; that our true
happiness is to be in Him, and our sole evil to be separated
from Him; it must recognise that we are full of darkness
which hinders us from knowing and loving Him; and that
thus, as our duties compel us to love God, and our lusts turn
us away from Him, we are full of unrighteousness. It must
give us an explanation of our opposition to God and to our
own good. It must teach us the remedies for these infirmities, and the means of obtaining these remedies. Let us
therefore examine all the religions of the world, and see if
there be any other than the Christian which is sufficient for
this purpose.

Shall it be that of the philosophers, who put forward as
the chief good, the good which is in ourselves? Is this the
true good? Have they found the remedy for our ills? Is
man's pride cured by placing him on an equality with God?
Have those who have made us equal to the brutes, or the
Mahomedans who have offered us earthly pleasures as the
chief good even in eternity, produced the remedy for our
lusts? What religion then will teach us to cure pride and

lust? What religion will in fact teach us our good, our duties, the weakness which turns us from them, the cause of this weakness, the remedies which can cure it, and the means of obtaining these remedies?

All other religions have not been able to do so. Let us see what the wisdom of God will do.

" Expect neither truth," she says, " nor consolation from men. I am she who formed you, and who alone can teach you what you are. But you are now no longer in the state in which I formed you. I created man holy, innocent, perfect. I filled him with light and intelligence. I communicated to him my glory and my wonders. The eye of man saw then the majesty of God. He was not then in the darkness which blinds him, nor subject to mortality and the woes which afflict him. But he has not been able to sustain so great glory without falling into pride. He wanted to make himself his own centre, and independent of my help. He withdrew himself from my rule; and, on his making himself equal to me by the desire of finding his happiness in himself, I abandoned him to himself. And setting in revolt the creatures that were subject to him, I made them his enemies; so that man is now become like the brutes, and so estranged from me that there scarce remains to him a dim vision of his Author. So far has all his knowledge been extinguished or disturbed! The senses, independent of reason, and often the masters of reason, have led him into pursuit of pleasure. All creatures either torment or tempt him, and domineer over him, either subduing him by their strength, or fascinating him by their charms, a tyranny more awful and more imperious.

" Such is the state in which men now are. There remains to them some feeble instinct of the happiness of their former state; and they are plunged in the evils of their blindness and their lust, which have become their second nature.

" From this principle which I disclose to you, you can recognize the cause of those contradictions which have astonished all men, and have divided them into parties holding so different views. Observe now all the feelings of greatness and glory which the experience of so many woes cannot stifle, and see if the cause of them must not be in another nature."

For Port Royal to-morrow (*Prosopopœa*).—" It is in vain O men, that you seek within yourselves the remedy for your ills. All your light can only reach the knowledge that not in yourselves will you find truth or good. The philosophers have promised you that, and have been unable to do it. They neither know what is your true good, nor what is your true state. How could they have given remedies for your ills, when they did not even know them? Your chief maladies are pride, which takes you away from God, and lust, which binds you to earth; and they have done nothing else but cherish one or other of these diseases. If they gave you God as an end, it was only to administer to your pride; they made you think that you are by nature like Him, and conformed to Him. And those who saw the absurdity of this claim put you on another precipice, by making you understand that your nature was like that of the brutes, and led you to seek your good in the lusts which are shared by the animals. This is not the way to cure you of your unrighteousness, which these wise men never knew. I alone can make you understand who you are. . . ."

Adam, Jesus Christ.

If you are united to God, it is by grace, not by nature. If you are humbled, it is by penitence, not by nature.

Thus this double capacity. . . .

You are not in the state of your creation.

As these two states are open, it is impossible for you not to recognise them. Follow your own feelings, observe yourselves, and see if you do not find the lively characteristics of these two natures. Could so many contradictions be found in a simple subject?

—Incomprehensible.—Not all that is incomprehensible ceases to exist. Infinite number. An infinite space equal to a finite.

—Incredible that God should unite Himself to us.—This consideration is drawn only from the sight of our vileness. But if you are quite sincere over it, follow it as far as I have done, and recognise that we are indeed so vile that we are incapable in ourselves of knowing if His mercy cannot make us capable of Him. For I would know how this animal, who knows himself to be so weak, has the right to measure the mercy of God, and set limits to it, suggested by his own fancy. He has so little knowledge of what God is, that he does not know what he himself is, and, completely disturbed at the sight of his own state, dares to say that God cannot make him capable of communion with Him.

But I would ask him if God demands anything else from him than the knowledge and love of Him, and why, since his nature is capable of love and knowledge, he believes that God cannot make Himself known and loved by him. Doubtless he knows at least that he exists, and that he loves something. Therefore, if he sees anything in the darkness wherein he is, and if he finds some object of his love among the things on earth, why, if God impart to him some ray of His essence, will he not be capable of knowing and of loving Him in the manner in which it shall please Him to communicate Himself to us? There must then be certainly an intolerable presumption in these sort of arguments, although they seem founded on an apparent humility, which is neither sincere nor reasonable, if it does not make us admit that, not knowing of ourselves what we are, we can only learn it from God.

" I do not mean that you should submit your belief to me without reason, and I do not aspire to overcome you by tyranny. In fact I do not claim to give you a reason for everything. And to reconcile these contradictions, I intend to make you see clearly, by convincing proofs, those divine signs in me, which may convince you of what I am, and may gain authority for me by wonders and proofs which you cannot reject; so that you may then believe without . . . the things which I teach you, since you will find no other ground for rejecting them, except that you cannot know of yourselves if they are true or not.

" God has willed to redeem men, and to open salvation to those who seek it. But men render themselves so unworthy of it, that it is right that God should refuse to some, because of their obduracy, what He grants to others from a compassion which is not due to them. If He had willed to overcome the obstinacy of the most hardened, He could have done so by revealing Himself so manifestly to them that they could not have doubted of the truth of His essence; as it will appear at the last day, with such thunders and such a convulsion of nature, that the dead will rise again, and the blindest will see Him.

" It is not in this manner that He has willed to appear in His advent of mercy, because, as so many make themselves unworthy of His mercy, He has willed to leave them in the loss of the good which they do not want. It was not then right that He should appear in a manner manifestly divine, and completely capable of convincing all men; but it was also not right that He should come in so hidden a manner that He could not be known by those who should sincerely seek Him. He has willed to make Himself quite recognisable by those; and thus, willing to appear openly to those who seek Him with all their heart, and to be hidden from those who flee from Him with all their heart, He so regulates the knowledge of Himself that He has given signs of Himself, visible to those who seek Him, and not to those who seek Him not. There is enough light for those who only desire to see, and enough obscurity for those who have a contrary disposition."

431

No other religion has recognised that man is the most excellent creature. Some, which have quite recognised the reality of his excellence, have considered as mean and ungrateful the low opinions which men naturally have of themselves; and others, which have thoroughly recognised how real is this vileness, have treated with proud ridicule those feelings of greatness, which are equally natural to man.

"Lift your eyes to God," say the first; "see Him whom you resemble, and who has created you to worship Him. You can make yourselves like unto Him; wisdom will make you equal to Him, if you will follow it." "Raise your heads, free men," says Epictetus. And others say, "Bend your eyes to the earth, wretched worm that you are, and consider the brutes whose companion you are."

What then will man become? Will he be equal to God

or the brutes? What a frightful difference! What then shall we be? Who does not see from all this that man has gone astray, that he has fallen from his place, that he anxiously seeks it, that he cannot find it again? And who shall then direct him to it? The greatest men have failed.

432

Scepticism is true; for, after all, men before Jesus Christ did not know where they were, nor whether they were great or small. And those who have said the one or the other, knew nothing about it, and guessed without reason and by chance. They also erred always in excluding the one or the other.

Quod ergo ignorantes quæritis, religio annuntiat vobis.[1]

433

After having understood the whole nature of man.—That a religion may be true, it must have knowledge of our nature. It ought to know its greatness and littleness, and the reason of both. What religion but the Christian has known this?

434

The chief arguments of the sceptics—I pass over the lesser ones—are that we have no certainty of the truth of these principles apart from faith and revelation, except in so far as we naturally perceive them in ourselves. Now this natural intuition is not a convincing proof of their truth; since, having no certainty, apart from faith, whether man was created by a good God, or by a wicked demon, or by chance, it is doubtful whether these principles given to us are true, or false, or uncertain, according to our origin. Again, no person is certain, apart from faith, whether he is awake or sleeps, seeing that during sleep we believe as firmly as we do that we are awake; we believe that we see space, figure, and motion; we are aware of the passage of time, we measure it; and in fact we act as if we were awake. So that half of our life being passed in sleep, we have on

[1] "What therefore ye ignorantly seek, religion proclaims to you."— Cf. Acts, xvii. 23.

our own admission no idea of truth, whatever we may imagine. As all our intuitions are then illusions, who knows whether the other half of our life, in which we think we are awake, is not another sleep a little different from the former, from which we awake when we suppose ourselves asleep?

[And who doubts that, if we dreamt in company, and the dreams chanced to agree, which is common enough, and if we were always alone when awake, we should believe that matters were reversed? In short, as we often dream that we dream, heaping dream upon dream, may it not be that this half of our life, wherein we think ourselves awake, is itself only a dream on which the others are grafted, from which we wake at death, during which we have as few principles of truth and good as during natural sleep, these different thoughts which disturb us being perhaps only illusions like the flight of time and the vain fancies of our dreams?]

These are the chief arguments on one side and the other.

I omit minor ones, such as the sceptical talk against the impressions of custom, education, manners, country, and the like. Though these influence the majority of common folk, who dogmatise only on shallow foundations, they are upset by the least breath of the sceptics. We have only to see their books if we are not sufficiently convinced of this, and we shall very quickly become so, perhaps too much.

I notice the only strong point of the dogmatists, namely, that, speaking in good faith and sincerely, we cannot doubt natural principles. Against this the sceptics set up in one word the uncertainty of our origin, which includes that of our nature. The dogmatists have been trying to answer this objection ever since the world began.

So there is open war among men, in which each must take a part, and side either with dogmatism or scepticism. For he who thinks to remain neutral is above all a sceptic. This neutrality is the essence of the sect; he who is not against them is essentially for them. [In this appears their advantage.] They are not for themselves; they are neutral, indifferent, in suspense as to all things, even themselves being no exception.

What then shall man do in this state? Shall he doubt

everything? Shall he doubt whether he is awake, whether he is being pinched, or whether he is being burned? Shall he doubt whether he doubts? Shall he doubt whether he exists? We cannot go so far as that; and I lay it down as a fact there never has been a real complete sceptic. Nature sustains our feeble reason, and prevents it raving to this extent.

Shall he then say, on the contrary, that he certainly possesses truth—he who, when pressed ever so little, can show no title to it, and is forced to let go his hold?

What a chimera then is man! What a novelty! What a monster, what a chaos, what a contradiction, what a prodigy! Judge of all things, imbecile worm of the earth; depositary of truth, a sink of uncertainty and error; the pride and refuse of the universe!

Who will unravel this tangle? Nature confutes the sceptics, and reason confutes the dogmatists. What then will you become, O men! who try to find out by your natural reason what is your true condition? You cannot avoid one of these sects, nor adhere to one of them.

Know then, proud man, what a paradox you are to yourself. Humble yourself, weak reason; be silent, foolish nature; learn that man infinitely transcends man, and learn from your Master your true condition, of which you are ignorant. Hear God.

For in fact, if man had never been corrupt, he would enjoy in his innocence both truth and happiness with assurance; and if man had always been corrupt, he would have no idea of truth or bliss. But, wretched as we are, and more so than if there were no greatness in our condition, we have an idea of happiness, and cannot reach it. We perceive an image of truth, and possess only a lie. Incapable of absolute ignorance and of certain knowledge, we have thus been manifestly in a degree of perfection from which we have unhappily fallen.

It is, however, an astonishing thing that the mystery furthest removed from our knowledge, namely, that of the transmission of sin, should be a fact without which we can have no knowledge of ourselves. For it is beyond doubt that there is nothing which more shocks our reason than to say that the sin of the first man has rendered guilty those, who, being so removed from this source, seem incapable of participation in it. This transmission does not only seem to us impossible, it seems also very unjust. For what is more contrary to the rules of our miserable justice than to damn eternally an infant incapable of will, for a sin wherein he seems to have so little a share, that it was committed six thousand years before he was in existence? Certainly nothing offends us more rudely than this doctrine; and yet, without this mystery, the most incomprehensible of all, we are incomprehensible to ourselves. The knot of our condition takes its twists and turns in this abyss, so that man is more inconceivable without this mystery than this mystery is inconceivable to man.

[Whence it seems that God, willing to render the difficulty of our existence unintelligible to ourselves, has concealed the knot so high, or, better speaking, so low, that we are quite incapable of reaching it; so that it is not by the proud exertions of our reason, but by the simple submission of reason, that we can truly know ourselves.

These foundations, solidly established on the inviolable authority of religion, make us know that there are two truths of faith equally certain: the one, that man, in the state of creation, or in that of grace, is raised above all nature, made like unto God and sharing in His divinity; the other, that in the state of corruption and sin, he is fallen from this state and made like unto the beasts.

These two propositions are equally sound and certain. Scripture manifestly declares this to us, when it says in some places: *Deliciæ meæ esse cum filiis hominum.*[2] *Effundum spiritum meum super omnem carnem.*[3] *Dii estis,*[4] &c.; and in other places, *Omnis caro fœnum.*[5] *Homo assimilatus est jumentis insipientibus, et similis factus est illis.*[6] *Dixi in corde meo de filiis hominum.* Eccles. iii.

Whence it clearly seems that man by grace is made like unto God, and a partaker in His divinity, and that without grace he is like unto the brute beasts.]

[2] Proverbs, viii. 31.   [3] Isaiah, xliv. 3; Joel, ii. 28.   [4] Psalms, lxxxii. 6.
[5] Isaiah, xl. 6.   [6] Psalms, xlix. 20.

435

Without this divine knowledge what could men do but either become elated by the inner feeling of their past greatness which still remains to them, or become despondent at the sight of their present weakness? For, not seeing the whole truth, they could not attain to perfect virtue. Some considering nature as incorrupt, others as incurable, they could not escape either pride or sloth, the two sources of all vice; since they cannot but either abandon themselves to it through cowardice, or escape it by pride. For if they knew the excellence of man, they were ignorant of his corruption; so that they easily avoided sloth, but fell into pride. And if they recognised the infirmity of nature, they were ignorant of its dignity; so that they could easily avoid vanity, but it was to fall into despair. Thence arise the different schools of the Stoics and Epicureans, the Dogmatists, Academicians, &c.

The Christian religion alone has been able to cure these two vices, not by expelling the one through means of the other according to the wisdom of the world, but by expelling both according to the simplicity of the Gospel. For it teaches the righteous that it raises them even to a participation in divinity itself; that in this lofty state they still carry the source of all corruption, which renders them during all their life subject to error, misery, death, and sin; and it proclaims to the most ungodly that they are capable of the grace of their Redeemer. So making those tremble whom it justifies, and consoling those whom it condemns, religion so justly tempers fear with hope through that double capacity of grace and of sin, common to all, that it humbles infinitely more than reason alone can do, but without despair; and it exalts infinitely more than natural pride, but without inflating: thus making it evident that alone being exempt from error and vice, it alone fulfils the duty of instructing and correcting men.

Who then can refuse to believe and adore this heavenly light? For is it not clearer than day that we perceive within ourselves ineffaceable marks of excellence? And is it not equally true that we experience every hour the re-

sults of our deplorable condition? What does this chaos
and monstrous confusion proclaim to us but the truth of
these two states, with a voice so powerful that it is impossible to resist it?

436

Weakness.—Every pursuit of men is to get wealth; and
they cannot have a title to show that they possess it justly,
for they have only that of human caprice; nor have they
strength to hold it securely. It is the same with knowledge,
for disease takes it away. We are incapable both of truth
and goodness.

437

We desire truth, and find within ourselves only uncertainty.

We seek happiness, and find only misery and death.

We cannot but desire truth and happiness, and are incapable of certainty or happiness. This desire is left to us,
partly to punish us, partly to make us perceive wherefrom
we are fallen.

438

If man is not made for God, why is he only happy in
God? If man is made for God, why is he so opposed to
God?

439

Nature corrupted.—Man does not act by reason, which
constitutes his being.

440

The corruption of reason is shown by the existence of
so many different and extravagant customs. It was necessary that truth should come, in order that man should no
longer dwell within himself.

441

For myself, I confess that so soon as the Christian religion
reveals the principle that human nature is corrupt and
fallen from God, that opens my eyes to see everywhere the
mark of this truth: for nature is such that she testifies

everywhere, both within man and without him, to a lost God and a corrupt nature.

442

Man's true nature, his true good, true virtue, and true religion, are things of which the knowledge is inseparable.

443

Greatness, wretchedness.—The more light we have, the more greatness and the more baseness we discover in man. Ordinary men—those who are more educated: philosophers, they astonish ordinary men—Christians, they astonish philosophers.

Who will then be surprised to see that religion only makes us know profoundly what we already know in proportion to our light?

444

This religion taught to her children what men have only been able to discover by their greatest knowledge.

445

Original sin is foolishness to men, but it is admitted to be such. You must not then reproach me for the want of reason in this doctrine, since I admit it to be without reason. But this foolishness is wiser than all the wisdom of men, *sapientius est hominibus.* For without this, what can we say that man is? His whole state depends on this imperceptible point. And how should it be perceived by his reason, since it is a thing against reason, and since reason, far from finding it out by her own ways, is averse to it when it is presented to her?

446

Of original sin. Ample tradition of original sin according to the Jews.

On the word in Genesis, viii. 21. The imagination of man's heart is evil from his youth.

R. Moses Haddarschan: This evil leaven is placed in man from the time that he is formed.

Massechet Succa: This evil leaven has seven names in

Scripture. It is called *evil, the foreskin, uncleanness, an enemy, a scandal, a heart of stone, the north wind;* all this signifies the malignity which is concealed and impressed in the heart of man.

Midrasch Tillim says the same thing, and that God will deliver the good nature of man from the evil.

This malignity is renewed every day against man, as it is written, Psalm xxxvii. 32: "The wicked watcheth the righteous, and seeketh to slay him;" but God will not abandon him. This malignity tries the heart of man in this life, and will accuse him in the other. All this is found in the *Talmud.*

Midrasch Tillim on Psalm iv. 4: "Stand in awe and sin not." Stand in awe and be afraid of your lust, and it will not lead you into sin. And on Psalm xxxvi. 1: "The wicked has said within his own heart, Let not the fear of God be before me." That is to say that the malignity natural to man has said that to the wicked.

Midrasch el Kohelet: "Better is a poor and wise child than an old and foolish king who cannot foresee the future." The child is virtue, and the king is the malignity of man. It is called king because all the members obey it, and old because it is in the human heart from infancy to old age, and foolish because it leads man in the way of [*perdition*], which he does not foresee. The same thing is in *Midrasch Tillim.*

Bereschist Rabba on Psalm xxxv. 10: "Lord, all my bones shall bless Thee, which deliverest the poor from the tyrant." And is there a greater tyrant than the evil leaven? And on Proverbs xxv. 21: "If thine enemy be hungry, give him bread to eat." That is to say, if the evil leaven hunger, give him the bread of wisdom of which it is spoken in Proverbs ix., and if he be thirsty, give him the water of which it is spoken in Isaiah lv.

Midrasch Tillim says the same thing, and that Scripture in that passage, speaking of the enemy, means the evil leaven; and that, in giving him that bread and that water, we heap coals of fire on his head.

Midrasch el Kohelet on Ecclesiastes ix. 14: "A great king besieged a little city." This great king is the evil leaven; the great bulwarks built against it are temptations; and there has been found a poor wise man who has delivered it—that is to say, virtue.

And on Psalm xli. 1: "Blessed is he that considereth the poor."

And on Psalm lxxviii. 39: "The spirit passeth away, and cometh not again"; whence some have erroneously argued against the immortality of the soul. But the sense is that this spirit is the evil leaven, which accompanies man till death, and will not return at the resurrection.

And on Psalm ciii. the same thing.

And on Psalm xvi.

Principles of Rabbinism: two Messiahs.

447

Will it be said that, as men have declared that righteousness has departed the earth, they therefore knew of original sin?—*Nemo ante obitum beatus est*[7]—that is to say, they knew death to be the beginning of eternal and essential happiness?

448

[*Miton*] sees well that nature is corrupt, and that men are averse to virtue; but he does not know why they cannot fly higher.

449

Order.—After corruption to say: "It is right that all those who are in that state should know it, both those who are content with it, and those who are not content with it; but it is not right that all should see Redemption."

450

If we do not know ourselves to be full of pride, ambition, lust, weakness, misery, and injustice, we are indeed blind. And if, knowing this, we do not desire deliverance, what can we say of a man. . . .?

What, then, can we have but esteem for a religion which knows so well the defects of man, and desire for the truth of a religion which promises remedies so desirable?

[7] "No one is happy before he is dead."

451

All men naturally hate one another. They employ lust as far as possible in the service of the public weal. But this is only a pretence and a false image of love; for at bottom it is only hate.

452

To pity the unfortunate is not contrary to lust. On the contrary, we can quite well give such evidence of friendship, and acquire the reputation of kindly feeling, without giving anything.

453

From lust men have found and extracted excellent rules of policy, morality, and justice; but in reality this vile root of man, this *figmentum malum*,[8] is only covered, it is not taken away.

454

Injustice.—They have not found any other means of satisfying lust without doing injury to others.

455

Self is hateful. You, Miton, conceal it; you do not for that reason destroy it; you are, then, always hateful.

—No; for in acting as we do to oblige everybody, we give no more occasion for hatred of us.—That is true, if we only hated in self the vexation which comes to us from it. But if I hate it because it is unjust, and because it makes itself the centre of everything, I shall always hate it.

In a word, the Self has two qualities: it is unjust in itself since it makes itself the centre of everything; it is inconvenient to others since it would enslave them; for each self is the enemy, and would like to be the tyrant of all others. You take away its inconvenience, but not its injustice, and so you do not render it lovable to those who hate injustice; you render it lovable only to the unjust, who do not any longer find in it an enemy. And thus you remain unjust, and can please only the unjust.

8 " Evil creation."

456

It is a perverted judgment that makes every one place himself above the rest of the world, and prefer his own good, and the continuance of his own good fortune and life, to that of the rest of the world.

457

Each one is all in all to himself; for he being dead, all is dead to him. Hence it comes that each believes himself to be all in all to everybody. We must not judge of nature by ourselves, but by it.

458

" All that is in the world is the lust of the flesh, or the lust of the eyes, or the pride of life; *libido sentiendi, libido sciendi, libido dominandi.*" Wretched is the cursed land which these three rivers of fire enflame rather than water! Happy they who, on these rivers, are not overwhelmed nor carried away, but are immovably fixed, not standing but seated on a low and secure base, whence they do not rise before the light, but, having rested in peace, stretch out their hands to Him, who must lift them up, and make them stand upright and firm in the porches of the holy Jerusalem! There pride can no longer assail them nor cast them down; and yet they weep, not to see all those perishable things swept away by the torrents, but at the remem--brance of their loved country, the heavenly Jerusalem, which they remember without ceasing during their prolonged exile.

459

The rivers of Babylon rush and fall and sweep away.
O holy Sion, where all is firm and nothing falls!
We must sit upon the waters, not under them or in them, but on them; and not standing but seated; being seated to be humble, and being above them to be secure. But we shall stand in the porches of Jerusalem.

Let us see if this pleasure is stable or transitory; if it pass away, it is a river of Babylon.

460

The lust of the flesh, the lust of the eyes, pride, &c.— There are three orders of things: the flesh, the spirit, and the will. The carnal are the rich and kings; they have the body as their object. Inquirers and scientists; they have the mind as their object. The wise; they have right-eousness as their object.

God must reign over all, and all men must be brought back to Him. In things of the flesh lust reigns specially; in intellectual matters, inquiry specially; in wisdom, pride specially. Not that a man cannot boast of wealth or knowl-edge, but it is not the place for pride; for in granting to a man that he is learned, it is easy to convince him that he is wrong to be proud. The proper place for pride is in wisdom, for it cannot be granted to a man that he has made himself wise, and that he is wrong to be proud; for that is right. Now God alone gives wisdom, and that is why *Qui gloriatur, in Domino glorietur.*[9]

461

The three lusts have made three sects; and the phi-losophers have done no other thing than follow one of the three lusts.

462

Search for the true good.—Ordinary men place the good in fortune and external goods, or at least in amusement. Philosophers have shown the vanity of all this, and have placed it where they could.

463

[*Against the philosophers who believe in God without Jesus Christ.*]

Philosophers.—They believe that God alone is worthy to be loved and admired; and they have desired to be loved

1 Cor., i. 31.

and admired of men, and do not know their own corruption. If they feel full of feelings of love and adoration, and find therein their chief delight, very well, let them think themselves good. But if they find themselves averse to Him, if they have no inclination but the desire to establish themselves in the esteem of men, and if their whole perfection consists only in making men—but without constraint—find their happiness in loving them, I declare that this perfection is horrible. What! they have known God, and have not desired solely that men should love Him, but that men should stop short at them! They have wanted to be the object of the voluntary delight of men.

464

Philosophers.—We are full of things which take us out of ourselves.

Our instinct makes us feel that we must seek our happiness outside ourselves. Our passions impel us outside, even when no objects present themselves to excite them. External objects tempt us of themselves, and call to us, even when we are not thinking of them. And thus philosophers have said in vain, " Retire within yourselves, you will find your good there." We do not believe them, and those who believe them are the most empty and the most foolish.

465

The Stoics say, " Retire within yourselves; it is there you will find your rest." And that is not true.

Others say, " Go out of yourselves; seek happiness in amusement." And this is not true. Illness comes.

Happiness is neither without us nor within us. It is in God, both without us and within us.

466

Had Epictetus seen the way perfectly, he would have said to men, " You follow a wrong road "; he shows that there is another, but he does not lead to it. It is the way of

willing what God wills. Jesus Christ alone leads to it:
Via, veritas.[10]

The vices of Zeno himself.

467

The reason of effects.—Epictetus. Those who say, "You
have a headache;" this is not the same thing. We are
assured of health, and not of justice; and in fact his own
was nonsense.

And yet he believed it demonstrable, when he said, "It is
either in our power or it is not." But he did not perceive
that it is not in our power to regulate the heart, and he was
wrong to infer this from the fact that there were some
Christians.

468

No other religion has proposed to men to hate themselves. No other religion then can please those who hate
themselves, and who seek a Being truly lovable. And these,
if they had never heard of the religion of a God humiliated,
would embrace it at once.

469

I feel that I might not have been; for the Ego consists
in my thoughts. Therefore I, who think, would not have
been, if my mother had been killed before I had life. I am
not then a necessary being. In the same way I am not
eternal or infinite; but I see plainly that there exists in
nature a necessary Being, eternal and infinite.

470

"Had I seen a miracle," say men, "I should become
converted." How can they be sure they would do a thing
of the nature of which they are ignorant? They imagine
that this conversion consists in a worship of God, which
is like commerce, and in a communion such as they picture
to themselves. True religion consists in annihilating self
before that Universal Being, whom we have so often provoked, and who can justly destroy us at any time; in recog-

[10] John xiv. 6.

nising that we can do nothing without Him, and have deserved nothing from Him but His displeasure. It consists
in knowing that there is an unconquerable opposition between us and God, and that without a mediator there can
be no communion with Him.

471

It is unjust that men should attach themselves to me, even
though they do it with pleasure and voluntarily. I should
deceive those in whom I had created this desire; for I am
not the end of any, and I have not the wherewithal to satisfy them. Am I not about to die? And thus the object of
their attachment will die. Therefore, as I would be blamable in causing a falsehood to be believed, though I should
employ gentle persuasion, though it should be believed with
pleasure, and though it should give me pleasure; even so
I am blamable in making myself loved, and if I attract
persons to attach themselves to me. I ought to warn those
who are ready to consent to a lie, that they ought not to believe it, whatever advantage comes to me from it; and
likewise that they ought not to attach themselves to me;
for they ought to spend their life and their care in pleasing
God, or in seeking Him.

472

Self-will will never be satisfied, though it should have
command of all it would; but we are satisfied from the
moment we renounce it. Without it we cannot be discontented; with it we cannot be content.

473

Let us imagine a body full of thinking members.

474

Members. To commence with that.—To regulate the love
which we owe to ourselves, we must imagine a body full
of thinking members, for we are members of the whole, and
must see how each member should love itself, &c. . . .

475

If the feet and the hands had a will of their own, they could only be in their order in submitting this particular will to the primary will which governs the whole body. Apart from that, they are in disorder and mischief; but in willing only the good of the body, they accomplish their own good.

476

We must love God only and hate self only.

If the foot had always been ignorant that it belonged to the body, and that there was a body on which it depended, if it had only had the knowledge and the love of self, and if it came to know that it belonged to a body on which it depended, what regret, what shame for its past life, for having been useless to the body which inspired its life, which would have annihilated it if it had rejected it and separated it from itself, as it kept itself apart from the body! What prayers for its preservation in it! And with what submission would it allow itself to be governed by the will which rules the body, even to consenting, if necessary, to be cut off, or it would lose its character as member! For every member must be quite willing to perish for the body, for which alone the whole is.

477

It is false that we are worthy of the love of others; it is unfair that we should desire it. If we were born reasonable and impartial, knowing ourselves and others, we should not give this bias to our will. However, we are born with it; we are therefore born unjust, for all tends to self. This is contrary to all order. We must consider the general good; and the propensity to self is the beginning of all disorder, in war, in politics, in economy, and in the particular body of man. The will is therefore depraved.

If the members of natural and civil communities tend towards the weal of the body, the communities themselves ought to look to another more general body of which they are members. We ought therefore to look to the whole. We are therefore born unjust and depraved.

478

When we want to think of God, is there nothing which turns us away, and tempts us to think of something else? All this is bad, and is born in us.

479

If there is a God, we must love Him only, and not the creatures of a day. The reasoning of the ungodly in the *Book of Wisdom* is only based upon the non-existence of God. "On that supposition," say they, "let us take delight in the creatures." That is the worst that can happen. But if there were a God to love, they would not have come to this conclusion, but to quite the contrary. And this is the conclusion of the wise: "There is a God, let us therefore not take delight in the creatures."

Therefore all that incites us to attach ourselves to the creatures is bad; since it prevents us from serving God if we know Him, or from seeking Him if we know Him not. Now we are full of lust. Therefore we are full of evil; therefore we ought to hate ourselves and all that excites us to attach ourselves to any other object than God only.

480

To make the members happy, they must have one will, and submit it to the body.

481

The examples of the noble deaths of the Lacedæmonians and others scarce touch us. For what good is it to us? But the example of the death of the martyrs touches us; for they are "our members." We have a common tie with them. Their resolution can form ours, not only by example, but because it has perhaps deserved ours. There is nothing of this in the examples of the heathen. We have no tie with them; as we do not become rich by seeing a stranger who is so, but in fact by seeing a father or a husband who is so.

482

Morality.—God having made the heavens and the earth, which do not feel the happiness of their being, He has willed to make beings who should know it, and who should compose a body of thinking members. For our members do not feel the happiness of their union, of their wonderful intelligence, of the care which nature has taken to infuse into them minds, and to make them grow and endure. How happy they would be if they saw and felt it! But for this they would need to have intelligence to know it, and good-will to consent to that of the universal soul. But if, having received intelligence, they employed it to retain nourishment for themselves without allowing it to pass to the other members, they would be not only unjust, but also miserable, and would hate rather than love themselves; their blessed-ness, as well as their duty, consisting in their consent to the guidance of the whole soul to which they belong, which loves them better than they love themselves.

483

To be a member is to have neither life, being, nor move-ment, except through the spirit of the body, and for the body.

The separate member, seeing no longer the body to which it belongs, has only a perishing and dying existence. Yet it believes it is a whole, and seeing not the body on which it depends, it believes it depends only on self, and desires to make itself both centre and body. But not having in itself a principle of life, it only goes astray, and is astonished in the uncertainty of its being; perceiving in fact that it is not a body, and still not seeing that it is a member of a body. In short, when it comes to know itself, it has re-turned as it were to its own home, and loves itself only for the body. It deplores its past wanderings.

It cannot by its nature love any other thing, except for itself and to subject it to self, because each thing loves itself more than all. But in loving the body, it loves itself, because it only exists in it, by it, and for it. *Qui adhæret Deo unus spiritus est.*[11]

The body loves the hand; and the hand, if it had a will, should love itself in the same way as it is loved by the soul. All love which goes beyond this is unfair.

Adhærens Deo unus spiritus est. We love ourselves, because we are members of Jesus Christ. We love Jesus Christ, because He is the body of which we are members. All is one, one is in the other, like the Three Persons.

484

Two laws suffice to rule the whole Christian Republic better than all the laws of statecraft.

485

The true and only virtue then is to hate self (for we are hateful on account of lust), and to seek a truly lovable being to love. But as we cannot love what is outside ourselves, we must love a being who is in us, and is not ourselves; and that is true of each and all men. Now only the Universal Being is such. The kingdom of God is within us; the universal good is within us, is ourselves—and not ourselves.

486

The dignity of man in his innocence consisted in using and having dominion over the creatures, but now in separating himself from them, and subjecting himself to them.

487

Every religion is false, which as to its faith does not worship one God as the origin of everything, and which as to its morality does not love one only God as the object of everything.

488

. . . But it is impossible that God should ever be the end, if He is not the beginning. We lift our eyes on high,

[11] I Cor., vi. 17.

but lean upon the sand; and the earth will dissolve, and we shall fall whilst looking at the heavens.

489

If there is one sole source of everything, there is one sole end of everything; everything through Him, everything for Him. The true religion then must teach us to worship Him only, and to love Him only. But as we find ourselves unable to worship what we know not, and to love any other object but ourselves, the religion which instructs us in these duties must instruct us also of this inability, and teach us also the remedies for it. It teaches us that by one man all was lost, and the bond broken between God and us, and that by one man the bond is renewed.

We are born so averse to this love of God, and it is so necessary that we must be born guilty, or God would be unjust.

490

Men, not being accustomed to form merit, but only to recompense it where they find it formed, judge of God by themselves.

491

The true religion must have as a characteristic the obligation to love God. This is very just, and yet no other religion has commanded this; ours has done so. It must also be aware of human lust and weakness; ours is so. It must have adduced remedies for this; one is prayer. No other religion has asked of God to love and follow Him.

492

He who hates not in himself his self-love, and that instinct which leads him to make himself God, is indeed blinded. Who does not see that there is nothing so opposed to justice and truth? For it is false that we deserve this, and it is unfair and impossible to attain it, since all demand the same thing. It is then a manifest injustice which is innate in us, of which we cannot get rid, and of which we must get rid.

Yet no religion has indicated that this was a sin; or that we were born in it; or that we were obliged to resist it; or has thought of giving us remedies for it.

493

The true religion teaches our duties; our weaknesses, pride, and lust; and the remedies, humility and mortification.

494

The true religion must teach greatness and misery; must lead to the esteem and contempt of self, to love and to hate.

495

If it is an extraordinary blindness to live without investigating what we are, it is a terrible one to live an evil life, while believing in God.

496

Experience makes us see an enormous difference between piety and goodness.

497

Against those who, trusting to the mercy of God, live heedlessly, without doing good works.—As the two sources of our sins are pride and sloth, God has revealed to us two of His attributes to cure them, mercy and justice. The property of justice is to humble pride, however holy may be our works, *et non intres in judicium,* &c.;[12] and the property of mercy is to combat sloth by exhorting to good works, according to that passage: "The goodness of God leadeth to repentance," and that other of the Ninevites: "Let us do penance to see if peradventure He will pity us." And thus mercy is so far from authorising slackness, that it is on the contrary the quality which formally attacks it; so that instead of saying, "If there were no mercy in God we should have to make every kind of effort after virtue," we must say, on the contrary, that it is because there is mercy in God, that we must make every kind of effort.

[12] Psalms, clxiii. 2.

498

It is true there is difficulty in entering into godliness. But this difficulty does not arise from the religion which begins in us, but from the irreligion which is still there. If our senses were not opposed to penitence, and if our corruption were not opposed to the purity of God, there would be nothing in this painful to us. We suffer only in proportion as the vice which is natural to us resists supernatural grace. Our heart feels torn asunder between these opposed efforts. But it would be very unfair to impute this violence to God, who is drawing us on, instead of to the world, which is holding us back. It is as a child, which a mother tears from the arms of robbers, in the pain it suffers, should love the loving and legitimate violence of her who procures its liberty, and detest only the impetuous and tyrannical violence of those who detain it unjustly. The most cruel war which God can make with men in this life is to leave them without that war which He came to bring. " I came to send war," He says, " and to teach them of this war. I came to bring fire and the sword." Before Him the world lived in this false peace.

499

External works.—There is nothing so perilous as what pleases God and man. For those states, which please God and man, have one property which pleases God, and another which pleases men; as the greatness of Saint Theresa. What pleased God was her deep humility in the midst of her revelations; what pleased men was her light. And so we torment ourselves to imitate her discourses, thinking to imitate her conditions, and not so much to love what God loves, and to put ourselves in the state which God loves.

It is better not to fast, and be thereby humbled, than to fast and be self-satisfied therewith. The Pharisee and the Publican.

What use will memory be to me, if it can alike hurt and help me, and all depends upon the blessing of God, who gives only to things done for Him, according to His rules and in His ways, the manner being thus as important as the thing, and perhaps more; since God can bring forth good out of evil, and without God we bring forth evil out of good?

500

The meaning of the words, good and evil.

501

First step: to be blamed for doing evil, and praised for doing good.

Second step: to be neither praised nor blamed.

502

Abraham took nothing for himself, but only for his servants. So the righteous man takes for himself nothing of the world, nor of the applause of the world, but only for his passions, which he uses as their master, saying to the one, "Go," and to another, "Come." *Sub te erit appetitus tuus.*[13] The passions thus subdued are virtues. Even God attributes to Himself avarice, jealousy, anger; and these are virtues as well as kindness, pity, constancy, which are also passions. We must employ them as slaves, and, leaving to them their food, prevent the soul from taking any of it. For, when the passions become masters, they are vices; and they give their nutriment to the soul, and the soul nourishes itself upon it, and is poisoned.

503

Philosophers have consecrated the vices by placing them in God Himself. Christians have consecrated the virtues.

504

The just man acts by faith in the least things; when he reproves his servants, he desires their conversion by the Spirit of God, and prays God to correct them; and he expects as much from God as from his own reproofs, and prays God to bless his corrections. And so in all his other actions he proceeds with the Spirit of God; and his actions

[13] Genesis, iv. 7.

deceive us by reason of the . . . or suspension of the Spirit of God in him; and he repents in his affliction.

505

All things can be deadly to us, even the things made to serve us; as in nature walls can kill us, and stairs can kill us, if we do not walk circumspectly.

The least movement affects all nature; the entire sea changes because of a rock. Thus in grace, the least action affects everything by its consequences; therefore everything is important.

In each action we must look beyond the action at our past, present, and future state, and at others whom it affects, and see the relations of all those things. And then we shall be very cautious.

506

Let God not impute to us our sins, that is to say, all the consequences and results of our sins, which are dreadful, even those of the smallest faults, if we wish to follow them out mercilessly!

507

The spirit of grace; the hardness of the heart; external circumstances.

508

Grace is indeed needed to turn a man into a saint; and he who doubts it does not know what a saint or a man is.

509

Philosophers.—A fine thing to cry to a man who does not know himself, that he should come of himself to God! And a fine thing to say so to a man who does know himself!

510

Man is not worthy of God, but he is not incapable of being made worthy.

It is unworthy of God to unite Himself to wretched man; but it is not unworthy of God to pull him out of his misery.

511

If we would say that man is too insignificant to deserve communion with God, we must indeed be very great to judge of it.

512

It is, in peculiar phraseology, wholly the body of Jesus Christ, but it cannot be said to be the whole body of Jesus Christ. The union of two things without change does not enable us to say that one becomes the other; the soul thus being united to the body, the fire to the timber, without change. But change is necessary to make the form of the one become the form of the other; thus the union of the Word to man. Because my body without my soul would not make the body of a man; therefore my soul united to any matter whatsoever will make my body. It does not distinguish the necessary condition from the sufficient condition; the union is necessary, but not sufficient. The left arm is not the right.

Impenetrability is a property of matter.

Identity of number in regard to the same time requires the identity of matter.

Thus if God united my soul to a body in China, the same body, *idem numero,* would be in China.

The same river which runs there is *idem numero* as that which runs at the same time in China.

513

Why God has established prayer.

1. To communicate to His creatures the dignity of causality.

2. To teach us from whom our virtue comes.

3. To make us deserve other virtues by work.

But to keep His own pre-eminence, He grants prayer to whom He pleases.

Objection: But we believe that we hold prayer of ourselves.

This is absurd; for since, though having faith, we cannot

have virtues, how should we have faith? Is there a greater distance between infidelity and faith than between faith and virtue?

Merit. This word is ambiguous.

Meruit habere Redemptorem.[14]

Meruit tam sacra membra tangere.[15]

Digno tam sacra membra tangere.[16]

Non sum dignus.[17]

Qui manducat indignus.[18]

Dignus est accipere.[19]

Dignare me.[20]

God is only bound according to His promises. He has promised to grant justice to prayers; He has never promised prayer only to the children of promise.

Saint Augustine has distinctly said that strength would be taken away from the righteous. But it is by chance that he said it; for it might have happened that the occasion of saying it did not present itself. But his principles make us see that when the occasion for it presented itself, it was impossible that he should not say it, or that he should say anything to the contrary. It is then rather that he was forced to say it, when the occasion presented itself, than that he said it, when the occasion presented itself, the one being of necessity, the other of chance. But the two are all that we can ask.

514

"Work out your own salvation with fear."

Proofs of prayer. *Petenti dabitur.*[21]

Therefore it is in our power to ask. On the other hand, there is God. So it is not in our power, since the obtaining of (the grace) to pray to Him in not in our power. For since salvation is not in us, and the obtaining of such grace is from Him, prayer is not in our power.

The righteous man should then hope no more in God, for he ought not to hope, but to strive to obtain what he wants.

[14] "He deserved to have a Redeemer."
[15] "He deserved to touch members so sacred."
[16] "I deem him worthy to touch, etc."
[17] "I am not worthy."—Luke, vii. 6.   [18] 1 Cor., xi. 27.
[19] Revel., iv. 11.   [20] "To deem me worthy."   [21] Matt., vii. 7.

Let us conclude then that, since man is now unrighteous since the first sin, and God is unwilling that he should thereby not be estranged from Him, it is only by a first effect that he is not estranged.

Therefore, those who depart from God have not this first effect without which they are not estranged from God, and those who do not depart from God have this first effect. Therefore, those whom we have seen possessed for some time of grace by this first effect, cease to pray, for want of this first effect.

Then God abandons the first in this sense.

515

The elect will be ignorant of their virtues, and the outcast of the greatness of their sins: "Lord, when saw we Thee an hungered, thirsty?" &c.

516

Romans iii. 27. Boasting is excluded. By what law? Of works? nay, but by faith. Then faith is not within our power like the deeds of the law, and it is given to us in another way.

517

Comfort yourselves. It is not from yourselves that you should expect grace; but, on the contrary, it is in expecting nothing from yourselves, that you must hope for it.

518

Every condition, and even the martyrs, have to fear, according to Scripture.

The greatest pain of purgatory is the uncertainty of the judgment. *Deus absconditus.*[22]

519

John viii. *Multi crediderunt in eum. Dicebat ergo Jesus: " Si manseritis . . . vere mei discipuli eritis, et veritas*

[22] " A hidden God."

*liberabit vos." Responderunt: "Semen Abrahæ sumus, et
nemini servimus unquam."*

There is a great difference between disciples and true
disciples. We recognise them by telling them that the
truth will make them free; for if they answer that they are
free, and that it is in their power to come out of slavery to
the devil, they are indeed disciples, but not true disciples.

520

The law has not destroyed nature, but has instructed it;
grace has not destroyed the law, but has made it act. Faith
received at baptism is the source of the whole life of
Christians and of the converted.

521

Grace will always be in the world, and nature also;
so that the former is in some sort natural. And thus there
will always be Pelagians, and always Catholics, and always
strife; because the first birth makes the one, and the grace
of the second birth the other.

522

The law imposed what it did not give. Grace gives what
it imposes.

523

All faith consists in Jesus Christ and in Adam, and all
morality in lust and in grace.

524

There is no doctrine more appropriate to man than this,
which teaches him his double capacity of receiving and of
losing grace, because of the double peril to which he is exposed, of despair or of pride.

525

The philosophers did not prescribe feelings suitable to
the two states.

They inspired feelings of pure greatness, and that is not man's state.

They inspired feelings of pure littleness, and that is not man's state.

There must be feelings of humility, not from nature, but from penitence, not to rest in them, but to go on to greatness. There must be feelings of greatness, not from merit, but from grace, and after having passed through humiliation.

526

Misery induces despair, pride induces presumption. The Incarnation shows man the greatness of his misery by the greatness of the remedy which he required.

527

The knowledge of God without that of man's misery causes pride. The knowledge of man's misery without that of God causes despair. The knowledge of Jesus Christ constitutes the middle course, because in Him we find both God and our misery.

528

Jesus Christ is a God whom we approach without pride, and before whom we humble ourselves without despair.

529

. . . Not a degradation which renders us incapable of good, nor a holiness exempt from evil.

530

A person told me one day that on coming from confession he felt great joy and confidence. Another told me that he remained in fear. Whereupon I thought that these two together would make one good man, and that each was wanting in that he had not the feeling of the other. The same often happens in other things.

531

He who knows the will of his master will be beaten with more blows, because of the power he has by his knowledge. *Qui justus est, justificetur adhuc,*[23] because of the power he has by justice. From him who has received most, will the greatest reckoning be demanded, because of the power he has by this help.

532

Scripture has provided passages of consolation and of warning for all conditions.

Nature seems to have done the same thing by her two infinities, natural and moral; for we shall always have the higher and the lower, the more clever and the less clever, the most exalted and the meanest, in order to humble our pride, and exalt our humility.

533

Comminutum cor[24] (Saint Paul). This is the Christian character. *Alba has named you, I know you no more* (Corneille). That is the inhuman character. The human character is the opposite.

534

There are only two kinds of men: the righteous, who believe themselves sinners; the rest, sinners, who believe themselves righteous.

535

We owe a great debt to those who point out faults. For they mortify us. They teach us that we have been despised. They do not prevent our being so in the future; for we have many other faults for which we may be despised. They prepare for us the exercise of correction and freedom from fault.

536

Man is so made that by continually telling him he is a fool he believes it, and by continually telling it to himself

[23] Revel., xxii. 11.   [24] "A broken heart."

he makes himself believe it. For man holds an inward talk
with his self alone, which it behoves him to regulate well:
Corrumpunt mores bonos colloquia prava.[25] We must keep
silent as much as possible, and talk with ourselves only of
God, whom we know to be true; and thus we convince ourselves of the truth.

537

Christianity is strange. It bids man recognise that he
is vile, even abominable, and bids him desire to be like God.
Without such a counterpoise, this dignity would make him
horribly vain, or this humiliation would make him terribly
abject.

538

With how little pride does a Christian believe himself
united to God! With how little humiliation does he place
himself on a level with the worms of earth!

A glorious manner to welcome life and death, good and
evil!

539

What difference in point of obedience is there between
a soldier and a Carthusian monk? For both are equally
under obedience and dependent, both engage in equally
painful exercises. But the soldier always hopes to command, and never attains this, for even captains and princes
are ever slaves and dependents; still he ever hopes and ever
works to attain this. Whereas the Carthusian monk makes
a vow to be always dependent. So they do not differ in
their perpetual thraldom, in which both of them always
exist, but in the hope, which one always has, and the other
never.

540

The hope which Christians have of possessing an infinite
good is mingled with real enjoyment as well as with fear;
for it is not as with those who should hope for a kingdom,
of which they, being subjects, would have nothing; but they
hope for holiness, for freedom from injustice, and they have
something of this.

[25] I Cor., xv. 33.

541

None is so happy as a true Christian, nor so reasonable, virtuous, or amiable.

542

The Christian religion alone makes man altogether *lovable and happy*. In honesty, we cannot perhaps be altogether lovable and happy.

543

Preface.—The metaphysical proofs of God are so remote from the reasoning of men, and so complicated, that they make little impression; and if they should be of service to some, it would be only during the moment that they see such demonstration; but an hour afterwards they fear they have been mistaken.

Quod curiositate cognoverunt superbia amiserunt.[26]

This is the result of the knowledge of God obtained without Jesus Christ; it is communion without a mediator with the God whom they have known without a mediator. Whereas those who have known God by a mediator know their own wretchedness.

544

The God of the Christians is a God who makes the soul feel that He is her only good, that her only rest is in Him, that her only delight is in loving Him; and who makes her at the same time abhor the obstacles which keep her back, and prevent her from loving God with all her strength. Self-love and lust, which hinder us, are unbearable to her. Thus God makes her feel that she has this root of self-love which destroys her, and which He alone can cure.

545

Jesus Christ did nothing but teach men that they loved themselves, that they were slaves, blind, sick, wretched, and sinners; that He must deliver them, enlighten, bless, and heal them; that this would be effected by hating self, and

[26] " What they knew by searching they have lost by pride."—St. Augustine.

by following Him through suffering and the death on the cross.

546

Without Jesus Christ man must be in vice and misery; with Jesus Christ man is free from vice and misery; in Him is all our virtue and all our happiness. Apart from Him there is but vice, misery, darkness, death, despair.

547

We know God only by Jesus Christ. Without this mediator all communion with God is taken away; through Jesus Christ we know God. All those who have claimed to know God, and to prove Him without Jesus Christ, have had only weak proofs. But in proof of Jesus Christ we have the prophecies, which are solid and palpable proofs. And these prophecies, being accomplished and proved true by the event, mark the certainty of these truths, and therefore the divinity of Christ. In Him then, and through Him, we know God. Apart from Him, and without the Scripture, without original sin, without a necessary Mediator promised and come, we cannot absolutely prove God, nor teach right doctrine and right morality. But through Jesus Christ, and in Jesus Christ, we prove God, and teach morality and doctrine. Jesus Christ is then the true God of men.

But we know at the same time our wretchedness; for this God is none other than the Saviour of our wretchedness. So we can only know God well by knowing our iniquities. Therefore those who have known God, without knowing their wretchedness, have not glorified Him, but have glorified themselves. *Quia . . . non cognovit per sapientiam . . . placuit Deo per stultitiam prædicationis salvos facere.*[27]

548

Not only do we know God by Jesus Christ alone, but we know ourselves only by Jesus Christ. We know life and death only through Jesus Christ. Apart from Jesus Christ, we do not know what is our life, nor our death, nor God, nor ourselves.

[27] 1 Cor., i. 21.

Thus without the Scripture, which has Jesus Christ alone
for its object, we know nothing, and see only darkness and
confusion in the nature of God, and in our own nature.

549

It is not only impossible but useless to know God without
Jesus Christ. They have not departed from Him, but ap-
proached; they have not humbled themselves, but . . .
*Quo quisque optimus est, pessimus, si hoc ipsum, quod
optimus est, adscribat sibi.*[28]

550

I love poverty because He loved it. I love riches because
they afford me the means of helping the very poor. I keep
faith with everybody; I do not render evil to those who
wrong me, but I wish them a lot like mine, in which I receive neither evil nor good from men. I try to be just, true,
sincere, and faithful to all men; I have a tender heart for
those to whom God has more closely united me; and whether
I am alone, or seen of men, I do all my actions in the sight
of God, who must judge of them, and to whom I have consecrated them all.

These are my sentiments; and every day of my life I bless
my Redeemer, who has implanted them in me, and who, of a
man full of weaknesses, of miseries, of lust, of pride, and of
ambition, has made a man free from all these evils by the
power of His grace, to which all the glory of it is due, as
of myself I have only misery and error.

551

Dignior plagis quam osculis non timeo quia amo.[29]

552

The Sepulchre of Jesus Christ.—Jesus Christ was dead,
but seen on the Cross. He was dead, and hidden in the
Sepulchre.

[28] "The quality which makes any one best makes him worst, if he claims
it for himself."
[29] "Though I deserve blows rather than kisses, I do not fear, because I
love."

Jesus Christ was buried by the saints alone.

Jesus Christ wrought no miracle at the Sepulchre.

Only the saints entered it.

It is there, not on the Cross, that Jesus Christ takes a new life.

It is the last mystery of the Passion and the Redemption.

Jesus Christ had nowhere to rest on earth but in the Sepulchre.

His enemies only ceased to persecute Him at the Sepulchre.

553

The Mystery of Jesus.—Jesus suffers in His passion the torments which men inflict upon Him; but in His agony He suffers the torments which He inflicts on Himself; *turbare semitipsum.*[30] This is a suffering from no human, but an almighty hand, for He must be almighty to bear it.

Jesus seeks some comfort at least in His three dearest friends, and they are asleep. He prays them to bear with Him for a little, and they leave Him with entire indifference, having so little compassion that it could not prevent their sleeping even for a moment. And thus Jesus was left alone to the wrath of God.

Jesus is alone on the earth, without any one not only to feel and share His sufferings, but even to know of it; He and Heaven were alone in that knowledge.

Jesus is in a garden, not of delight as the first Adam, where he lost himself and the whole human race, but in one of agony, where He saved Himself and the whole human race.

He suffers this affliction and this desertion in the horror of night.

I believe that Jesus never complained but on this single occasion; but then He complained as if he could no longer bear His extreme suffering. "My soul is sorrowful, even unto death."

Jesus seeks companionship and comfort from men. This is the sole occasion in all His life, as it seems to me. But He receives it not, for His disciples are asleep.

[30] John, xi. 33.

Jesus will be in agony even to the end of the world. We must not sleep during that time.

Jesus, in the midst of this universal desertion, including that of His own friends chosen to watch with Him, finding them asleep, is vexed because of the danger to which they expose, not Him, but themselves; He cautions them for their own safety and their own good, with a sincere tenderness for them during their ingratitude, and warns them that the spirit is willing and the flesh weak.

Jesus, finding them still asleep, without being restrained by any consideration for themselves or for Him, has the kindness not to waken them, and leaves them in repose.

Jesus prays, uncertain of the will of His Father, and fears death; but, when He knows it, He goes forward to offer Himself to death. *Eamus. Processit*[31] (John).

Jesus asked of men and was not heard.

Jesus, while His disciples slept, wrought their salvation. He has wrought that of each of the righteous while they slept, both in their nothingness before their birth, and in their sins after their birth.

He prays only once that the cup pass away, and then with submission; and twice that it come if necessary.

Jesus is weary.

Jesus, seeing all His friends asleep and all His enemies wakeful, commits Himself entirely to His Father.

Jesus does not regard in Judas his enmity, but the order of God, which He loves and admits, since He calls him friend.

Jesus tears Himself away from His disciples to enter into His agony; we must tear ourselves away from our nearest and dearest to imitate Him.

Jesus being in agony and in the greatest affliction, let us pray longer.

We implore the mercy of God, not that He may leave us at peace in our vices, but that He may deliver us from them.

If God gave us masters by His own hand, Oh! how necessary for us to obey them with a good heart! Necessity and events follow infallibly.

[31] John, xviii. 4.

—" Console thyself, thou wouldst not seek Me, if thou hadst not found Me.

" I thought of thee in Mine agony, I have sweated such drops of blood for thee.

" It is tempting Me rather than proving thyself, to think if thou wouldst do such and such a thing on an occasion which has not happened; I shall act in thee if it occur.

" Let thyself be guided by My rules; see how well I have led the Virgin and the saints who have let Me act in them.

" The Father loves all that I do.

" Dost thou wish that it always cost Me the blood of My humanity, without thy shedding tears?

" Thy conversion is My affair; fear not, and pray with confidence as for Me.

" I am present with thee by My Word in Scripture, by My Spirit in the Church and by inspiration, by My power in the priests, by My prayer in the faithful.

" Physicians will not heal thee, for thou wilt die at last. . But it is I who heal thee, and make the body immortal.

" Suffer bodily chains and servitude, I deliver thee at present only from spiritual servitude.

" I am more a friend to thee than such and such an one, for I have done for thee more than they; they would not have suffered what I have suffered from thee, and they would not have died for thee as I have done in the time of thine infidelities and cruelties, and as I am ready to do, and do, among my elect and at the Holy Sacrament."

" If thou knewest thy sins, thou wouldst lose heart."

—I shall lose it then, Lord, for on Thy assurance I believe their malice.

—" No, for I, by whom thou learnest, can heal thee of them, and what I say to thee is a sign that I will heal thee. In proportion to thy expiation of them, thou wilt know them, and it will be said to thee: ' Behold, thy sins are forgiven thee.' Repent, then, for thy hidden sins, and for the secret malice of those which thou knowest."

—Lord, I give Thee all.

— " I love thee more ardently than thou hast loved thine abominations, *ut immundus pro luto*.[32]

" To Me be the glory, not to thee, worm of the earth.

" Ask thy confessor, when My own words are to thee occasion of evil, vanity, or curiosity."

—I see in me depths of pride, curiosity and lust. There is no relation between me and God nor Jesus Christ the Righteous. But He has been made sin for me; all Thy scourges are fallen upon Him. He is more abominable than I, and, far from abhorring me, He holds Himself honoured that I go to Him and succor Him.

But He has healed Himself, and still more so will He heal me.

I must add my wounds to His, and join myself to Him; and He will save me in saving Himself. But this must not be postponed to the future.

Eritis sicut dii scientes bonum et malum.[33] Each one creates his god, when judging, " This is good or bad; " and men mourn or rejoice too much at events.

Do little things as though they were great, because of the majesty of Jesus Christ who does them in us, and who lives our life; and do the greatest things as though they were little and easy, because of His omnipotence.

554

It seems to me that Jesus Christ only allowed His wounds to be touched after His resurrection: *Noli me tangere*.[34] We must unite ourselves only to His sufferings.

At the Last Supper He gave Himself in communion as about to die; to the disciples at Emmaus as risen from the dead; to the whole Church as ascended into heaven.

555

" Compare not thyself with others, but with Me. If thou dost not find Me in those with whom thou comparest thyself, thou comparest thyself to one who is abominable. If thou findest Me in them, compare thyself to Me. But whom wilt

[32] " As foul with clay."   [33] Genesis, iii. 5.   [34] John, xx. 17.

thou compare? Thyself, or Me in thee? If it is thyself, it is one who is abominable. If it is I, thou comparest Me to Myself. Now I am God in all.

"I speak to thee, and often counsel thee, because thy director cannot speak to thee, for I do not want thee to lack a guide.

"And perhaps I do so at his prayers, and thus he leads thee without thy seeing it. Thou wouldst not seek Me, if thou didst not possess Me.

"Be not therefore troubled."

SECTION VIII

The Fundamentals of the Christian Religion

556

MEN blaspheme what they do not know. The Christian religion consists in two points. It is of equal concern to men to know them, and it is equally dangerous to be ignorant of them. And it is equally of God's mercy that He has given indications of both.

And yet they take occasion to conclude that one of these points does not exist, from that which should have caused them to infer the other. The sages who have said there is only one God have been persecuted, the Jews were hated, and still more the Christians. They have seen by the light of nature that if there be a true religion on earth, the course of all things must tend to it as to a centre.

The whole course of things must have for its object the establishment and the greatness of religion. Men must have within them feelings suited to what religion teaches us. And, finally, religion must so be the object and centre to which all things tend, that whoever knows the principles of religion can give an explanation both of the whole nature of man in particular, and of the whole course of the world in general.

And on this ground they take occasion to revile the Christian religion, because they misunderstand it. They imagine that it consists simply in the worship of a God considered as great, powerful, and eternal; which is strictly deism, almost as far removed from the Christian religion as atheism, which is its exact opposite. And thence they conclude that this religion is not true, because they do not see that all things concur to the establishment of this point, that God does not manifest Himself to men with all the evidence which He could show.

184

But let them conclude what they will against deism, they will conclude nothing against the Christian religion, which properly consists in the mystery of the Redeemer, who, uniting in Himself the two natures, human and divine, has redeemed men from the corruption of sin in order to reconcile them in His divine person to God.

The Christian religion then teaches men these two truths; that there is a God whom men can know, and that there is a corruption in their nature which renders them unworthy of Him. It is equally important to men to know both these points; and it is equally dangerous for man to know God without knowing his own wretchedness, and to know his own wretchedness without knowing the Redeemer who can free him from it. The knowledge of only one of these points gives rise either to the pride of philosophers, who have known God, and not their own wretchedness, or to the despair of atheists, who know their own wretchedness, but not the Redeemer.

And, as it is alike necessary to man to know these two points, so is it alike merciful of God to have made us know them. The Christian religion does this; it is in this that it consists.

Let us herein examine the order of the world, and see if all things do not tend to establish these two chief points of this religion: Jesus Christ is the end of all, and the centre to which all tends. Whoever knows Him knows the reason of everything.

Those who fall into error err only through failure to see one of these two things. We can then have an excellent knowledge of God without that of our own wretchedness, and of our own wretchedness without that of God. But we cannot know Jesus Christ without knowing at the same time both God and our own wretchedness.

Therefore I shall not undertake here to prove by natural reasons either the existence of God, or the Trinity, or the immortality of the soul, or anything of that nature; not only because I should not feel myself sufficiently able to find in nature arguments to convince hardened atheists, but also because such knowledge without Jesus Christ is useless and barren. Though a man should be convinced that numerical proportions are immaterial truths, eternal and dependent on a first truth, in which they subsist, and which is called God, I should not think him far advanced towards his own salvation.

The God of Christians is not a God who is simply the author of mathematical truths, or of the order of the elements; that is the view of heathens and Epicureans. He is not merely a God who exercises His providence over the life and fortunes of men, to bestow on those who worship Him a long and happy life. That was the portion of the Jews. But the God of Abraham, the God of Isaac, the God of Jacob, the God of Christians, is a God of love and of comfort, a God who fills the soul and heart of those whom He possesses, a God who makes them conscious of their inward wretchedness, and His infinite mercy, who unites Himself to their inmost soul, who fills it with humility and joy, with confidence and love, who renders them incapable of any other end than Himself.

All who seek God without Jesus Christ, and who rest in nature, either find no light to satisfy them, or come to form for themselves a means of knowing God and serving Him without a mediator. Thereby they fall either into atheism, or into deism, two things which the Christian religion abhors almost equally.

Without Jesus Christ the world would not exist; for it should needs be either that it would be destroyed or be a hell.

If the world existed to instruct man of God, His divinity would shine through every part in it in an indisputable manner; but as it exists only by Jesus Christ, and for Jesus Christ, and to teach men both their corruption and their redemption, all displays the proofs of these two truths.

All appearance indicates neither a total exclusion nor a manifest presence of divinity, but the presence of a God who hides Himself. Everything bears this character.

. . . Shall he alone who knows his nature know it only to be miserable? Shall he alone who knows it be alone unhappy?

. . . He must not see nothing at all, nor must he see sufficient for him to believe he possesses it; but he must see enough to know that he has lost it. For to know of his loss, he must see and not see; and that is exactly the state in which he naturally is.

. . . Whatever part he takes, I shall not leave him at rest . . .

557

. . . It is then true that everything teaches man his condition, but he must understand this well. For it is not true that all reveals God, and it is not true that all conceals God. But it is at the same time true that He hides Himself from those who tempt Him, and that He reveals Himself to those who seek Him, because men are both unworthy and capable of God; unworthy by their corruption, capable by their original nature.

558

What shall we conclude from all our darkness, but our unworthiness?

559

If there never had been any appearance of God, this eternal deprivation would have been equivocal, and might have as well corresponded with the absence of all divinity, as with the unworthiness of men to Know Him; but His occasional, though not continual, appearances remove the ambiguity. If He appeared once, He exists always; and thus we cannot but conclude both that there is a God, and that men are unworthy of Him.

560

We do not understand the glorious state of Adam, nor the nature of his sin, nor the transmission of it to us. These are matters which took place under conditions of a nature altogether different from our own, and which transcend our present understanding.

The knowledge of all this is useless to us as a means of escape from it; and all that we are concerned to know, is that we are miserable, corrupt, separated from God, but ransomed by Jesus Christ, whereof we have wonderful proofs on earth.

So the two proofs of corruption and redemption are drawn

from the ungodly, who live in indifference to religion, and from the Jews who are irreconcilable enemies.

561

There are two ways of proving the truths of our religion; one by the power of reason, the other by the authority of him who speaks.

We do not make use of the latter, but of the former. We do not say, "This must be believed, for Scripture, which says it, is divine." But we say that it must be believed for such and such a reason, which are feeble arguments, as reason may be bent to everything.

562

There is nothing on earth that does not show either the wretchedness of man, or the mercy of God; either the weakness of man without God, or the strength of man with God.

563

It will be one of the confusions of the damned to see that they are condemned by their own reason, by which they claimed to condemn the Christian religion.

564

The prophecies, the very miracles and proofs of our religion, are not of such a nature that they can be said to be absolutely convincing. But they are also of such a kind that it cannot be said that it is unreasonable to believe them. Thus there is both evidence and obscurity to enlighten some and confuse others. But the evidence is such that it surpasses, or at least equals, the evidence to the contrary; so that it is not reason which can determine men not to follow it, and thus it can only be lust or malice of heart. And by this means there is sufficient evidence to condemn, and insufficient to convince; so that it appears in those who follow it, that it is grace, and not reason, which makes them follow it; and in those who shun it, that it is lust, not reason, which makes them shun it.

Vere discipuli, vere Israëlita, vere liberi, vere cibus.[1]

565

Recognise, then, the truth of religion in the very obscurity of religion, in the little light we have of it, and in the indifference which we have to knowing it.

566

We understand nothing of the works of God, if we do not take as a principle that He has willed to blind some, and enlighten others.

567

The two contrary reasons. We must begin with that; without that we understand nothing, and all is heretical; and we must even add at the end of each truth that the opposite truth is to be remembered.

568

Objection. The Scripture is plainly full of matters not dictated by the Holy Spirit.—*Answer.* Then they do not harm faith.—*Objection.* But the Church has decided that all is of the Holy Spirit.—*Answer.* I answer two things: first, the Church has not so decided; secondly, if she should so decide, it could be maintained.

Do you think that the prophecies cited in the Gospel are related to make you believe? No, it is to keep you from believing.

569

Canonical.—The heretical books in the beginning of the Church serve to prove the canonical.

570

To the chapter on the *Fundamentals* must be added that on *Typology* touching the reason of types: why Jesus Christ

[1] In allusion to John. viii. 31; i. 47; viii. 36; vi. 32: " Verily disciples, verily an Israelite, verily children, verily food."

was prophesied as to His first coming; why prophesied
obscurely as to the manner.

571

The reason why. Types.—[They had to deal with a
carnal people and to render them the depositary of the
spiritual covenant.] To give faith to the Messiah, it was
necessary there should have been precedent prophecies, and
that these should be conveyed by persons above suspicion,
diligent, faithful, unusually zealous, and known to all the
world.

To accomplish all this, God chose this carnal people, to
whom He entrusted the prophecies which foretell the Messiah as a deliverer, and as a dispenser of those carnal goods
which this people loved. And thus they have had an extraordinary passion for their prophets, and, in sight of the
whole world, have had charge of these books which foretell
their Messiah, assuring all nations that He should come, and
in the way foretold in the books, which they held open to
the whole world. Yet this people, deceived by the poor and
ignominious advent of the Messiah, have been His most
cruel enemies. So that they, the people least open to suspicion in the world of favouring us, the most strict and
most zealous that can be named for their law and their
prophets, have kept the books incorrupt. Hence those
who have rejected and crucified Jesus Christ, who has
been to them an offence, are those who have charge of
the books which testify of Him, and state that He will
be an offence and rejected. Therefore they have shown
it was He by rejecting Him, and He has been alike
proved both by the righteous Jews who received Him, and
by the unrighteous who rejected Him, both facts having been foretold.

Wherefore the prophecies have a hidden and spiritual
meaning, to which this people were hostile, under the carnal
meaning which they loved. If the spiritual meaning had
been revealed, they would not have loved it, and, unable to
bear it, they would not have been zealous of the preservation of their books and their ceremonies; and if they had
loved these spiritual promises, and had preserved them in-

corrupt till the time of the Messiah, their testimony would have had no force, because they had been his friends.

Therefore it was well that the spiritual meaning should be concealed; but, on the other hand, if this meaning had been so hidden as not to appear at all, it could not have served as a proof of the Messiah. What then was done? In a crowd of passages it has been hidden under the temporal meaning, and in a few has been clearly revealed; besides that the time and the state of the world have been so clearly foretold that it is clearer than the sun. And in some places this spiritual meaning is so clearly expressed, that it would require a blindness like that which the flesh imposes on the spirit when it is subdued by it, not to recognise it.

See then what has been the prudence of God. This meaning is concealed under another in an infinite number of passages, and in some, though rarely, it is revealed; but yet so that the passages in which it is concealed are equivocal, and can suit both meanings; whereas the passages where it is disclosed are unequivocal, and can only suit the spiritual meaning.

So that this cannot lead us into error, and could only be misunderstood by so carnal a people.

For when blessings are promised in abundance, what was to prevent them from understanding the true blessings, but their covetousness, which limited the meaning to worldly goods? But those whose only good was in God referred them to God alone. For there are two principles, which divide the wills of men, covetousness and charity. Not that covetousness cannot exist along with faith in God, nor charity with worldly riches; but covetousness uses God, and enjoys the world, and charity is the opposite.

Now the ultimate end gives names to things. All which prevents us from attaining it, is called an enemy to us. Thus the creatures, however good, are the enemies of the righteous, when they turn them away from God, and God Himself is the enemy of those whose covetousness He confounds.

Thus as the significance of the word "enemy" is dependent on the ultimate end, the righteous understood by it their passions, and the carnal the Babylonians; and so these

terms were obscure only for the unrighteous. And this is
what Isaiah says: *Signa legem in electis meis,*[2] and that
Jesus Christ shall be a stone of stumbling. But, "Blessed
are they who shall not be offended in him." Hosea, *ult.*,
says excellently, "Where is the wise? and he shall understand what I say. The righteous shall know them, for the
ways of God are right; but the transgressors shall fall
therein."

572

Hypothesis that the apostles were impostors.—The time
clearly, the manner obscurely.—Five typical proofs.

$$2000 \begin{cases} 1600 \text{ prophets.} \\ 400 \text{ scattered.} \end{cases}$$

573

Blindness of Scripture.—"The Scripture," said the Jews,
"says that we shall not know whence Christ will come
(John vii. 27 and xii. 34). The Scripture says that Christ
abideth for ever, and He said that He should die." Therefore, says Saint John, they believed not, though He had
done so many miracles, that the word of Isaiah might be
fulfilled: "*He hath blinded them,*" &c.

574

Greatness.—Religion is so great a thing that it is right
that those who will not take the trouble to seek it, if it be
obscure, should be deprived of it. Why then do any complain, if it be such as can be found by seeking?

575

All things work together for good to the elect, even the
obscurities of Scripture; for they honour them because of
what is divinely clear. And all things work together for
evil to the rest of the world, even what is clear; for they
revile such, because of the obscurities which they do not
understand.

[2] Isaiah, viii. 16.

576

The general conduct of the world towards the Church: God willing to blind and to enlighten.—The event having proved the divinity of these prophecies, the rest ought to be believed. And thereby we see the order of the world to be of this kind. The miracles of the Creation and the Deluge being forgotten, God sends the law and the miracles of Moses, the prophets who prophesied particular things; and to prepare a lasting miracle, He prepares prophecies and their fulfilment; but, as the prophecies could be suspected, He desires to make them above suspicion, &c.

577

God has made the blindness of this people subservient to the good of the elect.

578

There is sufficient clearness to enlighten the elect, and sufficient obscurity to humble them. There is sufficient obscurity to blind the reprobate, and sufficient clearness to condemn them, and make them inexcusable.—*Saint Augustine, Montaigne, Sebond.*

The genealogy of Jesus Christ in the Old Testament is intermingled with so many others that are useless, that it cannot be distinguished. If Moses had kept only the record of the ancestors of Christ, that might have been too plain. If he had not noted that of Jesus Christ, it might not have been sufficiently plain. But, after all, whoever looks closely sees that of Jesus Christ expressly traced through Tamar, Ruth, &c.

Those who ordained these sacrifices, knew their uselessness; those who have declared their uselessness have not ceased to practise them.

If God had permitted only one religion, it had been too easily known; but when we look at it closely, we clearly discern the truth amidst this confusion.

The premiss.—Moses was a clever man. If then he ruled

himself by his reason, he would say nothing clearly which
was directly against reason.

Thus all the very apparent weaknesses are strength. Example: the two genealogies in Saint Matthew and Saint
Luke. What can be clearer than that this was not con-
certed?

579

God (and the Apostles), foreseeing that the seeds of pride
would make heresies spring up, and being unwilling to give
them occasion to arise from correct expressions, has put in
Scripture and the prayers of the Church contrary words
and sentences to produce their fruit in time.

So in morals He gives charity, which produces fruits contrary to lust.

580

Nature has some perfections to show that she is the
image of God, and some defects to show that she is only
His image.

581

God prefers rather to incline the will than the intellect.
Perfect clearness would be of use to the intellect, and would
harm the will. To humble pride.

582

We make an idol of truth itself; for truth apart from
charity is not God, but His image and idol, which we must
neither love nor worship; and still less must we love or
worship its opposite, namely, falsehood.

I can easily love total darkness; but if God keeps me in
a state of semi-darkness, such partial darkness displeases
me, and, because I do not see therein the advantage of total
darkness, it is unpleasant to me. This is a fault, and a
sign that I make for myself an idol of darkness, apart from
the order of God. Now only His order must be worshipped.

583

The feeble-minded are people who know the truth, but only affirm it so far as consistent with their own interest. But, apart from that, they renounce it.

584

The world exists for the exercise of mercy and judgment, not as if men were placed in it out of the hands of God, but as hostile to God; and to them He grants by grace sufficient light, that they may return to Him, if they desire to seek and follow Him; and also that they may be punished, if they refuse to seek or follow Him.

585

That God has willed to hide Himself.—If there were only one religion, God would indeed be manifest. The same would be the case, if there were no martyrs but in our religion.

God being thus hidden, every religion which does not affirm that God is hidden, is not true; and every religion which does not give the reason of it, is not instructive. Our religion does all this: *Vere tu es Deus absconditus.*[3]

586

If there were no obscurity, man would not be sensible of his corruption; if there were no light, man would not hope for a remedy. Thus, it is not only fair, but advantageous to us, that God be partly hidden and partly revealed; since it is equally dangerous to man to know God without knowing his own wretchedness, and to know his own wretchedness without knowing God.

587

This religion, so great in miracles, saints, blameless Fathers, learned and great witnesses, martyrs, established kings as David, and Isaiah, a prince of the blood, and so

[3] " Truly thou art a hidden God."

great in science, after having displayed all her miracles and all her wisdom, rejects all this, and declares that she has neither wisdom nor signs, but only the cross and foolishness.

For those, who, by these signs and that wisdom, have deserved your belief, and who have proved to you their character, declare to you that nothing of all this can change you, and render you capable of knowing and loving God, but the power of the foolishness of the cross without wisdom and signs, and not the signs without this power. Thus our religion is foolish in respect to the effective cause, and wise in respect to the wisdom which prepares it.

588

Our religion is wise and foolish. Wise, because it is the most learned, and the most founded on miracles, prophecies, &c. Foolish, because it is not all this which makes us belong to it. This makes us indeed condemn those who do not belong to it; but it does not cause belief in those who do belong to it. It is the cross that makes them believe, *ne evacuata sit crux.*[a] And so Saint Paul, who came with wisdom and signs, says that he has come neither with wisdom nor with signs; for he came to convert. But those who come only to convince, can say that they come with wisdom and with signs.

[a] I Cor., i. 17.

SECTION IX

PERPETUITY

589

ON the fact that the Christian religion is not the only religion.—So far is this from being a reason for believing that it is not the true one, that, on the contrary, it makes us see that it is so.

590

Men must be sincere in all religions; true heathens, true Jews, true Christians.

591

592

The falseness of other religions.—They have no witnesses. The Jews have. God defies other religions to produce such signs: Isaiah xviii. 9; xliv. 8.

593

History of China.—I believe only the histories, whose witnesses got themselves killed.

[Which is the more credible of the two, Moses or China?]

It is not a question of seeing this summarily. I tell you there is in it something to blind, and something to enlighten.

By this one word I destroy all your reasoning. "But China obscures," say you; and I answer, "China obscures, but there is clearness to be found; seek it."

197

Thus all that you say makes for one of the views, and not at all against the other. So this serves, and does no harm.

We must then see this in detail; we must put the papers on the table.

594

Against the history of China. The historians of Mexico, the five suns, of which the last is only eight hundred years old.

The difference between a book accepted by a nation, and one which makes a nation.

595

Mahomet was without authority. His reasons then should have been very strong, having only their own force. What does he say then, that we must believe him?

596

The Psalms are chanted throughout the whole world.

Who renders testimony to Mahomet? Himself. Jesus Christ desires His own testimony to be as nothing.

The quality of witnesses necessitates their existence always and everywhere; and he, miserable creature, is alone.

597

Against Mahomet.—The Koran is not more of Mahomet than the Gospel is of Saint Matthew, for it is cited by many authors from age to age. Even its very enemies, Celsus and Porphyry, never denied it.

The Koran says Saint Matthew was an honest man. Therefore Mahomet was a false prophet for calling honest men wicked, or for not agreeing with what they have said of Jesus Christ.

598

It is not by that which is obscure in Mahomet, and which may be interpreted in a mysterious sense, that I would have him judged, but by what is clear, as his paradise and the rest. In that he is ridiculous. And since what is clear is ridiculous, it is not right to take his obscurities for mysteries.

It is not the same with the Scripture. I agree that there are in it obscurities as strange as those of Mahomet; but there are admirably clear passages, and the prophecies are manifestly fulfilled. The cases are therefore not on a par. We must not confound, and put on one level things which only resemble each other in their obscurity, and not in the clearness, which requires us to reverence the obscurities.

599

The difference between Jesus Christ and Mahomet.— Mahomet was not foretold; Jesus Christ was foretold.

Mahomet slew; Jesus Christ caused His own to be slain. Mahomet forbade reading; the Apostles ordered reading.

In fact the two are so opposed, that if Mahomet took the way to succeed from a worldly point of view, Jesus Christ, from the same point of view, took the way to perish. And instead of concluding that, since Mahomet succeeded, Jesus Christ might well have succeeded, we ought to say that since Mahomet succeeded, Jesus Christ should have failed.

600

Any man can do what Mahomet has done; for he performed no miracles, he was not foretold. No man can do what Christ has done.

601

The heathen religion has no foundation [at the present day. It is said once to have had a foundation by the oracles which spoke. But what are the books which assure us of this? Are they so worthy of belief on account of the virtue of their authors? Have they been preserved with such care that we can be sure that they have not been meddled with?]

The Mahomedan religion has for a foundation the Koran and Mahomet. But has this prophet, who was to be the last hope of the world, been foretold? What sign has he that every other man has not, who chooses to call himself a prophet? What miracles does he himself say that he has done? What mysteries has he taught, even according to his own tradition? What was the morality, what the happiness held out by him?

The Jewish religion must be differently regarded in the tradition of the Holy Bible, and in the tradition of the people. Its morality and happiness are absurd in the tradition of the people, but are admirable in that of the Holy Bible. (And all religion is the same; for the Christian religion is very different in the Holy Bible and in the casuists.) The foundation is admirable; it is the most ancient book in the world, and the most authentic; and whereas Mahomet, in order to make his own book continue in existence, forbade men to read it, Moses, for the same reason, ordered every one to read his.

Our religion is so divine that another divine religion has only been the foundation of it.

602

Order.—To see what is clear and indisputable in the whole state of the Jews.

603

The Jewish religion is wholly divine in its authority, its duration, its perpetuity, its morality, its doctrine, and its effects.

604

The only science contrary to common sense and human nature is that alone which has always existed among men.

605

The only religion contrary to nature, to common sense, and to our pleasure, is that alone which has always existed.

606

No religion but our own has taught that man is born in sin. No sect of philosophers has said this. Therefore none have declared the truth.

No sect or religion has always existed on earth, but the Christian religion.

607

Whoever judges of the Jewish religion by its coarser forms will misunderstand it. It is to be seen in the Holy Bible, and in the tradition of the prophets, who have made it plain enough that they did not interpret the law according to the letter. So our religion is divine in the Gospel, in the Apostles, and in tradition; but it is absurd in those who tamper with it.

The Messiah, according to the carnal Jews, was to be a great temporal prince. Jesus Christ, according to carnal Christians, has come to dispense us from the love of God, and to give us sacraments which shall do everything without our help. Such is not the Christian religion, nor the Jewish. True Jews and true Christians have always expected a Messiah who should make them love God, and by that love triumph over their enemies.

608

The carnal Jews hold a midway place between Christians and heathens. The heathens know not God, and love the world only. The Jews know the true God, and love the world only. The Christians know the true God, and love not the world. Jews and heathens love the same good. Jews and Christians know the same God.

The Jews were of two kinds; the first had only heathen affections, the other had Christian affections.

609

There are two kinds of men in each religion: among the heathen, worshippers of beasts, and the worshippers of the one only God of natural religion; among the Jews, the carnal, and the spiritual, who were the Christians of the old law; among Christians, the coarser-minded, who are the Jews of the new law. The carnal Jews looked for a carnal Messiah; the coarser Christians believe that the Messiah has dispensed them from the love of God; true Jews and true Christians worship a Messiah who makes them love God.

610

*To show that the true Jews and the true Christians have
but the same religion.*—The religion of the Jews seemed
to consist essentially in the fatherhood of Abraham, in circumcision, in sacrifices, in ceremonies, in the Ark, in the
temple, in Jerusalem, and, finally, in the law, and in the
covenant with Moses.

I say that it consisted in none of those things, but only
in the love of God, and that God disregarded all the other
things.

That God did not accept the posterity of Abraham.

That the Jews were to be punished like strangers, if they
transgressed. *Deut.* viii. 19: "If thou do at all forget
the Lord thy God, and walk after other gods, I testify
against you this day that ye shall surely perish, as the
nations which the Lord destroyeth before your face."

That strangers, if they loved God, were to be received
by Him as the Jews. *Isaiah,* lvi. 3: "Let not the stranger
say, 'The Lord will not receive me.' The strangers who
join themselves unto the Lord to serve Him and love Him,
will I bring unto my holy mountain, and accept therein
sacrifices, for mine house is a house of prayer."

That the true Jews considered their merit to be from
God only, and not from Abraham. *Isaiah,* lxiii. 16: "Doubtless thou art our Father, though Abraham be ignorant of
us, and Israel acknowledge us not. Thou art our Father
and our Redeemer."

Moses himself told them that God would not accept
persons. *Deut.* x. 17: "God," said he, "regardeth neither
persons nor sacrifices."

The Sabbath was only a sign, *Exod.* xxxi. 13; and in memory of the escape from Egypt, *Deut.* v. 19. Therefore it is
no longer necessary, since Egypt must be forgotten.

Circumcision was only a sign, *Gen.* xvii. 11. And thence
it came to pass that, being in the desert, they were not
circumcised, because they could not be confounded with
other peoples; and after Jesus Christ came, it was no
longer necessary.

That the circumcision of the heart is commanded. *Deut.*

x. 16; *Jeremiah,* iv. 4: "Be ye circumcised in heart; take away the superfluities of your heart, and harden yourselves not. For your God is a mighty God, strong and terrible, who accepteth not persons."

That God said He would one day do it. *Deut.* xxx. 6: "God will circumcise thine heart, and the heart of thy seed, that thou mayest love Him with all thine heart."

That the uncircumcised in heart shall be judged. *Jeremiah,* ix. 26: For God will judge the uncircumcised peoples, and all the people of Israel, because he is "uncircumcised in heart."

That the external is of no avail apart from the internal. *Joel,* ii. 13; *Scindite corda vestra,* &c. *Isaiah,* lviii. 3, 4, &c.

The love of God is enjoined in the whole of Deuteronomy. *Deut.* xxx. 19: "I call heaven and earth to record that I have set before you life and death, that you should choose life, and love God, and obey Him, for God is your life."

That the Jews, for lack of that love, should be rejected for their offences, and the heathen chosen in their stead. *Hosea,* i. 10; *Deut.* xxxii. 20. "I will hide myself from them in view of their latter sins, for they are a froward generation without faith. They have moved me to jealousy with that which is not God, and I will move them to jealousy with those which are not a people, and with an ignorant and foolish nation." *Isaiah,* lxv. 1.

That temporal goods are false, and that the true good is to be united to God. *Psalm,* cxliii. 15.

That their feasts are displeasing to God. *Amos,* v. 21.

That the sacrifices of the Jews displeased God. *Isaiah,* lxvi. 1-3; i. 11; *Jer.,* vi. 20; David, *Miserere.*—Even on the part of the good, *Expectavi. Psalm* xlix. 8, 9, 10, 11, 12, 13, and 14.

That He has established them only for their hardness. *Micah,* admirably, vi.; 1 *Kings,* xv. 22; *Hosea,* vi. 6.

That the sacrifices of the Gentiles will be accepted of God, and that God will take no pleasure in the sacrifices of the Jews. *Malachi,* i. 11.

That God will make a new covenant with the Messiah, and the old will be annulled. *Jer.* xxxi. 31. *Mandata non bona. Ezek.*

That the old things will be forgotten. *Isaiah,* xliii. 18, 19; lxv. 17, 18.

That the Ark will no longer be remembered. *Jer.* iii. 15.

That the temple should be rejected. *Jer.* vii. 12, 13, 14.

That the sacrifices should be rejected, and other pure sacrifices established. *Malachi,* i. 11.

That the order of Aaron's priesthood should be rejected, and that of Melchizedek introduced by the Messiah. *Ps. Dixit Dominus.*

That this priesthood should be eternal. *Ibid.*

That Jerusalem should be rejected, and Rome admitted. *Ps. Dixit Dominus.*

That the name of the Jews should be rejected, and a new name given. *Isaiah,* lxv. 15.

That this last name should be more excellent than that of the Jews, and eternal. *Isaiah,* lvi. 5

That the Jews should be without prophets (Amos), without a king, without princes, without sacrifice, without an idol.

That the Jews should nevertheless always remain a people. *Jer.* xxxi. 36.

611

Republic.—The Christian Republic—and even the Jewish —has only had God for ruler, as Philo the Jew notices, *On Monarchy.*

When they fought, it was for God only; their chief hope was in God only; they considered their towns as belonging to God only, and kept them for God. 1 *Chron.* xix. 13.

612

Gen. xvii. 7. *Statuam pactum meum inter me et te fœdere sempiterno ut sim Deus tuus.*

9. *Et tu ergo custodies pactum meum.*

613

Perpetuity.—That religion has always existed on earth, which consists in believing that man has fallen from a state of glory and of communion with God into a state of sorrow, penitence, and estrangement from God, but that after this life we shall be restored by a Messiah who should have come. All things have passed away, and this has endured, for which all things are.

Men have in the first age of the world been carried away into every kind of debauchery, and yet there were saints, as Enoch, Lamech, and others, who waited patiently for the Christ promised from the beginning of the world. Noah saw the wickedness of men at its height; and he was held worthy to save the world in his person, by the hope of the Messiah of whom he was the type. Abraham was surrounded by idolaters, when God made known to him the mystery of the Messiah, whom he welcomed from afar. In the time of Isaac and Jacob abomination was spread over all the earth; but these saints lived in faith; and Jacob, dying and blessing his children, cried in a transport which made him break off his discourse, "I await, O my God, the Saviour whom Thou hast promised. *Salutare tuum expectabo, Domine.*" The Egyptians were infected both with idolatry and magic; the very people of God were led astray by their example. Yet Moses and others believed Him whom they saw not, and worshipped Him, looking to the eternal gifts which He was preparing for them.

The Greeks and Latins then set up false deities; the poets made a hundred different theologies, while the philosophers separated into a thousand different sects; and yet in the heart of Judæa there were always chosen men who foretold the coming of this Messiah, which was known to them alone.

He came at length in the fulness of time, and time has since witnessed the birth of so many schisms and heresies, so many political revolutions, so many changes in all things; yet this Church, which worships Him who has always been worshipped, has endured uninterruptedly. It is a wonderful, incomparable, and altogether divine fact that this religion, which has always endured, has always been attacked. It has been a thousand times on the eve of universal destruction, and every time it has been in that state, God has restored it by extraordinary acts of His power.

This is astonishing, as also that it has preserved itself without yielding to the will of tyrants. For it is not strange that a State endures, when its laws are sometimes made to give way to necessity, but that . . . (See the passage indicated in Montaigne.)

614

States would perish if they did not often make their laws give way to necessity. But religion has never suffered this, or practised it. Indeed there must be these compromises, or miracles. It is not strange to be saved by yielding, and this is not strictly self-preservation; besides, in the end they perish entirely. None has endured a thousand years. But the fact that this religion has always maintained itself, inflexible as it is, proves its divinity.

615

Whatever may be said, it must be admitted that the Christian religion has something astonishing in it. Some will say, "This is because you were born in it." Far from it; I stiffen myself against it for this very reason, for fear this prejudice bias me. But although I am born in it, I cannot help finding it so.

616

Perpetuity.—The Messiah has always been believed in. The tradition from Adam was still fresh in Noah and in Moses. Since then the prophets have foretold him, while at the same time foretelling other things, which, being from time to time fulfilled in the sight of men, showed the truth of their mission, and consequently that of their promises touching the Messiah. Jesus Christ performed miracles, and the Apostles also, who converted all the heathen; and all the prophecies being thereby fulfilled, the Messiah is for ever proved.

617

Perpetuity.—Let us consider that since the beginning of the world the expectation or worship of the Messiah has existed uninterruptedly; that there have been found men, who said that God had revealed to them that a Redeemer was to be born, who should save His people; that Abraham came afterwards, saying that he had had a revelation that the Messiah was to spring from him by a son, whom he should have; that Jacob declared that, of his twelve sons, the Messiah would spring from Judah; that Moses and the prophets then came to declare the time and the manner of His coming; that they said their law was only temporary till that of the Messiah, that it should endure till then, but that the other should last for ever; that thus either their law, or that of the Messiah, of which it was the promise, would be always upon the earth; that, in fact, it has always endured; that at last Jesus Christ came with all the circumstances foretold. This is wonderful.

618

This is positive fact. While all philosophers separate into different sects, there is found in one corner of the world the most ancient people in it, declaring that all the world is in error, that God has revealed to them the truth, that they will always exist on the earth. In fact, all other sects come to an end, this one still endures, and has done so for four thousand years.

They declare that they hold from their ancestors that man has fallen from communion with God, and is entirely estranged from God, but that He has promised to redeem them; that this doctrine shall always exist on the earth; that their law has a double signification; that during sixteen hundred years they have had people, whom they believed prophets, foretelling both the time and the manner; that four hundred years after they were scattered everywhere, because Jesus Christ was to be everywhere announced; that Jesus Christ came in the manner, and at the time foretold; that the Jews have since been scattered abroad under a curse, and nevertheless still exist.

619

I see the Christian religion founded upon a preceding religion, and this is what I find as a fact.

I do not here speak of the miracles of Moses, of Jesus Christ, and of the Apostles, because they do not at first seem convincing, and because I only wish here to put in evidence all those foundations of the Christian religion which are beyond doubt, and which cannot be called in question by any person whatsoever. It is certain that we see in many places of the world a peculiar people, separated from all other peoples of the world, and called the Jewish people.

I see then a crowd of religions in many parts of the world and in all times; but their morality cannot please me, nor can their proofs convince me. Thus I should equally have rejected the religion of Mahomet and of China, of the ancient Romans and of the Egyptians, for the sole reason, that none having more marks of truth than another, nor anything which should necessarily persuade me, reason cannot incline to one rather than the other.

But, in thus considering this changeable and singular variety of morals and beliefs at different times, I find in one corner of the world a peculiar people, separated from all other peoples on earth, the most ancient of all, and whose histories are earlier by many generations than the most ancient which we possess.

I find then this great and numerous people, sprung from a single man, who worship one God, and guide themselves by a law which they say that they obtained from His own hand. They maintain that they are the only people in the world to whom God has revealed His mysteries; that all men are corrupt and in disgrace with God; that they are all abandoned to their senses and their own imagination, whence come the strange errors and continual changes which happen among them, both of religions and of morals, whereas they themselves remain firm in their conduct; but that God will not leave other nations in this darkness for ever; that there will come a Saviour for all; that they are in the world to announce Him to men; that they are ex-

pressly formed to be forerunners and heralds of this great
event, and to summon all nations to join with them in the
expectation of this Saviour.

To meet with this people is astonishing to me, and seems
to me worthy of attention. I look at the law which they
boast of having obtained from God, and I find it admirable.
It is the first law of all, and is of such a kind that, even
before the term *law* was in currency among the Greeks, it
had, for nearly a thousand years earlier, been uninterruptedly accepted and observed by the Jews. I likewise
think it strange that the first law of the world happens to
be the most perfect; so that the greatest legislators have
borrowed their laws from it, as is apparent from the law of
the Twelve Tables at Athens, afterwards taken by the
Romans, and as it would be easy to prove, if Josephus and
others had not sufficiently dealt with this subject.

620

Advantages of the Jewish people.—In this search the
Jewish people at once attract my attention by the number
of wonderful and singular facts which appear about them.

I first see that they are a people wholly composed of
brethren, and whereas all others are formed by the assem-
blage of an infinity of families, this, though so wonderfully fruitful, has all sprung from one man alone, and,
being thus all one flesh, and members one of another, they
constitute a powerful state of one family. This is unique.

This family, or people, is the most ancient within human
knowledge, a fact which seems to me to inspire a peculiar
veneration for it, especially in view of our present inquiry;
since if God has from all time revealed Himself to men,
it is to these we must turn for knowledge of the tradition.

This people is not eminent solely by their antiquity, but
is also singular by their duration, which has always continued from their origin till now. For whereas the nations
of Greece and of Italy, of Lacedæmon, of Athens and of
Rome, and others who came long after, have long since
perished, these ever remain, and in spite of the endeavours
of many powerful kings who have a hundred times tried

to destroy them, as their historians testify, and as it is easy to conjecture from the natural order of things during so long a space of years, they have nevertheless been preserved (and this preservation has been foretold) ; and extending from the earliest times to the latest, their history comprehends in its duration all our histories [which it preceded by a long time].

The law by which this people is governed is at once the most ancient law in the world, the most perfect, and the only one which has been always observed without a break in a state. This is what Josephus admirably proves, *against Apion,* and also Philo the Jew, in different places where they point out that it is so ancient that the very name of *law* was only known by the oldest nation more than a thousand years afterwards; so that Homer, who has written the history of so many states, has never used the term. And it is easy to judge of its perfection by simply reading it; for we see that it has provided for all things with so great wisdom, equity and judgment, that the most ancient legislators, Greek and Roman, having had some knowledge of it, have borrowed from it their principal laws; this is evident from what are called the Twelve Tables, and from the other proofs which Josephus gives.

But this law is at the same time the severest and strictest of all in respect to their religious worship, imposing on this people, in order to keep them to their duty, a thousand peculiar and painful observances, on pain of death. Whence it is very astonishing that it has been constantly preserved during many centuries by a people, rebellious and impatient as this one was; while all other states have changed their laws from time to time, although these were far more lenient.

The book which contains this law, the first of all, is itself the most ancient book in the world, those of Homer, Hesiod, and others, being six or seven hundred years later.

621

The creation and the deluge being past, and God no longer requiring to destroy the world, nor to create it anew, nor to give such great signs of Himself, He began to establish a people on the earth, purposely formed, who were to last until the coming of the people whom the Messiah should fashion by His spirit.

622

The creation of the world beginning to be distant, God provided a single contemporary historian, and appointed a whole people as guardians of this book, in order that this history might be the most authentic in the world, and that all men might thereby learn a fact so necessary to know, and which could only be known through that means.

623

[Japhet begins the genealogy.]
Joseph folds his arms, and prefers to keep silent.

624

Why should Moses make the lives of men so long, and their generations so few?

Because it is not the length of years, but the multitude of generations, which renders things obscure. For truth is perverted only by the change of men. And yet he puts two things, the most memorable that were ever imagined, namely, the creation and the deluge, so near that we reach from one to the other.

625

Shem, who saw Lamech, who saw Adam, saw also Jacob, who saw those who saw Moses; therefore the deluge and the creation are true. This is conclusive among certain people who understand it rightly.

626

The longevity of the patriarchs, instead of causing the loss of past history, conduced, on the contrary, to its preservation. For the reason why we are sometimes insufficiently instructed in the history of our ancestors, is that we have never lived long with them, and that they are often dead before we have attained the age of reason. Now, when men lived so long, children lived long with their parents. They conversed long with them. But what else could be the subject of their talk save the history of their ancestors, since to that all history was reduced, and men did not study science or art, which now form a large part of daily conversation? We see also that in these days tribes took particular care to preserve their genealogies.

627

I believe that Joshua was the first of God's people to have this name, as Jesus Christ was the last of God's people.

628

Antiquity of the Jews.—What a difference there is between one book and another! I am not astonished that the Greeks made the Iliad, nor the Egyptians and the Chinese their histories.

We have only to see how this originates. These fabulous historians are not contemporaneous with the facts about which they write. Homer composes a romance, which he gives out as such, and which is received as such; for nobody doubted that Troy and Agamemnon no more existed than did the golden apple. Accordingly he did not think of making a history, but solely a book to amuse; he is the only writer of his time; the beauty of the work has made it last, every one learns it and talks of it, it is necessary to know it, and each one knows it by heart. Four hundred years afterwards the witnesses of these facts are no longer alive, no one knows of his own knowledge if it be a fable or a history; one has only learnt it from his ancestors, and this can pass for truth.

Every history which is not contemporaneous, as the books of the Sibyls and Trismegistus, and so many others which have been believed by the world, are false, and found to be false in the course of time. It is not so with contemporaneous writers.

There is a great difference between a book which an individual writes, and publishes to a nation, and a book which itself creates a nation. We cannot doubt that the book is as old as the people.

629

Josephus hides the shame of his nation.
Moses does not hide his own shame.
Quis mihi det ut omnes prophetent? [1]
He was weary of the multitude.

630

The sincerity of the Jews.—Maccabees, after they had no more prophets; the Masorah, since Jesus Christ.

This book will be a testimony for you.

Defective and final letters.

Sincere against their honour, and dying for it; this has no example in the world, and no root in nature.

631

Sincerity of the Jews.—They preserve lovingly and carefully the book in which Moses declares that they have been all their life ungrateful to God, and that he knows they will be still more so after his death; but that he calls heaven and earth to witness against them, and that he has [taught] them enough.

He declares that God, being angry with them, shall at last scatter them among all the nations of the earth; that as they have offended Him by worshipping gods who were not their God, so He will provoke them by calling a people who are not His people; that He desires that all His words be preserved for ever, and that His book be placed in the Ark of the Covenant to serve for ever as a witness against them.

Isaiah says the same thing, xxx.

[1] Numbers, xi. 29.

632

On Esdras.—The story that the books were burnt with
the temple proved false by Maccabees: " Jeremiah gave them
the law."

The story that he recited the whole by heart. Josephus
and Esdras point out *that he read the book.* Baronius, *Ann.*,
p. 180: *Nullus penitus Hebræorum antiquorum reperitur qui
tradiderit libros periisse et per Esdram esse restitutos, nisi
in IV. Esdræ.*[2]

The story that he changed the letters.

Philo, *in Vita Moysis: Illa lingua ac character quo anti-
quitus scripta est lex sic permansit usque ad LXX.*[3]

Josephus says that the Law was in Hebrew when it was
translated by the Seventy.

Under Antiochus and Vespasian, when they wanted to
abolish the books, and when there was no prophet, they
could not do so. And under the Babylonians, when no
persecution had been made, and when there were so many
prophets, would they have let them be burnt?

Josephus laughs at the Greeks who would not bear . . .

Tertullian.—*Perinde potuit abolefactam eam violentia
cataclysmi in spiritu rursus reformare, quemadmodum et
Hierosolymis Babylonia expugnatione deletis, omne instru-
mentum Judaicæ literaturæ per Esdram constat restaura-
tum.*[4]

He says that Noah could as easily have restored in spirit
the book of Enoch, destroyed by the Deluge, as Esdras
could have restored the Scriptures lost during the Captivity.

(Θεὸς) ἐν τῇ ἐπὶ Ναβουχοδόνοσορ αἰχμαλωσίᾳ τοῦ λαοῦ, δια-
φθαρεισῶν τῶν γραφῶν . . . ἐνέπνευσε Εσδρᾷ τῷ ἱερεῖ ἐκ τῆς
φυλῆς Λευὶ τοὺς τῶν προγεγονότων προφητῶν πάντας ἀνατάξασθαι
λόγους, καὶ ἀποκαταστῆσαι τῷ λαῷ τὴν διὰ Μωυσέως νομοθεσίαν.[5]
He alleges this to prove that it is not incredible that the
Seventy may have explained the holy Scriptures with that

---

[2] " Nothing is found within the ancient Hebrew writings which recorded
that the books perished and were restored through Esdras, except in
Esdras, IV."

[3] " The same language and character in which the Law was written in
ancient times remained till the Septuagint."

[4] Tertullian, *De cultu femin.*, ii. 3.

[5] Eusebius, *Hist. lib.*, v., c. 8.

uniformity which we admire in them. And he took that from Saint Irenæus.

Saint Hilary, in his preface to the Psalms, says that Esdras arranged the Psalms in order.

The origin of this tradition comes from the 14th chapter of the fourth book of *Esdras. Deus glorificatus est, et Scripturæ vere divinæ creditæ sunt, omnibus eandem et eisdem verbis et eisdem nominibus recitantibus ab initio usque ad finem, uti et præsentes gentes cognoscerent quoniam per inspirationem Dei interpretatæ sunt Scripturæ et non esset mirabile Deum hoc in eis operatum: quando in ea captivitate populi quæ facta est a Nabuchodonosor, corruptis scripturis et post 70 annos Judæis descendentibus in regionem suam, et post deinde temporibus Artaxercis Persarum regis, inspiravit Esdræ sacerdoti tribus Levi præteritorum prophetarum omnes rememorare sermones, et restituere populo eam legem quæ data est per Moysen.*

633

Against the story in Esdras, II. *Maccab.,* ii.;—Josephus *Antiquities,* II. i.—Cyrus took occasion from the prophecy of Isaiah to release the people. The Jews held their property in peace under Cyrus in Babylon; hence they could well have the Law.

Josephus, in the whole history of Esdras, does not say one word about this restoration.—II. Kings, xvii. 27.

634

If the story in Esdras is credible, then it must be believed that the Scripture is Holy Scripture; for this story is based only on the authority of those who assert that of the Seventy, which shows that the Scripture is holy.

Therefore if this account be true, we have what we want therein; if not, we have it elsewhere. And thus those who would ruin the truth of our religion, founded on Moses, establish it by the same authority by which they attack it. So by this providence it still exists.

635

Chronology of Rabbinism. (The citations of pages are from the book *Pugio.*)

Page 27. R. Hakadosch (*anno* 200), author of the *Mischna,* or vocal law, or second law.

Commentaries on the *Mischna* (*anno* 340): The one *Siphra.*

Barajetot.

Talmud Hierosol.

Tosiphtot.

Bereschit Rabah, by R. Osaiah Rabah, commentary on the *Mischna.*

Bereschit Rabah, Bar Naconi, are subtle and pleasant discourses, historical and theological. This same author wrote the books called *Rabot.*

A hundred years after the *Talmud Hierosol,* 440 A. D., was composed the *Babylonian Talmud,* by R. Ase, by the universal consent of all the Jews, who are necessarily obliged to observe all that is contained therein.

The addition of R. Ase is called the *Gemara,* that is to say, the "commentary" on the *Mischna.* And the Talmud includes together the *Mischna* and the *Gemara.*

636

If does not indicate indifference: Malachi, Isaiah.

Is., Si volumus, &c.

In quacumque die.

637

Prophecies.—The sceptre was not interrupted by the captivity in Babylon, because the return was promised and foretold.

638

Proofs of Jesus Christ.—Captivity, with the assurance of deliverance within seventy years, was not real captivity. But now they are captives without any hope.

God has promised them that even though He should scatter them to the ends of the earth, nevertheless if they were faithful to His law, He would assemble them together again. They are very faithful to it, and remain oppressed.

639

When Nebuchadnezzar carried away the people, for fear they should believe that the sceptre had departed from Judah, they were told beforehand that they would be there for a short time, and that they would be restored. They were always consoled by the prophets; and their kings continued. But the second destruction is without promise of restoration, without prophets, without kings, without consolation, without hope, because the sceptre is taken away for ever.

640

It is a wonderful thing, and worthy of particular attention, to see this Jewish people existing so many years in perpetual misery, it being necessary as a proof of Jesus Christ, both that they should exist to prove Him, and that they should be miserable because they crucified Him; and though to be miserable and to exist are contradictory, they nevertheless still exist in spite of their misery.

641

They are visibly a people expressly created to serve as a witness to the Messiah (*Isaiah,* xliii. 9; xliv. 8). They keep the books, and love them, and do not understand them. And all this was foretold; that God's judgments are entrusted to them, but as a sealed book.

SECTION X

TYPOLOGY

642

PROOF of the two Testaments at once.—To prove the two at one stroke, we need only see if the prophecies in one are fulfilled in the other. To examine the prophecies, we must understand them. For if we believe they have only one meaning, it is certain that the Messiah has not come; but if they have two meanings, it is certain that He has come in Jesus Christ.

The whole problem then is to know if they have two meanings.

That the Scripture has two meanings, which Jesus Christ and the Apostles have given, is shown by the following proofs:

1. Proof by Scripture itself.

2. Proof by the Rabbis. Moses Maimonides says that it has two aspects, and that the prophets have prophesied Jesus Christ only.

3. Proof by the Kabbala.

4. Proof by the mystical interpretation which the Rabbis themselves give to Scripture.

5. Proof by the principles of the Rabbis, that there are two meanings; that there are two advents of the Messiah, a glorious and humiliating one, according to their desert; that the prophets have prophesied of the Messiah only—the Law is not eternal, but must change at the coming of the Messiah—that then they shall no more remember the Red Sea; that the Jews and the Gentiles shall be mingled.

[6. Proof by the key which Jesus Christ and the Apostles give us.]

643

Isaiah, li. The Red Sea an image of the Redemption. *Ut sciatis quod filius hominis habet potestatem remittendi peccata, tibi dico:*[1] *Surge.* God, wishing to show that He could form a people holy with an invisible holiness, and fill them with an eternal glory, made visible things. As nature is an image of grace, He has done in the bounties of nature what He would do in those of grace, in order that we might judge that He could make the invisible, since He made the visible excellently.

Therefore He saved this people from the deluge; He has raised them up from Abraham, redeemed them from their enemies, and set them at rest.

The object of God was not to save them from the deluge, and raise up a whole people from Abraham, only in order to bring them into a rich land.

And even grace is only the type of glory, for it is not the ultimate end. It has been symbolised by the law, and itself symbolises [*glory*]. But it is the type of it, and the origin or cause.

The ordinary life of men is like that of the saints. They all seek their satisfaction, and differ only in the object in which they place it; they call those their enemies who hinder them, &c. God has then shown the power which He has of giving invisible blessings, by that which He has shown Himself to have over things visible.

644

Types.—God, wishing to form for Himself an holy people, whom He should separate from all other nations, whom He should deliver from their enemies and should put into a place of rest, has promised to do so, and has foretold by His prophets the time and the manner of His coming. And yet, to confirm the hope of His elect, He has made them see it in an image through all time, without leaving them devoid of assurances of His power and of His will to save them. For, at the creation of man, Adam was the witness,

[1] Mark, ii. 10, 11.

and guardian of the promise of a Saviour, who should be
born of woman, when men were still so near the creation
that they could not have forgotten their creation and their
fall. When those who had seen Adam were no longer in
the world, God sent Noah whom He saved, and drowned
the whole earth by a miracle which sufficiently indicated the
power which He had to save the world, and the will which
He had to do so, and to raise up from the seed of woman
Him whom He had promised. This miracle was enough to
confirm the hope of men.

The memory of the deluge being so fresh among men,
while Noah was still alive, God made promises to Abraham,
and, while Shem was still living, sent Moses, &c. . . .

645

Types.—God, willing to deprive His own of perishable
blessings, created the Jewish people in order to show that
this was not owing to lack of power.

646

The Synagogue did not perish, because it was a type.
But because it was only a type, it fell into servitude. The
type existed till the truth came, in order that the Church
should be always visible, either in the sign which promised
it, or in substance.

647

That the law was figurative.

648

Two errors: 1. To take everything literally. 2. To take
everything spiritually.

649

To speak against too greatly figurative language.

650

There are some types clear and demonstrative, but others
which seem somewhat far-fetched, and which convince

only those who are already persuaded. These are like the
Apocalyptics. But the difference is that they have none
which are certain, so that nothing is so unjust as to claim
that theirs are as well founded as some of ours; for they
have none so demonstrative as some of ours. The comparison is unfair. We must not put on the same level, and
confound things, because they seem to agree in one point,
while they are so different in another. The clearness in
divine things requires us to revere the obscurities in them.

[It is like men, who employ a certain obscure language
among themselves. Those who should not understand it,
would understand only a foolish meaning.]

651

*Extravagances of the Apocalyptics, Preadamites, Millen-
arians, &c.*—He who would base extravagant opinions on
Scripture, will, for example, base them on this. It is said
that "this generation shall not pass till all these things be
fulfilled." Upon that I will say that after that generation
will come another generation, and so on ever in succession.

Solomon and the King are spoken of in the second book
of Chronicles, as if they were two different persons. I will
say that they were two.

652

Particular Types.—A double law, double tables of the law,
a double temple, a double captivity.

653

Types.—The prophets prophesied by symbols of a girdle,
a beard and burnt hair, &c.

654

Difference between dinner and supper.

In God the word does not differ from the intention, for
He is true; nor the word from the effect, for He is powerful; nor the means from the effect, for He is wise. Bern.,
ult. sermo in Missam.

Augustine, *de Civit. Dei,* v. 10. This rule is general. God can do everything, except those things, which if He could do, He would not be almighty, as dying, being deceived, lying, &c.

Many Evangelists for the confirmation of the truth: their difference useful.

The Eucharist after the Lord's Supper. Truth after the type.

The ruin of Jerusalem, a type of the ruin of the world, forty years after the death of Jesus. " I know not," as a man, or as an ambassador (Mark xiii. 32).

Jesus condemned by the Jews and the Gentiles.

The Jews and the Gentiles typified by the two sons. Aug. *de Civ.* xx. 29.

655

The six ages, the six Fathers of the six ages, the six wonders at the beginning of the six ages, the six mornings at the beginning of the six ages.

656

'Adam *forma futuri.*[2] The six days to form the one, the six ages to form the other. The six days, which Moses represents for the formation of Adam, are only the picture of the six ages to form Jesus Christ and the Church. If Adam had not sinned, and Jesus Christ had not come, there had been only one covenant, only one age of men, and the creation would have been represented as accomplished at one single time.

657

Types.—The Jewish and Egyptian peoples were plainly foretold by the two individuals whom Moses met; the Egyptian beating the Jew, Moses avenging him and killing the Egyptian, and the Jew being ungrateful.

658

The symbols of the Gospel for the state of the sick soul are sick bodies; but because one body cannot be sick enough

[2] Romans, v. 14.

to express it well, several have been needed. Thus there are the deaf, the dumb, the blind, the paralytic, the dead Lazarus, the possessed. All this crowd is in the sick soul.

659

Types.—To show that the Old Testament is only figurative, and that the prophets understood by temporal blessings other blessings, this is the proof:—

First, that this would be unworthy of God.

Secondly, that their discourses express very clearly the promise of temporal blessings, and that they say nevertheless that their discourses are obscure, and that their meaning will not be understood. Whence it appears that this secret meaning was not that which they openly expressed, and that consequently they meant to speak of other sacrifices, of another deliverer, &c. They say that they will be understood only in the fulness of time (Jer. xxx. *ult.*).

The third proof is that their discourses are contradictory, and neutralise each other; so that if we think that they did not mean by the words " law " and " sacrifice " anything else than that of Moses, there is a plain and gross contradiction. Therefore they meant something else, sometimes contradicting themselves in the same chapter. Now to understand the meaning of an author . . .

660

Lust has become natural to us, and has made our second nature. Thus there are two natures in us—the one good, the other bad. Where is God? Where you are not, and the kingdom of God is within you. The Rabbis.

661

Penitence, alone of all these mysteries, has been manifestly declared to the Jews, and by Saint John, the Forerunner; and then the other mysteries; to indicate that in each man, as in the entire world, this order must be observed.

662

The carnal Jews understood neither the greatness nor the humiliation of the Messiah foretold in their prophecies. They misunderstood Him in His foretold greatness, as when He said that the Messiah should be lord of David, though his son, and that He was before Abraham, who had seen Him. They did not believe Him so great as to be eternal, and they likewise misunderstood Him in His humiliation and in His death. "The Messiah," said they, "abideth for ever, and this man says that he shall die." Therefore they believed Him neither mortal nor eternal; they only sought in Him for a carnal greatness.

663

Typical.—Nothing is so like charity as covetousness, and nothing is so opposed to it. Thus the Jews, full of possessions which flattered their covetousness, were very like Christians, and very contrary. And by this means they had the two qualities which it was necessary they should have, to be very like the Messiah to typify Him, and very contrary not to be suspected witnesses.

664

Typical.—God made use of the lust of the Jews to make them minister to Jesus Christ, [who brought the remedy for their lust].

665

Charity is not a figurative precept. It is dreadful to say that Jesus Christ, who came to take away types in order to establish the truth, came only to establish the type of charity, in order to take away the existing reality which was there before.

"If the light be darkness, how great is that darkness!"

666

Fascination. *Somnum suum*.[3] *Figura hujus mundi*.[4]
The Eucharist. *Comedes panem tuum*.[5] *Panem nostrum*.[6]
Inimici Dei terram lingent.[7] Sinners lick the dust, that is
to say, love earthly pleasures.

The Old Testament contained the types of future joy, and
the New contains the means of arriving at it. The types
were of joy; the means of penitence; and nevertheless the
Paschal Lamb was eaten with bitter herbs, *cum amaritudi-
nibus*.[8]

Singularis sum ego donec transeam.[9]—Jesus Christ before
His death was almost the only martyr.

667

Typical.—The expressions, sword, shield. *Potentissime*.

668

We are estranged, only by departing from charity. Our
prayers and our virtues are abominable before God, if they
are not the prayers and the virtues of Jesus Christ. And
our sins will never be the object of [mercy], but of the
justice of God, if they are not [those of] Jesus Christ. He
has adopted our sins, and has [admitted] us into union [with
Him], for virtues are [His own, and] sins are foreign to
Him; while virtues [are] foreign to us, and our sins are
our own.

Let us change the rule which we have hitherto chosen
for judging what is good. We had our own will as our
rule. Let us now take the will of [God]; all that He wills is
good and right to us, all that He does not will is [bad].

All that God does not permit is forbidden. Sins are forbidden by the general declaration that God has made, that
He did not allow them. Other things which He has left
without general prohibition, and which for that reason are
said to be permitted, are nevertheless not always permitted.

---

[3] Psalms, lxxvi. 5.   [4] 1 Cor., vii. 31.   [5] Deut., viii. 9.   [6] Luke, xi. 3.
[7] Psalms, lxxii. 9.   [8] Exodus, xii. 8.   [9] Psalms, cxli. 10.

For when God removes some one of them from us, and when, by the event, which is a manifestation of the will of God, it appears that God does not will that we should have a thing, that is then forbidden to us as sin; since the will of God is that we should not have one more than another. There is this sole difference between these two things, that it is certain that God will never allow sin, while it is not certain that He will never allow the other. But so long as God does not permit it, we ought to regard it as sin; so long as the absence of God's will, which alone is all goodness and all justice, renders it unjust and wrong.

669

To change the type, because of our weakness.

670

Types.—The Jews had grown old in these earthly thoughts, that God loved their father Abraham, his flesh and what sprung from it; that on account of this He had multiplied them, and distinguished them from all other nations, without allowing them to intermingle; that when they were languishing in Egypt, He brought them out with all these great signs in their favour; that He fed them with manna in the desert, and led them into a very rich land; that He gave them kings and a well-built temple, in order to offer up beasts before Him, by the shedding of whose blood they should be purified; and that at last He was to send them the Messiah to make them masters of all the world, and foretold the time of His coming.

The world having grown old in these carnal errors, Jesus Christ came at the time foretold, but not with the expected glory; and thus men did not think it was He. After His death, Saint Paul came to teach men that all these things had happened in allegory; that the kingdom of God did not consist in the flesh, but in the spirit; that the enemies of men were not the Babylonians, but the passions; that God delighted not in temples made with hands, but in a pure and contrite heart; that the circumcision of the body was unprofitable, but that of the heart was needed; that Moses had not given them the bread from heaven, &c.

But God, not having desired to reveal these things to this people who were unworthy of them, and having nevertheless desired to foretell them, in order that they might be believed, foretold the time clearly, and expressed the things sometimes clearly, but very often in figures, in order that those who loved symbols might consider them, and those who loved what was symbolized might see it therein.

All that tends not to charity is figurative.

The sole aim of the Scripture is charity.

All which tends not to the sole end is the type of it. For since there is only one end, all which does not lead to it in express terms is figurative.

God thus varies that sole precept of charity to satisfy our curiosity, which seeks for variety, by that variety which still leads us to the one thing needful. For one thing alone is needful, and we love variety; and God satisfies both by these varieties, which lead to the one thing needful.

The Jews have so much loved the shadows, and have so strictly expected them, that they have misunderstood the reality, when it came in the time and manner foretold..

The Rabbis take the breasts of the Spouse for types, and all that does not express the only end they have, namely, temporal good.

And Christians take even the Eucharist as a type of the glory at which they aim.

671

The Jews, who have been called to subdue nations and kings, have been the slaves of sin; and the Christians, whose calling has been to be servants and subjects, are free children.

672

A formal point.—When Saint Peter and the Apostles deliberated about abolishing circumcision, where it was a question of acting against the law of God, they did not heed the prophets, but simply the reception of the Holy Spirit in the persons uncircumcised.

They thought it more certain that God approved of those whom He filled with His Spirit, than it was that the law must be obeyed. They knew that the end of the law was only the Holy Spirit; and that thus, as men certainly had this without circumcision, it was not necessary.

673

Fac secundum exemplar quod tibi ostensum est in monte.[10] —The Jewish religion then has been formed on its likeness to the truth of the Messiah; and the truth of the Messiah has been recognised by the Jewish religion, which was the type of it.

Among the Jews the truth was only typified; in heaven it is revealed.

In the Church it is hidden, and recognised by its resemblance to the type.

The type has been made according to the truth, and the truth has been recognised according to the type.

Saint Paul says himself that people will forbid to marry, and he himself speaks of it to the Corinthians in a way which is a snare. For if a prophet has said the one, and Saint Paul had then said the other, he would have been accused.

674

Typical.—" Do all things according to the pattern which has been shown thee on the mount." On which Saint Paul says that the Jews have shadowed forth heavenly things.

675

. . . And yet this Covenant, made to blind some and enlighten others, indicated in those very persons, whom it blinded, the truth which should be recognised by others. For the visible blessings which they received from God were so great and so divine, that He indeed appeared able to give them those that are invisible, and a Messiah.

For nature is an image of grace, and visible miracles are images of the invisible. *Ut sciatis . . . tibi dico: Surge.*[11]

[10] Exodus, xxv. 40. [11] Matt., ix. 6.

Isaiah says that Redemption will be as the passage of the Red Sea.

God has then shown by the deliverance from Egypt, and from the sea, by the defeat of kings, by the manna, by the whole genealogy of Abraham, that He was able to save, to send down bread from heaven, &c.; so that the people hostile to Him are the type and the representation of the very Messiah whom they know not, &c.

He has then taught us at last that all these things were only types, and what is "true freedom," a "true Israelite," "true circumcision," "true bread from heaven," &c.

In these promises each one finds what he has most at heart, temporal benefits or spiritual, God or the creatures; but with this difference, that those who therein seek the creatures find them, but with many contradictions, with a prohibition against loving them, with the command to worship God only, and to love Him only, which is the same thing, and, finally, that the Messiah came not for them; whereas those who therein seek God find Him, without any contradiction, with the command to love Him only, and that the Messiah came in the time foretold, to give them the blessings which they ask.

Thus the Jews had miracles and prophecies, which they saw fulfilled, and the teaching of their law was to worship and love God only; it was also perpetual. Thus it had all the marks of the true religion; and so it was. But the Jewish teaching must be distinguished from the teaching of the Jewish law. Now the Jewish teaching was not true, although it had miracles and prophecy and perpetuity, because it had not this other point of worshipping and loving God only.

676

The veil, which is upon these books for the Jews, is there also for evil Christians, and for all who do not hate themselves.

But how well disposed men are to understand them and to know Jesus Christ, when they truly hate themselves!

677

A type conveys absence and presence, pleasure and pain.

A cipher has a double meaning, one clear, and one in which it is said that the meaning is hidden.

678

Types.—A portrait conveys absence and presence, pleasure and pain. The reality excludes absence and pain.

To know if the law and the sacrifices are a reality or a type, we must see if the prophets, in speaking of these things, confined their view and their thought to them, so that they saw only the old covenant; or if they saw therein something else of which they were the representation, for in a portrait we see the thing figured. For this we need only examine what they say of them.

When they say that it will be eternal, do they mean to speak of that covenant which they say will be changed; and so of the sacrifices, &c.?

A cipher has two meanings. When we find out an important letter in which we discover a clear meaning, and in which it is nevertheless said that the meaning is veiled and obscure, that it is hidden, so that we might read the letter without seeing it, and interpret it without understanding it, what must we think but that here is a cipher with a double meaning, and the more so if we find obvious contradictions in the literal meaning? The prophets have clearly said that Israel would be always loved by God, and that the law would be eternal; and they have said that their meaning would not be understood, and that it was veiled.

How greatly then ought we to value those who interpret the cipher, and teach us to understand the hidden meaning, especially if the principles which they educe are perfectly clear and natural! This is what Jesus Christ did, and the Apostles. They broke the seal; He rent the veil, and revealed the spirit. They have taught us through this that the enemies of man are his passions; that the Redeemer would be spiritual, and His reign spiritual; that there would

be two advents, one in lowliness to humble the proud, the
other in glory to exalt the humble; that Jesus Christ would be
both God and man.

679

Types.—Jesus Christ opened their mind to understand
the Scriptures.

Two great revelations are these. (1.) All things happened to them in types: *vere Israelitæ, vere liberi,* true bread
from Heaven. (2.) A God humbled to the Cross. It was
necessary that Christ should suffer in order to enter into
glory, "that He should destroy death through death." Two
advents.

680

Types.—When once this secret is disclosed, it is impossible
not to see it. Let us read the Old Testament in this light,
and let us see if the sacrifices were real; if the fatherhood
of Abraham was the true cause of the friendship of God;
and if the promised land was the true place of rest. No.
They are therefore types. Let us in the same way examine
all those ordained ceremonies, all those commandments which
are not of charity, and we shall see that they are types.

All these sacrifices and ceremonies were then either types
or nonsense. Now there are things clear, and too lofty,
to be thought nonsense.

To know if the prophets confined their view in the Old
Testament, or saw therein other things.

681

Typical.—The key of the cipher. *Veri adoratores.*[12]—
Ecce agnus Dei qui tollit peccata mundi.[13]

682

Is. i. 21. Change of good into evil, and the vengeance
of God. Is. x. 1; xxvi. 20; xxviii. i. Miracles: Is. xxxiii.
9; xl. 17; xli. 26; xliii. 13.

Jer. xi. 21; xv. 12; xvii. 9. *Pravum est cor omnium et
incrustabile; quis cognoscet illud?* that is to say, Who can

[12] John, iv. 23.   [13] John, i. 29.

know all its evil? For it is already known to be wicked.
Ego dominus, &c.—*vii.* 14. *Faciam domui huic,* &c.—Trust
in external sacrifices—vii. 22. *Quia non sum locutus,* &c.
Outward sacrifice is not the essential point—xi. 13. *Secundum numerum,* &c. A multitude of doctrines.

Is. xliv. 20-24; liv. 8; lxiii. 12-17; lxvi. 17. Jer. ii.. 35;
iv. 22-24; v. 4, 29-31; vi. 16; xxiii. 15-17.

683

Types.—The letter kills. All happened in types. Here is
the cipher which Saint Paul gives us. Christ must suffer.
An humiliated God. Circumcision of the heart, true fast-
ing, true sacrifice, a true temple. The prophets have shown
that all these must be spiritual.

Not the meat which perishes, but that which does not
perish.

"Ye shall be free indeed." Then the other freedom was
only a type of freedom.

"I am the true bread from Heaven."

684

Contradiction.—We can only describe a good character
by reconciling all contrary qualities, and it is not enough to
keep up a series of harmonious qualities without reconciling
contradictory ones. To understand the meaning of an author,
we must make all the contrary passages agree.

Thus, to understand Scripture, we must have a meaning
in which all the contrary passages are reconciled. It is
not enough to have one which suits many concurring passages; but it is necessary to have one which reconciles even
contradictory passages.

Every author has a meaning in which all the contradictory
passages agree, or he has no meaning at all. We cannot
affirm the latter of Scripture and the prophets; they undoubtedly are full of good sense. We must then seek for a
meaning which reconciles all discrepancies.

The true meaning then is not that of the Jews; but in
Jesus Christ all the contradictions are reconciled.

The Jews could not reconcile the cessation of the royalty and principality, foretold by Hosea, with the prophecy of Jacob.

If we take the law, the sacrifices, and the kingdom as realities, we cannot reconcile all the passages. They must then necessarily be only types. We cannot even reconcile the passages of the same author, nor of the same book, nor sometimes of the same chapter, which indicates copiously what was the meaning of the author. As when Ezekiel, chap. xx., says that man will live by the commandments of God and will not live by them.

685

Types.—If the law and the sacrifices are the truth, it must please God, and must not displease Him. If they are types, they must be both pleasing and displeasing.

Now in all the Scripture they are both pleasing and displeasing. It is said that the law shall be changed; that the sacrifice shall be changed; that they shall be without law, without a prince, and without a sacrifice; that a new covenant shall be made; that the law shall be renewed; that the precepts which they have received are not good; that their sacrifices are abominable; that God has demanded none of them.

It is said, on the contrary, that the law shall abide for ever; that this covenant shall be for ever; that sacrifice shall be eternal; that the sceptre shall never depart from among them, because it shall not depart from them till the eternal King comes.

Do all these passages indicate what is real? No. Do they then indicate what is typical? No, but what is either real or typical. But the first passages, excluding as they do reality, indicate that all this is only typical.

All these passages together cannot be applied to reality; all can be said to be typical; therefore they are not spoken of reality, but of the type.

Agnus occisus est ab origine mundi.[14] A sacrificing judge.

[14] Revel., xiii. 8.

686

Contradictions.—The sceptre till the Messiah,—without king or prince.

The eternal law,—changed.

The eternal covenant,—a new covenant.

Good laws,—bad precepts. Ezekiel.

687

Types.—When the word of God, which is really true, is false literally, it is true spiritually. *Sede a dextris meis :*[15] this is false literally, therefore it is true spiritually.

In these expressions, God is spoken of after the manner of men; and this means nothing else but that the intention which men have in giving a seat at their right hand, God will have also. It is then an indication of the intention of God, not of His manner of carrying it out.

Thus when it is said, "God has received the odour of your incense, and will in recompense give you a rich land," that is equivalent to saying that the same intention which a man would have, who, pleased with your perfumes, should in recompense give you a rich land, God will have towards you, because you have had towards [Him] the same intention as a man has towards him, to whom he presents perfumes. So *iratus est,* a "jealous God," &c. For, the things of God being inexpressible, they cannot be spoken of otherwise, and the Church makes use of them even to-day: *Quia confortavit seras,* &c.[16]

It is not allowable to attribute to Scripture the meaning which it has not revealed to us that it has. Thus, to say that the closed *mem*[17] of Isaiah signifies six hundred, has not been revealed. It might be said that the final *tsadé* and the *he deficientes* may signify mysteries. But it is not allowable to say so, and still less to say this is the way of the philosopher's stone. But we say that the literal meaning is not the true meaning, because the prophets have themselves said so.

---

[15] Psalms, cx. 1.   [16] Psalms, cxlvii. 13.
[17] In allusion to certain features in Hebrew writing.

688

I do not say that the *mem* is mystical.

689

Moses (*Deut.* xxx.) promises that God will circumcise their heart to render them capable of loving Him.

690

One saying of David, or of Moses, as for instance that " God will circumcise the heart," enables us to judge of their spirit. If all their other expressions were ambiguous, and left us in doubt whether they were philosophers or Christians, one saying of this kind would in fact determine all the rest, as one sentence of Epictetus decides the meaning of all the rest to be the opposite. So far ambiguity exists, but not afterwards.

691

If one of two persons, who are telling silly stories, uses language with a double meaning, understood in his own circle, while the other uses it with only one meaning, any one not in the secret, who hears them both talk in this manner, will pass upon them the same judgment. But if afterwards, in the rest of their conversation one says angelic things, and the other always dull common-places, he will judge that the one spoke in mysteries, and not the other; the one having sufficiently shown that he is incapable of such foolishness, and capable of being mysterious; and the other that he is incapable of mystery, and capable of foolishness.

The Old Testament is a cipher.

692

There are some who see clearly that man has no other enemy than lust, which turns him from God, and not God; and that he has no other good than God, and not a rich land. Let those who believe that the good of man is in the flesh,

and evil in what turns him away from sensual pleasures,
[satiate] themselves with them, and [die] in them. But let
those who seek God with all their heart, who are only
troubled at not seeing Him, who desire only to possess Him,
and have as enemies only those who turn them away from
Him, who are grieved at seeing themselves surrounded and
overwhelmed with such enemies, take comfort. I proclaim
to them happy news. There exists a Redeemer for them.
I shall show Him to them. I shall show that there is a God
for them. I shall not show Him to others. I shall make
them see that a Messiah has been promised, who should deliver them from their enemies, and that One has come to
free them from their iniquities, but not from their enemies.

When David foretold that the Messiah would deliver His
people from their enemies, one can believe that in the flesh
these would be the Egyptians; and then I cannot show
that the prophecy was fulfilled. But one can well believe
also that the enemies would be their sins; for indeed the
Egyptians were not their enemies, but their sins were so.
This word, enemies, is therefore ambiguous. But if he says
elsewhere, as he does, that He will deliver His people from
their sins, as indeed do Isaiah and others, the ambiguity is
removed, and the double meaning of enemies is reduced to
the simple meaning of iniquities. For if he had sins in his
mind, he could well denote them as enemies; but if he thought
of enemies, he could not designate them as iniquities.

Now Moses, David, and Isaiah used the same terms. Who
will say then that they have not the same meaning, and that
David's meaning, which is plainly iniquities when he spoke
of enemies, was not the same as [that of] Moses when speaking of enemies?

Daniel (ix.) prays for the deliverance of the people
from the captivity of their enemies. But he was thinking
of sins, and to show this, he says that Gabriel came to tell
him that his prayer was heard, and that there were only
seventy weeks to wait, after which the people would be freed
from iniquity, sin would have an end, and the Redeemer, the
Holy of Holies, would bring *eternal* justice, not legal, but
eternal.

SECTION XI

THE PROPHECIES

693

WHEN I see the blindness and the wretchedness of man, when I regard the whole silent universe, and man without light, left to himself, and, as it were, lost in this corner of the universe, without knowing who has put him there, what he has come to do, what will become of him at death, and incapable of all knowledge, I become terrified, like a man who should be carried in his sleep to a dreadful desert island, and should awake without knowing where he is, and without means of escape. And thereupon I wonder how people in a condition so wretched do not fall into despair. I see other persons around me of a like nature. I ask them if they are better informed than I am. They tell me that they are not. And thereupon these wretched and lost beings, having looked around them, and seen some pleasing objects, have given and attached themselves to them. For my own part, I have not been able to attach myself to them, and, considering how strongly it appears that there is something else than what I see, I have examined whether this God has not left some sign of Himself.

I see many contradictory religions, and consequently all false save one. Each wants to be believed on its own authority, and threatens unbelievers. I do not therefore believe them. Every one can say this; every one can call himself a prophet. But I see the Christian religion wherein prophecies are fulfilled; and that is what every one cannot do.

694

And what crowns all this is prediction, so that it should not be said that it is chance which has done it.

Whosoever, having only a week to live, will not find out that it is expedient to believe that all this is not a stroke of chance . . .

Now, if the passions had no hold on us, a week and a hundred years would amount to the same thing.

695

Prophecies.—Great Pan is dead.

696

Susceperunt verbum cum omni aviditate, scrutantes Scripturas, si ita se haberent.[1]

697

Prodita lege.—Impleta cerne.—Implenda collige.[2]

698

We understand the prophecies only when we see the events happen. Thus the proofs of retreat, discretion, silence, &c., are proofs only to those who know and believe them.

Joseph so internal in a law so external.

Outward penances dispose to inward, as humiliations to humility. Thus the . . .

699

The synagogue has preceded the church; the Jews, the Christians. The prophets have foretold the Christians; Saint John, Jesus Christ.

700

It is glorious to see with the eyes of faith the history of Herod and of Cæsar.

701

The zeal of the Jews for their law and their temple (*Josephus,* and *Philo the Jew, ad Caïum*). What other people had such a zeal? It was necessary they should have it.

[1] Acts, xvii. 11.
[2] " Read what has been handed down.—Note what has been fulfilled.—Bring together what is to be fulfilled."

Jesus Christ foretold as to the time and the state of the world. The ruler taken from the thigh, and the fourth monarchy. How lucky we are to see this light amidst this darkness!

How fine it is to see, with the eyes of faith, Darius and Cyrus, Alexander, the Romans, Pompey and Herod working, without knowing it, for the glory of the Gospel!

702

Zeal of the Jewish people for the law, especially after there were no more prophets.

703

While the prophets were for maintaining the law, the people were indifferent. But since there have been no more prophets, zeal has succeeded them.

704

The devil troubled the zeal of the Jews before Jesus Christ, because he would have been their salvation, but not since.

The Jewish people scorned by the Gentiles; the Christian people persecuted.

705

Proof.—Prophecies with their fulfilment; what has preceded and what has followed Jesus Christ.

706

The prophecies are the strongest proof of Jesus Christ. It is for them also that God has made most provision; for the event which has fulfilled them is a miracle existing since the birth of the Church to the end. So God has raised up prophets during sixteen hundred years, and, during four hundred years afterwards, He has scattered all these prophecies among all the Jews, who carried them into all parts of the world. Such was the preparation for the birth of Jesus Christ, and, as His Gospel was to be believed by all the world, it was not only necessary that there should be prophecies to make it believed, but that these prophecies should exist throughout the whole world, in order to make it embraced by the whole world.

707

But it was not enough that the prophecies should exist. It was necessary that they should be distributed throughout all places, and preserved throughout all times. And in order that this agreement might not be taken for an effect of chance, it was necessary that this should be foretold.

It is far more glorious for the Messiah that the Jews should be the spectators, and even the instruments of His glory, besides that God had reserved them.

708

Prophecies.—The time foretold by the state of the Jewish people, by the state of the heathen, by the state of the temple, by the number of years.

709

One must be bold to predict the same thing in so many ways. It was necessary that the four idolatrous or pagan monarchies, the end of the kingdom of Judah, and the seventy weeks, should happen at the same time, and all this before the second temple was destroyed.

710

Prophecies.—If one man alone had made a book of predictions about Jesus Christ, as to the time and the manner, and Jesus Christ had come in conformity to these prophecies, this fact would have infinite weight.

But there is much more here. Here is a succession of men during four thousand years, who, constantly and without variation, come, one after another, to foretell this same event. Here is a whole people who announce it, and who have existed for four thousand years, in order to give corporate testimony of the assurances which they have, and from which they cannot be diverted by whatever threats and persecutions people may make against them. This is far more important.

711

Predictions of particular things.—They were strangers in Egypt, without any private property, either in that country or elsewhere. [There was not the least appearance, either of the royalty which had previously existed so long, or of that supreme council of seventy judges which they called the *Sanhedrin,* and which, having been instituted by Moses, lasted to the time of Jesus Christ. All these things were as far removed from their state at that time as they could be], when Jacob, dying, and blessing his twelve children, declared to them, that they would be proprietors of a great land, and foretold in particular to the family of Judah, that the kings, who would one day rule them, should be of his race; and that all his brethren should be their subjects; [and that even the Messiah, who was to be the expectation of nations, should spring from him; and that the kingship should not be taken away from Judah, nor the ruler and law-giver of his descendants, till the expected Messiah should arrive in his family].

This same Jacob, disposing of this future land as though he had been its ruler, gave a portion to Joseph more than to the others. "I give you," said he, "one part more than to your brothers." And blessing his two children, Ephraim and Manasseh, whom Joseph had presented to him, the elder, Manasseh, on his right, and the young Ephraim on his left, he put his arms crosswise, and placing his right hand on the head of Ephraim, and his left on Manasseh, he blessed them in this manner. And, upon Joseph's representing to him that he was preferring the younger, he replied to him with admirable resolution: "I know it well, my son; but Ephraim will increase more than Manasseh." This has been indeed so true in the result, that, being alone almost as fruitful as the two entire lines which composed a whole kingdom, they have been usually called by the name of Ephraim alone.

This same Joseph, when dying, bade his children carry his bones with them when they should go into that land, to which they only came two hundred years afterwards.

Moses, who wrote all these things so long before they happened, himself assigned to each family portions of that land before they entered it, as though he had been its ruler. [In fact he declared that God was to raise up from their nation and their race a prophet, of whom he was the type; and he foretold them exactly all that was to happen to them in the land which they were to enter after his death, the victories which God would give them, their ingratitude towards God, the punishments which they would receive for it, and the rest of their adventures.] He gave them judges who should make the division. He prescribed the entire form of political government which they should observe, the cities of refuge which they should build, and . . .

712

The prophecies about particular things are mingled with those about the Messiah, so that the prophecies of the Messiah should not be without proofs, nor the special prophecies without fruit.

713

Perpetual captivity of the Jews.—Jer. xi. 11 : "I will bring evil upon Judah from which they shall not be able to escape."

Types.—Is. v.: "The Lord had a vineyard, from which He looked for grapes; and it brought forth only wild grapes. I will therefore lay it waste, and destroy it; the earth shall only bring forth thorns, and I will forbid the clouds from [raining] upon it. The vineyard of the Lord is the house of Israel, and the men of Judah His pleasant plant. I looked that they should do justice, and they bring forth only iniquities."

Is. viii.: "Sanctify the Lord with fear and trembling; let Him be your only dread, and He shall be to you for a sanctuary, but for a stone of stumbling and a rock of offence to both the houses of Israel, for a gin and for a snare to the inhabitants of Jerusalem; and many among them shall stumble against that stone, and fall, and be broken, and be snared, and perish. Hide my words, and cover my law for my disciples.

"I will then wait in patience upon the Lord that hideth and concealeth Himself from the house of Jacob."

Is. xxix.: "Be amazed and wonder, people of Israel; stagger and stumble, and be drunken, but not with wine; stagger, but not with strong drink. For the Lord hath poured out upon you the spirit of deep sleep. He will close your eyes; He will cover your princes and your prophets that have visions." (Daniel xii.: "The wicked shall not understand, but the wise shall understand." Hosea, the last chapter, the last verse, after many temporal blessings, says: "Who is wise, and he shall understand these things, &c.?") "And the visions of all the prophets are become unto you as a sealed book, which men deliver to one that is learned, and who can read; and he saith, I cannot read it, for it is sealed. And when the book is delivered to them that are not learned, they say, I am not learned.

"Wherefore the Lord said, Forasmuch as this people with their lips do honour me, but have removed their heart far from me,"—there is the reason and the cause of it; for if they adored God in their hearts, they would understand the prophecies,—"and their fear towards me is taught by the precept of man. Therefore, behold, I will proceed to do a marvellous work among this people, even a marvellous work and a wonder; for the wisdom of their wise men shall perish, and their understanding shall be [hid]."

Prophecies. Proofs of Divinity.—Is. xli.: "Shew the things that are to come hereafter, that we may know that ye are gods: we will incline our heart unto your words. Teach us the things that have been at the beginning, and declare us things for to come.

"By this we shall know that ye are gods. Yea, do good or do evil, if you can. Let us then behold it and reason together. Behold, ye are of nothing, and only an abomination, &c. Who," (among contemporary writers), "hath declared from the beginning that we may know of the things done from the beginning and origin? that we may say, You are righteous. There is none that teacheth us, yea, there is none that declareth the future."

Is. xlii.: "I am the Lord, and my glory will I not give to another. I have foretold the things which have come to pass, and things that are to come do I declare. Sing unto God a new song in all the earth.

"Bring forth the blind people that have eyes and see not, and the deaf that have ears and hear not. Let all the nations be gathered together. Who among them can declare this, and shew us former things, and things to come? Let them bring forth their witnesses, that they may be justified; or let them hear, and say, It is truth.

"Ye are my witnesses, saith the Lord, and my servant whom I have chosen; that ye may know and believe me, and understand that I am He.

"I have declared, and have saved, and I alone have done wonders before your eyes: ye are my witnesses, said the Lord, that I am God.

"For your sake I have brought down the forces of the Babylonians. I am the Lord, your Holy One and creator.

"I have made a way in the sea, and a path in the mighty waters. I am He that drowned and destroyed for ever the mighty enemies that have resisted you.

"Remember ye not the former things, neither consider the things of old.

"Behold, I will do a new thing; now it shall spring forth; shall ye not know it? I will even make a way in the wilderness, and rivers in the desert.

"This people have I formed for myself; I have established them to shew forth my praise, &c.

"I, even I, am He that blotteth out thy transgressions for mine own sake, and will not remember thy sins. Put in remembrance your ingratitude: see thou, if thou mayest be justified. Thy first father hath sinned, and thy teachers have transgressed against me."

Is. xliv.: "I am the first, and I am the last, saith the Lord. Let him who will equal himself to me, declare the order of things since I appointed the ancient people, and the things that are coming. Fear ye not: have I not told you all these things? Ye are my witnesses."

Prophecy of Cyrus.—Is. xlv. 4: "For Jacob's sake, mine elect, I have called thee by thy name."

Is. xlv. 21: "Come and let us reason together. Who hath declared this from ancient time? Who hath told it from that time? Have not I, the Lord?"

Is. xlvi.: "Remember the former things of old, and know there is none like me, declaring the end from the beginning, and from ancient times the things that are not yet done, saying, My counsel shall stand, and I will do all my pleasure."

Is. xlii.: "Behold, the former things are come to pass, and new things do I declare; before they spring forth I tell you of them."

Is. xlviii. 3: "I have declared the former things from the beginning; I did them suddenly; and they came to pass. Because I know that thou art obstinate, that thy spirit is rebellious, and thy brow brass; I have even declared it to thee before it came to pass: lest thou shouldst say that it was the work of thy gods, and the effect of their commands.

"Thou hast seen all this; and will not ye declare it? I have shewed thee new things from this time, even hidden things, and thou didst not know them. They are created now, and not from the beginning; I have kept them hidden from thee; lest thou shouldst say, Behold, I knew them.

"Yea, thou knewest not; yea, thou heardest not; yea, from that time that thine ear was not opened: for I knew that thou wouldst deal very treacherously, and wast called a transgressor from the womb."

Reprobation of the Jews and conversion of the Gentiles. —Is. lxv.: "I am sought of them that asked not for me; I am found of them that sought me not: I said, Behold me, behold me, unto a nation that did not call upon my name.

"I have spread out my hands all the day unto an unbelieving people, which walketh in a way that was not good, after their own thoughts; a people that provoketh me to anger continually by the sins they commit in my face; that sacrificeth to idols, &c.

"These shall be scattered like smoke in the day of my wrath, &c.

"Your iniquities, and the iniquities of your fathers, will I assemble together, and will recompense you for all according to your works.

"Thus saith the Lord, As the new wine is found in the cluster, and one saith, Destroy it not, for a blessing is in it [and the promise of fruit]: for my servants' sake I will not destroy all Israel.

"Thus I will bring forth a seed out of Jacob and out of Judah, an inheritor of my mountains, and mine elect and my servants shall inherit it, and my fertile and abundant plains; but I will destroy all others, because you have forgotten your God to serve strange gods. I called, and ye did not answer; I spake, and ye did not hear; and ye did choose the thing which I forbade.

"Therefore thus saith the Lord, Behold, my servants shall eat, but ye shall be hungry; my servants shall rejoice, but ye shall be ashamed; my servants shall sing for joy of heart, but ye shall cry and howl for vexation of spirit.

"And ye shall leave your name for a curse unto my chosen: for the Lord shall slay thee, and call His servants by another name, that he who blesseth himself in the earth shall bless himself in God, &c., because the former troubles are forgotten.

"For, behold, I create new heavens and a new earth; and the former things shall not be remembered, nor come into mind.

"But be ye glad and rejoice for ever in that which I create; for, behold, I create Jerusalem a rejoicing, and her people a joy.

"And I will rejoice in Jerusalem and joy in my people; and the voice of weeping shall no more be heard in her, nor the voice of crying.

"Before they call, I will answer; and while they are yet speaking, I will hear. The wolf and the lamb shall feed together, and the lion shall eat straw like the bullock; and dust shall be the serpent's meat. They shall not hurt nor destroy in all my holy mountain."

Is. lvi. 3: "Thus saith the Lord, keep ye judgment, and do justice: for my salvation is near to come, and my righteousness to be revealed.

"Blessed is the man that doeth this, that keepeth the Sabbath, and keepeth his hand from doing any evil.

"Neither let the strangers that have joined themselves to me, say, God will separate me from His people. For thus saith the Lord: Whoever will keep my Sabbath, and choose the things that please me, and take hold of my covenant; even unto them will I give in mine house a place and a name better than that of sons and of daughters: I will give them an everlasting name, that shall not be cut off."

Is. lix. 9: "Therefore for our iniquities is justice far from us: we wait for light, but behold obscurity; for brightness, but we walk in darkness. We grope for the wall like the blind; we stumble at noon day as in the night: we are in desolate places as dead men.

"We roar all like bears, and mourn sore like doves; we look for judgment, but there is none; for salvation, but it is far from us."

Is. lxvi. 18: "But I know their works and their thoughts; it shall come that I will gather all nations and tongues, and they shall see my glory.

"And I will set a sign among them, and I will send those that escape of them unto the nations, to Africa, to Lydia, to Italy, to Greece, and to the people that have not heard my fame, neither have seen my glory. And they shall bring your brethren."

Jer. vii. *Reprobation of the Temple:* "Go ye unto Shiloth, where I set my name at the first, and see what I did to it for the wickedness of my people. And now, because ye have done all these works, saith the Lord, I will do unto this house, wherein my name is called upon, wherein ye trust, and unto the place which I gave to your priests, as I have done to Shiloth." (For I have rejected it, and made myself a temple elsewhere.)

"And I will cast you out of my sight, as I have cast out all your brethren, even the seed of Ephraim." (Rejected for ever.) "Therefore pray not for this people."

Jer. vii. 22: "What avails it you to add sacrifice to sacrifice? For I spake not unto your fathers, when I brought them out of the land of Egypt, concerning burnt offerings or sacrifices. But this thing commanded I them, saying,

Obey and be faithful to my commandments, and I will be
your God, and ye shall be my people." (It was only after
they had sacrificed to the golden calf that I gave myself
sacrifices to turn into good an evil custom.)

Jer. vii. 4: "Trust ye not in lying words, saying, The
temple of the Lord, the temple of the Lord, the temple of
the Lord, are these."

714

The Jews witnesses for God. Is. xliii. 9; xliv. 8.

Prophecies fulfilled.—1 Kings, xiii. 2.—1 Kings, xxiii.
16.—Jos. vi. 26.—1 Kings, xvi. 34.—Deut. xxiii.

Malachi i. 11. The sacrifice of the Jews rejected, and the
sacrifice of the heathen, (even out of Jerusalem,) and in all
places.

Moses, before dying, foretold the calling of the Gentiles,
Deut. xxxii. 21, and the reprobation of the Jews.

Moses foretold what would happen to each tribe.

Prophecy.—"Your name shall be a curse unto mine elect,
and I will give them another name."

"Make their heart fat," and how? by flattering their lust
and making them hope to satisfy it.

715

Prophecy.—Amos and Zechariah. They have sold the
just one, and therefore will not be recalled.—Jesus Christ
betrayed.

They shall no more remember Egypt. See Is. xliii. 16,
17, 18, 19. Jerem. xxiii. 6, 7.

Prophecy.—The Jews shall be scattered abroad. Is. xxvii.
6.—A new law, Jerem. xxxi. 32.

Malachi. Grotius.—The second temple glorious.—Jesus
Christ will come. (Haggai, ii. 7, 8, 9, 10.)

The calling of the Gentiles. Joel, ii. 28. Hosea, ii. 24.
Deut. xxxii. 21. Malachi, i. 11.

716

Hosea, iii.—Is. xlii., xlviii., liv., lx., lxi., last verse. "I
foretold it long since that they might know that it is I."
Jaddus to Alexander.

717

[*Prophecies.*—The promise that David will always have descendants. Jer. xiii. 13.]

718

The external reign of the race of David, 2 Chron., by all the prophecies, and with an oath. And it was not temporally fulfilled. Jerem. xxiii. 20.

719

We might perhaps think that, when the prophets foretold that the sceptre should not depart from Judah until the eternal King came, they spoke to flatter the people, and that their prophecy was proved false by Herod. But to show that this was not their meaning, and that, on the contrary, they knew well that this temporal kingdom should cease, they said that they would be without a king and without a prince, and for a long time. Hosea iii. 4.

720

Non habemus regem nisi Cæsarem.[3] Therefore Jesus Christ was the Messiah, since they had no longer any king but a stranger, and would have no other.

721

We have no king but Cæsar.

722

Daniel ii.: "All thy soothsayers and wise men cannot show unto thee the secret which thou hast demanded. But there is a God in heaven who can do so, and that hath revealed to thee in thy dream what shall be in the latter days." (This dream must have caused him much misgiving.)

"And it is not by my own wisdom that I have knowledge of this secret, but by the revelation of this same God, that hath revealed it to me, to make it manifest in thy presence.

"Thy dream was then of this kind. Thou sawest a great

---

[3] John, xix. 15.

image, high and terrible, which stood before thee. His head was of gold, his breast and arms of silver, his belly and his thighs of brass, his legs of iron, his feet part of iron and part of clay. Thus thou sawest till that a stone was cut out without hands, which smote the image upon his feet, that were of iron and of clay, and brake them to pieces.

"Then was the iron, the clay, the brass, the silver, and the gold broken to pieces together, and the wind carried them away; but this stone that smote the image became a great mountain, and filled the whole earth. This is the dream, and now I will give thee the interpretation thereof.

"Thou who art the greatest of kings, and to whom God hath given a power so vast that thou art renowned among all peoples, art the head of gold which thou hast seen. But after thee shall arise another kingdom inferior to thee, and another third kingdom of brass, which shall bear rule over all the earth.

"But the fourth kingdom shall be strong as iron, and even as iron breaketh in pieces and subdueth all things, so shall this empire break in pieces and bruise all.

"And whereas thou sawest the feet and toes, part of clay and part of iron, the kingdom shall be divided; but there shall be in it of the strength of iron and of the weakness of clay.

"But as iron cannot be firmly mixed with clay, so they who are represented by the iron and by the clay, shall not cleave one to another though united by marriage.

"Now in the days of these kings shall God set up a kingdom, which shall never be destroyed, nor ever be delivered up to other people. It shall break in pieces and consume all these kingdoms, and it shall stand for ever, according as thou sawest that the stone was cut out of the mountain without hands, and that it fell from the mountain, and brake in pieces, the iron, the clay, the silver, and the gold. God hath made known to thee what shall come to pass hereafter. This dream is certain, and the interpretation thereof sure.

"Then Nebuchadnezzar fell upon his face towards the earth," &c.

Daniel viii. 8. "Daniel having seen the combat of the ram

and of the he-goat, who vanquished him and ruled over the earth, whereof the principal horn being broken four others came up toward the four winds of heaven, and out of one of them came forth a little horn, which waxed exceeding great toward the south, and toward the east, and toward the land of Israel, and it waxed great even to the host of heaven; and it cast down some of the stars, and stamped upon them, and at last overthrew the prince, and by him the daily sacrifice was taken away, and the place of his sanctuary was cast down.

"This is what Daniel saw. He sought the meaning of it, and a voice cried in this manner, 'Gabriel, make this man to understand the vision.' And Gabriel said—

"The ram which thou sawest is the king of the Medes and Persians, and the he-goat is the king of Greece, and the great horn that is between his eyes is the first king of this monarchy.

"Now that being broken, whereas four stood up for it, four kingdoms shall stand up out of the nation, but not in his power.

"And in the latter time of their kingdom, when iniquities are come to the full, there shall arise a king, insolent and strong, but not by his own power, to whom all things shall succeed after his own will; and he shall destroy the holy people, and through his policy also he shall cause craft to prosper in his hand, and he shall destroy many. He shall also stand up against the Prince of princes, but he shall perish miserably, and nevertheless by a violent hand."

Daniel ix. 20. "Whilst I was praying with all my heart, and confessing my sin and the sin of all my people, and prostrating myself before my God, even Gabriel, whom I had seen in the vision at the beginning, came to me and touched me about the time of the evening oblation, and he informed me and said, O Daniel, I am now come forth to give thee the knowledge of things. At the beginning of thy supplications I came to shew that which thou didst desire, for thou art greatly beloved: therefore understand the matter, and consider the vision. Seventy weeks are determined upon thy people, and upon thy holy city, to finish the transgression, and to make an end of sins, and to abolish iniquity, and to bring in everlasting righteousness; to accomplish the vision and the prophecies, and to anoint the Most Holy. (After which this people shall be no more thy people, nor this city the holy city. The times of wrath shall be passed, and the years of grace shall come for ever.)

"Know therefore, and understand, that, from the going forth of the commandment to restore and to build Jerusalem unto the Messiah the Prince, shall be seven weeks, and three score and two weeks." (The Hebrews were accustomed to divide numbers, and to place the small first. Thus, 7 and 62 make 69. Of this 70 there will then remain the 70th, that is to say, the 7 last years of which he will speak next.)

"The street shall be built again, and the wall, even in troublous times. And after three score and two weeks," (which have followed the first seven. Christ will then be killed after the sixty-nine weeks, that is to say, in the last week), "the Christ shall be cut off, and a people of the prince that shall come shall destroy the city and the sanctuary, and overwhelm all, and the end of that war shall accomplish the desolation."

"Now one week," (which is the seventieth, which remains), "shall confirm the covenant with many, and in the midst of the week," (that is to say, the last three and a half years), "he shall cause the sacrifice and the oblation to cease, and for the overspreading of abominations he shall make it desolate, even until the consummation, and that determined shall be poured upon the desolate."

Daniel, xi. The angel said to Daniel: "There shall stand up yet," (after Cyrus, under whom this still is), "three kings in Persia," (Cambyses, Smyrdis, Darius); "and the fourth who shall then come," (Xerxes) "shall be far richer than they all, and far stronger, and shall stir up all his people against the Greeks.

"But a mighty king shall stand up," (Alexander), "that shall rule with great dominion, and do according to his will. And when he shall stand up, his kingdom shall be broken, and shall be divided in four parts toward the four winds of heaven," (as he had said above, vi, 6, viii, 8), "but not his posterity; and his successors shall not equal his power, for his kingdom shall be plucked up, even for others besides these," (his four chief successors).

" And the king of the south," (Ptolemy, son of Lagos, Egypt), " shall be strong; but one of his princes shall be strong above him, and his dominion shall be a great dominion," (Seleucus, King of Syria. Appian says that he was the most powerful of Alexander's successors).

" And in the end of years they shall join themselves together, and the king's daughter of the south," (Berenice, daughter of Ptolemy Philadelphus, son of the other Ptolemy), " shall come to the king of the north," (to Antiochus Deus, King of Syria and of Asia, son of Seleucus Lagidas), " to make peace between these princes.

" But neither she nor her seed shall have a long authority; for she and they that brought her, and her children, and her friends, shall be delivered to death." (Berenice and her son were killed by Seleucus Callinicus.)

" But out of a branch of her roots shall one stand up," (Ptolemy Euergetes was the issue of the same father as Berenice), " which shall come with a mighty army into the land of the king of the north, where he shall put all under subjection, and he shall also carry captive into Egypt their gods, their princes, their gold, their silver, and all their precious spoils," (if he had not been called into Egypt by domestic reasons, says Justin, he would have entirely stripped Seleucus) ; " and he shall continue several years when the king of the north can do nought against him.

" And so he shall return into his kingdom. But his sons shall be stirred up, and shall assemble a multitude of great forces," (Seleucus Ceraunus, Antiochus the Great). " And their army shall come and overthrow all; wherefore the king of the south shall be moved with choler, and shall also form a great army, and fight him," (Ptolemy Philopator against Antiochus the Great at Raphia), " and conquer; and his troops shall become insolent, and his heart shall be lifted up," (this Ptolemy desecrated the temple: Josephus) : " he shall cast down many ten thousands, but he shall not be strengthened by it. For the king of the north," (Antiochus the Great), " shall return with a greater multitude than before, and in those times also a great number of enemies shall stand up against the king of the south," (during the reign of the young Ptolemy Epiphanes), "also the apostates and robbers of thy people shall exalt themselves to establish the vision; but they shall fall." (Those who abandon their religion to please Euergetes, when he will send his troops to Scopas; for Antiochus will again take Scopas, and conquer them.) "And the king of the north shall destroy the fenced cities, and the arms of the south shall not withstand, and all shall yield to his will; he shall stand in the land of Israel, and it shall yield to him. And thus he shall think to make himself master of all the empire of Egypt," (despising the youth of Epiphanes, says Justin). "And for that he shall make alliance with him, and give his daughter" (Cleopatra, in order that she may betray her husband. On which Appian says the doubting his ability to make himself master of Egypt by force, because of the protection of the Romans, he wished to attempt it by cunning). "He shall wish to corrupt her, but she shall not stand on his side, neither be for him. Then he shall turn his face to other designs, and shall think to make himself master of some isles," (that is to say, seaports), "and shall take many," (as Appian says).

"But a prince shall oppose his conquests," (Scipio Africanus, who stopped the progress of Antiochus the Great, because he offended the Romans in the person of their allies), "and shall cause the reproach offered by him to cease. He shall then return into his kingdom and there perish, and be no more." (He was slain by his soldiers.)

"And he who shall stand up in his estate," (Seleucus Philopator or Soter, the son of Antiochus the Great), "shall be a tyrant, a raiser of taxes in the glory of the kingdom," (which means the people), "but within a few days he shall be destroyed, neither in anger nor in battle. And in his place shall stand up a vile person, unworthy of the honour of the kingdom, but he shall come in cleverly by flatteries. All armies shall bend before him; he shall conquer them, and even the prince with whom he has made a covenant. For having renewed the league with him, he shall work deceitfully, and enter with a small people into his province, peaceably and without fear. He shall take the fattest places, and

shall do that which his fathers have not done, and ravage on
all sides. He shall forecast great devices during his time."

723

Prophecies.—The seventy weeks of Daniel are ambiguous
as regards the term of commencement, because of the terms
of the prophecy; and as regards the term of conclusion, because of the differences among chronologists. But all this
difference extends only to two hundred years.

724

Predictions.—That in the fourth monarchy, before the
destruction of the second temple, before the dominion of the
Jews was taken away, in the seventieth week of Daniel,
during the continuance of the second temple, the heathen
should be instructed, and brought to the knowledge of the
God worshipped by the Jews; that those who loved Him
should be delivered from their enemies, and filled with His
fear and love.

And it happened that in the fourth monarchy, before the
destruction of the second temple, &c., the heathen in great
number worshipped God, and led an angelic life. Maidens
dedicated their virginity and their life to God. Men renounced their pleasures. What Plato could only make acceptable to a few men, specially chosen and instructed, a
secret influence imparted, by the power of a few words, to
a hundred million ignorant men.

The rich left their wealth. Children left the dainty homes
of their parents to go into the rough desert. (See Philo the
Jew.) All this was foretold a great while ago. For two
thousand years no heathen had worshipped the God of the
Jew; and at the time foretold, a great number of the heathen
worshipped this only God. The temples were destroyed.
The very kings made submission to the cross. All this was
due to the Spirit of God, which was spread abroad upon the
earth.

No heathen, since Moses until Jesus Christ, believed according to the very Rabbis. A great number of the heathen,

after Jesus Christ, believed in the books of Moses, kept
them in substance and spirit, and only rejected what was
useless.

725

Prophecies.—The conversion of the Egyptians (Isaiah,
xix. 19) ; an altar in Egypt to the true God.

726

Prophecies.—In Egypt.—Pugio Fidei, p. 659. *Talmud.*

" It is a tradition among us, that, when the Messiah shall
come, the house of God, destined for the dispensation of
His Word, shall be full of filth and impurity; and that the
wisdom of the scribes shall be corrupt and rotten. Those
who shall be afraid to sin, shall be rejected by the people, and
treated as senseless fools."

Is. xlix.: " Listen, O isles, unto me, and hearken, ye people,
from afar: The Lord hath called me by my name from the
womb of my mother; in the shadow of His hand hath He hid
me, and hath made my words like a sharp sword, and said
unto me, Thou art my servant in whom I will be glorified.
Then I said, Lord, have I laboured in vain? have I spent my
strength for nought? yet surely my judgment is with Thee,
O Lord, and my work with Thee. And now, saith the Lord,
that formed me from the womb to be His servant, to bring
Jacob and Israel again to Him: Thou shalt be glorious in
my sight, and I will be thy strength. It is a light thing that
thou shouldst convert the tribes of Jacob; I have raised thee
up for a light to the Gentiles, that thou mayest be my salvation unto the ends of the earth. Thus saith the Lord to
him whom man despiseth, to him whom the nation abhorreth,
to a servant of rulers. Princes and kings shall worship thee,
because the Lord is faithful that hath chosen thee.

" Again saith the Lord unto me, I have heard thee in
the days of salvation and of mercy, and I will preserve thee
for a covenant of the people, to cause to inherit the desolate
nations, that thou mayest say to the prisoners: Go forth;
to them that are in darkness show yourselves, and possess
these abundant and fertile lands. They shall not hunger

nor thirst, neither shall the heat nor sun smite them; for he that hath mercy upon them shall lead them, even by the springs of waters shall he guide them, and make the mountains a way before them. Behold, the peoples shall come from all parts, from the east and from the west, from the north and from the south. Let the heavens give glory to God; let the earth be joyful; for it hath pleased the Lord to comfort His people, and He will have mercy upon the poor who hope in Him.

"Yet Sion dared to say: The Lord hath forsaken me, and hath forgotten me. Can a woman forget her child, that she should not have compassion on the son of her womb? but if she forget, yet will not I forget thee, O Sion. I will bear thee always between my hands, and thy walls are continually before me. They that shall build thee are come, and thy destroyers shall go forth of thee. Lift up thine eyes round about, and behold; all these gather themselves together, and come to thee. As I live, saith the Lord, thou shalt surely clothe thee with them all, as with an ornament, thy waste and thy desolate places, and the land of thy destruction, shall even now be too narrow by reason of the inhabitants, and the children thou shalt have after thy barrenness shall say again in thy ears: The place is too strait for me: give place to me that I may dwell. Then shalt thou say in thy heart: who hath begotten me these, seeing I have lost my children, and am desolate, a captive, and removing to and fro? and who brought up these? Behold, I was left alone; there, where had they been? And the Lord shall say to thee: Behold, I will lift up mine hand to the Gentiles, and set up my standard to the people; and they shall bring thy sons in their arms and in their bosoms. And kings shall be their nursing fathers, and queens their nursing mothers: they shall bow down to thee with their face toward the earth, and lick up the dust of thy feet; and thou shalt know that I am the Lord; for they shall not be ashamed that wait for me. Shall the prey be taken from the mighty? But even if the captives be taken away from the strong, nothing shall hinder me from saving thy children, and from destroying thy enemies; and all flesh shall know that I am the Lord, thy Saviour and thy Redeemer, the mighty One of Jacob.

"Thus saith the Lord: What is the bill of this divorcement, wherewith I have put away the synagogue? and why have I delivered it into the hands of your enemies? Is it not for your iniquities and for your transgressions that I have put it away?

"For I came, and no man received me; I called, and there was none to hear. Is my arm shortened that I cannot redeem?

"Therefore I will show the tokens of mine anger; I will clothe the heavens with darkness, and make sack cloth their covering.

"The Lord hath given me the tongue of the learned that I should know how to speak a word in season to him that is weary. He hath opened mine ear, and I have listened to Him as a master.

"The Lord hath revealed His will, and I was not rebellious.

"I gave my body to the smiters, and my cheeks to outrage; I hid not my face from shame and spitting. But the Lord hath helped me; therefore I have not been confounded.

"He is near that justifieth me; who will contend with me? who will be mine adversary, and accuse me of sin, God himself being my protector?

"All men shall pass away, and be consumed by time; let those that fear God hearken to the voice of His servant; let him that languisheth in darkness put his trust in the Lord. But as for you, ye do but kindle the wrath of God upon you; ye walk in the light of your fire and in the sparks that ye have kindled. This shall ye have of mine hand; ye shall lie down in sorrow.

"Hearken to me, ye that follow after righteousness, ye that seek the Lord: look unto the rock whence ye are hewn, and to the hole of the pit whence ye are digged. Look unto Abraham, your father, and unto Sarah that bare you: for I called him alone, when childless, and increased him. Behold, I have comforted Zion, and heaped upon her blessings and consolations.

"Hearken unto me, my people, and give ear unto me; for a law shall proceed from me, and I will make my judgment to rest for a light of the Gentiles."

Amos, viii. The prophet, having enumerated the sins of Israel, said that God had sworn to take vengeance on them.

He says this: "And it shall come to pass in that day, saith the Lord, that I will cause the sun to go down at noon, and I will darken the earth in the clear day; and I will turn your feasts into mourning, and all your songs into lamentation.

"You all shall have sorrow and suffering, and I will make this nation mourn as for an only son, and the end therefore as a bitter day. Behold, the days come, saith the Lord, that I will send a famine in the land, not a famine of bread, nor a thirst for water, but of hearing the words of the Lord. And they shall wander from sea to sea, and from the north even to the east; they shall run to and fro to seek the word of the Lord, and shall not find it.

"In that day shall the fair virgins and young men faint for thirst. They that have followed the idols of Samaria, and sworn by the god of Dan, and followed the manner of Beersheba, shall fall, and never rise up again."

Amos, iii. 2: "Ye only have I known of all the families of the earth for my people."

Daniel, xii. 7. Having described all the extent of the reign of the Messiah, he says: "All these things shall be finished, when the scattering of the people of Israel shall be accomplished."

Haggai, ii. 4: "Ye who, comparing this second house with the glory of the first, despise it, be strong, saith the Lord, be strong, O Zerubbabel, and O Jesus, the high priest, be strong, all ye people of the land, and work. For I am with you, saith the Lord of hosts; according to the word that I covenanted with you when ye came out of Egypt, so my spirit remaineth among you. Fear ye not. For thus saith the Lord of hosts: Yet one little while, and I will shake the heavens, and the earth, and the sea, and the dry land," (a way of speaking to indicate a great and an extraordinary change); "and I will shake all nations, and the desire of all the Gentiles shall come; and I will fill this house with glory, saith the Lord.

"The silver is mine, and the gold is mine, saith the Lord," (that is to say, it is not by that that I wish to be honoured;

as it is said elsewhere: All the beasts of the field are mine,
what advantages me that they are offered me in sacrifice?).
"The glory of this latter house shall be greater than of
the former, saith the Lord of hosts; and in this place will
I establish my house, saith the Lord.

"According to all that thou desiredst in Horeb in the
day of the assembly, saying, Let us not hear again the voice
of the Lord, neither let us see this fire any more, that we
die not. And the Lord said unto me, Their prayer is just.
I will raise them up a prophet from among their brethren,
like unto thee, and will put my words in his mouth; and
he shall speak unto them all that I shall command him. And
it shall come to pass, that whosoever will not hearken unto
my words which he will speak in my name, I will require it
of him."

Genesis, xlix. "Judah, thou art he whom thy brethren
shall praise, and thou shalt conquer thine enemies; thy
father's children shall bow down before thee. Judah is
a lion's whelp: from the prey, my son, thou art gone up,
and art couched as a lion, and as a lioness that shall be
roused up.

"The sceptre shall not depart from Judah, nor a law-
giver from between his feet, until Shiloh come; and unto
him shall the gathering of the people be."

727

*During the life of the Messiah.—Ænigmatis.—*Ezek. xvii.
His forerunner. Malachi, iii.

He will be born an infant. Is. ix.

He will be born in the village of Bethlehem. Micah, v.
He will appear chiefly in Jerusalem, and will be a descendant
of the family of Judah and of David.

He is to blind the learned and the wise, Is. vi., viii., xxix.,
&c.; and to preach the Gospel to the lowly, Is. xxix.; to
open the eyes of the blind, give health to the sick, and bring
light to those that languish in darkness. Is. lxi.

He is to show the perfect way, and be the teacher of the
Gentiles. Is. lv.; xlii. 1—7.

The prophecies are to be unintelligible to the wicked, Dan.

xii.; Hosea, xiv. 10; but they are to be intelligible to those who are well informed.

The prophecies, which represent Him as poor, represent Him as master of the nations. Is. lii. 14, &c.; liii.; Zech. ix. 9.

The prophecies, which foretell the time, foretell Him only as master of the nations and suffering, and not as in the clouds nor as judge. And those, which represent Him thus as judge and in glory, do not mention the time. When the Messiah is spoken of as great and glorious, it is as the judge of the world, and not its Redeemer.

He is to be the victim for the sins of the world. Is. xxxix., liii., &c.

He is to be the precious corner-stone. Is. xxviii., 16.

He is to be a stone of stumbling and offence. Is. viii. Jerusalem is to dash against this stone.

The builders are to reject this stone. Ps. cxvii. 22.

God is to make this stone the chief corner-stone.

And this stone is to grow into a huge mountain, and fill the whole earth. Dan. ii.

So He is to be rejected, despised, betrayed, (Ps. cviii. 8), sold (Zech. xi. 12), spit upon, buffeted, mocked, afflicted in innumerable ways, given gall to drink (Ps. lxviii.), pierced (Zech. xii.), His feet and His hands pierced, slain, and lots cast for His raiment.

He will rise again (Ps. xv.) the third day (Hosea, vi. 3).

He will ascend to heaven to sit on the right hand. Ps. cx.

The kings will arm themselves against Him. Ps. ii.

Being on the right hand of the Father, He will be victorious over His enemies.

The kings of the earth and all nations will worship Him. Is. lx.

The Jews will continue as a nation. Jeremiah.

They will wander, without kings, &c. (Hosea iii.), without prophets (Amos), looking for salvation and finding it not (Isaiah).

Calling of the Gentiles by Jesus Christ. Is lii. 15; lv. 5; lx., &c. Ps. lxxxi.

Hosea, i. 9: "Ye are not my people, and I will not be your God, when ye are multiplied after the dispersion. In the places where it was said, Ye are not my people, I will call them my people."

728

It was not lawful to sacrifice outside of Jerusalem, which was the place that the Lord has chosen, nor even to eat the tithes elsewhere. Deut. xii. 5, &c.; Deut. xiv. 23, &c.; xv. 20; xvi. 2, 7, 11, 15.

Hosea foretold that they should be without a king, without a prince, without a sacrifice, and without an idol; and this prophecy is now fulfilled, as they cannot make a lawful sacrifice out of Jerusalem.

729

Predictions.—It was foretold that, in the time of the Messiah, He should come to establish a new covenant, which should make them forget the escape from Egypt (Jer. xxiii. 5; Is. xliii. 16) that He should place His law not in externals, but in the heart; that He should put His fear, which had only been from without, in the midst of the heart. Who does not see the Christian law in all this?

730

. . . That then idolatry would be overthrown; that this Messiah would cast down all idols, and bring men into the worship of the true God.

That the temples of the idols would be cast down, and that among all nations, and in all places of the earth, He would be offered a pure sacrifice, not of beasts.

That He would be king of the Jews and Gentiles. And we see this king of the Jews and Gentiles oppressed by both, who conspire His death; and ruler of both, destroying the worship of Moses in Jerusalem, which was its centre, where He made His first Church; and also the worship of idols in Rome, the centre of it, where He made His chief Church.

731

Prophecies.—That Jesus Christ will sit on the right hand, till God has subdued His enemies.

Therefore He will not subdue them Himself.

732

". . . Then they shall teach no more every man his
neighbor, saying, Here is the Lord, *for God shall make Himself known to all*."

". . . Your sons shall prophesy." "I will put my spirit
and my fear *in your heart*."

All that is the same thing. To prophesy is to speak of
God, not from outward proofs, but from an inward and immediate feeling.

733

That He would teach men the perfect way.

And there has never come, before Him nor after Him,
any man who has taught anything divine approaching to
this.

734

. . . That Jesus Christ would be small in His beginning,
and would then increase. The little stone of Daniel.

If I had in no wise heard of the Messiah, nevertheless,
after such wonderful predictions of the course of the world
which I see fulfilled, I see that He is divine. And if I
knew that these same books foretold a Messiah, I should be
sure that He would come; and seeing that they place His
time before the destruction of the second temple, I should
say that He had come.

735

Prophecies.—That the Jews would reject Jesus Christ, and
would be rejected of God, for this reason, that the chosen
vine brought forth only wild grapes. That the chosen people
would be faithless, ungrateful, and unbelieving, *populum non
credentem et contradicentem.*[a] That God would strike them
with blindness, and in full noon they would grope like the
blind; and that a forerunner would go before Him.

736

Transfixerunt. Zech. xii. 10.

That a deliverer should come, who would crush the

[a] Isaiah, lxv. 2; Romans, x. 21.

demon's head, and free His people from their sins, *ex omnibus iniquitatibus;* that there should be a New Covenant, which would be eternal; that there should be another priesthood after the order of Melchisedek, and it should be eternal; that the Christ should be glorious, mighty, strong, and yet so poor that He would not be recognised, nor taken for what He is, but rejected and slain; that His people who denied Him should no longer be His people; that the idolaters should receive Him, and take refuge in Him; that He should leave Zion to reign in the centre of idolatry; that nevertheless the Jews should continue for ever; that He should be of Judah, and when there should be no longer a king.

SECTION XII

Proofs of Jesus Christ

737

THEREFORE I reject all other religions. In that way I find an answer to all objections. It is right that a God so pure should only reveal Himself to those whose hearts are purified. Hence this religion is lovable to me, and I find it now sufficiently justified by so divine a morality. But I find more in it.

I find it convincing that, since the memory of man has lasted, it was constantly announced to men that they were universally corrupt, but that a Redeemer should come; that it was not one man who said it, but innumerable men, and a whole nation, expressly made for the purpose, and prophesying for four thousand years. This is a nation which is more ancient than every other nation. Their books, scattered abroad, are four thousand years old.

The more I examine them, the more truths I find in them: an entire nation foretell Him before His advent, and an entire nation worship Him after His advent; what has preceded and what has followed; in short, people without idols and kings, this synagogue which was foretold, and these wretches who frequent it, and who, being our enemies, are admirable witnesses of the truth of these prophecies, wherein their wretchedness and even their blindness are foretold.

I find this succession, this religion, wholly divine in its authority, in its duration, in its perpetuity, in its morality, in its conduct, in its doctrine, in its effects. The frightful darkness of the Jews was foretold. *Eris palpans in meridie.*[1] *Dabitur liber scienti literas, et dicet: Non possum legere.*[2] While the sceptre was still in the hands of the first foreign usurper, there is the report of the coming of Jesus Christ.

[1] Deut., xxviii. 29.   [2] Isaiah, xxix. 12.

So I hold out my arms to my *Redeemer,* who, having been foretold for four thousand years, has come to suffer and to die for me on earth, at the time and under all the circumstances foretold. By His grace, I await death in peace, in the hope of being eternally united to Him. Yet I live with joy, whether in the prosperity which it pleases Him to bestow upon me, or in the adversity which He sends for my good, and which He has taught me to bear by His example.

738

The prophecies having given different signs which should all happen at the advent of the Messiah, it was necessary that all these signs should occur at the same time. So it was necessary that the fourth monarchy should have come, when the seventy weeks of Daniel were ended; and that the sceptre should have then departed from Judah. And all this happened without any difficulty. Then it was necessary that the Messiah should come; and Jesus Christ then came, who was called the Messiah. And all this again was without difficulty. This indeed shows the truth of the prophecies.

739

The prophets foretold, and were not foretold. The saints again were foretold, but did not foretell. Jesus Christ both foretold and was foretold.

740

Jesus Christ, whom the two Testaments regard, the Old as its hope, the New as its model, and both as their centre.

741

The two oldest books in the world are those of Moses and Job, the one a Jew and the other a Gentile. Both of them look upon Jesus Christ as their common centre and object: Moses in relating the promises of God to Abraham, Jacob, &c., and his prophecies; and Job, *Quis mihi det ut,* &c. *Scio enim quod redemptor meus vivit,* &c.[3]

[3] Job, xix. 23-25.

742

The Gospel only speaks of the virginity of the Virgin up to the time of the birth of Jesus Christ. All with reference to Jesus Christ.

743

Proofs of Jesus Christ.
Why was the book of Ruth preserved?
Why the story of Tamar?

744

" Pray that ye enter not into temptation." It is dangerous to be tempted; and people are tempted because they do not pray.

Et tu conversus confirma fratres tuos.[4] But before, *conversus Jesus respexit Petrum.*[5]

Saint Peter asks permission to strike Malchus, and strikes before hearing the answer. Jesus Christ replies afterwards.

The word, *Galilee,* which the Jewish mob pronounced as if by chance, in accusing Jesus Christ before Pilate, afforded Pilate a reason for sending Jesus Christ to Herod. And thereby the mystery was accomplished, that He should be judged by Jews and Gentiles. Chance was apparently the cause of the accomplishment of the mystery.

745

Those who have a difficulty in believing seek a reason in the fact that the Jews do not believe. " Were this so clear," say they, " why did the Jews not believe?" And they almost wish that they had believed, so as not to be kept back by the example of their refusal. But it is their very refusal that is the foundation of our faith. We should be much less disposed to the faith, if they were on our side. We should then have a more ample pretext. The wonderful thing is to have made the Jews great lovers of the things foretold, and great enemies of their fulfilment.

4 Luke, xxii. 32.   5 Luke, xxii. 61.

746

The Jews were accustomed to great and striking miracles, and so, having had the great miracles of the Red Sea and of the land of Canaan as an epitome of the great deeds of their Messiah, they therefore looked for more striking miracles, of which those of Moses were only the patterns.

747

The carnal Jews and the heathen have their calamities, and Christians also. There is no Redeemer for the heathen, for they do not so much as hope for one. There is no Redeemer for the Jews; they hope for Him in vain. There is a Redeemer only for Christians. (*See* Perpetuity.)

748

In the time of the Messiah the people divided themselves. The spiritual embraced the Messiah, and the coarser-minded remained to serve as witnesses of Him.

749

"If this was clearly foretold to the Jews, how did they not believe it, or why were they not destroyed for resisting a fact so clear?"

I reply: in the first place, it was foretold both that they would not believe a thing so clear, and that they would not be destroyed. And nothing is more to the glory of the Messiah; for it was not enough that there should be prophets; their prophets must be kept above suspicion. Now, &c.

750

If the Jews had all been converted by Jesus Christ, we should have none but questionable witnesses. And if they had been entirely destroyed, we should have no witnesses at all.

751

What do the prophets say of Jesus Christ? That He will be clearly God? No; but that He is a God truly hidden; that He will be slighted; that none will think that it is He; that He will be a stone of stumbling, upon which many will stumble, &c. Let people then reproach us no longer for want of clearness, since we make profession of it.

But, it is said, there are obscurities.—And without that, no one would have stumbled over Jesus Christ, and this is one of the formal pronouncements of the prophets: *Excæca*.[6]

752

Moses first teaches the Trinity, original sin, the Messiah.

David: a great witness; a king, good, merciful, a beautiful soul, a sound mind, powerful. He prophesies, and his wonder comes to pass. This is infinite.

He had only to say that he was the Messiah, if he had been vain; for the prophecies are clearer about him than about Jesus Christ. And the same with Saint John.

753

Herod was believed to be the Messiah. He had taken away the sceptre from Judah, but he was not of Judah. This gave rise to a considerable sect.

Curse of the Greeks upon those who count three periods of time.

In what way should the Messiah come, seeing that through Him the sceptre was to be eternally in Judah, and at His coming the sceptre was to be taken away from Judah?

In order to effect that seeing they should not see, and hearing they should not understand, nothing could be better done.

754

Homo existens te Deum facit.[7]
Scriptum est, Dii estis, et non potest solvi Scriptura.[8]

---

[6] Isaiah, vi. 10.   [7] "Man existing makes thee God."
[8] "It is written, 'You are Gods,' and the Scripture cannot be overthrown."

Hæc infirmitas non est ad vitam et est ad mortem.[9]
Lazarus dormit, et deinde dixit: Lazarus mortuus est[10]

755

The apparent discrepancy of the Gospels.

736

What can we have but reverence for a man who foretells plainly things which come to pass, and who declares his intention both to blind and to enlighten, and who intersperses obscurities among the clear things which come to pass?

757

The time of the first advent was foretold; the time of the second is not so; because the first was to be obscure, and the second is to be brilliant, and so manifest that even His enemies will recognise it. But, as He was first to come only in obscurity, and to be known only of those who searched the Scriptures. . . .

758

God, in order to cause the Messiah to be known by the good and not to be known by the wicked, made Him to be foretold in this manner. If the manner of the Messiah had been clearly foretold, there would have been no obscurity, even for the wicked. If the time had been obscurely foretold, there would have been obscurity, even for the good. For their [goodness of heart] would not have made them understand, for instance, that the closed *mem* signifies six hundred years. But the time has been clearly foretold, and the manner in types.

By this means, the wicked, taking the promised blessings for material blessings, have fallen into error, in spite of the clear prediction of the time; and the good have not fallen into error. For the understanding of the promised bless-

---

[9] " This sickness is not unto life, and is unto death."
[10] John, xi. 11, 14.

ings depends on the heart, which calls "good" that which it loves; but the understanding of the promised time does not depend on the heart. And thus the clear prediction of the time, and the obscure prediction of the blessings, deceive the wicked alone.

759

Either the Jews or the Christians must be wicked.

760

The Jews reject Him, but not all. The saints receive Him, and not the carnal-minded. And so far is this from being against His glory, that it is the last touch which crowns it. For their argument, the only one found in all their writings, in the Talmud and in the Rabbinical writings, amounts only to this, that Jesus Christ has not subdued the nations with sword in hand, *gladium tuum, potentissime.*[11] Is this all they have to say? Jesus Christ has been slain, say they. He has failed. He has not subdued the heathen with His might. He has not bestowed upon us their spoil. He does not give riches. Is this all they have to say? It is in this respect that He is lovable to me. I would not desire Him whom they fancy. It is evident that it is only His life which has prevented them from accepting Him; and through this rejection they are irreproachable witnesses, and, what is more, they thereby accomplish the prophecies.

[By means of the fact that this people have not accepted Him, this miracle here has happened. The prophecies were the only lasting miracles which could be wrought, but they were liable to be denied.]

761

The Jews, in slaying Him in order not to receive Him as the Messiah, have given Him the final proof of being the Messiah.

And in continuing not to recognise Him, they made themselves irreproachable witnesses. Both in slaying Him, and in continuing to deny Him, they have fulfilled the prophecies (Isa. lx.; Ps. lxxi.).

[11] Psalms, xlv. 3.

762

What could the Jews, His enemies, do? If they receive Him, they give proof of Him by their reception; for then the guardians of the expectation of the Messiah receive Him. If they reject Him, they give proof of Him by their rejection.

763

The Jews, in testing if He were God, have shown that He was man.

764

The Church has had as much difficulty in showing that Jesus Christ was man, against those who denied it, as in showing that he was God; and the probabilities were equally great.

765

Source of contradictions.—A God humiliated, even to the death on the cross; a Messiah triumphing over death by his own death. Two natures in Jesus Christ, two advents, two states of man's nature.

766

Types.—Saviour, father, sacrificer, offering, food, king, wise, law-giver, afflicted, poor, having to create a people whom He must lead and nourish and bring into His land . . .

Jesus Christ. Offices.—He alone had to create a great people, elect, holy, and chosen; to lead, nourish, and bring it into the place of rest and holiness; to make it holy to God; to make it the temple of God; to reconcile it to, and save it from the wrath of God; to free it from the slavery of sin, which visibly reigns in man; to give laws to this people, and engrave these laws on their heart; to offer Himself to God for them, and sacrifice Himself for them; to be a victim without blemish, and Himself the sacrificer, having to offer Himself, His body, and His blood, and yet to offer bread and wine to God . . .

Ingrediens mundum.[12]

" Stone upon stone."

What preceded and what followed. All the Jews exist still, and are wanderers.

767

Of all that is on earth, He partakes only of the sorrows, not of the joys. He loves His neighbours, but His love does not confine itself within these bounds, and overflows to His own enemies, and then to those of God.

768

Jesus Christ typified by Joseph, the beloved of his father, sent by his father to see his brethren, &c., innocent, sold by his brethren for twenty pieces of silver, and thereby becoming their lord, their saviour, the saviour of strangers, and the saviour of the world; which had not been but for their plot to destroy him, their sale and their rejection of him.

In prison Joseph innocent between two criminals; Jesus Christ on the cross between two thieves. Joseph foretells freedom to the one, and death to the other, from the same omens. Jesus Christ saves the elect, and condemns the outcast for the same sins. Joseph foretells only; Jesus Christ acts. Joseph asks him who will be saved to remember him, when he comes into his glory; and he whom Jesus Christ saves asks that He will remember him, when He comes into His kingdom.

769

The conversion of the heathen was only reserved for the grace of the Messiah. The Jews have been so long in opposition to them without success; all that Solomon and the prophets said has been useless. Sages, like Plato and Socrates, have not been able to persuade them.

770

After many persons had gone before, Jesus Christ at last came to say: " Here am I, and this is the time. That which the prophets have said was to come in the fulness of

[12] Hebrews, x. 5.

time, I tell you My apostles will do. The Jews shall be cast
out. Jerusalem shall be soon destroyed. And the heathen
shall enter into the knowledge of God. My apostles shall
do this after you have slain the heir of the vineyard."

Then the apostles said to the Jews: "You shall be
accursed," (*Celsus laughed at it*) ; and to the heathen, "You
shall enter into the knowledge of God." And this then
came to pass.

771

Jesus Christ came to blind those who saw clearly, and to
give sight to the blind; to heal the sick, and leave the healthy
to die; to call to repentance, and to justify sinners, and to
leave the righteous in their sins; to fill the needy, and leave
the rich empty.

772

Holiness.—*Effundum spiritum meum.*[13] All nations were
in unbelief and lust. The whole world now became fervent
with love. Princes abandoned their pomp; maidens suffered
martyrdom. Whence came this influence? The Messiah was
come. These were the effect and signs of His coming.

773

Destruction of the Jews and heathen by Jesus Christ:
Omnes gentes venient et adorabunt eum.[14] *Parum est ut,*
&c.[15] *Postula a me.*[16] *Adorabunt eum omnes reges.*[17] *Testes
iniqui.*[18] *Dabit maxillam percutienti.*[19] *Dederunt fel in
escam.*[20]

774

Jesus Christ for all, Moses for a nation.

The Jews blessed in Abraham: "I will bless those that
bless thee." But: "All nations blessed in his seed." *Parum
est ut,* &c.

Lumen ad revelationem gentium.[21]

Non fecit taliter omni nationi,[22] said David, in speaking
of the Law. But, in speaking of Jesus Christ, we must say:

[13] Joel, ii. 28.   [14] Psalms xxii. 27.   [15] Isaiah xlix. 6.   [16] Psalms ii. 8.
[17] Psalms lxxii. 11.   [18] Psalms xxxv. 11.   [19] Lament. iii. 30.
[20] Psalms lxix. 21.   [21] Luke ii. 31.   [22] Psalms cxlvii. 20.

Fecit taliter omni nationi. Parum est ut, &c., Isaiah. So it belongs to Jesus Christ to be universal. Even the Church offers sacrifice only for the faithful. Jesus Christ offered that of the cross for all.

775

There is heresy in always explaining *omnes* by " all," and heresy in not explaining it sometimes by " all." *Bibite ex hoc omnes;*[23] the Huguenots are heretics in explaining it by " all." *In quo omnes peccaverunt;*[24] the Huguenots are heretics in excepting the children of true believers. We must then follow the Fathers and tradition in order to know when to do so, since there is heresy to be feared on both sides.

776

Ne timeas pusillus grex.[25] *Timore et tremore.—Quid ergo? Ne timeas* [modo] *timeas.* Fear not, provided you fear; but if you fear not, then fear.

Qui me recipit, non me recipit, sed eum qui me misit.[26]
Nemo scit, neque Filius.[27]
Nubes lucida obumbravit.[28]

Saint John was to turn the hearts of the fathers to the children, and Jesus Christ to plant division. There is no contradiction.

777

The effects *in communi* and *in particulari.*[29] The semi-Pelagians err in saying of *in communi* what is true only *in particulari;* and the Calvinists in saying *in particulari* what is true *in communi.* Such is my opinion.

778

Omnis Judæa regio, et Jerosolomytæ universi, et baptizabantur.[30] Because of all the conditions of men who came there.

From these stones there *can* come children unto Abraham.

[23] Matt. xxvi. 27.   [24] Rom. v. 12.   [25] Luke xii. 32.   [26] Matt. x. 40.
[27] Matt. xi. 27.   [28] Matt. xvii. 5.   [29] " In general," " in particular."
[30] Mark i. 5.

779

If men knew themselves, God would heal and pardon them. *Ne convertantur et sanem eos, et dimittantur eis peccata.*[31]

780

Jesus Christ never condemned without hearing. To Judas: *Amice, ad quid venisti?*[32] To him that had not on the wedding garment, the same.

781

The types of the completeness of the Redemption, as that the sun gives light to all, indicate only completeness; but [*the types*] of exclusions, as of the Jews elected to the exclusion of the Gentiles, indicate exclusion.

"Jesus Christ the Redeemer of all."—Yes, for He has offered, like a man who has ransomed all those who were willing to come to Him. If any die on the way, it is their misfortune; but, so far as He was concerned, He offered them redemption.—That holds good in this example, where he who ransoms and he who prevents death are two persons, but not of Jesus Christ, who does both these things.—No, for Jesus Christ, in the quality of Redeemer, is not perhaps Master of all; and thus, in so far as it is in Him, He is the Redeemer of all.

When it is said that Jesus Christ did not die for all, you take undue advantage of a fault in men who at once apply this exception to themselves; and this is to favour despair, instead of turning them from it to favour hope. For men thus accustom themselves to inward virtues by outward customs.

782

The victory over death. What is a man advantaged if he gain the whole world and lose his own soul? Whosoever will save his soul, shall lose it.

"I am not come to destroy the law, but to fulfil."

[31] Mark iv. 12.   [32] Matt. xxvi. 50.

"Lambs took not away the sins of the world, but I am the lamb which taketh away the sins."

"Moses gave you not the bread from heaven. Moses hath not led you out of captivity, and made you truly free."

783

. . . Then Jesus Christ comes to tell men that they have no other enemies but themselves; that it is their passions which keep them apart from God; that He comes to destroy these, and give them His grace, so as to make of them all one Holy Church; that He comes to bring back into this Church the heathen and Jews; that He comes to destroy the idols of the former and the superstition of the latter. To this all men are opposed, not only from the natural opposition of lust; but, above all, the kings of the earth, as had been foretold, join together to destroy this religion at its birth. (*Proph.: Quare fermerunt gentes . . . reges terræ*[88] *. . . adversus Christum.*)

All that is great on earth is united together; the learned, the wise, the kings. The first write; the second condemn; the last kill. And notwithstanding all these oppositions, these men, simple and weak, resist all these powers, subdue even these kings, these learned men and these sages, and remove idolatry from all the earth. And all this is done by the power which had foretold it.

784

Jesus Christ would not have the testimony of devils, nor of those who were not called, but of God and John the Baptist.

785

I consider Jesus Christ in all persons and in ourselves: Jesus Christ as a Father in His Father, Jesus Christ as a Brother in His Brethren, Jesus Christ as poor in the poor, Jesus Christ as rich in the rich, Jesus Christ as Doctor and Priest in priests, Jesus Christ as Sovereign in princes, &c. For by His glory He is all that is great, being God; and by

[88] Psalms ii. 1-2. (Taken as a prophecy of Christ.)

His mortal life He is all that is poor and abject. Therefore
He has taken this unhappy condition, so that He could
be in all persons, and the model of all conditions.

786

Jesus Christ is an obscurity (according to what the world
calls obscurity), such that historians, writing only of important matters of states, have hardly noticed Him.

787

*On the fact that neither Josephus, nor Tacitus, nor other
historians have spoken of Jesus Christ.*—So far is this from
telling against Christianity, that on the contrary it tells for
it. For it is certain that Jesus Christ has existed; that His
religion has made a great talk; and that these persons were
not ignorant of it. Thus it is plain that they purposely
concealed it, or that, if they did speak of it, their account
has been suppressed or changed.

788

"I have reserved me seven thousand." I love the worshippers unknown to the world and to the very prophets.

789

As Jesus Christ remained unknown among men, so His
truth remains among common opinions without external
difference. Thus the Eucharist among ordinary bread.

790

Jesus would not be slain without the forms of justice; for
it is far more ignominious to die by justice than by an
unjust sedition.

791

The false justice of Pilate only serves to make Jesus
Christ suffer; for he causes Him to be scourged by his false
justice, and afterwards puts Him to death. It would have
been better to have put Him to death at once. Thus it is

with the falsely just. They do good and evil works to please the world, and to show that they are not altogether of Jesus Christ; for they are ashamed of Him. And at last, under great temptations and on great occasions, they kill Him.

792

What man ever had more renown? The whole Jewish people foretell Him before His coming. The Gentile people worship Him after His coming. The two peoples, Gentile and Jewish, regard Him as their centre.

And yet what man enjoys this renown less? Of thirty-three years, He lives thirty without appearing. For three years He passes as an impostor; the priests and the chief people reject Him; His friends and His nearest relatives despise Him. Finally, He dies, betrayed by one of His own disciples, denied by another, and abandoned by all.

What part, then, has He in this renown? Never had man so much renown; never had man more ignominy. All that renown has served only for us, to render us capable of recognising Him; and He had none of it for Himself.

793

The infinite distance between body and mind is a symbol of the infinitely more infinite distance between mind and charity; for charity is supernatural.

All the glory of greatness has no lustre for people who are in search of understanding.

The greatness of clever men is invisible to kings, to the rich, to chiefs, and to all the worldly great.

The greatness of wisdom, which is nothing if not of God, is invisible to the carnal-minded and to the clever. These are three orders differing in kind.

Great geniuses have their power, their glory, their greatness, their victory, their lustre, and have no need of worldly greatness, with which they are not in keeping. They are seen, not by the eye, but by the mind; this is sufficient.

The saints have their power, their glory, their victory, their lustre, and need no worldly or intellectual greatness, with which they have no affinity; for these neither add anything to them, nor take away anything from them. They are seen of God and the angels, and not of the body, nor of the curious mind. God is enough for them.

Archimedes, apart from his rank, would have the same veneration. He fought no battles for the eyes to feast upon; but he has given his discoveries to all men. Oh! how brilliant he was to the mind!

Jesus Christ, without riches, and without any external exhibition of knowledge, is in His own order of holiness. He did not invent; He did not reign. But He was humble, patient, holy, holy to God, terrible to devils, without any sin. Oh! in what great pomp, and in what wonderful splendour, He is come to the eyes of the heart, which perceive wisdom!

It would have been useless for Archimedes to have acted the prince in his books on geometry, although he was a prince.

It would have been useless for our Lord Jesus Christ to come like a king, in order to shine forth in His kingdom of holiness. But He came there appropriately in the glory of His own order.

It is most absurd to take offence at the lowliness of Jesus Christ, as if His lowliness were in the same order as the greatness which He came to manifest. If we consider this greatness in His life, in His passion, in His obscurity, in His death, in the choice of His disciples, in their desertion, in His secret resurrection, and the rest, we shall see it to be so immense, that we shall have no reason for being offended at a lowliness which is not of that order.

But there are some who can only admire worldly greatness, as though there were no intellectual greatness; and others who only admire intellectual greatness, as though there were not infinitely higher things in wisdom.

All bodies, the firmament, the stars, the earth and its kingdoms, are not equal to the lowest mind; for mind knows all these and itself; and these bodies nothing.

All bodies together, and all minds together, and all their products, are not equal to the least feeling of charity. This is of an order infinitely more exalted.

From all bodies together, we cannot obtain one little thought; this is impossible, and of another order. From all bodies and minds, we cannot produce a feeling of true charity; this is impossible, and of another and supernatural order.

794

Why did Jesus Christ not come in a visible manner, instead of obtaining testimony of Himself from preceding prophecies? Why did He cause Himself to be foretold in types?

795

If Jesus Christ had only come to sanctify, all Scripture and all things would tend to that end; and it would be quite easy to convince unbelievers. If Jesus Christ had only come to blind, all His conduct would be confused; and we would have no means of convincing unbelievers. But as he came *in sanctificationem et in scandalum*,[34] as Isaiah says, we cannot convince unbelievers, and they cannot convince us. But by this very fact we convince them; since we say that in his whole conduct there is no convincing proof on one side or the other.

796

Jesus Christ does not say that He is not of Nazareth, in order to leave the wicked in their blindness; nor that He is not Joseph's son.

797

Proofs of Jesus Christ.—Jesus Christ said great things so simply, that it seems as though He had not thought them great; and yet so clearly that we easily see what He thought of them. This clearness, joined to this simplicity, is wonderful.

798

The style of the gospel is admirable in so many ways, and among the rest in hurling no invectives against the persecutors and enemies of Jesus Christ. For there is no such invective in any of the historians against Judas, Pilate, or any of the Jews.

If this moderation of the writers of the Gospels had been assumed, as well as many other traits of so beautiful a char-

---

[34] Isaiah viii. 14.

acter, and they had only assumed it to attract notice, even
if they had not dared to draw attention to it themselves,
they would not have failed to secure friends, who would
have made such remarks to their advantage. But as they
acted thus without pretence, and from wholly disinterested
motives, they did not point it out to any one; and I believe
that many such facts have not been noticed till now, which
is evidence of the natural disinterestedness with which the
thing has been done.

799

An artisan who speaks of wealth, a lawyer who speaks of
war, of royalty, &c.; but the rich man rightly speaks of
wealth, a king speaks indifferently of a great gift he has
just made, and God rightly speaks of God.

800

Who has taught the evangelists the qualities of a perfectly
heroic soul, that they paint it so perfectly in Jesus Christ?
Why do they make Him weak in His agony? Do they not
know how to paint a resolute death? Yes, for the same
Saint Luke paints the death of Saint Stephen as braver
than that of Jesus Christ.

They make Him therefore capable of fear, before the
necessity of dying has come, and then altogether brave.

But when they make Him so troubled, it is when He afflicts
Himself; and when men afflict Him, He is altogether strong.

801

Proof of Jesus Christ.—The supposition that the apostles
were impostors is very absurd. Let us think it out. Let
us imagine those twelve men, assembled after the death of
Jesus Christ, plotting to say that He was risen. By this
they attack all the powers. The heart of man is strangely
inclined to fickleness, to change, to promises, to gain. However little any of them might have been led astray by all
these attractions, nay more, by the fear of prisons, tortures,
and death, they were lost. Let us follow up this thought.

802

The apostles were either deceived or deceivers. Either supposition has difficulties; for it is not possible to mistake a man raised from the dead . . .

While Jesus Christ was with them, He could sustain them. But, after that, if He did not appear to them, who inspired them to act?

SECTION XIII

The Miracles

803

*T*HE *beginning*.—Miracles enable us to judge of doctrine, and doctrine enables us to judge of miracles.

There are false miracles and true. There must be a distinction, in order to know them; otherwise they would be useless. Now they are not useless; on the contrary, they are fundamental. Now the rule which is given to us must be such, that it does not destroy the proof which the true miracles give of the truth, which is the chief end of the miracles.

Moses has given two rules: that the prediction does not come to pass (Deut. xviii.), and that they do not lead to idolatry (Deut. xiii.); and Jesus Christ one.

If doctrine regulates miracles, miracles are useless for doctrine.

If miracles regulate . . .

Objection to the rule.—The distinction of the times. One rule during the time of Moses, another at present.

804

Miracle.—It is an effect, which exceeds the natural power of the means which are employed for it; and what is not a miracle is an effect, which does not exceed the natural power of the means which are employed for it. Thus, those who heal by invocation of the devil do not work a miracle; for that does not exceed the natural power of the devil. But . . .

805

The two fundamentals; one inward, the other outward; grace and miracles; both supernatural.

806

Miracles and truth are necessary, because it is necessary to convince the entire man, in body and soul.

807

In all times, either men have spoken of the true God, or the true God has spoken to men.

808

Jesus Christ has verified that He was the Messiah, never in verifying His doctrine by Scripture and the prophecies, but always by His miracles.

He proves by a miracle that He remits sins.

Rejoice not in your miracles, said Jesus Christ, but because your names are written in heaven.

If they believe not Moses, neither will they believe one risen from the dead.

Nicodemus recognises by His miracles that His teaching is of God. *Scimus quia venisti a Deo magister; nemo enim potest hæc signa facere quæ tu facis nisi Deus fuerit cum eo.*[1] He does not judge of the miracles by the teaching, but of the teaching by the miracles.

The Jews had a doctrine of God as we have one of Jesus Christ, and confirmed by miracles. They were forbidden to believe every worker of miracles; and they were further commanded to have recourse to the chief priests, and to rely on them.

And thus, in regard to their prophets, they had all those reasons which we have for refusing to believe the workers of miracles.

And yet they were very sinful in rejecting the prophets, and Jesus Christ, because of their miracles; and they would not have been culpable, if they had not seen the miracles. *Nisi fecissem . . . peccatum non haberent.*[2] Therefore all belief rests upon miracles.

Prophecy is not called miracle; as Saint John speaks of the first miracle in Cana, and then of what Jesus Christ says

[1] John iii. 2.   [2] John xv. 24.

to the woman of Samaria, when He reveals to her all her hidden life. Then He heals the centurion's son; and Saint John calls this "the second miracle."

809

The combinations of miracles.

810

The second miracle can suppose the first, but the first cannot suppose the second.

811

Had it not been for the miracles, there would have been no sin in not believing in Jesus Christ.

812

I should not be a Christian, but for the miracles, said Saint Augustine.

813

Miracles.—How I hate those who make men doubt of miracles! Montaigne speaks of them as he should in two places. In one, we see how careful he is; and yet, in the other he believes, and makes sport of unbelievers.

However it may be, the Church is without proofs if they are right.

814

Montaigne against miracles.
Montaigne for miracles.

815

It is not possible to have a reasonable belief against miracles.

816

Unbelievers the most credulous. They believe the miracles of Vespasian, in order not to believe those of Moses.

817

Title: How it happens that men believe so many liars, who say that they have seen miracles, and do not believe any of those who say that they have secrets to make men immortal, or restore youth to them.—Having considered how it happens that so great credence is given to so many impostors, who say they have remedies, often to the length of men putting their lives into their hands, it has appeared to me that the true cause is that there are true remedies. For it would not be possible that there should be so many false remedies, and that so much faith should be placed in them, if there were none true. If there had never been any remedy for any ill, and all ills had been incurable, it is impossible that men should have imagined that they could give remedies, and still more impossible that so many others should have believed those who boasted of having remedies; in the same way as did a man boast of preventing death, no one would believe him, because there is no example of this. But as there were a number of remedies found to be true by the very knowledge of the greatest men, the belief of men is thereby induced; and, this being known to be possible, it has been therefore concluded that it was. For people commonly reason thus: " A thing is possible, therefore it is "; because the thing cannot be denied generally, since there are particular effects which are true, the people, who cannot distinguish which among these particular effects are true, believe them all. In the same way, the reason why so many false effects are credited to the moon, is that there are some true, as the tide.

It is the same with prophecies, miracles, divination by dreams, sorceries, &c. For if there had been nothing true in all this, men would have believed nothing of them; and thus, instead of concluding that there are no true miracles because there are so many false, we must, on the contrary, say that there certainly are true miracles, since there are false, and that there are false miracles only because some are true. We must reason in the same way about religion; for it would not be possible that men should have imagined so many false religions, if there had not been a true one. The objection to this is that savages have a religion; but the answer is that they have heard the true spoken of, as appears by the deluge, circumcision, the cross of Saint Andrew, &c.

818

Having considered how it comes that there are so many false miracles, false revelations, sorceries, &c., it has seemed to me that the true cause is that there are some true; for it would not be possible that there should be so many false miracles, if there were none true, nor so many false revelations, if there were none true, nor so many false religions, if there were not one true. For if there had never been all this, it is almost impossible that men should have imagined it, and still more impossible that so many others should have believed it. But as there have been very great things true, and as they have been believed by great men, this impression has been the cause that nearly everybody is rendered capable of believing also the false. And thus, instead of concluding that there are no true miracles, since there are so many false, it must be said, on the contrary, that there are true miracles, since there are so many false; and that there are false ones only because there are true; and that in the same way there are false religions because there is one true.—Objection to this: savages have a religion. But this is because they have heard the true spoken of, as appears by the cross of Saint Andrew, the deluge, circumcision, &c. —This arises from the fact that the human mind, finding itself inclined to that side by the truth, becomes thereby susceptible of all the falsehoods of this . . .

819

Jeremiah, xxiii. 32. The *miracles* of the false prophets. In the Hebrew and Vatable[8] they are the *tricks*.

Miracle does not always signify miracle. 1 Sam., xiv. 15; *miracle* signifies *fear,* and is so in the Hebrew. The same evidently in Job, xxxiii. 7; and also Isaiah, xxi. 4; Jeremiah, xliv. 12. *Portentum* signifies *simulacrum,* Jeremiah, l. 38;

[8] Professor of Hebrew in the College Royal in the 16th Century.

and it is so in the Hebrew and Vatable. Isaiah, viii. 18.
Jesus Christ says that He and His will be in *miracles*.

820

If the devil favoured the doctrine which destroys him,
he would be divided against himself, as Jesus Christ said.
If God favoured the doctrine which destroys the Church,
He would be divided against Himself. *Omne regnum
divisum.*[4] For Jesus Christ wrought against the devil, and
destroyed his power over the heart, of which exorcism is
the symbolisation, in order to establish the kingdom of God.
And thus He adds, *Si in digito Dei regnum Dei ad vos.*[5]

821

There is a great difference between tempting and leading
into error. God tempts, but He does not lead into error.
To tempt is to afford opportunities, which impose no necessity; if men do not love God, they will do a certain thing.
To lead into error is to place a man under the necessity
of inferring and following out what is untrue.

822

Abraham and Gideon are above revelation. The Jews
blinded themselves in judging of miracles by the Scripture.
God has never abandoned His true worshippers.

I prefer to follow Jesus Christ than any other, because
He has miracle, prophecy, doctrine, perpetuity, &c.

The Donatists. No miracle which obliges them to say it
is the devil.

The more we particularise God, Jesus Christ, the
Church . . .

823

If there were no false miracles, there would be certainty.
If there were no rule to judge of them, miracles would be
useless, and there would be no reason for believing.

Now there is, humanly speaking, no human certainty, but
we have reason.

[4] Matt. xii. 25.   [5] Luke xi. 20.

824

Either God has confounded the false miracles, or He has foretold them; and in both ways He has raised Himself above what is supernatural with respect to us, and has raised us to it.

825

Miracles serve not to convert, but to condemn. (Q. 113, A. 10, *Ad.* 2.)

826

Reasons why we do not believe.

John, xii. 37. *Cum autem tanta signa fecisset, non credebant in eum, ut sermo Isayæ impleretur. Excæcavit,* &c.

Hæc dixit Isaias, quando vidit gloriam ejus et locutus est de eo.

Judæi signa petunt et Græci sapientiam quærunt, nos autem Jesum crucifixum. Sed plenum signis, sed plenum sapientia; vos autem Christum non crucifixum et religionem sine miraculis et sine sapientia.[6]

What makes us not believe in the true miracles, is want of love. John: *Sed vos non creditis, quia non estis ex ovibus.*[7] What makes us believe the false is want of love. 1 Thess. ii.

The foundation of religion. It is the miracles. What then? Does God speak against miracles, against the foundations of the faith which we have in Him?

If there is a God, faith in God must exist on earth. Now the miracles of Jesus Christ are not foretold by Antichrist, but the miracles of Antichrist are foretold by Jesus Christ. And so if Jesus Christ were not the Messiah, He would have indeed led into error; but Antichrist cannot surely lead into error. When Jesus Christ foretold the miracles of Antichrist, did He think of destroying faith in His own miracles?

Moses foretold Jesus Christ, and bade to follow Him. Jesus Christ foretold Antichrist, and forbade to follow him.

It was impossible that in the time of Moses men should

<hr />

[6] 1 Cor. i. 22.   [7] John x. 26.

keep their faith for Antichrist, who was unknown to them. But it is quite easy, in the time of Antichrist, to believe in Jesus Christ, already known.

There is no reason for believing in Antichrist, which there is not for believing in Jesus Christ. But there are reasons for believing in Jesus Christ, which there are not for believing in the other.

827

Judges xiii. 23: "If the Lord were pleased to kill us, He would not have shewed us all these things."

Hezekiah, Sennacherib.

Jeremiah. Hananiah, the false prophet, dies in seven months.

2 Macc. iii. The temple, ready for pillage, miraculously succored.—2 Macc. xv.

1 Kings, xvii. The widow to Elijah, who had restored her son, "By this I know that thy words are true."

1 Kings, xviii. Elijah with the prophets of Baal.

In the dispute concerning the true God and the truth of religion, there has never happened any miracle on the side of error, and not of truth.

828

Opposition.—Abel, Cain; Moses, the Magicians; Elijah, the false prophets: Jeremiah, Hananiah; Micaiah, the false prophets; Jesus Christ, the Pharisees; St. Paul, Bar-jesus; the Apostles, the Exorcists; Christians, unbelievers; Catholics, heretics; Elijah, Enoch; Antichrist.

829

Jesus Christ says that the Scriptures testify of Him. But He does not point out in what respect.

Even the prophecies could not prove Jesus Christ during His life; and so, men would not have been culpable for not believing in Him before His death, had the miracles not sufficed without doctrine. Now those who did not believe in Him, when He was still alive, were sinners, as He said

Himself, and without excuse. Therefore they must have
had proof beyond doubt, which they resisted. Now, they
had not the prophecies, but only the miracles. Therefore
the latter suffice, when the doctrine is not inconsistent with
them; and they ought to be believed.

John, vii. 40. *Dispute among the Jews as among the
Christians of to-day.* Some believed in Jesus Christ; others
believed Him not, because of the prophecies which said that
He should be born in Bethlehem. They should have considered more carefully whether He was not. For His miracles being convincing, they should have been quite sure of
these supposed contradictions of His teaching to Scripture;
and this obscurity did not excuse, but blinded them. Thus
those who refuse to believe in the miracles in the present
day on account of a supposed contradiction, which is unreal, are not excused.

The Pharisees said to the people, who believed in Him,
because of His miracles: "This people who knoweth not
the law are cursed. But have any of the rulers or of the
Pharisees believed on him? For we know that out of Galilee ariseth no prophet." Nicodemus answered: "Doth our
law judge any man before it hear him, [and specially, such
a man who works such miracles]?"

830

The prophecies were ambiguous; they are no longer so.

831

The five propositions were ambiguous; they are no longer
so.

832

Miracles are no longer necessary, because we have had
them already. But when tradition is no longer minded; when
the Pope alone is offered to us; when he has been imposed
upon; and when the true source of truth, which is tradition, is thus excluded; and the Pope, who is its guardian, is
biassed; the truth is no longer free to appear. Then, as men

speak no longer of truth, truth itself must speak to men. This is what happened in the time of Arius. (Miracles under Diocletian and under Arius.)

833

Miracle.—The people conclude this of themselves; but if the reason of it must be given to you . . .

It is unfortunate to be in exception to the rule. The same must be strict, and opposed to exception. But yet, as it is certain that there are exceptions to a rule, our judgment must, though strict, be just.

834

John, vi. 26: *Non quia vidisti signum, sed quia saturati estis.*

Those who follow Jesus Christ because of His miracles honour His power in all the miracles which it produces. But those who, making profession to follow Him because of His miracles, follow Him in fact only because He comforts them and satisfies them with worldly blessings, discredit His miracles, when they are opposed to their own comforts.

John, ix: *Non est hic homo a Deo, quia sabbatum non custodit. 'Alii: Quomodo potest homo peccator hæc signa facere?*

Which is the most clear?

This house is not of God; for they do not there believe that the five propositions are in Jansenius. Others: This house is of God; for in it there are wrought strange miracles.

Which is the most clear?

Tu quid dicis? Dico quia propheta est.—Nisi esset hic a Deo, non poterat facere quidquam.[s]

835

In the Old Testament, when they will turn you from God. In the New, when they will turn you from Jesus Christ. These are the occasions for excluding particular miracles from belief. No others need be excluded.

[s] John ix. 17, 33.

Does it therefore follow that they would have the right to exclude all the prophets who came to them? No; they would have sinned in not excluding those who denied God, and would have sinned in excluding those who did not deny God. For they must needs be convinced at their first sight of Jesus Christ.

So soon, then, as we see a miracle, we must either assent to it, or have striking proofs to the contrary. We must see if it denies a God, or Jesus Christ, or the Church.

836

There is a great difference between not being for Jesus Christ and saying so, and not being for Jesus Christ and pretending to be so. The one party can do miracles, not the others. For it is clear of the one party, that they are opposed to the truth, but not of the others; and thus miracles are clearer.

837

That we must love one God only is a thing so evident, that it does not require miracles to prove it.

838

Jesus Christ performed miracles, then the apostles, and the first saints in great number; because the prophecies not being yet accomplished but in the process of being accomplished by them, the miracles alone bore witness to them. It was foretold that the Messiah should convert the nations. How could this prophecy be fulfilled without the conversion of the nations? And how could the nations be converted to the Messiah, if they did not see this final effect of the prophecies which prove Him? Therefore, till He had died, risen again, and converted the nations, all was not accomplished; and so miracles were needed during all this time. Now they are no longer needed against the Jews; for the accomplished prophecies constitute a lasting miracle.

839

"Though ye believe not Me, believe at least the works." He refers them, as it were, to the strongest proof.

It had been told to the Jews, as well as to Christians, that they should not always believe the prophets; but yet the Pharisees and Scribes are greatly concerned about His miracles, and try to show that they are false, or wrought by the devil. For they must needs be convinced, if they acknowledge that they are of God.

At the present day we are not troubled to make this distinction. Still it is very easy to do: those who deny neither God nor Jesus Christ do no miracles which are not certain. *Nemo facit virtutem in nomine meo, et cito possit de me male loqui.*[9]

But we have not to draw this distinction. Here is a sacred relic. Here is a thorn from the crown of the Saviour of the world, over whom the prince of this world has no power, which works miracles by the peculiar power of the blood shed for us. Now God Himself chooses this house in order to display conspicuously therein His power.

These are not men who do miracles by an unknown and doubtful virtue, which makes a decision difficult for us. It is God Himself. It is the instrument of the Passion of His only Son, who, being in many places, chooses this, and makes men come from all quarters there to receive these miraculous alleviations in their weaknesses.

840

The Church has three kinds of enemies: the Jews, who have never been of her body; the heretics, who have withdrawn from it; and the evil Christians, who rend her from within.

These three kinds of different adversaries usually attack her in different ways. But here they attack her in one and the same way. As they are all without miracles, and as the Church has always had miracles against them, they have all had the same interest in evading them; and they all make use of this excuse, that doctrine must not be judged by miracles, but miracles by doctrine. There were two parties among those who heard Jesus Christ: those who followed His teaching on account of His miracles; others who said

[9] Mark ix. 39.

. . . There were two parties in the time of Calvin . . .
There are now the Jesuits, &c.

841

Miracles furnish the test in matters of doubt, between
Jews and heathens, Jews and Christians, Catholics and heretics, and slandered and slanderers, between the two crosses.

But miracles would be useless to heretics; for the Church,
authorised by miracles which have already obtained belief,
tells us that they have not the true faith. There is no doubt
that they are not in it, since the first miracles of the Church
exclude belief in theirs. Thus there is miracle against
miracle, both the first and greatest being on the side of the
Church.

These nuns, astonished at what is said, that they are in the
way of perdition; that their confessors are leading them to
Geneva; that they suggest to them that Jesus Christ is not
in the Eucharist, nor on the right hand of the Father; know
that all this is false, and therefore offer themselves to God
in this state. *Vide si via iniquitatis in me est.*[10] What happens thereupon? This place, which is said to be the temple
of the devil, God makes His own temple. It is said that the
children must be taken away from it. God heals them there.
It is said that it is the arsenal of hell. God makes of it the
sanctuary of His grace. Lastly, they are threatened with all
the fury and vengeance of heaven; and God overwhelms
them with favours. A man would need to have lost his
senses to conclude from this that they are therefore in the
way of perdition.

(We have without doubt the same signs as Saint
Athanasius.)

842

Si tu es Christus, dic nobis.

*Opera quæ ego facio in nomine patris mei, hæc testimonium
perhibent de me. Sed vos non creditis quia non estis ex
ovibus meis. Oves mei vocem meam audiunt.*[11]

John, vi. 30. *Quod ergo tu facis signum ut videamus et
credamus tibi?—Non dicunt: Quam doctrinam prædicas?*

[10] Psalms cxxxix. 24.   [11] Luke xxii. 67.

Nemo potest facere signa quæ tu facis nisi Deus.

2 Macc. xiv. 15. *Deus qui signis evidentibus suam portionem protegit.*

Volumus signum videre de cælo, tentantes eum. Luke, xi. 16.

Generatio prava signum quærit; et non dabitur.[12]

Et ingemiscens ait: Quid generatio ista signum quærit? (Mark, viii. 12.) They asked a sign with an evil intention.

Et non poterat facere.[13] And yet he promises them the sign of Jonah, the great and wonderful miracle of his resurrection.

Nisi videritis signa, non creditis.[14] He does not blame them for not believing unless there are miracles, but for not believing unless they are themselves spectators of them.

Antichrist *in signis mendacibus,* says Saint Paul, 2 Thess. ii.

Secundum operationem Satanæ, in seductione iis qui pereunt et quod charitatem veritatis non receperunt ut salvi fierent, ideo mittet illis Deus operationes erroris ut credant mendacio.[15]

As in the passage of Moses: *Tentat enim vos Deus, utrum diligatis eum.*

Ecce prædixi vobis: vos ergo videte.

843

Here is not the country of truth. She wanders unknown amongst men. God has covered her with a veil, which leaves her unrecognised by those who do not hear her voice. Room is opened for blasphemy, even against the truths that are at least very likely. If the truths of the Gospel are published the contrary is published too, and the questions are obscured, so that the people cannot distinguish. And they ask, "What have you to make you believed rather than others? What sign do you give? You have only words, and so have we. If you had miracles, good and well." That doctrine ought to be supported by miracles is a truth, which they misuse in order to revile doctrine. And if miracles happen, it is said that miracles are not enough

[12] Matt. xii. 39.   [13] Mark vi. 5.   [14] John iv. 8, 48.   [15] Thess. ii. 9-11.

without doctrine; and this is another truth, which they misuse in order to revile miracles.

Jesus Christ cured the man born blind, and performed a number of miracles on the Sabbath day. In this way He blinded the Pharisees, who said that miracles must be judged by doctrine.

"We have Moses: but, as for this fellow, we know not from whence he is." It is wonderful that you know not whence He is, and yet He does such miracles.

Jesus Christ spoke neither against God, nor against Moses.

Antichrist and the false prophets, foretold by both Testaments, will speak openly against God and against Jesus Christ. Who is not hidden . . . God would not allow him, who would be a secret enemy, to do miracles openly.

In a public dispute where the two parties profess to be for God, for Jesus Christ, for the Church, miracles have never been on the side of the false Christians, and the other side has never been without a miracle.

"He hath a devil." John, x. 21. And others said, "Can a devil open the eyes of the blind?"

The proofs which Jesus Christ and the apostles draw from Scripture are not conclusive; for they say only that Moses foretold that a prophet should come. But they do not thereby prove that this is He; and that is the whole question. These passages therefore serve only to show that they are not contrary to Scripture, and that there appears no inconsistency, but not that there is agreement. Now this is enough, namely, exclusion of inconsistency, along with miracles.

There is a mutual duty between God and men. We must pardon Him this saying: Quid debui? "Accuse me," said God in Isaiah.

"God must fulfil His promises," &c.

Men owe it to God to accept the religion which He sends. God owes it to men not to lead them into error. Now, they would be led into error, if the workers of miracles announced a doctrine which should not appear evidently false to the light of common sense, and if a greater worker of miracles had not already warned men not to believe them.

Thus, if there were divisions in the Church, and the Arians, for example, who declared themselves founded on Scripture just as the Catholics, had done miracles, and not the Catholics, men should have been led into error.

For, as a man, who announces to us the secrets of God, is not worthy to be believed on his private authority, and that is why the ungodly doubt him; so when a man, as a token of the communion which he has with God, raises the dead, foretells the future, removes the seas, heals the sick, there is none so wicked as not to bow to him, and the incredulity of Pharaoh and the Pharisees is the effect of a supernatural obduracy.

When therefore we see miracles and a doctrine not suspicious, both on one side, there is no difficulty. But when we see miracles and suspicious doctrine on the same side, we must then see which is the clearest. Jesus Christ was suspected.

Barjesus blinded. The power of God surpasses that of His enemies.

The Jewish exorcists beaten by the devils, saying, " Jesus I know, and Paul I know; but who are ye?"

Miracles are for doctrine, and not doctrine for miracles.

If the miracles are true, shall we be able to persuade men of all doctrine? No; for this will not come to pass. *Si angelus* . . .[16]

Rule: we must judge of doctrine by miracles; we must judge of miracles by doctrine. All this is true, but contains no contradiction.

For we must distinguish the times.

How glad you are to know the general rules, thinking thereby to set up dissension, and render all useless! We shall prevent you, my father; truth is one and constant.

It is impossible, from the duty of God to men, that a man, hiding his evil teaching, and only showing the good, saying that he conforms to God and the Church, should do miracles so as to instil insensibly a false and subtle doctrine. This cannot happen.

And still less, that God, who knows the heart, should perform miracles in favour of such an one.

[16] Galatians i. 8.

844

The three marks of religion: perpetuity, a good life, miracles. They destroy perpetuity by their doctrine of probability; a good life by their morals; miracles by destroying either their truth or the conclusions to be drawn from them.

If we believe them, the Church will have nothing to do with perpetuity, holiness, and miracles. The heretics deny them, or deny the conclusions to be drawn from them; they do the same. But one would need to have no sincerity in order to deny them, or again to lose one's senses in order to deny the conclusions to be drawn from them.

Nobody has ever suffered martyrdom for the miracles which he says he has seen; for the folly of men goes perhaps to the length of martyrdom, for those which the Turks believe by tradition, but not for those which they have seen.

845

The heretics have always attacked these three marks, which they have not.

846

First objection: "An angel from heaven. We must not judge of truth by miracles, but of miracles by truth. Therefore the miracles are useless."

Now they are of use, and they must not be in opposition to the truth. Therefore what Father Lingende has said, that "God will not permit that a miracle may lead into error . . ."

When there shall be a controversy in the same Church, miracle will decide.

Second objection: "But Antichrist will do miracles."

The magicians of Pharaoh did not entice to error. Thus we cannot say to Jesus respecting Antichrist, "You have led me into error." For Antichrist will do them against Jesus Christ, and so they cannot lead into error. Either God will not permit false miracles, or He will procure greater.

[Jesus Christ has existed since the beginning of the world: this is more impressive than all the miracles of Antichrist.]

If in the same Church there should happen a miracle on the side of those in error, men would be led into error. Schism is visible; a miracle is visible. But schism is more a sign of error than a miracle is a sign of truth. Therefore a miracle cannot lead into error.

But apart from schism, error is not so obvious as a miracle is obvious. Therefore a miracle could lead into error.

Ubi est Deus tuus?[17] Miracles show Him, and are a light.

847

One of the anthems for Vespers at Christmas: *Exortum est in tenebris lumen rectis corde.*[18]

848

If the compassion of God is so great that He instructs us to our benefit, even when He hides Himself, what light ought we not to expect from Him when He reveals Himself?

849

Will *Est et non est*[19] be received in faith itself as well as in miracles? And if it is inseparable in the others . . .

When Saint Xavier works miracles.—[Saint Hilary. Ye wretches, who oblige us to speak of miracles.]

Unjust judges, make not your own laws on the moment; judge by those which are established, and by yourselves. *Væ qui conditis leges iniquas.*[20]

Miracles endless, false.

In order to weaken your adversaries, you disarm the whole Church.

If they say that our salvation depends upon God, they are "heretics." If they say that they are obedient to the Pope, that is "hypocrisy." If they are ready to subscribe to all the articles, that is not enough. If they say that a man must not be killed for an apple, "they attack the mor-

ality of Catholics." If miracles are done among them, it is
not a sign of holiness, and is, on the contrary, a symptom
of heresy.

The way in which the Church has existed is that truth
has been without dispute, or, if it has been contested, there
has been the Pope, or, failing him, there has been the
Church.

850

The five propositions condemned, but no miracle; for the
truth was not attacked. But the Sorbonne . . . but the
bull . . .

It is impossible that those who love God with all their
heart should fail to recognise the Church; so evident is she.
—It is impossible that those who do not love God should
be convinced of the Church.

Miracles have such influence that it was necessary that
God should warn men not to believe in them in opposition
to Him, all clear as it is that there is a God. Without
this they would have been able to disturb men.

And thus so far from these passages, Deut. xiii., making
against the authority of the miracles, nothing more indicates
their influence. And the same in respect of Antichrist. "To
seduce, if it were possible, even the elect."

851

The history of the man born blind.

What says Saint Paul? Does he continually speak of
the evidence of the prophecies? No, but of his own miracle.
What says Jesus Christ? Does He speak of the evidence
of the prophecies? No; His death had not fulfilled them,
But He says, *Si non fecissem.*[21] Believe the works.

Two supernatural foundations of our wholly supernatural
religion; one visible, the other invisible; miracles with
grace, miracles without grace.

The synagogue, which has been treated with love as a
type of the Church, and with hatred, because it was only
the type, has been restored, being on the point of falling
when it was well with God, and thus a type.

[21] John xv. 24.

Miracles prove the power which God has over hearts, by that which He exercises over bodies.

The Church has never approved a miracle among heretics.

Miracles a support of religion: they have been the test of Jews; they have been the test of Christians, saints, innocents, and true believers.

A miracle among schismatics is not so much to be feared; for schism, which is more obvious than a miracle, visibly indicates their error. But when there is no schism, and error is in question, miracle decides.

Si non fecissem quæ alius non fecit.[31] The wretches who have obliged us to speak of miracles.

Abraham and Gideon confirm faith by miracles.

Judith. God speaks at last in their greatest oppression.

If the cooling of love leaves the Church almost without believers, miracles will rouse them. This is one of the last effects of grace.

If one miracle were wrought among the Jesuits!

When a miracle disappoints the expectation of those in whose presence it happens, and there is a disproportion between the state of their faith and the instrument of the miracle, it ought then to induce them to change. But with you it is otherwise. There would be as much reason in saying that, if the Eucharist raised a dead man, it would be necessary for one to turn a Calvinist rather than remain a Catholic. But when it crowns the expectation, and those who hoped that God would bless the remedies, see themselves healed without remedies . . .

The ungodly.—No sign has ever happened on the part of the devil without a stronger sign on the part of God, or even without it having been foretold that such would happen.

852

Unjust persecutors of those whom God visibly protects. If they reproach you with your excesses, " they speak as the heretics." If they say that the grace of Jesus Christ distinguishes us, " they are heretics." If they do miracles, " it is the mark of their heresy."

Ezekiel.—They say: These are the people of God who speak thus.

It is said, "Believe in the Church"; but it is not said, "Believe in miracles"; because the last is natural, and not the first. The one had need of a precept, not the other. Hezekiah.

The synagogue was only a type, and thus it did not perish; and it was only a type, and so it is decayed. It was a type which contained the truth, and thus it has lasted until it no longer contained the truth.

My reverend father, all this happened in types. Other religions perish; this one perishes not.

Miracles are more important than you think. They have served for the foundation, and will serve for the continuation of the Church till Antichrist, till the end.

The two witnesses.

In the Old Testament and the New, miracles are performed in connection with types. Salvation, or an useless thing, if not to show that we must submit to the Scriptures: type of the sacrament.

853

[We must judge soberly of divine ordinances, my father, Saint Paul in the isle of Malta.]

854

The hardness of the Jesuits then surpasses that of the Jews, since those refused to believe Jesus Christ innocent only because they doubted if His miracles were of God. Whereas the Jesuits, though unable to doubt that the miracles of Port Royal are of God, do not cease to doubt still the innocence of that house.

855

I suppose that men believe miracles. You corrupt religion either in favour of your friends, or against your enemies. You arrange it at your will.

856

On the miracle.—As God has made no family more happy, let it also be the case that He find none more thankful.

SECTION XIV

Appendix: Polemical Fragments

857

*C*LEARNESS, *obscurity.*—There would be too great darkness, if truth had not visible signs. This is a wonderful one, that it has always been preserved in one Church and one visible assembly [of men]. There would be too great clearness, if there were only one opinion in this Church. But in order to recognise what is true, one has only to look at what has always existed; for it is certain that truth has always existed, and that nothing false has always existed.

858

The history of the Church ought properly to be called the history of truth.

859

There is a pleasure in being in a ship beaten about by a storm, when we are sure that it will not founder. The persecutions which harass the Church are of this nature.

860

In addition to so many other signs of piety, they are also persecuted, which is the best sign of piety.

861

The Church is an excellent state, when it is sustained by God only.

862

The Church has always been attacked by opposite errors, but perhaps never at the same time, as now. And if she

305

suffer more because of the multiplicity of errors, she derives this advantage from it, that they destroy each other.

She complains of both, but far more of the Calvinists, because of the schism.

It is certain that many of the two opposite sects are deceived. They must be disillusioned.

Faith embraces many truths which seem to contradict each other. *There is a time to laugh, and a time to weep,* &c. *Responde. Ne respondeas,* &c.[1]

The source of this is the union of the two natures in Jesus Christ; and also the two worlds (the creation of a new heaven and a new earth; a new life and a new death; all things double, and the same names remaining); and finally the two natures that are in the righteous, (for they are the two worlds, and a member and image of Jesus Christ. And thus all the names suit them: righteous, yet sinners; dead, yet living; living, yet dead; elect, yet outcast, &c.).

There are then a great number of truths, both of faith and of morality, which seem contradictory, and which all hold good together in a wonderful system. The source of all heresies is the exclusion of some of these truths; and the source of all the objections which the heretics make against us is the ignorance of some of our truths. And it generally happens that, unable to conceive the connection of two opposite truths, and believing that the admission of one involves the exclusion of the other, they adhere to the one, exclude the other, and think of us as opposed to them. Now exclusion is the cause of their heresy; and ignorance that we hold the other truth causes their objections.

1st example: Jesus Christ is God and man. The Arians, unable to reconcile these things, which they believe incompatible, say that He is man; in this they are Catholics. But they deny that He is God; in this they are heretics. They allege that we deny His humanity; in this they are ignorant.

2nd example: On the subject of the Holy Sacrament. We believe that, the substance of the bread being changed, and being consubstantial with that of the body of our Lord, Jesus Christ is therein really present. That is one truth. Another is that this Sacrament is also a type of the cross

[1] Proverbs xxvi. 4, 5,

and of glory, and a commemoration of the two. That is the Catholic faith, which comprehends these two truths which seem opposed.

The heresy of to-day, not conceiving that this Sacrament contains at the same time both the presence of Jesus Christ and a type of Him, and that it is a sacrifice and a commemoration of a sacrifice, believes that neither of these truths can be admitted without excluding the other for this reason.

They fasten to this point alone, that this Sacrament is typical; and in this they are not heretics. They think that we exclude this truth; hence it comes that they raise so many objections to us out of the passages of the Fathers which assert it. Finally, they deny the presence; and in this they are heretics.

3rd example: Indulgences.

The shortest way, therefore, to prevent heresies is to instruct in all truths; and the surest way to refute them is to declare them all. For what will the heretics say?

In order to know whether an opinion is a Father's . . .

863

All err the more dangerously, as they each follow a truth. Their fault is not in following a falsehood, but in not following another truth.

864

Truth is so obscure in these times, and falsehood so established, that unless we love the truth, we cannot know it.

865

If there is ever a time in which we must make profession of two opposite truths, it is when we are reproached for omitting one. Therefore the Jesuits and Jansenists are wrong in concealing them, but the Jansenists more so, for the Jesuits have better made profession of the two.

866

Two kinds of people make things equal to one another, as feasts to working days, Christians to priests, all things among them, &c. And hence the one party conclude that what is then bad for priests is also so for Christians, and the other that what is not bad for Christians is lawful for priests.

867

If the ancient Church was in error, the Church is fallen. If she should be in error to-day, it is not the same thing; for she has always the superior maxim of tradition from the hand of the ancient Church; and so this submission and this conformity to the ancient Church prevail and correct all. But the ancient Church did not assume the future Church, and did not consider her, as we assume and consider the ancient.

868

That which hinders us in comparing what formerly occurred in the Church with what we see there now, is that we generally look upon Saint Athanasius, Saint Theresa, and the rest, as crowned with glory, and acting towards us as gods. Now that time has cleared up things, it does so appear. But at the time when he was persecuted, this great saint was a man called Athanasius; and Saint Theresa was a nun. "Elias was a man subject to like passions as we are," says Saint James, to disabuse Christians of that false idea which makes us reject the example of the saints, as disproportioned to our state. "They were saints," say we, "they are not like us." What then actually happened? Saint Athanasius was a man called Athanasius, accused of many crimes, condemned by such and such a council for such and such a crime. All the bishops assented to it, and finally the Pope. What said they to those who opposed this? That they disturbed the peace, that they created schism, &c.

Zeal, light. Four kinds of persons: zeal without knowledge; knowledge without zeal; neither knowledge nor zeal; both zeal and knowledge. The first three condemned him. The last acquitted him, were excommunicated by the Church, and yet saved the Church.

869

If Saint Augustine came at the present time, and was as little authorised as his defenders, he would accomplish nothing. God directs his Church well, by having sent him before with authority.

870

God has not wanted to absolve without the Church. As she has part in the offence, He desires her to have part in the pardon. He associates her with this power, as kings their parliaments. But if she absolves or binds without God, she is no longer the Church. For, as in the case of parliament, even if the king have pardoned a man, it must be ratified; but if parliament ratifies without the king, or refuses to ratify on the order of the king, it is no longer the parliament of the king, but a rebellious assembly.

871

The Church, the Pope. Unity, plurality.—Considering the Church as a unity, the Pope, who is its head, is as the whole. Considering it as a plurality, the Pope is only a part of it. The Fathers have considered the Church now in the one way, now in the other. And thus they have spoken differently of the Pope. (Saint Cyprian: *Sacerdos Dei.*) But in establishing one of these truths, they have not excluded the other. Plurality which is not reduced to unity is confusion; unity which does not depend on plurality is tyranny. There is scarcely any other country than France in which it is permissible to say that the Council is above the Pope.

872

The Pope is head. Who else is known of all? Who else is recognised by all, having power to insinuate himself into all the body, because he holds the principal shoot, which insinuates itself everywhere? How easy it was to make this degenerate into tyranny! That is why Christ has laid down for them this precept: *Vos autem non sic.*[2]

[2] Luke xxii. 26.

873

The Pope hates and fears the learned, who do not submit to him at will.

874

We must not judge of what the Pope is by some words of the Fathers—as the Greeks said in a council, important rules—but by the acts of the Church and the Fathers, and by the canons.

Duo aut tres in unum.[3] Unity and plurality. It is an error to exclude one of the two, as the papists do who exclude plurality, or the Huguenots who exclude unity.

875

Would the Pope be dishonoured by having his knowledge from God and tradition; and is it not dishonouring him to separate him from this holy union?

876

God does not perform miracles in the ordinary conduct of His Church. It would be a strange miracle if infallibility existed in one man. But it appears so natural for it to reside in a multitude, since the conduct of God is hidden under nature, as in all His other works.

877

Kings dispose of their own power; but the Popes cannot dispose of theirs.

878

Summum jus, summa injuria.[4]

The majority is the best way, because it is visible, and has strength to make itself obeyed. Yet it is the opinion of the least able.

If men could have done it, they would have placed might in the hands of justice. But as might does not allow itself

[3] John x. 30; 1 John v. 8.   [4] "The greatest law, the greatest injury."

to be managed as men want, because it is a palpable quality, whereas justice is a spiritual quality of which men dispose as they please, they have placed justice in the hands of might. And thus that is called just which men are forced to obey.

Hence comes the right of the sword, for the sword gives a true right. Otherwise we should see violence on one side and justice on the other. End of the twelfth *Provincial*. Hence comes the injustice of the Fronde, which raises its alleged justice against power. It is not the same in the Church, for there is a true justice and no violence.

879

Injustice.—Jurisdiction is not given for the sake of the judge, but for that of the litigant. It is dangerous to tell this to the people. But the people have too much faith in you; it will not harm them, and may serve you. It should therefore be made known. *Pasce oveas meas, non tuas.*[5] You owe me pasturage.

880

Men like certainty. They like the Pope to be infallible in faith, and grave doctors to be infallible in morals, so as to have certainty.

881

The Church teaches, and God inspires, both infallibly. The work of the Church is of use only as a preparation for grace or condemnation. What it does is enough for condemnation, not for inspiration.

882

Every time the Jesuits may impose upon the Pope, they will make all Christendom perjured.

The Pope is very easily imposed upon, because of his occupations, and the confidence which he has in the Jesuits;

[5] John xxi. 17.

and the Jesuits are very capable of imposing upon him by means of calumny.

883

The wretches who have obliged me to speak of the basis of religion.

884

Sinners purified without penitence; the righteous justified without love; all Christians without the grace of Jesus Christ; God without power over the will of men; a predestination without mystery; a redemption without certitude!

885

Any one is made a priest, who wants to be so, as under Jeroboam.

It is a horrible thing that they propound to us the discipline of the Church of to-day as so good, that it is made a crime to desire to change it. Formerly it was infallibly good, and it was thought that it could be changed without sin; and now, such as it is, we cannot wish it changed! It has indeed been permitted to change the custom of not making priests without such great circumspection, that there were hardly any who were worthy; and it is not allowed to complain of the custom which makes so many who are unworthy!

886

Heretics.—Ezekiel. All the heathen, and also the Prophet, spoke evil of Israel. But the Israelites were so far from having the right to say to him, "You speak like the heathen," that he is most forcible upon this, that the heathens say the same as he.

887

The Jansenists are like the heretics in the reformation of morality; but you are like them in evil.

888

You are ignorant of the prophecies, if you do not know that all this must happen; princes, prophets, Pope, and even

the priests. And yet the Church is to abide. By the grace
of God we have not come to that. Woe to these priests!
But we hope that God will bestow His mercy upon us that
we shall not be of them.

Saint Peter, ii.: false prophets in the past, the image of
future ones.

889

. . . So that if it is true, on the one hand, that some
lax monks, and some corrupt casuists, who are not members
of the hierarchy, are steeped in these corruptions, it is, on
the other hand, certain that the true pastors of the Church,
who are the true guardians of the Divine Word, have preserved it unchangeably against the efforts of those who have
attempted to destroy it.

And thus true believers have no pretext to follow that
laxity, which is only offered to them by the strange hands
of these casuists, instead of the sound doctrine which is
presented to them by the fatherly hands of their own
pastors. And the ungodly and heretics have no ground
for publishing these abuses as evidence of imperfection
in the providence of God over His Church; since, the
Church consisting properly in the body of the hierarchy,
we are so far from being able to conclude from the
present state of matters that God has abandoned her to
corruption, that it has never been more apparent than at
the present time that God visibly protects her from
corruption.

For if some of these men, who, by an extraordinary vocation, have made profession of withdrawing from the world
and adopting the monks' dress, in order to live in a more perfect state than ordinary Christians, have fallen into excesses
which horrify ordinary Christians, and have become to us
what the false prophets were among the Jews; this is a
private and personal misfortune, which must indeed be de-
plored, but from which nothing can be inferred against
the care which God takes of His Church; since all these
things are so clearly foretold, and it has been so long since
announced that these temptations would arise from these
kind of people; so that when we are well instructed, we see

in this rather evidence of the care of God than of His forgetfulness in regard to us.

890

Tertullian: *Nunquam Ecclesia reformabitur.*[6]

891

Heretics, who take advantage of the doctrine of the Jesuits, must be made to know that it is not that of the Church . . . the doctrine of the Church; and that our divisions do not separate us from the altar.

892

If in differing we condemned, you would be right. Uniformity without diversity is useless to others; diversity without uniformity is ruinous for us. The one is harmful outwardly; the other inwardly.

893

By showing the truth, we cause it to be believed; but by showing the injustice of ministers, we do not correct it. Our mind is assured by a proof of falsehood; our purse is not made secure by proof of injustice.

894

Those who love the Church lament to see the corruption of morals; but laws at least exist. But these corrupt the laws. The model is damaged.

895

Men never do evil so completely and cheerfully as when they do it from religious conviction.

896

It is in vain that the Church has established these words, anathemas, heresies, &c. They are used against her.

[6] "The Church will never be reformed."

897

The servant knoweth not what his lord doeth, for the master tells him only the act and not the intention. And this is why he often obeys slavishly, and defeats the intention. But Jesus Christ has told us the object. And you defeat that object.

898

They cannot have perpetuity, and they seek universality; and therefore they make the whole Church corrupt, that they may be saints.

899

Against those who misuse passages of Scripture, and who pride themselves in finding one which seems to favour their error.—The chapter for Vespers, Passion Sunday, the prayer for the king.

Explanation of these words: "He that is not with me is against me." And of these others: "He that is not against you is for you." A person who says: "I am neither for nor against;" we ought to reply to him . . .

900

He who will give the meaning of Scripture, and does not take it from Scripture, is an enemy of Scripture. (Aug.: *De Doct. Christ.*)

901

Humilibus dat gratiam; an ideo non dedit humilitatem?[7]
Sui eum non receperunt; quotquot autem non receperunt an non erant sui?[8]

902

"It must indeed be," says Feuillant, "that this is not so certain; for controversy indicates uncertainty, (Saint Athanasius, Saint Chrysostom, morals, unbelievers)."

The Jesuits have not made the truth uncertain, but they have made their own ungodliness certain.

Contradiction has always been permitted, in order to

[7] James iv. 6.   [8] John i. 11, 12.

blind the wicked; for all that offends truth or love is evil.
This is the true principle.

903

All religions and sects in the world have had natural
reason for a guide. Christians alone have been constrained
to take their rules from without themselves, and to acquaint
themselves with those which Jesus Christ bequeathed to men
of old to be handed down to true believers. This constraint
wearies these good Fathers. They desire, like other people,
to have liberty to follow their own imaginations. It is in
vain that we cry to them, as the prophets said to the Jews
of old: "Enter into the Church; acquaint yourselves with
the precepts which the men of old left to her, and follow
those paths." They have answered like the Jews: "We
will not walk in them; but we will follow the thoughts of our
hearts;" and they have said, "We will be as the other
nations."

904

They make a rule of exception.

Have the men of old given absolution before penance?
Do this as exceptional. But of the exception you make a
rule without exception, so that you do not even want the
rule to be exceptional.

905

On confessions and absolutions without signs of regret.
God regards only the inward; the Church judges only
by the outward. God absolves as soon as He sees penitence
in the heart; the Church when she sees it in works. God
will make a Church pure within, which confounds, by its
inward and entirely spiritual holiness, the inward impiety of
proud sages and Pharisees; and the Church will make an
assembly of men whose external manners are so pure as to
confound the manners of the heathen. If there are hypo-
crites among them, but so well disguised that she does not
discover their venom, she tolerates them; for, though they
are not accepted of God, whom they cannot deceive, they
are of men, whom they do deceive. And thus she is not dis-

honoured by their conduct, which appears holy. But you want the Church to judge neither of the inward, because that belongs to God alone, nor of the outward, because God dwells only upon the inward; and thus, taking away from her all choice of men, you retain in the Church the most dissolute, and those who dishonour her so greatly, that the synagogues of the Jews and sects of philosophers would have banished them as unworthy; and have abhorred them as impious.

906

The easiest conditions to live in according to the world are the most difficult to live in according to God, and *vice versâ*. Nothing is so difficult according to the world as the religious life; nothing is easier than to live it according to God. Nothing is easier, according to the world, than to live in high office and great wealth; nothing is more difficult than to live in them according to God, and without acquiring an interest in them and a liking for them.

907

The casuists submit the decision to the corrupt reason, and the choice of decisions to the corrupt will, in order that all that is corrupt in the nature of man may contribute to his conduct.

908

But is it *probable* that *probability* gives assurance?
Difference between rest and security of conscience. Nothing gives certainty but truth; nothing gives rest but the sincere search for truth.

909

The whole society itself of their casuists cannot give assurance to a conscience in error, and that is why it is important to choose good guides.
Thus they will be doubly culpable, both in having followed ways which they should not have followed, and in having listened to teachers to whom they should not have listened.

910

Can it be anything but compliance with the world which makes you find things probable? Will you make us believe that it is truth, and that if duelling were not the fashion, you would find it probable that they might fight, considering the matter in itself?

911

Must we kill to prevent there being any wicked? This is to make both parties wicked instead of one. *Vince in bono malum.*[9] (Saint Augustine.)

912

Universal.—Ethics and language are special, but universal sciences.

913

Probability.—Each one can employ it; no one can take it away.

914

They allow lust to act, and check scruples; whereas they should do the contrary.

915

Montalte.—Lax opinions please men so much, that it is strange that theirs displease. It is because they have exceeded all bounds. Again, there are many people who see the truth, and who cannot attain to it; but there are few who do not know that the purity of religion is opposed to our corruptions. It is absurd to say that an eternal recompense is offered to the morality of Escobar.

916

Probability.—They have some true principles; but they misuse them. Now, the abuse of truth ought to be as much punished as the introduction of falsehood.

As if there were two hells, one for sins against love, the other for those against justice!

[9] Romans xii. 21.

917

Probability.—The earnestness of the saints in seeking the truth was useless, if the probable is trustworthy. The fear of the saints who have always followed the surest way, (Saint Theresa having always followed her confessor).

918

Take away *probability,* and you can no longer please the world; give *probability,* and you can no longer displease it.

919

These are the effects of the sins of the peoples and of the Jesuits. The great have wished to be flattered. The Jesuits have wished to be loved by the great. They have all been worthy to be abandoned to the spirit of lying, the one party to deceive, the others to be deceived. They have been avaricious, ambitious, voluptuous. *Coacervabunt tibi magistræ.*[10] Worthy disciples of such masters, they have sought flatterers, and have found them.

920

If they do not renounce their doctrine of probability, their good maxims are as little holy as the bad, for they are founded on human authority; and thus, if they are more just, they will be more reasonable, but not more holy. They take after the wild stem on which they are grafted.

If what I say does not serve to enlighten you, it will be of use to the people.

If these are silent, the stones will speak.

Silence is the greatest persecution; the saints were never silent. It is true that a call is necessary; but it is not from the decrees of the Council that we must learn whether we are called, it is from the necessity of speaking. Now, after Rome has spoken, and we think that she has condemned the truth, and that they have written it, and after the books which have said the contrary are censured; we must cry out

[10] 2 Tim. iv. 3.

so much the louder, the more unjustly we are censured, and the more violently they would stifle speech, until there come a Pope who hears both parties, and who consults antiquity to do justice. So the good Popes will find the Church still in outcry.

The Inquisition and the Society are the two scourges of the truth.

Why do you not accuse them of Arianism? For, though they have said that Jesus Christ is God, perhaps they mean by it not the natural interpretation, but as it is said, *Dii estis*.[11]

If my Letters are condemned at Rome, that which I condemn in them is condemned in heaven. *Ad tuum, Domine Jesu, tribunal appello*.[12]

You yourselves are corruptible.

I feared that I had written ill, seeing myself condemned; but the example of so many pious writings makes me believe the contrary. It is no longer allowable to write well, so corrupt or ignorant is the Inquisition!

"It is better to obey God than men."

I fear nothing; I hope for nothing. It is not so with the bishops. Port Royal fears, and it is bad policy to disperse them; for they will fear no longer and will cause greater fear. I do not even fear your like censures, if they are not founded on those of tradition. Do you censure all? What! even my respect? No. Say then what, or you will do nothing, if you do not point out the evil, and why it is evil. And this is what they will have great difficulty in doing.

Probability.—They have given a ridiculous explanation of certitude; for, after having established that all their ways are sure, they have no longer called that sure which leads to heaven without danger of not arriving there by it, but that which leads there without danger of going out of that road.

921

. . . The saints indulge in subtleties in order to think themselves criminals, and impeach their better actions. And

[11] " Ye are Gods."   [12] " To thy judgment-seat, Lord Jesus, I appeal."

these indulge in subtleties in order to excuse the most wicked.

The heathen sages erected a structure equally fine outside, but upon a bad foundation; and the devil deceives men by this apparent resemblance based upon the most different foundation.

Man never had so good a cause as I; and others have never furnished so good a capture as you . . .

The more they point out weakness in my person, the more they authorise my cause.

You say that I am a heretic. Is that lawful? And if you do not fear that men do justice, do you not fear that God does justice?

You will feel the force of the truth, and you will yield to it . . .

There is something supernatural in such a blindness. *Digna necessitas.*[13] *Mentiris impudentissime*[14] . . .

Doctrina sua noscitur vir[15] . . .

False piety, a double sin.

I am alone against thirty thousand. No. Protect, you, the court; protect, you, deception; let me protect the truth. It is all my strength. If I lose it, I am undone. I shall not lack accusations, and persecutions. But I possess the truth, and we shall see who will take it away.

I do not need to defend religion, but you do not need to defend error and injustice. Let God, out of His compassion, having no regard to the evil which is in me, and having regard to the good which is in you, grant us all grace that truth may not be overcome in my hands, and that falsehood . . .

922

Probable.—Let us see if we seek God sincerely, by comparison of the things which we love. It is *probable* that this food will not poison me. It is *probable* that I shall not lose my action by not prosecuting it . . .

---

[13] " Their desert by necessity was drawing nigh." Wisdom, xix. 4.
[14] " You lie most impudently."   [15] " A man is known by his doctrine."

923

It is not absolution only which remits sins by the sacrament of penance, but contrition, which is not real if it does not seek the sacrament.

924

People who do not keep their word, without faith, without honour, without truth, deceitful in heart, deceitful in speech; for which that amphibious animal in fable was once reproached, which held itself in a doubtful position between the fish and the birds . . .

It is important to kings and princes to be considered pious; and therefore they must confess themselves to you.

LETTERS OF PASCAL

TRANSLATED BY

M. L. BOOTH

MINOR WORKS OF PASCAL

TRANSLATED BY

O. W. WIGHT

LETTERS OF PASCAL

From Pascal to His Sister Jacqueline

January 26, 1648.

My Dear Sister,

WE have received your letters. I intended to reply
to the first that you wrote me more than four
months since, but my indisposition and some other
things prevented me. Since then I have not been in a condition to write, either on account of my illness, for want of
leisure, or for some other reason. I have few hours of
leisure and health together; I shall however endeavor to
finish this letter without forcing myself; I know not whether
it will be long or short. My principal design is to make
you understand the truth of the visit which you know of,
in which I hoped to have wherewith to satisfy you and to
reply to your last letters. I can commence with nothing
else than the expression of the pleasure which they have
given me; I have received satisfactions so sensible from
them that I cannot tell them to you by word of mouth. I
entreat you to believe that, though I may not have written
to you, there has not been an hour in which you have not
been present to me, in which I have not made wishes for
the continuation of the great designs with which Heaven
has inspired you.[1] I have felt new transports of joy at all
the letters which bore testimony of it, and I have been delighted to see the continuance of it without your receiving
any news on our part. This has made me judge that there
was a more than human support, since there was no need
of human means to sustain it. I should be glad neverthe-

[1] An allusion to the design of Jacqueline to become a nun.

less to contribute something to it; but I have none of the capacities necessary for that purpose. My weakness is so great that, if I should undertake it, I should do an act of temerity rather than of charity, and I should have a right to fear for us both the calamity that menaces the blind led by the blind. I have felt my incapacity incomparably more since the visits which are in question; and far from having brought back enough of light for others, I have brought nothing but confusion and trouble for myself, which God alone can calm, and in which I shall work with care, but without impatience and disquietude, knowing well that both would remove me from it. I repeat that God alone can calm it, and that I shall work for this, since I find nothing but occasions for making it spring up and increase in those from whom I had expected its dissipation; so that, seeing myself reduced to myself alone, it remains to me only to pray to God that he may bless it with success. For this I shall have need of the aid of scholars and disinterested persons: the first will not afford it; I seek no longer but for the latter; and hence I desire infinitely to see you, for letters are long, inconvenient, and almost useless on such occasions. Nevertheless I will write you something of it.

The first time I saw M. Rebours,[2] I made myself known to him and was received with as much civility as I could wish. This was due to my father, since I received it on his account. After the first compliments, I asked permission to see him again from time to time; he granted it to me: thus I was at liberty to see him, so that I do not account this first sight as a visit, since it was only the permission for such. I was there for some time, and among other conversation, I told him with my usual frankness and *naïveté,* that we had seen their books and those of their adversaries, which was sufficient to make him understand that we were of their sentiments. He expressed some pleasure at this. I then told him that I thought that many things could be demonstrated upon the mere principles of common-sense that their adversaries said were contrary to it, and that well-directed reasoning led to a belief in them, although it was

[2] One of the confessors of Port-Royal.

necessary to believe in them without the aid of reasoning. These were my own words, in which I think there was not wherewith to wound the most severe modesty. But as you know that all actions may have two sources, and that such language might proceed from a principle of vanity and of confidence in reasoning, this suspicion, which was increased by the knowledge that he had of my studies in geometry, sufficed to make him find this language strange, and he expressed it to me by a repartee so full of humility and gentleness that it would doubtless have confounded the pride that he wished to refute. Still I endeavored to make him understand my motive; but my justification increased his suspicions and he took my excuses for obstinacy. I acknowledge that his discourse was so beautiful that if I had been in the state in which he believed me, he would have drawn me from it; but as I did not think myself in this disease, I opposed the remedy which he presented me; but he insisted on it the more, the more I seemed to evade it, because he took my refusal for obstinacy; and the more he strove to continue, the more my thanks testified to him that I did not consider it necessary; so that the whole of this interview passed in this equivocation and in an embarrassment which continued in all the rest, and which could not be unravelled. I shall not relate the others word for word, since it would not be necessary to my purpose; I shall only tell you in substance the purport of what was said on them, or rather, the principle of their restraint.

But I entreat you before all things to draw no conclusions from what I write, for things may escape me without sufficient precision; and this may cause some suspicion to spring up in you as disadvantageous as unjust. For indeed, after having reflected on it carefully, I find in it only an obscurity which it would be difficult and dangerous to decide, and for myself, I suspend my judgment entirely, as much from my weakness as from my want of knowledge.

2

LETTER FROM PASCAL AND HIS SISTER JACQUELINE TO THEIR
SISTER, MADAME PERIER

April 1, 1648.

WE do not know whether this letter will be interminable,
like the rest, but we know that we would gladly write to you
without end. We have here the letter of M. de Saint-
Cyran, *de la Vocation,* lately published without approba-
tion or privilege, which has shocked many. We are reading
it; we will send it afterwards to you. We should be glad
to know your opinion of it, and that of my father. It
takes high ground.

We have several times begun to write to you, but I
have been deterred from it by the example and the speeches,
or, if you like, the rebuffs of which you know; but, since
we have been enlightened upon the matter as much as possible, I believe that it is necessary to use some circumspection in it, and if there are occasions in which we ought
not to speak of these things, we may now dispense with
them; for we do not doubt each other, and as we are, as
it were, mutually assured that we have, in all these discourses, nothing but the glory of God for our object, and
scarcely any communication outside of ourselves, I do
not see that we should have any scruple, so long as he
shall give us these sentiments. If we add to these considerations that of the union which nature has made between us, and to this last that which grace has made, I
think that, far from finding a prohibition, we shall find an
obligation to it; for I find that our happiness has been so
great in being united in the latter way that we ought to
unite to acknowledge and to rejoice at it. For it must be
confessed that it is properly since this time (which M. de
Saint-Cyran wishes should be called the commencement of
life), that we should consider ourselves as truly related,
and that it has pleased God to join us in his new world
by the spirit, as he had done in the terrestrial world by
the flesh.

We beg you that there may not be a day in which you

do not revolve this in memory, and often acknowledge the way which God has used in this conjunction, in which he has not only made us brothers of each other, but children of the same father; for you know that my father has foreseen us all, and, as it were, conceived us in this design. It is in this that we should marvel, that God has given us both the type and the reality of this union; for, as we have often said among ourselves, corporeal things are nothing but an image of spiritual, and God has represented invisible things in the visible. This thought is so general and so useful that we ought not to let much time pass without thinking of it with attention. We have discoursed particularly enough of the relation of these two sorts of things, for which reason we shall not speak of it here; for it is too long to write, and too beautiful not to have remained in your memory, and, what is more, is absolutely necessary according to my opinion. For, as our sins hold us wrapped in things corporeal and terrestrial, and as these are not only the penalty of our sins, but also the occasion of committing new ones, and the cause of the first, it is necessary that we should make use of the same position into which we have fallen to raise us from our overthrow. For this reason, we should use carefully the advantage which the goodness of God bestows upon us in having always before our eyes an image of the good that we have lost, and in surrounding us in the very captivity to which his justice has reduced us, with so many objects that serve to us as an ever-present lesson.

So that we should consider ourselves as criminals in a prison filled with images of their liberator, and instructions necessary to escape from their bondage; but it must be acknowledged that we cannot perceive these sacred characters without a supernatural light; for as all things speak of God to those who know him, and as they reveal him to all those who love him, these same things conceal him from all those who know him not. Thus it is seen, that in the darkness of the world men follow them in a brutal blindness, and cling to them, and make of them the final end of their desires, which they cannot do without sacrilege, for there is nothing but God that should be the final end, as he alone is the principle. For whatever resemblance created nature may have to its Creator, and although the most trifling things, and the smallest and the vilest portions of the world represent at least by their unity the perfect unity that is found only in God, we cannot legitimately bear to them sovereign respect, since there is nothing so abominable in the eyes of God and man as idolatry, because it renders to the creature the honor that is due to none but the Creator. The Scripture is full of the vengeance that God executes on all those who have been guilty of it, and the first commandment of the Decalogue, which includes all the rest, prohibits above everything the adoration of his images. But as he is much more jealous of our affections than our respect, it is evident that there is no crime more injurious or more detestable to him than to bestow sovereign love upon created things, although they represent him.

This is why those to whom God has made known these great truths ought to use these images to enjoy that which they represent, and not remain eternally in that carnal and Judaical blindness which causes the type to be taken for the reality. And those whom God, by regeneration, has drawn freely from sin (which is the veritable nothingness, since it is opposed to God, who is the veritable being) to give them a place in his Church, which is his real temple, after having drawn them freely from nothingness to the point of their creation, in order to give them a place in the universe, have a double obligation to honor him and serve him; since as created beings they should remain in the order of created beings, and not profane the place that they fill, and as Christians they should aspire without ceasing to render themselves worthy to form part of the body of Jesus Christ. But as whilst the created things that compose the world acquit themselves of their obligation by remaining within a limited perfection, because the perfection of the world is also limited, the children of God should set no bounds to their purity and their perfection, because they form part of a body wholly divine, and infinitely perfect; as it is evident that Jesus Christ does not limit the commandment of perfection, and that he proposes

it to us as a model wherein it exists infinite when he says:
" Be ye also perfect as your Father in heaven is perfect."
Thus it is a very prejudicial and very common error among
Christians, and even among those who make a profession
of piety, to persuade themselves that there may be a degree of perfection in which they can be with assurance,
and which it is not necessary to pass, since there is none
at which it will not be wrong to stop, and from which we
can only avoid falling by mounting still higher.

3

LETTER FROM PASCAL AND HIS SISTER JACQUELINE TO THEIR
SISTER, MADAME PERIER

Paris, November 5, afternoon, 1648.

MY DEAR SISTER,

Your letter has recalled to us a misunderstanding of
which we had lost recollection, so absolutely had it passed
from us. The somewhat too diffuse explanations that we
have received have brought to light the general and former
subject of our complaints, and the satisfaction that we
have given has softened the harshness which my father
had conceived for them. We said what you had already
said, without knowing that you had said it, and then we
excused verbally what you had afterwards excused in
writing, without knowing that you had done so; and we
knew not what you had done until after we had acted ourselves; for as we have hidden nothing from my father,
he has revealed every thing, and thus cured all our suspicions. You know how much such troubles disturb the
peace of the family both within and without, and what need
we have in these junctures of the warnings which you
have given us a little too late.

We have some to give you on the subject of your own.
The first is in respect to what you say, that we have instructed you as to what you should write to us. 1°. I do
not remember to have spoken to you of it, so that this was
a novelty to me; and, besides, even though this were true,

I should fear that you had not retained this humanly, if you had not forgotten the person of whom you learned it to remember only God, who alone could have truly instructed you in it. If you remember it as a good thing, you cannot think to hold it from any other, since neither you nor the others can learn it except from God alone. For, although in this kind of gratitude, we do not stop at the men whom we address as though they were the authors of the good that we receive through their means, this nevertheless forms a partial opposition to the views of God, and chiefly in the persons who are not entirely divested of the carnal impressions which make them consider as the source of good the objects that transmit it.

Not that we ought not to remember those persons from whom we have received any instructions, when these persons have been authorized to make them, as fathers, bishops, and confessors, because they are the masters of whom others are the disciples. But as to us, it is different; for as the angel refused the adoration of a holy servant like himself, we tell you, in entreating you no longer to use these terms of human gratitude, to refrain from paying us such compliments, since we are disciples like yourself.

The second is in respect to what you say of its being unnecessary to repeat these things to us, since we know them perfectly already; which causes us to fear that you do not distinguish clearly enough here between the things of which you speak and those of which the world speaks, since it is doubtless quite enough to have learned the latter once and retained them well to be no further instructed in them, while it does not suffice to have comprehended once those of the other kind and to have known them well, that is, by the internal impulse of God, to preserve the knowledge of them in the same degree, although we may retain the memory. Not that we may not remember and as easily retain an epistle of St. Paul as a book of Virgil; but the knowledge that we acquire in this manner, as well as its continuation, is only an effect of memory, while to understand this secret language, unknown to those who are not of Heaven, it is necessary that the same grace, which alone can give the first knowledge of it, shall continue and render it ever present by retracing it without ceasing in the hearts of the faithful to keep it constantly existing there; as God continually renews their beatitude in the blessed, which is an effect and a consequence of grace; as likewise the Church holds that the Father perpetually produces the Son and maintains the eternity of this essence by an effusion of his substance, which is without interruption as well as without end.

Thus the continuation of the justice of the faithful is nothing else than the continuation of the infusion of grace, and not a single grace that subsists continually; and this it is that teaches us perfectly our perpetual dependence on the mercy of God, since if he suspends the course of it ever so slightly, barrenness necessarily becomes the result. In this necessity, it is easy to see that it is necessary to make new efforts continually to acquire this continual newness of spirit, since we can only preserve the former grace by the acquisition of a new grace, and since otherwise we shall lose what we think to retain, as those who wish to shut in the light shut in nothing but darkness. Thus we should watch unceasingly to purify the interior, which is constantly sullied by new spots while retaining the old ones, since without this assiduous renovation we shall be incapable of receiving that new wine that cannot be put into old bottles.

For this reason you should not fear to place before our eyes the things which we have in our memory, and which it is necessary to cause to enter into the heart, since it is unquestionable that your discourse can better serve as the instrument of grace than can the impression of it that remains in our memory, since grace is especially accorded to prayer, and since this charity that you have had for us is among those prayers that ought never to be interrupted. Thus we never should refuse to read or to hear holy things, however common or well-known they may be; for our memory as well as the instructions which it contains, is only an inanimate and Judaical body without the spirit that should vivify them. And it often happens that God avails himself of these exterior means to make them understood and to leave so much the less food for the vanity of men when they thus receive grace in themselves. Thus, a book or a sermon, however common it may be, brings much more profit to him who hears or reads it with better disposition than does the excellence of the most elevated discourses which usually bring more pleasure than instruction; and it is sometimes seen that those who listen as they ought, although ignorant and almost stupid, are touched by the simple name of God and the words that menace them with hell, although these may be all that they comprehend and although they knew it as well before.

The third is in respect to what you say about only writing things to make us understand that you share the same feeling. We have equally to praise and to thank you on this subject; we praise you for your perseverance and thank you for the testimony that you give us of it. We had already drawn this confession from M. Périer, and the things that we induced him to say had assured us of it: we can only tell you how much we are pleased by representing to you the joy which you would receive if you should hear the same thing of us.

We have nothing in particular to tell you, except touching the design of your house.[1] We know that M. Périer is too earnest in what he undertakes to fully think of two things at once, and that the entire design is of such magnitude that, in order to complete it, he must remain a long time without thinking of any thing else. We know, too, that his project is only for a part of the building; but this, besides being only too large alone, engages for the completion of the rest as soon as there shall be no farther obstacles to it, however determined he may be to the contrary, especially if he employs the time in building that it would take to undeceive him of the secret pleasure that he finds in it. Thus we have counselled him to build much less than he intended, and only what is actually necessary, although according to the same design, in order that he may not have cause to become absorbed in it, nor yet deprive himself of the opportunity of doing so. We entreat you to think seriously of it, and to resolve to

[1] A country house built by M. Périer, which is still standing, at Bienassis, near the gates of Clermont.—*Faugère*.

counsel him likewise, lest it may happen that he may be
far more prudent and bestow much more care and pains
in the building of an earthly house than he is obliged to
bestow on that mystic tower, of which you know St. Augustine speaks in one of his letters, which he has promised
to finish in his conversations. Adieu. B. P.—J. P.

Postscript of Jacqueline.—I hope shortly to write you the
particulars of my own affair, of which I shall send you the
details; meanwhile, pray to God for the result.

If you know any pious soul, let him pray to God for me
also.[2]

4

LETTER TO MADAME PERIER AND HER HUSBAND,[1] ON THE
DEATH OF M. PASCAL, PERE

OCTOBER 17, 1651.

As you are both now informed of our common misfortune, and as the letter which we commenced has given
you some consolation by the recital of the happy circumstances that accompanied the subject of our affliction, I
cannot refuse to you those which remain in my mind, and
which I pray God to give me, and to recall to me several
which we formerly received from his grace, and which have
been newly given to us by our friends on this occasion.

I know not now where my first letter ended. My sister
sent it away without noticing that it was not finished. It
only seems to me that it contained in substance some particulars of the conduct of God over life and sickness, which
I would repeat to you here, so deeply are they engraven
in my heart, and so solid is the consolation that they bring
me, if you could not have seen them yourselves in the
preceding letter, and if my sister did not intend to make
to you a more exact recital of them at her earliest con-

[2] This last sentence is in the handwriting of Pascal; usually Jacqueline
wrote under the dictation of her brother.—W.
[1] Fragments of this letter have figured in a great number of the editions
of Pascal, under the title of: *Thoughts upon Death, extracted from a letter
written by M. Pascal upon the subject of the death of his father.* M.
Cousin, upon this indication, sought for and found the letter, such as we
publish it here.—W.

venience. I shall, therefore, only speak to you here of the conclusion which I draw from them, which is that, except those who are interested by the feelings of nature, there is not a Christian who should not rejoice at it.

Upon this great foundation, I shall commence what I have to say to you by a remark that is very consoling to those who have sufficient liberty of spirit to conceive it in the midst of grief. It is that we should seek consolation in our ills, not in ourselves, not in men, not in any thing that is created; but in God. And the reason is, that all creatures are not the first cause of the accidents that we call evils; but that the providence of God being the only and veritable cause, the arbiter and the sovereign of them, it is indubitable that we must resort directly to the source, and go back to the origin to find a solid alleviation. If we follow this precept, and if we regard this event, not as an effect of chance, not as a fatal necessity of nature, not as the play of the elements and parts of which man is composed (for God has not abandoned his elect to caprice and chance), but as a result indispensable, inevitable, just, holy, useful to the good of the Church, and to the exaltation of the name and the greatness of God, of a decree of his providence conceived from all eternity to be executed in the plenitude of its time in such a year, such a day, such an hour, such a place, such a manner; and, in short, that all that has happened has been from all time foreknown and foreordained of God; if, I say, through a transport of grace, we regard this accident, not in itself and apart from God, but apart from itself, and in the inmost part of the will of God, in the justice of his decree, in the order of his providence, which is the true cause of it, without which it would not have happened, through which alone it has happened, and in the manner in which it has happened; we shall adore in humble silence the impenetrable loftiness of his secrets, we shall venerate the sanctity of his decrees, we shall bless the acts of his providence, and, uniting our will to that of God himself, we shall wish with him, in him, and for him, the thing that he has willed in us and for us from all eternity.

Let us regard it, then, in this manner, and let us practice this precept, which I learned of a great man in the time of our deepest affliction, that there is no consolation except in truth alone. It is certain that Socrates and Seneca have nothing consolatory on such an occasion as this. They have been in the error that has blinded all men in the beginning: they have all taken death as natural to man; and all the discourses which they have founded upon this false principle are so futile that they only serve to demonstrate by their inutility how weak man is in general, since the most elevated productions of the greatest among men are so weak and puerile. It is not the same with Jesus Christ, it is not thus in the canonical books: the truth is there revealed, and consolation is also as infallibly joined with it as it is infallibly separated from error.

Let us, then, consider death in the truth which the Holy Spirit has taught us. We have this admirable advantage, of knowing that death is really and actually a penalty of sin imposed on man in order to expiate his crime, necessary to man to purge him from sin; that it is the only one that can deliver the soul from the concupiscence of the members, without which saints come not into the world. We know that life, and the life of Christians, is a continual sacrifice, that can only be completed by death; we know that as Jesus Christ, being in the world, regarded and offered himself to God as a sacrifice, and a veritable victim; as his birth, his life, his death, his resurrection, his ascension, his presence in the Eucharist, and his eternal seat at the right hand, are only a sole and single sacrifice; we know that what has been accomplished in Jesus Christ should be accomplished also in all his members.

Let us, then, consider life as a sacrifice; and let the accidents of life make no impression upon the minds of Christians, except in proportion as they interrupt or accomplish this sacrifice. Let us only call that evil which renders the victim of God the victim of the devil, but let us call that good which renders the victim of the devil in Adam the victim of God; and by this rule let us examine the nature of death.

For this consideration it is necessary to have recourse to the person of Jesus Christ, for all that is in men is

abominable, and as God looks upon men only through the
mediator Jesus Christ, men should also look neither upon
others nor themselves except mediately through Jesus Christ.
For if we do not take this course, we shall find in ourselves nothing but veritable misfortunes, or abominable pleasures; but if we regard all things in Jesus Christ, we shall
find full consolation, full satisfaction, and full edification.

Let us, then, consider death in Jesus Christ, and not without Jesus Christ. Without Jesus Christ it is horrible, detestable, the horror of nature. In Jesus Christ it is altogether different; it is benignant, holy, the joy of the faithful.
Every thing is sweet in Jesus Christ, even to death: and this
is why he suffered and died to sanctify death and suffering;
and, in common with God and man, he has been all that was
great, and all that was abject, in order to sanctify in himself
all things except sin, and to be the model of every condition.

To consider the nature of death, and of death in Jesus
Christ, it is necessary to see what rank it holds in his continual and uninterrupted sacrifice, and for this to remark
that in sacrifices the most important part is the death of
the victim. The oblation and sanctification which precede
are the details; but the accomplishment is the death, in
which, by the annihilation of life, the creature renders to
God all the homage of which it is capable, in annihilating
itself before the face of his majesty, and in adoring his
sovereign existence, which alone exists in reality. It is true
that there is another part, after the death of the victim,
without which its death would be useless, that is, God's ac-
ceptance of the sacrifice. This is what is said in the Scripture: *Et odoratus est Dominus suavitatem.* "And the Lord
smelled a sweet sacrifice." This it is that really consum-
mates the oblation; but it is rather an action of God towards the creature than of the creature towards God, and
does not hinder the last act of the creature from being
death.

All these things have been accomplished in Jesus Christ.
In entering the world, he offered himself: *Obtulit semetipsum
per Spiritum Sanctum. Ingrediens mundum, dixit: Hostiam
noluisti ... Tunc dixi: Ecce venio. In capite,* etc. "Through

the Eternal Spirit he offered himself. When he cometh into the world, he saith, sacrifice and offering thou wouldst not. Then said I, Lo, I come." This is his oblation. His sanctification was immediate upon his oblation. This sacrifice lasted all his life, and was accomplished by his death. "Ought he not to have suffered these things, and to enter into his glory?" "Though he were a son, yet learned he obedience by the things which he suffered." But "in the days of his flesh, when he had offered up prayers and supplications, with strong cries and tears unto him that was able to save, he was heard in that he feared:" and God raised him from the dead, and sent him his glory, prefigured formerly by the fire from heaven that fell upon the victim to burn and consume his body, and to make it live the spiritual life of glory. This is what Jesus Christ has obtained, and what has been accomplished through his resurrection.

Thus this sacrifice being perfected by the death of Christ, and consummated even in his body by his resurrection, in which the image of sinful flesh was absorbed by glory, Jesus Christ had wholly finished his part; it remained only that the sacrifice should be accepted of God, that, as the smoke ascended and carried the odor to the throne of God, thus Jesus Christ was, in this state of perfect immolation, offered, carried to, and accepted at the throne of God himself: and this it is that has been accomplished in the ascension, in which he mounted on high and by his own power and by the power of his Holy Spirit, which surrounded him on every side, was carried away; as the smoke of the victims, the emblem of Jesus Christ, was carried on high by the air that sustained it, the type of the Holy Spirit: and the Acts of the Apostles indicate to us expressly that he was received up into heaven, in order to assure us that this holy sacrifice accomplished on earth was welcome and acceptable to God, and was received into the bosom of God, to shine in glory through ages upon ages.

This is the state of things as regards our sovereign Lord. Let us consider them now in ourselves. From the moment we enter the Church, which is the world of the Faithful and especially of the elect, into which Jesus Christ entered at the moment of his incarnation by a privilege peculiar to the only Son of God, we are offered and sacrificed. This sacrifice is continued by life and completed at death, in which the soul truly quitting all vices, and the love of the world, with the contagion of which it is always infected throughout life, achieves its immolation and is received into the bosom of God.

Let us not grieve then like the heathen who have no hope. We did not lose our father at the moment of his death: we lost him, so to say, when he entered the Church through baptism. From that time, he belonged to God; his life was devoted to God; his actions regarded the world only for God. In his death, he became totally separated from sin, and it was at that moment that he was accepted by God, and that his sacrifice received its accomplishment and its consummation. He has performed therefore what he had vowed: he has finished the work that God had given him to do; he has accomplished the only thing for which he was created. The will of God is accomplished in him, and his will is absorbed in God. Let not our will then separate what God has joined together; and let us stifle or moderate, by the understanding of truth, the feelings of a corrupt and fallen nature which has only false images, and which troubles by its illusions the sanctity of the feelings which truth and the Gospel should give us.

Let us then no longer look upon death like the heathen, but like Christians, that is with hope, as St. Paul commands, since this is the especial privilege of Christians. Let us no longer regard a corpse as putrid carrion because deceitful nature figures it thus; but as the inviolable and eternal temple of the Holy Spirit, as faith teaches. For we know that sainted bodies are inhabited by the Holy Spirit until the resurrection, which will be caused by virtue of this spirit which dwells in them for this effect. It is for this reason that we honor the relics of the dead, and it was on this true principle that the Eucharist was formerly placed in the mouth of the dead, since, as it was known that they were the temple of the Holy Spirit, it was believed that they also merited to be united to this holy sacrament. But the Church has changed this custom, not in order that these bodies shall not be holy, but for the reason that the Eucharist being the bread of life and of the living, it ought not to be given to the dead.

Let us no longer regard a man as having ceased to live although nature suggests it; but as beginning to live, as truth assures. Let us no longer regard his soul as perished and reduced to nothingness, but as quickened and united to the sovereign life; and let us thus correct, by attention to these truths, the sentiments of error so deeply imprinted in ourselves and those emotions of honor so natural to mankind.

To subdue this dread more effectually, it is necessary fully to comprehend its origin; and to paint it to you in a few words, I am forced to tell you in general what is the source of all vice and all sin. This I have learned from two very great and holy personages. The truth covered by this mystery is that God has created man with two loves, the one for God, the other for himself; but with this law, that the love for God shall be infinite, that is without any other limits than God himself; and that the love for self shall be finite and relating to God.

Man in this state not only loves himself without sin, but could not do otherwise than love himself without sin.

Since, sin being come, man has lost the first of these loves; and the love for himself being left alone in this great soul capable of an infinite love, this self-love has extended and overflowed in the empty space which the love of God has quitted; and thus he loves himself alone, and all things for himself, that is, infinitely. This is the origin of self-love. It was natural to Adam and just in his innocence; but it became criminal and immoderate after his sin.

Here is the source of this love, and the cause of its defect and of its excess. It is the same with the passion of ruling, of indolence, and others. The application is easy. Let us come to our single subject. The dread of death was natural to innocent Adam, because, his life being pleasing to God, it must have been pleasing to man: and death was terrible when it ended a life conformed to the will of God. Since, man having sinned, his life has become corrupt, his body and soul enemies to each other, and both to God. This horrible change having infected so holy a life, the love of life has nevertheless remained; and the dread of death being equally felt, that which was just in Adam is unjust and criminal in us.

Such is the origin of the dread of death and the cause of its faultiness. Let us then illumine the error of nature by the light of faith. The dread of death is natural, but it is in the state of innocence; death in truth is terrible, but it is when it puts an end to a pure life. It was just to hate it when it separated a holy soul from a holy body; but it is just to love it when it separates a holy soul from an impure body. It was just to flee it, when it broke the peace between the body and the soul; but not when it calms the irreconcilable dissension between them. In short, when it afflicted an innocent body, when it took away from the body the liberty of honoring God, when it separated from the soul a body submissive to and co-operative with its will, when it put an end to all the good of which man is capable, it was just to abhor it; but when it puts an end to an impure life, when it takes away from the body the liberty of sinning, when it delivers the soul from a powerful rebel that contradicts all the motives for its salvation, it is very unjust to preserve the same feelings.

Let us not therefore relinquish this love for life which nature has given us, since we have received it from God; but let this be for the same life for which God has given it to us and not for a contrary object. In consenting to the love that Adam had for his innocent life and that Jesus Christ himself had for his own, let us bring ourselves to hate a life contrary to that which Jesus Christ has loved, and only to fear the death which Jesus Christ has feared, which comes to a body pleasing to God; but not to fear a death that, punishing a guilty body, and purging a vicious body, ought to give us quite contrary feelings, if we have any thing of faith, of hope, and of charity.

It is one of the great principles of Christianity that every thing that happened to Jesus Christ should take place in the soul and the body of each Christian: that as Jesus Christ suffered during his mortal life, died to this mortal life, was raised to a new life, ascended to heaven, and sitteth at the right hand of the Father; so the body and soul should suffer, die, be raised from the dead, ascend to heaven, and sit at the right hand of God. All these things are accomplished in the soul during life, but not in the body. The soul suffers and dies to sin in penitence and in baptism; the soul is raised again to a new life in the same baptism; the soul quits the earth and ascends to heaven at death, and takes its seat at the right hand of God at the time that he appoints. None of these things happen to the body during this life; but the same things befall it afterwards. For at death the body dies to its mortal life; at the judgment it will rise to a new life; after the judgment, it will ascend to heaven and will sit at the right hand of God. Thus the same things happen to the body and the soul, but at different times; and the changes of the body come only when those of the soul are accomplished, that is at the hour of death: so that death is the consummation of the beatitude of the soul and the commencement of the beatitude of the body.

These are the admirable ways of the wisdom of God for the salvation of his saints, and St. Augustine teaches us on this subject, that God has arranged them in this wise for fear that if the body of man should die and rise again forever at baptism, men would only enter into the obedience of the Gospel through the love of life; whilst the grandeur of faith shines forth far more when it tends to immortality through the shades of death.

This is, certainly, our belief and the faith that we profess, and I believe that there is in this more than is needed to aid your consolations by my small efforts. I should not undertake to carry you this aid of myself; but as these are only repetitions of what I have learned, I give them with assurance, praying God to bless these seeds, and to give them growth, for without him we can do nothing, and his most holy words will not take root in us, as he himself has said.

It is not that I wish that you should be without feeling; the blow is too sensible; it would be even insupportable without supernatural aid. It is not therefore right that we should be without grief, like the angels who have no sentiment of nature; neither is it right that we should be without consolation, like the heathen who have no sentiment of grace: but it is right that we should be afflicted and consoled like Christians, and that the consolations of grace should overcome the feelings of nature; that we should say with the apostles: "We are afflicted but not cast down," in order that grace may not only be in us but victorious in us; that thus, in sanctifying the name of our Father, his will may be made ours; that his grace may reign and prevail over nature, and that our afflictions may be as the substance of a sacrifice which his grace perfects and annihilates for the glory of God; and that these individual sacrifices may honor and precede the universal sacrifice wherein all nature should be perfected by the power of Jesus Christ. Thus we derive advantage from our own imperfections, since they serve as material for this sacrifice; for it is the aim of true Christians to profit by their own imperfections, because "all things work together for good to the elect."

And if we pay close attention to this, we shall find great advantages for our edification, in considering the thing truly as we said just now. For, since it is true that the death of the body is only the type of that of the soul, and since we build upon the principle that in this chance we have all possible reason to hope for its sure salvation, it is certain that if we cannot arrest the progress of grief, we should derive this benefit, that since the death of the body is so terrible that it causes in us such emotions, that of the soul ought to cause in us those far more inconsolable. God sends us the first, God turns away the second. Let us then consider the greatness of our blessings in the greatness of our ills, and let the excess of our grief be in proportion to that of our joy.

There is nothing that can moderate it, except the fear that he may languish for some time in the pains which are destined to purge the remains of the sin of this life, and we ought carefully to apply ourselves to appease the anger of God towards him. Prayer and sacrifices are a sovereign remedy for his pains. But I have learned of a holy man in our affliction that one of the most solid and useful charities towards the dead is to do the things that they would command were they still in the world, to practise the holy advice which they have given us, and put ourselves, for their sakes, in the condition in which they would wish us at present. By this practice, we shall in some sort revive them in ourselves, since their counsels are still living and acting within us; and as heresiarchs are punished in the other life for the sins into which they have drawn their votaries, in whom their venom is still living, so the dead are recompensed, exclusive of their own merit, for those to whom they have given succession by their counsels and their example.

Let us strive then with all our power to revive him in us before God; and let us console ourselves in the union of our hearts, in which it seems to me that he still lives, and that our reunion in some sort restores to us his presence, as Jesus Christ makes himself present in the assembly of his faithful.

I pray God to form and to maintain these sentiments in us, and to continue those which it appears to me he has given me, of having more tenderness than ever for you and for my sister; for it seems to me that the love that we had for my father ought not to be lost, and that we should make a division of it among ourselves, and that we should chiefly inherit the affection which he bore to us, to love each other still more cordially if possible.

I pray God to strengthen us in these resolutions, and in this hope I entreat you to permit me to give you a counsel which indeed you could take without me; but I shall not refrain from giving it. It is that after having found grounds of consolation for him, we shall not come to lack them for ourselves by dwelling upon the need and the utility that we shall have of his presence.

It is I who am the most interested in it. If I had lost him six years ago, I should have lost myself, and although I believe my necessity of him at present to be less absolute, I know that he would still have been necessary to me ten years and useful all my life. But we should hope that God having ordered it in such a time, such a place and such a manner, it is doubtless the most expedient for his glory and for our salvation.

However strange this may appear, I believe that we should regard all events in the same manner, and that, however sinister they may appear to us, we should hope that God would draw from them a source of joy to us if we will but intrust the direction of them to him. We know of persons of condition who have feared the death of relatives which God has perhaps averted at their prayer, who have caused or been the occasion of so much misery that there was reason to wish that the prayers had not been granted.

Man is assuredly too weak to judge soundly of the result of future things. Let us therefore hope in God, and let us not weary ourselves by rash and indiscreet forecasts. Let us commit ourselves then to God for the direction of our lives, and that grief may not prevail within us.

St. Augustine teaches us that there is in every man a serpent, an Eve and an Adam. The serpent is the senses and our nature, the Eve is the concupiscible appetite, and the Adam is the reason. Nature tempts us continually, concupiscible appetite often fills us with desires, but the sin is not consummated if reason does not consent. Let the serpent and the Eve therefore act if we cannot hinder it; but let us pray to God that his grace may so strengthen our Adam that he may remain victorious; and that Jesus Christ may be the conqueror over him and may reign eternally in us. Amen.

5

EXTRACT FROM A LETTER OF M. PASCAL TO M. PERIER

PARIS, *Friday, June 6,* 1653

I HAVE just received your letter, inclosing that of my sister, which I have not had leisure to read, and moreover believe that this would be useless.

My sister made her profession yesterday, Thursday, the 5th of June, 1653. It was impossible for me to delay her: the Messieurs of Port Royal feared that a slight delay might bring on a greater one, and wished to hasten it for the reason that they hope ere long to put her in office; and consequently, it was necessary to hasten, because for this several years of profession are needed. This is the way they paid me. In fine, I could not, etc.

6

ExTRACT FROM A LETTER TO MADAME PERIER, UPON THE PRO-
JECTED MARRIAGE OF MADEMOISELLE JACQUELINE PERIER

1659.

IN general, their advice was that you could in no way,
without mortally wounding charity and your conscience, and
rendering yourself guilty of one of the greatest crimes,
pledge a child of her age and innocence, and even of her
piety, to the most perilous and lowest of the conditions of
Christianity. That indeed, according to the world, the affair
had no difficulty, and she was to conclude it without hesitation; but that according to God, she had less difficulty in it,
and she was to reject it without hesitation, because the condition of an advantageous marriage is as desirable in the
opinion of the world as it is vile and prejudicial in the sight
of God. That not knowing to what she may be called, nor
whether her temperament may not be so tranquil that she can
support her virginity with piety, it were little to know the
value of it to pledge her to lose this good so desirable to
every one in himself, and so desirable to fathers and mothers
for their children, since as they can no longer desire it for
themselves, it is in them that they should strive to render to
God what they have lost in general for other causes than for
God.

Besides, that husbands, although rich and wise in the
opinion of the world, are in truth complete pagans in the
sight of God; so that the last words of these gentlemen are
that to pledge a child to an ordinary man is a species of
homicide and a deicide as it were in their own persons.

7

NOTE FROM PASCAL TO THE MARCHIONESS DE SABLE

December, 1660.

ALTHOUGH I am much embarrassed, I can no longer defer
rendering you a thousand thanks for having procured me the

acquaintance of M. Menjot; for it is doubtless to you, Madame, that I owe it; and as I esteemed him highly already from the things which my sister had told me of him, I cannot tell you with how much joy I have received the favor which he has wished to render me. It is only necessary to read his letter to see how much intellect and judgment he possesses; and although I may not be capable of understanding the depth of the matters which he treats in his book, I will tell you, nevertheless, Madame, that I have learned much from the manner in which he reconciles in a few words the immateriality of the soul with the power of matter to change its functions and to cause delirium. I am very impatient to have the honor to converse with you on it.

8

FRAGMENT OF A LETTER TO M. PERIER

1661.

You give me pleasure by sending me all the details of your controversies, and chiefly because you are interested therein; for I imagine that you do not imitate our controversialists of this country, who avail themselves so badly, at least so it seems to me, of the advantage which God offers them of suffering something for the establishment of his truths. For, if this were for the establishment of their truths, they would not act differently; and it seems that they are ignorant that the same Providence that has inspired some with light, has refused it to others; and it seems that in laboring to persuade them of it they are serving another God than the one who permits the obstacles that oppose their progress. They think to render service to God by murmuring against the hindrances, as if this were another power that should excite their piety, and another that should give vigor to those who oppose them.

This is what comes of self-will. When we wish by our own efforts that something shall succeed, we become irritated with obstacles, because we feel in these hindrances that the motive that makes us act has not placed them there, and we find things in them which the self-will that makes us act has not formed there.

But when God inspires our actions, we never feel any thing outside that does not come from the same principle that causes us to act; there is no opposition in the motive that impels us; the same motive power which leads us to act, leads others to resist us, or permits them at least; so that as we find no difference in this, and as it is not our own will that combats external events, but the same will that produces the good and permits the evil, this uniformity does not trouble the peace of the soul, and is one of the best tokens that we are acting by the will of God, since it is much more certain that God permits the evil, however great it may be, than that God causes the good in us (and not some secret motive), however great it may appear to us; so that in order really to perceive whether it is God that makes us act, it is much better to test ourselves by our deportment without than by our motives within, since if we only examine ourselves within, although we may find nothing but good there, we cannot assure ourselves that this good comes truly from God. But when we examine ourselves without, that is when we consider whether we suffer external hindrances with patience, this signifies that there is a uniformity of will between the motive power that inspires our passions and the one that permits the resistance to them; and as there is no doubt that it is God who permits the one, we have a right humbly to hope that it is God who produces the other.

But what! we act as if it were our mission to make truth triumph whilst it is only our mission to combat for it. The desire to conquer is so natural that when it is covered by the desire of making the truth triumph, we often take the one for the other, and think that we are seeking the glory of God when in truth we are seeking our own. It seems to me that the way in which we support these hindrances is the surest token of it, for in fine if we wish only the order established by God, it is certain that we wish the triumph of his justice as much as that of his mercy, and that when it does not come of our negligence, we shall be in an equal mood, whether the truth be known or whether it be combated, since in the one the mercy of God triumphs, and in the other, his justice.

Pater juste, mundus te non cognovit. Righteous father, the world has not known thee. Upon which St. Augustine says that it is through his justice that the world has not known him. Let us pray, labor, and rejoice evermore, as St. Paul says.

If you had reproved me in my first faults, I should not have been guilty of this, and should have been moderate. But I shall not suppress this any more than the other; you can suppress it yourself if you wish. I could not refrain, so angry am I against those who insist absolutely that the truth shall be believed when they demonstrate it, which Jesus Christ did not do in his created humanity. It is a mockery, and it seems to me treating . . . I am grieved on account of the malady of M. de Laporte. I assure you that I honor him with all my heart. I, etc.

9

LETTER TO MADAME PERIER

(Addressed: A Mademoiselle Périer la Conseillère.)

ROUEN, Saturday, the last of January, 1643.

MY DEAR SISTER,

I doubt not that you have been greatly troubled at the length of time in which you have received no news from these parts. But I think that you must have suspected that the journey of the Elus has been the cause, as in fact it was. Had it not been for this, I should not have failed to write to you oftener. I have to tell you that Messieurs the commissioners being at Gizors, my father made me take a tour to Paris, where I found a letter which you had written, in which you say that you are surprised that I reproach you that you do not write often enough, and in which you tell me that you write to Rouen once every week. It is very certain, if this is so, that the letters are lost, for I do not receive one once in three weeks. On my return to Rouen, I found a letter from M. Périer, who writes that you are ill. He does not write whether your sickness is dangerous or whether you are better; and an unusual length of time has passed since without having received any letter, so that we are in an anxiety from which I pray you to relieve us as soon as possible; but I think the prayer I make you will be useless, for before you shall have received this letter, I hope that we shall have received letters from you or from M. Périer. The department is finished, God be praised. If I knew of any thing new, I would let you know it. I am, my dear sister, etc.

Postscript in the handwriting of Etienne Pascal, the father: " My dear daughter will excuse me if I do not write to her as I wished, having no leisure for it; for I have never been in a tenth part the perplexity that I am at present. I could not be more so without being overwhelmed; for the last four months I have not been in bed six times before two o'clock in the morning.

" I lately commenced a jesting letter upon the subject of your last, concerning the marriage of M. Desjeux, but I have never had leisure to finish it. For news, the daughter of M. de Paris, *maître des comptes,* the wife of M. de Neufirlle, also *maître des comptes,* is dead, as well as the daughter of Belair, the wife of young Lambert. Your little boy slept here last night. He is very well, thank God.

" I am ever your true and affectionate friend,
                                        " PASCAL."

Your very humble and affectionate servant and brother,
                                        PASCAL.

10

NOTE FROM PASCAL TO HIS SISTER, MADAME PERIER

(Superscribed, To Mademoiselle Périer, at Clermont, in Auvergne.)

MY DEAR SISTER,

I do not believe that it is quite right that you should be vexed; for, if you are not so because we have forgotten you, then you ought not to be at all. I tell you no news,

for there is too much that is general, and there must always
be too much that is private. I should have much to tell
you that happens in complete secrecy, but I regard it as
useless to send it to you; all that I pray you is, to mingle
acts of grace with the prayers which you make for me, and
which I entreat you to multiply at this time. I carried your
letter myself with the aid of God, in order that it might be
forwarded to Madame de Maubuisson. They gave me a little
book, in which this sentence was written with the hand.[1] I
know not whether it is in the little book of sentences, but
it is beautiful. I am so much hurried that I can say no more.
Do not fail in your fasts. Adieu.

II

LETTERS TO MADEMOISELLE DE ROANNEZ[1]

I

1656.

IN order to answer all the points upon which you address me, and, indeed, to write, although my time is
limited.

I am delighted that you like the book of M. de Laval,[2] and
the Meditations on Grace; I draw from this important conclusions for what I desire.

I send the details of this condemnation which had frightened[3] you: it is nothing at all, thank God, and it is a miracle
that nothing worse is done, since the enemies of truth have
the power and the will to oppress him. Perhaps you are of
those who merit not to be abandoned by God, and removed
from an undeserving world, and he is assured that you will
serve the Church by your prayers, if the Church has served
you by hers. For it is the Church that merits with Jesus

[1] It is wanting here.—W.
[1] Charlotte Gouffier de Roannez, sister of the duke of this name, the
friend of Pascal, and one of the editors of the *Thoughts*.
[2] Pseudonym under which the Duke de Luynes published different works
of piety, among others, *Sentences drawn from Holy Scripture and the
Fathers.*—W.
[3] The allusion is probably to the censure of the Sorbonne against Arnauld,
in 1656.—W.

Christ, who is inseparable from her, the conversion of all those who are not in the truth; and it is in turn these converted persons who succor the mother who has delivered them. I praise with all my heart the little zeal that I have recognized in your letter for the union with the pope. The body is not more living without the head, than the head without the body. Whoever separates himself from the one or the other is no longer of the body, and belongs no more to Jesus Christ. I know not whether there are persons in the Church more attached to this unity of body than those that you call ours. We know that all the virtues, martyrdom, the austerities and all good works are useless out of the Church, and out of communion with the head of the Church, which is the pope. I will never separate myself from his communion, at least I pray God to give me this grace, without which I should be lost forever.

I make to you a sort of profession of faith, and I know not wherefore; but I would neither efface it nor commence it again.

M. Du Gas has spoken to me this morning of your letter with as much astonishment and joy as it is possible to have: he knows not where you have taken what he has reported to me of your words; he has said to me surprising things, that no longer surprise me so much. I begin to accustom myself to you and to the grace that God gives you, and nevertheless I avow to you that it is to me always new, as it is always new in reality.

For it is a continual flow of graces that the Scripture compares to a river, and to the light which the sun continually emits from itself, and is always new, so that if it ceased an instant to emit them, all that we have received would disappear, and we should remain in darkness.

He has said to me that he had begun a response to you, and that he would transcribe it to render it more legible, and that, at the same time, he would extend it. But he has just sent it to me with a little note, wherein he informs me that he has been able neither to transcribe it nor to extend it; this makes me think that it will be ill-written. But I am a witness of his want of leisure, and of his desire that he had leisure for your sake.

I take part in the joy that the affair of the . . .[4] will afford you, for I see clearly that you are interested for the Church: you are indeed under obligations to her. For sixteen hundred years she has groaned for you. It is time to groan for her and for us altogether, and to give her all that remains to us of life, since Jesus Christ has assumed life only to lose it for her and for us.

II

OCTOBER, 1656.

IT seems to me that you take sufficient interest in the miracle to send you particular notice that its verification is consummated by the Church, as you will see by the sentence of the grand vicar.

There are so few persons to whom God would manifest himself by these extraordinary acts, that we ought indeed to profit by these occasions, since he does not leave the secrecy of the nature that covers him but to excite our faith to serve him with so much the more ardor as we know him with the more certainty.

If God discovered himself continually to men, there would be no merit in believing him; and, if he never discovered himself, there would be little faith. But he conceals himself ordinarily and discovers himself rarely to those whom he wishes to engage in his service. This strange secrecy, in which God is impenetrably withdrawn from the sight of men, is a great lesson to betake ourselves to solitude far from the sight of men. He remained concealed under the veil of the nature that covers him till the Incarnation; and when it was necessary that he should appear, he concealed himself still the more in covering himself with humanity. He was much more recognizable when he was invisible than when he rendered himself visible. And in fine, when he wished to fulfil the promise that he made to his apostles to remain with men until his final coming, he chose to remain in the strangest and most obscure secret of all, which are the species of the Eucharist. It is this sacrament that St. John calls in the Apoc-

[4] In the manuscript of the Oratory: *of the Nuns.—Faugère.*

arypse *a concealed manner;* and I believe that Isaiah saw it in that state, when he said in the spirit of prophecy: *Truly thou art a God concealed.* This is the last secrecy wherein he can be. The veil of nature that covers God has been penetrated by some of the unbelieving, who, as St. Paul says, have recognized an invisible God in visible nature. Heretical Christians have recognized him through his humanity and adored Jesus Christ God and man. But to recognize him under the species of bread is peculiar to Catholics alone: none but us are thus enlightened by God. We may add to these considerations the secrecy of the spirit of God concealed still in the Scripture. For there are two perfect senses, the literal and the mystical; and the Jews, stopping at the one, do not even think that there is another, and take no thought for searching it out, just as the impious, seeing natural effects, attribute them to nature, without thinking that there is another author, and, as the Jews, seeing a perfect man in Jesus Christ, have not thought to seek in him another nature: *We had not thought that it was he,* again says Isaiah: and just as, in fine, the heretics, seeing the perfect appearances of bread in the Eucharist, do not think to see it in another substance. All things cover some mystery; all things have veils that cover God. Christians ought to recognize him in every thing. Temporal afflictions cover eternal goods to which they lead. Temporal joys cover eternal ills that they cause. Let us pray God to make us recognize and serve him in every thing; let us give him countless thanks that, having concealed himself in all things for others, he has discovered himself in all things and in so many ways for us.

III

I know not how you have taken the loss of your letters. I could wish indeed that you may have taken it as you ought. It is time to begin to judge of what is good or bad by the will of God, who can be neither unjust nor blind, and not by our own, which is always full of malice and error. If you have had these sentiments, I shall be greatly pleased, inasmuch as you will have received consolation for a more valid reason than that which I have to communicate to you, which is that I hope that they are found again. That of the 5th has already been brought to me; and although it is not the most important (for that of M. du Gas is more so), nevertheless this makes me hope to recover the other.

I know not why you complain that I have written nothing for you,—I do not separate you two, and continually think of both. You see plainly that my other letters, and this also, refer sufficiently to you. In truth, I cannot refrain from telling you that I could wish to be infallible in my judgments; you would not be badly off if that were the case, for I am very much pleased with you; but my judgment is nothing. I say this with reference to the manner in which I see you speak of that good persecuted friar, and of what * * * does. I am not surprised to see M. N. interested in the matter, I am accustomed to his zeal, but yours is wholly new; this new language is usually the product of a new heart. Jesus Christ has given in the Church this sign whereby to recognize those who have faith,—that they shall speak a new language; and in fact the renewal of thoughts and desires causes that of discourse. What you say of days passed in solitude, and the consolation afforded you by reading, are things that M. N. will be extremely happy to know when I shall make him acquainted with them, and my sister also. These certainly are new things, but they must be unceasingly renewed, for this newness, which cannot be displeasing to God as the old man cannot be pleasing to him, is different from earthly novelties, inasmuch as worldly things, however new they may be, grow old as they endure; whilst this new spirit is renewed the more, the longer it endures. Our old man perishes, says St. Paul, and is renewed day by day, and will be perfectly new only in eternity, when shall be sung without ceasing that new song of which David speaks in the Psalms; that is the song that springs from the new spirit of love.

I will tell you for news, of what concerns these two persons, that I clearly perceive their zeal does not grow cold; this surprises me, for it is much more rare to see continuation in piety than to see entrance upon it. I have them always in mind, especially her of the miracle, because there is something in her case more extraordinary, although the other may be also very extraordinary and almost without example. It is certain that the graces conferred by God in this life are the measure of the glory prepared by him for the other. Thus when I foresee the end and crown of this work by the commencements that appear in pious persons, I feel a veneration that overcomes me with respect towards those whom he seems to have chosen for his elect. I confess to you that it seems to me that I see them already on one of those thrones where those who shall have left all will judge the world with Jesus Christ, according to the promise that he has made. But when I come to think that these same persons may fall, and be on the contrary, of the unfortunate number of the judged, and that there will be so many of them who will fall from glory and leave to others by their negligence the crown that God had offered them, I cannot bear the thought; and the distress that I should feel in seeing them in this eternal state of misery, after having imagined them with so much reason in the other state, makes me turn my mind from the idea and recur to God in order to pray him not to abandon the weak creatures that he has acquired, and to say to him for the two persons whom you know what the Church says to-day with St. Paul: *O Lord, do thou complete that work which thou thyself hast commenced.* St. Paul often regarded himself in these two states, and it is what makes him say elsewhere: *I keep under my body, and bring it into subjection; lest when I have preached to others, I myself be a castaway.* I end therefore with these words of Job: *I have always feared the Lord like the waves of a raging sea and swollen to engulf me.* And elsewhere: *Happy is the man that feareth always!*

IV

IT is very certain that separation never takes place without pain. We do not feel our bond when we voluntarily follow the object that leads us, as St. Augustine says; but when we begin to resist and draw back, we suffer; the bond stretches and suffers violence; and this bond is our body, which is broken but by death. Our Lord has said that *since the com-*

ing of John the Baptist, that is, since his coming in each of the faithful, *the kingdom of heaven suffers violence and the violent take it by storm.* Before we are touched by the spirit we feel nothing but the burden of concupiscence that presses us to the earth. When God draws us on high, these two opposing efforts cause that violence which he alone can enable us to overcome. *But we can do all things,* says St. Leon, *with him, without whom we can do nothing.* We must then resolve to endure this warfare all our lives; for here there is no peace. *Christ came not to bring peace, but a sword.* Nevertheless, it must be acknowledged that, as Scripture says, the *wisdom of this world is foolishness with God;* so it may be said that this warfare which appears hard to men is peace with God, for it is the peace which Jesus Christ himself has brought us. Yet it will not be perfected until the body shall be destroyed; and this it is which makes us wish for death, while we nevertheless cheerfully endure life for the love of him who has suffered both life and death for us, and who is able to give us more than we can ask or think, as says St. Paul in the Epistle of to-day.

v

GOD be praised, I have no more fears for you, but am full of hope! These are consoling words indeed of Jesus Christ: *To him that hath shall be given.* By this promise, those who have received much have the right to hope for more, and those who have received extraordinarily should hope extraordinarily. I try as much as I can to let nothing distress me, and to take every thing that happens as for the best. I believe that this is a duty, and that we sin in not doing so. For, in short, the reason why sins are sins is only because they are contrary to the will of God: and the essence of sin thus consisting in having a will opposed to that which we know to be of God, it is plain, it appears to me, that when he discovers his will to us by events, it would be a sin not to conform ourselves to it. I have learned that in every thing that happens there is something worthy of admiration, since the will of God is manifest in it. I praise him with all my heart for the continuation of his favors, for I see plainly that they do not diminish.

The affair of * * * does not go on very well: it is a thing that makes those tremble who are truly the children of God to see the persecution which is in preparation, not only against individuals (this would be little) but against the Truth. To speak truly, God is indeed abandoned. It appears to me that this is a time in which the service that we render him is very pleasing to him. He desires that we should judge of grace by nature, and thus we may be allowed to suppose that as a prince driven from his country by his subjects feels extreme tenderness for those who remain faithful to him amidst the public revolt, in the same manner, God looks with especial favor upon those who are at this time defending the purity of religion and morals, so warmly assailed. But there is this difference between the kings of the earth and the King of kings, that the princes do not render their subjects faithful, but find them so; whilst God never finds men other than unfaithful, and renders them faithful when they are so. So that while the kings of the earth are under signal obligations to those who adhere to their allegiance, it happens, on the contrary, that those who subsist in the service of God are themselves infinitely indebted to him. Let us continue then to praise him for this grace, if he has bestowed it upon us, for which we shall praise him throughout eternity, and let us pray that he may give us still more of it, and that he may look with pity upon us and upon the whole Church, outside of which there is nothing but malediction.

I am interested in the victim of persecution of whom you speak. I see plainly that God has reserved to himself some hidden servants, as he said to Elijah. I pray him that we may be of the number, and that in spirit, in sincerity, and in truth.

VI

WHATEVER may come of the affair of * * *, enough, thank God, has already been done to draw an admirable advantage from it against these accursed precepts. There is need that those who have taken any part in this should render great thanks to God, and that their relatives and friends should pray to God for them that they may not fall from the great happiness and honor which he has bestowed on them. All the honors of the world are but the image of this; this alone is solid and real, and nevertheless it is useless without the right frame of heart. It is not bodily austerities nor mental exercises, but good impulses of the heart, which are of merit and which sustain the sufferings of the body and the mind. For in short two things are necessary for sanctification— sufferings and joys. St. Paul says that *we must through much tribulation enter into the kingdom of God.* This should console those who experience tribulation, since, being warned that the path to heaven which they seek is filled with it, they should rejoice at meeting tokens that they are in the right way. But these very sufferings are not without joys, and are never surmounted but by pleasure. For as those who forsake God to return to the world do it only because they find more enjoyment in the pleasures of the world than in those of a union with God, and because this conquering charm leads them away and, making them repent of their first choice, renders them *penitents of the devil,* according to the saying of Tertullian; so none would ever quit the pleasures of the world to embrace the cross of Jesus Christ, did he not find more enjoyment in contempt, in poverty, in destitution, and in the scorn of men, than in the delights of sin. And thus, says Tertullian, *it must not be supposed that the Christian's life is a life of sadness.* We forsake pleasures only for others which are greater. *Pray without ceasing,* says St. Paul, *in every thing give thanks, rejoice evermore.* It is the joy of having found God that is the principle of the sorrow of having offended him, and of the whole change of life. He that finds a treasure in a field, according to Jesus Christ, has such joy that he goes directly and sells all that he has to purchase the field. The people of the world know nothing of this joy, *which the world can neither give nor take away,* as is said by Jesus Christ. The blessed have this joy without sorrow; the people of the world have their sorrows without this joy, and Christians have this joy mingled with the sorrow of having pursued other pleasures and the fear of losing it by the allurements of these same pleasures which tempt us without ceasing. And thus we should labor unceasingly to cherish this joy which moderates our fear, and to preserve this fear which preserves our joy, so that on feeling ourselves too much carried away by the one we may incline towards the other, and thus remain poised between the two. *In the day of prosperity be joyful; but in the day of adversity consider,* says the Scripture, and so it shall be till the promise of Jesus Christ shall be accomplished in us that our joy shall be full. Let us not then be cast down by sadness, nor believe that piety consists only in bitterness without consolation. The true piety, which is found perfect only in heaven, is so full of satisfactions that it overflows with them in its beginning, its progress, and its consummation. Its light is so shining that it is reflected on all about it; and if there is sadness mingled with it, especially at the outset, this comes from ourselves and not from virtue; for it is not the effect of the piety that is springing up in us, but of the impiety that still is there. Remove the impiety and the joy will be unalloyed. Let us not ascribe this then to devotion, but to ourselves and seek relief from it only through our correction.

VII

I AM very glad of the hope which you give me of the success of the affair which you fear may make you vain. There is something to fear in any case; for, were it successful, I should fear from it that evil sorrow of which St. Paul says that it leads to death, instead of that different one that leads to life.

It is certain that the matter was a thorny one, and that, if the person should be extricated from it, the result would give reason for some vanity, were it not that we had entreated it of God, and should therefore believe the good that comes of it his work. But if it should not succeed well, we ought not therefore to fall into despondency, for the same reason that having prayed to God in the affair, it is

evident that he has taken it into his own hand; thus he
must be regarded as the author of all good and of all
evil, with the exception of sin. Thereupon I would repeat
to the person the passage of Scripture to which I have
before referred: *In the day of prosperity rejoice, but in the
day of adversity consider.* Nevertheless, I must say to you
in respect to the other person whom you know, who sends
word that she has many things on her mind that trouble
her, that I am very sorry to see her in this state. I am
deeply grieved at her troubles, and should be glad to be able
to relieve them; I entreat her not to anticipate the future,
and to remember that, as our Lord has said, *Sufficient unto
the day is the evil thereof.*

The past ought not to trouble us, since we have only to
feel regret for our faults; but the future ought to concern
us still less, since it is wholly beyond our control, and since
perhaps we may not reach it at all. The present is the only
time that is truly our own, and this we ought to employ
according to the will of God. It is in this that our thoughts
ought chiefly to be centred. Yet the world is so restless
that men scarcely ever think of the present life and of the
moment in which they are living, but of that in which they
will live. In this manner we are always living in the future,
and never in the present. Our Lord has willed that our foresight should not extend beyond the present day. These are
the bounds within which we must keep both for our safety
and for our own repose. For in truth, the Christian precepts are those fullest of consolation, exceeding, I affirm,
the maxims of the world.

I also foresee many troubles, both for that person, for
others, and for myself. But I pray to God, when I find
myself absorbed in these forebodings, to restrain me within
my prescribed course. I call myself to an account, and I
find that I am neglecting to do many things that I ought at
present, in order to escape from useless thoughts of the
future on which, far from being obliged to dwell, it is on
the contrary my duty not to dwell at all. It is only for
want of not understanding how to know and study the
present that we undertake to study the future. What I
say here, I say for myself, and not for that person who has

assuredly more virtue and reflection than I; but I show
him my defect to hinder him from falling into it: we sometimes correct ourselves better by the sight of evil than by
the example of good; and it is well to accustom ourselves
to profit by evil, since this is so common while goodness is
so rare.

VIII

I PITY the person whom you know in the disquietude in
which I know she is, and in which I am not surprised
to see her. It is a little day of judgment which cannot
come without a universal emotion of the person, as the general judgment will cause a general emotion in the world,
those excepted who shall have already judged themselves, as
she pretends to have done. This temporal suffering would
guarantee her from the eternal, through the infinite merits
of Jesus Christ, who has endured it and rendered it his
own; this it is that should console her. Our yoke is also
his own; without this it would be insupportable.

Take my yoke upon you, says he. It is not our yoke;
it is his, and he also bears it. *Know,* says he, *that my
yoke is easy and light.* It is light only to him and to his
divine power. I would say to her that she should remember that these disquietudes come not from the good that
is springing up in her, but from the evil which is still
remaining and must be continually diminished; that she
must do like a child that is being torn by robbers from the
arms of its mother who will not let it go; for it should
not charge the mother that fondly holds it back with the
violence that it suffers, but its unjust ravishers. The whole
office of Advent is well fitted to give courage to the weak;
these words of Scripture: *Take courage, ye fearful and unbelieving, behold, your Redeemer cometh,* are often repeated there, and in the vesper service of to-day it is said:
"Take courage and fear not; for your God shall come to
save and deliver you."

IX

Your letter has given me the greatest joy. I confess that I was beginning to fear or at least to be astonished. I know not what was the beginning of the trouble of which you speak; but I know that trouble must come. I was reading the thirteenth chapter of St. Mark. I was thinking of writing you; and I will tell you therefore what I found in it. Jesus Christ is there addressing a solemn discourse to his disciples on his second coming; and as whatever happens to the Church happens also to each individual Christian, it is certain that this whole chapter predicts the state of each person in whom on conversion the old man is destroyed, as well as that of the whole universe which shall be destroyed to give place to a new heaven and a new earth, as the Scripture says. And thus I should think that the overthrow of the reprobate temple, which prefigures the overthrow of the reprobate man within us, and of which it is said that there shall not be one stone left upon another, indicates that no passion of the old man shall remain;[1] and these fierce contentions, both civil and domestic, represent so well the internal conflicts experienced by those who give themselves up to God, that nothing can be better depicted.

But very striking are these words: *When ye shall see the abomination of desolation in the holy place, let not him that is on the house-top go into the house.* It seems to me that this perfectly predicts the times in which we live, in which moral corruption is in the houses of sanctity and in the books of theologians and ecclesiastics, in which we should least expect it. We must shun such disorder; and woe to those with child and to those that give suck in those days, that is to those that are held back by worldly ties! The words of a sainted woman are applicable here: "We are not to consider whether we are called to quit the world, but solely whether we are called to remain in it, as we should not deliberate whether we were called to fly a house infected with plague or on fire."

[1] The two MSS. of the Bibliothéque Imp. say: "no passion *in us.*"— *Faugère.*

This chapter of the Evangelist, which I should like to read with you entire, concludes with an exhortation to watch and pray in order to shun all these misfortunes, and in truth, it is proper indeed that when the danger is continual the prayer should be continual also.

For this purpose I send the prayers which were asked of me; it is now three in the afternoon. Since your departure, a miracle has been performed upon a nun of Pontoise, who, without leaving her convent, has been cured of an extraordinary headache by an act of devotion to the holy Thorn. I will tell you more about it another time. But I must quote to you, in respect to this, an excellent saying of St. Augustine, very consoling to certain persons, that those alone really see miracles whom the miracles benefit; for they are not seen at all if they do not benefit.

I am under obligations that I cannot sufficiently express for the present which you have made me; I did not know what it could be, for I unfolded it before reading your letter, and I afterwards repented for not having rendered to it at first the respect that was due to it. It is a truth that the Holy Spirit reposes invisibly in the relics of those who have died in the grace of God, until they shall appear visibly in the resurrection, and this it is that renders the relics of the saints so worthy of veneration. For God never abandons his own, even in the sepulchre in which their bodies, though dead to the eyes of men, are more than ever living in the sight of God, since sin is no more in them; whilst it constantly resides in them during life, at least in its root, for the fruits of sin are not always in them; and this fatal root, which is inseparable from them in life, causes it to be forbidden us during life to honor them, since they are rather worthy of detestation. It is for this that death becomes necessary to mortify entirely this fatal root, and this it is that renders it desirable. But it is of no use to tell you what you know so well; it would be better to tell it to the other persons of whom you speak, but they would not listen to it.

12

LETTER FROM PASCAL TO QUEEN CHRISTINA, ON SENDING
HER THE ARITHMETICAL MACHINE, 1650

MADAME,

If I had as much health as zeal, I should go myself to
present to Your Majesty a work of several years which I
dare offer you from so far; and I should not suffer any other
hands than mine to have the honor of bearing it to the feet
of the greatest princess in the world. This work, Madame,
is a machine for making arithmetical calculations without
pen or counters. Your Majesty is not ignorant of the cost
of time and pains of new productions, above all when the
inventors wish to bring them themselves to their highest
perfection; this is why it would be useless to say how much
I have laboured upon this one, and I cannot better express
myself than by saying that I have devoted myself to it
with as much ardor as though I had foreseen that it would
one day appear before so august a person. But, Madame,
if this honor has not been the veritable motive of my work,
it will be at least its recompense; and I shall esteem myself
too happy if, after so many vigils, it can give Your Majesty
a few moments' satisfaction. I shall not importune Your
Majesty with the details of the parts which compose this
machine; if you have any curiosity in respect to it, you
can satisfy yourself in a discourse which I have addressed to
M. de Bourdelot; in which I have sketched in a few words
the whole history of this work, the object of its invention,
the occasion that led to its investigation, the utility of its
applications, the difficulty of its execution, the degree of its
progress, the success of its accomplishment, and the rules
for its use. I shall therefore only speak here of the motive
that led me to offer it to Your Majesty, which I consider as
the consummation and happiest fortune of its destiny. I
know, Madame, that I may be suspected of having sought
honor in presenting it to Your Majesty, since it can pass only
for something extraordinary when it is seen that it is
addressed to you: and that whilst it should only be offered to
you through the consideration of its excellence, it will be

judged that it is excellent for the sole reason that it is offered to you. It is not this hope, however, that has inspired me with such a design. It is too great, Madame, to have any other object than Your Majesty yourself. What has really determined me to this is the union that I find in your sacred person of two things that equally overwhelm me with admiration and respect—which are, sovereign authority and solid science; for I have an especial veneration for those who are elevated to the supreme degree either of power or of knowledge. The latter may, if I am not mistaken, as well as the former, pass for sovereigns. The same gradations are found in genius as in condition; and the power of kings over their subjects is, it seems to me, only an image of the power of minds over inferior minds, over whom they exercise the right of persuasion, which is with them what the right of command is in political government. This second empire even appears to me of an order so much the more elevated, as minds are of an order more elevated than bodies; and so much the more just, as it can be shared and preserved only by merit, whilst the other can be shared and preserved by birth and fortune. It must be acknowledged then that each of these empires is great in itself; but, Madame, let Your Majesty, who is not wounded by it, permit me to say, the one without the other appears to me defective. However powerful a monarch may be, something is wanting to his glory if he has not pre-eminence of mind; and however enlightened a subject may be, his condition is always lowered by dependence. Men who naturally desire what is most perfect, have hitherto continually aspired to meet this sovereign *par excellence*. All kings and scholars have hitherto been but faint outlines of it, only half performing their endeavor; this masterpiece has been reserved for our own times. And that this great marvel might appear accompanied with all possible subjects of wonder, the position that men could not attain is filled by a youthful queen, in whom are found combined the advantage of experience with the tenderness of youth, the leisure of study with the occupation of royal birth, and the eminence of science with the feebleness of sex. It is Your Majesty, Madame, that furnishes to the world this unique example that was wanting to it. You it is in whom power is dispensed by the light of science, and science exalted by the lustre of authority. It is from this marvellous union that, as Your Majesty sees nothing beneath your power, you also see nothing above your mind, and that you will be the admiration of every age. Reign then, incomparable princess, in a manner wholly new; let your genius subdue every thing that is not submissive to your arms; reign by right of birth during a long course of years over so many triumphant provinces; but reign continually by the force of your merit over the whole extent of the earth. As for me, not having been born under the former of your empires, I wish all the world to know that I glory in living under the latter; and it is to bear witness to this that I dare to raise my eyes to my queen, in giving her this first proof of my dependence.

This, Madame, is what leads me to make to Your Majesty this present, although unworthy of you. My weakness has not checked my ambition. I have figured to myself that although the name alone of Your Majesty seems to put away from you every thing that is disproportioned to your greatness, you will not however reject every thing that is inferior to yourself; as your greatness would thus be without homage and your glory without praise. You will be contented to receive a great mental effort, without exacting that it should be the effort of a mind as great as your own. It is by this condescension that you will deign to enter into communication with the rest of mankind; and all these joint considerations make me protest, with all the submission of which one of the greatest admirers of your heroic qualities is capable, that I desire nothing with so much ardor as to be able to be adopted, Madame, by Your Majesty, as your most humble, most obedient, and most faithful servant.

BLAISE PASCAL.

MINOR WORKS OF PASCAL

Epitaph of M. Pascal, Pere

HERE lies, etc.

Illustrious for his great knowledge which was recognized by the scholars of all Europe; more illustrious still for the great probity which he exercised in the offices and employments with which he was honored; but much more illustrious for his exemplary piety. He tasted good and bad fortune, that he might be known in every thing for what he was. He was seen temperate in prosperity and patient in adversity. He sought the aid of God in misfortune, and rendered him thanks in happiness. His heart was devoted to his God, his king, his family, and his friends. He had respect for the great and love for the small; it pleased God to crown all the graces of nature that he had bestowed on him with a divine grace which made his great love for God the foundation, the stay, and the consummation of all his other virtues.

Thou, who seest in this epitome the only thing that remains to us of so beautiful a life, admire the fragility of all present things, weep the loss that we have suffered; render thanks to God for having left for a time to earth the enjoyment of such a treasure; and pray his goodness to crown with his eternal glory him whom he crowned here below with more graces and virtues than the limits of an epitaph permit us to relate.

His grief-stricken children have placed this epitaph on this spot, which they have composed from the fulness of their hearts, in order to render homage to the truth and not to appear ingrates in the sight of God.

PRAYER

To Ask of God the Proper Use of Sickness

I. LORD, whose spirit is so good and so gentle in all things, and who art so merciful that not only the prosperity but the very disgrace that happens to thy elect is the effect of thy mercy, grant me the favor not to act towards me as towards a heathen in the condition to which thy justice has reduced me: that like a true Christian I may recognize thee for my Father and my God, in whatever condition I may find myself, since the change of my condition brings none to thine; as thou art always the same, however subject I may be to change, and as thou art none the less God when thou afflictest and punishest, than when thou comfortest and showest indulgence.

II. Thou gavest me health to serve thee, and I made a profane use of it. Thou sendest me sickness now to correct me; suffer not that I use it to irritate thee by my impatience. I made a bad use of my health, and thou hast justly punished me for it. Suffer not that I make a bad use of my punishment. And since the corruption of my nature is such that it renders thy favors pernicious to me, grant, O my God! that thy all-powerful grace may render thy chastisements salutary. If my heart was full of affection for the world while it retained its vigor, destroy this vigor for my salvation; and render me incapable of enjoying the world, either through weakness of body or through zeal of charity, that I may enjoy but thee alone.

III. O God, before whom I must render an exact account of all my actions at the end of my life and at the end of the world! O God, who lettest the world and all the things of the world subsist but to train thy elect or to punish sinners! O God, who allowest sinners hardened in the pleasurable and criminal use of the world! O God, who makest our bodies to die, and who at the hour of death separatest our soul from all that it loved in the world! O God, who wilt snatch me, at this last moment of my life, from all the things to which I am attached and on which I have set my heart! O God, who wilt consume at the last day the heavens and the earth with all the creatures they contain, to show to all mankind that nothing subsists save thee, and that thus nothing is worthy of love save thee, since nothing is durable save thee! O God, who wilt destroy all these vain idols and all these fatal objects of our passions! I praise thee, my God, and I will bless thee all the days of my life, that it has pleased thee to anticipate in my favor this terrible day, by destroying all things in respect to me through the weakness to which thou hast reduced me. I praise thee, my God, and I will bless thee all the days of my life, that it has pleased thee to reduce me to the incapacity of enjoying the sweets of health and the pleasures of the world, and that thou hast destroyed in some sort, for my advantage, the deceitful idols that thou wilt destroy effectively, for the confusion of the wicked, in the day of thy wrath. Grant, Lord, that I may judge myself, after the destruction that thou hast made with respect to me, that thou mayest not judge me thyself, after the entire destruction that thou wilt make of my life and of the world. For, Lord, as at the instant of my death I shall find myself separated from the world, stripped of all things, alone in thy presence, to answer to thy justice for all the emotions of my heart, grant that I may consider myself in this sickness as in a species of death, separated from the world, stripped of all the objects of my attachment, alone in thy presence, to implore of thy mercy the conversion of my heart; and that thus I may have extreme consolation in knowing that thou sendest me now a partial death in order to exercise thy mercy, before thou sendest me death effectively in order to exercise thy judgment. Grant then, O my God, that as thou hast anticipated my death, I may anticipate the rigor of thy sentence, and that I may examine myself before thy judgment, so that I may find mercy in thy presence.

IV. Grant, O my God! that I may adore in silence the order of thy adorable providence in the direction of my life; that this scourge may console me; and that, having lived during peace in the bitterness of my sins, I may taste the heavenly sweets of thy grace during the salutary evils with which thou afflictest me. But I perceive, my God, that my heart is so obdurate and full of the thoughts, the cares, the anxieties, and the attachments of the world, that sickness no more than health, nor discourses, nor books, nor thy sacred

Scriptures, nor thy Gospel, nor thy most holy mysteries, nor alms, nor fasts, nor mortifications, nor miracles, nor the use of sacraments, nor the sacrifice of thy body, nor all my efforts, nor those of all the world together, can do any thing at all for the commencement of my conversion, if thou dost not accompany all these things with an extraordinary assistance of thy grace. It is for this that I address myself to thee, all-powerful God, to ask of thee a gift which all created things together cannot accord to me. I should not have the boldness to address to thee my cries, if any other had power to grant them. But, my God, as the conversion of my heart, which I ask of thee, is a work which surpasses all the efforts of nature, I can only address myself to the all-powerful Author and Master of nature and of my heart. To whom shall I cry, O Lord, to whom shall I have recourse, if not to thee? Nothing that is less than God can fulfil my expectation. It is God himself that I ask and seek; and it is to thee alone, my God, that I address myself to obtain thee. Open my heart, O Lord; enter into the rebellious place which has been occupied by vices. They hold it subject. Enter into it as into the strong man's house; but first bind the strong and powerful enemy that has possession of it, and then take the treasures which are there. Lord, take my affections, which the world had stolen; take this treasure thyself, or rather retake it, since it belongs to thee as a tribute that I owe thee, since thy image is imprinted in it. Thou formedst it, O Lord, at the moment of my baptism, which was my second birth; but it is wholly effaced. The image of the world is so deeply engraven there that thine is no longer to be recognized. Thou alone couldst create my soul, thou alone canst create it anew; thou alone couldst form thy image, thou alone canst reform and reimprint thy effaced portrait, that is, my Saviour, Jesus Christ, who is thy image, and the expression of thy substance.

V. O my God! how happy is a heart that can love so charming an object, that does not dishonor it, and the attachment of which is so salutary to it! I feel that I cannot love the world without displeasing thee, and destroying and dishonoring myself; yet the world is still the object of my delight. O my God! how happy is the soul of which thou art the delight, since it can abandon itself to loving thee, not only without scruple, but also with merit! How firm and durable is its happiness, since its expectation will never be frustrated, because thou wilt never be destroyed, and neither life nor death will ever separate it from the object of its desires; and since the same moment that will plunge the wicked with their idols into a common ruin, will unite the just with thee in a common glory; and since, as the former will perish with the perishable objects to which they are attached, the latter will subsist eternally in the eternal and self-subsistent object to which they are closely bound! Oh! how happy are those who with an entire liberty, and irresistible inclination of their will, love perfectly and freely that which they are obliged to love necessarily!

VI. Perfect, O my God, the good impulses that thou givest me. Be their end as thou art their principle. Crown thy own gifts, for I recognize that they are from thee. Yes, my God, and far from pretending that my prayers may have some merit that forces thee to accord them of necessity, I humbly acknowledge that, having given to created things my heart, which thou hadst formed only for thyself, and not for the world, nor for myself, I can expect no grace except from thy mercy, since I have nothing in me that can oblige thee to it, and since all the natural impulses of my heart, whether tending towards created things, or towards myself, can only irritate thee. I, therefore, render thee thanks, my God, for the good impulses which thou givest me, and for the very one that thou hast given me to render thanks for them.

VII. Move my heart to repent of my faults, since, without this internal sorrow, the external ills with which thou affectest my body will be to me a new occasion of sin. Make me truly to know that the ills of the body are nothing else than the punishment and the symbol combined of the ills of the soul. But, Lord, grant also that they may be their remedy, by making me consider, in the pains which I feel, those that I did not feel in my soul, although wholly diseased, and covered with sores. For, Lord, the greatest of its diseases is this insensibility and extreme weakness, which had taken away from it all feeling of its own sufferings. Make me to feel them acutely, and grant that the portion of life that remains to me may be a continual penitence to wash away the offences that I have committed.

VIII. Lord, although my past life may have been exempt from great crimes, of which thou hast removed from me the occasions, it has nevertheless been most odious to thee by its continual negligence, by the bad use of thy most august sacraments, by the contempt of thy word and of thy inspirations, by the indolence and total uselessness of my actions and my thoughts, by the complete loss of the time which thou hadst given me only to adore thee, to seek in all my occupations the means of pleasing thee, and to repent of faults that are committed every day, and are even common to the most just; so that their life should be a continual penitence, without which they are in danger of falling from their justice. Thus, my God, I have always been opposed to thee.

IX. Yes, Lord, hitherto I have always been deaf to thy inspirations, I have despised thy oracles; I have judged the contrary of that which thou hast judged; I have contradicted the holy maxims which thou hast brought to the world from the bosom of thy eternal Father, and conformably to which thou wilt judge the world. Thou sayest: Blessed are those that mourn, and woe to those that are comforted! And I have said: Woe to those that mourn and blessed are those that are comforted! I have said: Blessed art those that enjoy an affluent fortune, a glorious reputation, and robust health! And why have I reputed them blessed, if not because all these advantages furnished them ample facility for enjoying created things, that is for offending thee! Yes, Lord, I confess that I have esteemed health a blessing, not because it is an easy means for serving thee with utility, for accomplishing more cares and vigils in thy service, and for the assistance of my neighbor; but because by its aid I could abandon myself with less restraint to the abundance of the delights of life, and better relish fatal pleasures. Grant me the favor, Lord, to reform my corrupt reason and to conform my sentiments to thine. Let me esteem myself happy in affliction, and, in the impotence of acting externally, purify my sentiments so that they may no longer be repugnant to thine; and let me thus find thee within myself, since I cannot seek thee without because of my weakness. For, Lord, thy kingdom is within thy faithful; and I shall find it within myself, if I find there thy spirit and thy sentiments.

X. But, Lord, what shall I do to force thee to diffuse thy spirit over this miserable earth? All that I am is odious to thee, and I find nothing in myself that can be pleasing to thee. I see nothing therein, Lord, but my sufferings, which bear some resemblance to thine. Consider then the ills that I suffer and those that menace me. Look with an eye of mercy upon the wounds that thy hand has made, O my Saviour, who lovedst thy sufferings in death! O God, who wert made man only to suffer more than any other man for the salvation of mankind! O God, who wert not incarnated until after the sin of mankind, and who only tookest upon thyself a body in order to suffer therein all the ills which our sins had merited! O God, who lovedst so much these suffering bodies that thou hast chosen for thyself a body more oppressed with suffering than any that has ever appeared on earth! Look with favor upon my body, not for itself, nor for all that it contains, for everything therein deserving of thy anger, but for the ills that it endures, which alone can be worthy of thy love. Love my sufferings, Lord, and let my ills invite thee to visit me. But to finish the preparation for thy abode, grant, O my Saviour, that if my body has this in common with thine—that it suffers for my offences, my soul may also have this in common with thine—that it may be plunged in sorrow for the same offences; and that thus I may suffer with thee, and like thee, both in my body and in my soul, for the sins that I have committed.

XI. Grant me the favor, Lord, to join thy consolations to my sufferings, that I may suffer like a Christian. I ask not to be exempt from sorrow, for this is the recompense of the saints; but I ask that I may not be abandoned to the sorrows of nature without the consolations of thy spirit; for this is the curse of the Jews and the heathen. I ask not to have a fulness of consolation without any suffering; for this is the life of glory. Neither do I ask to be in the fulness of evils without consolation; for this is the state of Judaism. But I ask, Lord, to feel at the same time both the sorrows of nature for my sins, and the consolations of thy spirit through thy grace; for this is the true condition of Christianity. Let me not feel sorrow without consolation; but let me feel sorrow and consolation together, that I may come at last to feel thy consolation without any sorrow. For, Lord, thou lettest the world languish in natural suffering without consolation, before the coming of thy only Son: now thou consolest and assuagest the sufferings of thy faithful through the grace of thy only Son: and thou crownest thy saints with a pure beatitude in the glory of thy only Son. Such are the admirable degrees through which thou conductest thy work. Thou hast drawn me from the first: make me pass through the second, to arrive at the third. Lord, this is the favor that I ask of thee.

XII. Suffer me not to be so far removed from thee, that I can consider thy soul sorrowful unto death, and thy body a prey to death for my own sins, without rejoicing to suffer both in my body and in my soul. For what is there more shameful, and yet more common in Christians and in myself, than that, whilst thou sweatest blood for the expiation of our offences, we live in delights; and that those Christians who profess to belong to thee, that those who by baptism have renounced the world to follow thee, that those who have sworn solemnly in the presence of the Church to live and die for thee, that those who profess to believe that the world has persecuted and crucified thee, that those who believe that thou wert exposed to the wrath of God and the cruelty of men to ransom them from their crimes; that those, I say, who believe all these truths, who consider thy body as the victim that was yielded up for their salvation, who consider the pleasures and the sins of the world as the only cause of thy sufferings, and the world itself as thy executioner, seek to flatter their bodies by these very pleasures, in this very world; and that those who cannot, without shuddering with horror, see a man caress and cherish the murderer of his father, who would devote himself to give him life, can live as I have done, with full joy, in the world that I know to have been veritably the murderer of him whom I acknowledge for my God and my Father, who has delivered himself up for my own salvation, and who has borne in his person the penalty of my iniquities? It is just, Lord, that thou shouldst have interrupted a joy so criminal as that in which I was reposing in the shadow of death.

XIII. Remove from me then, Lord, the sadness that the love of self might give me for my own sufferings and for the things of the world that do not succeed to the satisfaction of the inclinations of my heart, and that do not regard thy glory; but create in me a sadness in conformity with thine. Let my sufferings serve to appease thy wrath. Make of them an occasion for my salvation and my conversion. Let me henceforth desire health and life only to employ them and end them for thee, with thee, and in thee. I ask of thee neither health, nor sickness, nor life, nor death; but that thou wilt dispose of my health and my sickness, my life and my death, for thy glory, for my salvation, and for the utility of the Church and of thy saints, of whom I hope by thy grace to form a part. Thou alone knowest what is most expedient for me: thou art the sovereign master, do what thou wilt. Give to me, take from me; but conform my will to thine; and grant that in humble and perfect submission and in holy confidence, I may be disposed to receive the orders of thy eternal providence, and that I may adore alike all that comes to me from thee.

XIV. Grant, my God, that in a constantly equal uniformity of spirit I may receive all kinds of events, since we know not what we should ask, and since I cannot desire one more than another without presumption, and without rendering myself the judge of and responsible for the results that thy wisdom has rightly been pleased to hide from me. Lord, I know only that I know but one thing, that it is good to follow thee and that it is evil to offend thee. After this, I know not which is the better or worse of any thing; I know not which is more profitable to me, health or sickness, wealth or poverty, nor of all the things of the world. This is a discernment that exceeds the power of men or of angels, and that is hidden in the secrets of thy providence which I adore, and which I wish not to fathom.

XV. Grant then, Lord, that such as I am I may conform myself to thy will; and that being sick as I am, I may glorify thee in my sufferings. Without them I could not arrive at glory; and thou, too, my Saviour, hast only wished to attain

it through them. It was by the tokens of thy sufferings that
thou wert recognized by thy disciples; and it is by sufferings
also that thou wilt recognize thy disciples. Acknowledge me
then for thy disciple in the evils which I endure both in my
body and my mind, for the offences that I have committed.
And since nothing is pleasing to God if it be not offered
through thee, unite my will to thine, and my sorrows to
those which thou hast suffered. Grant that mine may become
thine. Unite me to thee; fill me with thyself and with thy
Holy Spirit. Enter into my heart and soul, to bear in them
my sufferings, and to continue to endure in me what remains
to thee to suffer of thy passion, that thou mayest complete in
thy members even the perfect consummation of thy body, so
that being full of thee, it may no longer be that I live and
suffer, but that it may be thou that livest and sufferest in me,
O my Saviour! And that thus having some small part in thy
sufferings, thou wilt fill me entirely with the glory that they
have acquired for thee, in which thou wilt live with the
Father and the Holy Spirit through ages upon ages. So
be it.

COMPARISON BETWEEN CHRISTIANS

Of Early Times and Those of To-day

In early times, Christians were perfectly instructed in all
the points necessary to salvation; whilst we see to-day so
gross an ignorance of them, that it makes all those mourn
who have sentiments of tenderness for the Church.

Men only entered then into the Church after great labors
and long desires; they find their way into it now without any
trouble, without care, and without labor.

They were only admitted to it after a strict examination.
They are received into it now before they are in a condition
to be examined.

They were not received then until after having abjured
their past life, until after having renounced the world, the
flesh, and the devil. They enter it now before they are in a
condition to do any of these things.

In short, it was necessary formerly to forsake the world in order to be received into the Church; whilst men enter now into the Church at the same time as into the world. By this process, an essential distinction was then known between the world and the Church. They were considered as two opposites, as two irreconcilable enemies, of which the one persecuted the other without cessation, and of which the weaker in appearance should one day triumph over the stronger; so that of these two antagonistic parties men quitted the one to enter the other; they abandoned the maxims of the one to embrace the maxims of the other; they put off the sentiments of the one to put on the sentiments of the other; in fine, they quitted, they renounced, they abjured this world in which they had received their first birth, to devote themselves entirely to the Church in which they received as it were their second birth and thus they conceived a terrible difference between the two; whilst they now find themselves almost at the same time in both; and the same moment that brings us forth into the world makes us acknowledged by the Church, so that the reason supervening, no longer makes a difference between these two opposite worlds. It is developed in both together. Men frequent the Sacraments, and enjoy the pleasures of the world; and thus whilst formerly they saw an essential difference between the two, they see them now confounded and blended together, so that they can no longer discriminate between them.

Hence it is that formerly none but well-instructed persons were to be seen among the Christians, whilst they are now in an ignorance that inspires one with horror; hence it is that those who had formerly been regenerated by baptism, and had forsaken the vices of the world to enter into the piety of the Church, fell back so rarely from the Church into the world; whilst nothing more common is to be seen at this time than the vices of the world in the hearts of Christians. The Church of the Saints is found defiled by the mingling of the wicked; and her children, whom she has conceived and nourished from childhood in her bosom, are the very ones who carry into her heart, that is to the participation in her most august mysteries, the most cruel of her enemies, the spirit of the world, the spirit of ambition, the spirit of vengeance, the spirit of impurity, the spirit of concupiscence and the love that she has for her children obliges her to admit into her very bowels the most cruel of her persecutors.

But it is not to the Church that should be imputed the misfortunes which have followed a change in such salutary discipline, for she has not changed in spirit, however she may have changed in conduct. Having therefore seen that the deferring of baptism left a great number of children in the curse of Adam, she wished to deliver them from this mass of perdition by hastening the aid which she could give them; and this good mother sees only with extreme regret that what she devised for the salvation of these children has become the occasion for the destruction of adults. Her true spirit is that those whom she withdraws at so tender an age from the contagion of the world, shall adopt sentiments wholly opposed to those of the world. She anticipates the use of reason to anticipate the vices into which corrupt reason will allure them; and before their mind has power to act, she fills them with her spirit, that they may live in ignorance of the world and in a condition so much the more remote from vice as they will never have known it. This appears from the ceremonies of baptism; for she does not accord baptism to children until after they have declared, by the mouth of sponsors, that they desire it, that they believe, that they renounce the world and Satan. And as she wishes that they should preserve these intentions throughout the whole course of their lives, she commands them expressly to keep them inviolate, and orders the sponsors, by an indispensable commandment, to instruct the children in all these things; for she does not wish that those whom she has nourished in her bosom should to-day be less instructed and less zealous than the adults whom she admitted in former times to the number of her own; she does not desire a less perfection in those whom she nourishes than in those whom she receives. . . . . Yet men use it in a manner so contrary to the intention of the Church, that one cannot think of it without horror. They scarcely reflect any longer upon so great a benefit, because they have never wished it, because they have never asked it, because they do not even remember having received it. . . . .

But as it is evident that the Church demands no less zeal

in those who have been brought up servants of the faith than in those who aspire to become such, it is necessary to place before their eyes the example of the catechumens, to consider their ardor, their devotion, their horror of the world, their generous renunciation of the world; and if they were not deemed worthy of receiving baptism without this disposition, those who do not find it in themselves.....................
They must therefore submit to receive the instruction that they would have had if they had begun to enter into the communion of the Church; they must moreover submit to a continual penitence, and have less aversion for the austerity or their mortification than pleasure in the use of delights poisoned by sin...

To dispose them to be instructed, they must be made to understand the difference of the customs that have been practised in the Church in conformity with the diversity of the times ....
As in the infant Church they taught the catechumens, that is those who aspired to baptism, before conferring it upon them; and only admitted them to it after full instruction in the mysteries of religion, after a penitence for their past lives, after profound knowledge of the greatness and excellence of the profession of the faith and of the Christian maxims into which they desired to enter forever, after eminent tokens of a genuine conversion of the heart, and after an extreme desire of baptism. These things being known to all the Church, the sacrament of incorporation was conferred upon them by which they became members of the Church; whilst in these times, baptism having been accorded to children before the use of reason, through very important considerations, it happens that the negligence of parents suffers Christians to grow old without any knowledge of the greatness of our religion.

When instruction preceded baptism, all were instructed; but now that baptism precedes instruction, the instruction that was necessary has become voluntary, and then neglected and almost abolished. The true reason of this conduct is that men are persuaded of the necessity of baptism, and they are not persuaded of the necessity of instruction. So that when instruction preceded baptism, the necessity of the one caused men to have recourse to the other necessarily; whilst

baptism at the present time preceding instruction, as men
have been made Christians without having been instructed,
they believe that they can remain Christians without seeking
instruction . . . . And whilst the early Christians testified
so much gratitude towards the Church for the favor which
she accorded only to their long prayers, they testify to-day
so much ingratitude for this same favor, which she accords
to them even before they are in a condition to ask it. And
if she detested so strongly the lapses of the former, although
so rare, how much must she hold in abomination the continual lapses and relapses of the latter, although they are
much more indebted to her, since she has drawn them much
sooner and much more unsparingly from the damnation to
which they were bound by their first birth. She cannot, without mourning, see the greatest of her favors abused, and what
she has done to secure their salvation becomes the almost
certain occasion of their destruction......................

DISCOURSES

ON THE CONDITION OF THE GREAT

I

In order to enter into a real knowledge of your condition,
consider it in this image:

A man was cast by a tempest upon an unknown island, the
inhabitants of which were in trouble to find their king, who
was lost; and having a strong resemblance both in form and
face to this king, he was taken for him, and acknowledged in
this capacity by all the people. At first he knew not what
course to take; but finally he resolved to give himself up
to his good fortune. He received all the homage that they
chose to render him, and suffered himself to be treated as
a king.

But as he could not forget his real condition, he was conscious, at the same time that he was receiving this homage,
that he was not the king whom this people had sought, and
that this kingdom did not belong to him. Thus he had a

double thought: the one by which he acted as king, the other by which he recognized his true state, and that it was accident alone that had placed him in his present condition. He concealed the latter thought, and revealed the other. It was by the former that he treated with the people, and by the latter that he treated with himself.

Do not imagine that it is less an accident by which you find yourself master of the wealth which you possess, than that by which this man found himself king. You have no right to it of yourself and by your own nature any more than he: and not only do you find yourself the son of a duke, but also do you find yourself in the world at all, only through an infinity of chances. Your birth depends on a marriage, or rather on the marriages of all those from whom you descend. But upon what do these marriages depend? A visit made by chance, an idle word, a thousand unforeseen occasions.

You hold, you say, your wealth from your ancestors; but was it not by a thousand accidents that your ancestors acquired it and that they preserved it? A thousand others, as capable as they, have either been unable to acquire it, or have lost it after having gained it. Do you imagine, too, that it may have been by some natural way that this wealth has passed from your ancestors to you? This is not true. This order is founded only upon the mere will of legislators who may have had good reasons, but none of which was drawn from a natural right that you have over these things. If it had pleased them to order that this wealth, after having been possessed by fathers during their life, should return to the republic after their death, you would have no reason to complain of it.

Thus the whole title by which you possess your property, is not a title of nature but of a human institution. Another turn of imagination in those who made the laws would have rendered you poor; and it is only this concurrence of chance which caused your birth with the caprice of laws favorable in your behalf, that puts you in possession of all this property. I will not say that it does not legitimately belong to you, and that it is permissible for another to wrest it from you; for God, who is its master, has permitted communities to make laws for its division, and when these laws are once established, it is unjust to violate them. This it is that distinguishes you somewhat from the man who possessed his kingdom only through the error of the people; because God did not authorize this possession, and required him to renounce it, whilst he authorizes yours. But what you have wholly in common with him is, that this right which you have, is not founded any more than his upon any quality or any merit in yourself which renders you worthy of it. Your soul and your body are, of themselves, indifferent to the state of boatman or that of duke; and there is no natural bond that attaches them to one condition rather than to another.

What follows from this? that you should have a double thought, like the man of whom we have spoken, and that, if you act externally with men in conformity with your rank, you should recognize, by a more secret but truer thought, that you have nothing naturally superior to them. If the public thought elevates you above the generality of men, let the other humble you, and hold you in a perfect equality with all mankind, for this is your natural condition.

The populace that admires you knows not, perhaps, this secret. It believes that nobility is real greatness, and it almost considers the great as being of a different nature from others. Do not discover to them this error, unless you choose; but do not abuse this elevation with insolence, and, above all, do not mistake yourself by believing that your being has something in it more exalted than that of others.

What would you say of that man who was made king by the error of the people, if he had so far forgotten his natural condition as to imagine that this kingdom was due to him, that he deserved it, and that it belonged to him of right? You would marvel at his stupidity and folly. But is there less in the people of rank who live in so strange a forgetfulness of their natural condition?

How important is this advice! For all the excesses, all the violence, and all the vanity of great men, come from the fact that they know not what they are: it being difficult for those who regard themselves at heart as equal with all men, and who are fully persuaded that they have nothing within themselves that merits these trifling advantages which God has given them over others, to treat them with insolence. For this it is necessary for one to forget himself, and to believe that he has some real excellence above them, in which consists this illusion that I am endeavoring to discover to you.

II

It is well, sir, that you should know what is due to you, that you may not pretend to exact from men that which is not due to you; for this is an obvious injustice; and nevertheless it is very common to those of your condition, because they are ignorant of the nature of it.

There is in the world two kinds of greatness: for there is greatness of institution, and natural greatness. Greatness of institution depends upon the will of men who have with reason thought it right to honor certain positions, and to attach to them certain marks of respect. Dignities and nobility are of this class. In one country the nobles are honored, in another the plebeians; in this the eldest, in the other the youngest. Why is this? because thus it has been pleasing to men. The thing was indifferent before the institution; since the institution it becomes just, because it is unjust to disturb it.

Natural greatness is that which is independent of the caprice of men, because it consists in the real and effective qualities of the soul or the body, which render the one or the other more estimable, as the sciences, the enlightenment of the mind, virtue, health, strength.

We owe something to both these kinds of greatness; but as they are of a different nature, we owe them likewise different respect. To the greatness of institution we owe the respect of institution, that is, certain external ceremonies which should be nevertheless accompanied, in conformity with reason, with an internal recognition of the justice of this order, but which do not make us conceive any real quality in those whom we honor after this manner. It is necessary to speak to kings on the bended knee, to remain standing in the presence-chamber of princes. It is a folly and baseness of spirit to refuse to them these duties.

But as for the natural homage which consists in esteem, we owe it only to natural greatness; and we owe, on the contrary, contempt and aversion to qualities contrary to this natural greatness. It is not necessary, because you are a duke, that I should esteem you; but it is necessary that I should salute you. If you are a duke and a gentleman, I shall render what I owe to both these qualities. I shall not refuse you the ceremonies that are merited by your quality of duke, nor the esteem that is merited by that of a gentleman. But if you were a duke without being a gentleman, I should still do you justice; for in rendering you the external homage which the order of men has attached to your birth, I should not fail to have for you the internal contempt that would be merited by your baseness of mind.

Therein consists the justice of these duties. And the injustice consists in attaching natural respect to greatness of condition, or in exacting respect of condition for natural greatness. M. N. . . . is a greater geometrician than I; in this quality, he wishes to take precedence of me: I will tell him that he understands nothing of the matter. Geometry is a natural greatness; it demands a preference of esteem; but men have not attached to it any external preference. I shall, therefore, take precedence of him, and shall esteem him greater than I in the quality of geometrician. In the same manner, if, being duke and peer, you would not be contented with my standing uncovered before you, but should also wish that I should esteem you, I should ask you to show me the qualities that merit my esteem. If you did this, you would gain it, and I could not refuse it to you with justice; but if you did not do it, you would be unjust to demand it of me; and assuredly you would not succeed, were you the greatest prince in the world.

III

I WISH, sir, to make known to you your true condition; for this is the thing of all others of which persons of your class are the most ignorant. What is it, in your opinion, to be a great nobleman? It is to be master of several objects that men covet, and thus to be able to satisfy the wants and the desires of many. It is these wants and these desires that attract them towards you, and that make them submit to you: were it not for these, they would not even look at you; but they hope, by these services, and this deference which they render you, to obtain from you some part of the good which they desire, and of which they see that you have the disposal.

God is surrounded with people full of love who demand of him the benefits of love which are in his power: thus he is properly the king of love. You are in the same manner surrounded with a small circle of persons, over whom you reign in your way. These men are full of desire. They demand of you the benefits of desire; it is desire that binds them to you. You are therefore properly the king of desire. Your kingdom is of small extent; but you are equal in this to the greatest kings of the earth: they are like you the sovereigns of desire. It is desire that constitutes their power; that is the possession of things that men covet.

But while knowing your natural condition, avail yourself of the means that it gives you, and do not pretend to rule by a different power than by that which makes you king. It is not your strength and your natural power that subjects all these people to you. Do not pretend then to rule them by force or to treat them with harshness. Satisfy their reasonable desires; alleviate their necessities; let your pleasure consist in being beneficent; advance them as much as you can, and you will act like the true king of desire.

What I tell you does not go very far; and if you stop there you will not save yourself from being lost; but at least you will be lost like an honest man. There are some men who expose themselves to damnation so foolishly by avarice, by brutality, by debauches, by violence, by excesses, by blasphemies! The way which I open to you is doubtless the most honorable; but in truth it is always a great folly for a man to expose himself to damnation; and therefore he must not stop at this. He must despise desire and its kingdom, and aspire to that kingdom of love in which all the subjects breathe nothing but love, and desire nothing but the benefits of love. Others than I will show you the way to this; it is sufficient for me to have turned you from those gross ways into which

I see many persons of your condition suffer themselves to be led, for want of knowing the true state of this condition.

ON THE CONVERSION OF THE SINNER.[1]

THE first thing with which God inspires the soul that he deigns to touch truly, is a knowledge and most extraordinary insight by which the soul considers things and herself in a manner wholly new.

This new light gives her fear, and brings her a trouble that penetrates the repose which she found in the things that made her delights.

She can no longer relish with tranquillity the things that charmed her. A continual scruple opposes her in this enjoyment, and this internal sight causes her to find no longer this accustomed sweetness among the things to which she abandoned herself with a full effusion of heart.

But she finds still more bitterness in the exercises of piety than in the vanities of the world. On one side, the vanity of the visible objects interests her more than the hope of the invisible, and on the other the solidity of the invisible interests her more than the vanity of the visible. And thus the presence of the one and the solidity of the other dispute her affection, and the vanity of the one and the absence of the other excite her aversion; so that a disorder and confusion spring up in her, that.............................
....
She considers perishable things as perishable and even already perished; and in the certain prospect of the annihilation of every thing that she loves, she is terrified by this consideration, in seeing that each moment snatches from her the enjoyment of her good, and that what is most dear to her glides away at every moment, and that finally a certain day will come in which she will find herself stripped of all the things in which she had placed her hope. So that she comprehends perfectly that her heart being attached only to vain and fragile things, her soul must be left alone and forsaken on quitting this life, since she has not taken

[1] By some scholars this fragment is attributed to Mlle. Pascal.

care to unite herself to a true and self-subsisting good which could sustain her both during and after this life.

Thence it comes that she begins to consider as nothingness all that must return to nothingness,—the heavens, the earth, her spirit, her body, her relatives, her friends, her enemies, wealth, poverty, disgrace, prosperity, honor, ignominy, esteem, contempt, authority, indigence, health, sickness, life itself. In fine, all that is less durable than her soul is incapable of satisfying the desire of this soul, which seeks earnestly to establish itself in a felicity as durable as herself.

She begins to be astonished at the blindness in which she has lived, and when she considers, on the one hand, the long time that she has lived without making these reflections, and the great number of people who live in the same way, and, on the other hand, how certain it is that the soul, being immortal as she is, cannot find her felicity among perishable things which will be taken away from her, at all events, by death, she enters into a holy confusion and an astonishment that brings to her a most salutary trouble.

For she considers that, however great may be the number of those who grow old in the maxims of the world, and whatever may be the authority of this multitude of examples of those who place their felicity in this world, it is nevertheless certain that, even though the things of the world should have some solid pleasure, which is recognized as false by an infinite number of fearful and continual examples, it is inevitable that we shall lose these things, or that death at last will deprive us of them; so that the soul having amassed treasures of temporal goods, of whatever nature they may be, whether gold, or science, or reputation, it is an indispensable necessity that she shall find herself stripped of all these objects of her felicity; and that thus, if they have had wherewith to satisfy her, they will not always have wherewith to satisfy her; and that, if it is to procure herself a real happiness, it is not to promise herself a very durable happiness, since it must be limited to the course of this life.

So that, by a holy humility which God exalts above pride, she begins to exalt herself above the generality of mankind: she condemns their conduct, she detests their maxims, she bewails their blindness; she devotes herself to the search for the true good; she comprehends that it is necessary that it should have the two following qualities: the one that it shall last as long as herself, and that it cannot be taken away from her except by her consent, and the other that there shall be nothing more lovely.

She sees that in the love she has had for the world, she found in it this second quality in her blindness; for she perceived nothing more lovely. But as she does not see the first in it, she knows that it is not the sovereign good. She seeks it, therefore, elsewhere, and knowing by a pure light that it is not in the things that are within her, or without her, or before her (in nothing, therefore, within or around her), she begins to seek it above her.

This elevation is so eminent and so transcendent that she does not stop at the heavens,—they have not wherewith to satisfy her,—nor above the heavens, nor at the angels, nor at the most perfect beings. She passes through all created things, and cannot stop her heart until she has rendered herself up at the throne of God, in which she begins to find her repose and that good which is such that there is nothing more lovely, and which cannot be taken away from her except by her own consent.

For although she does not feel those charms with which God recompenses continuance in piety, she comprehends, nevertheless, that created things cannot be more lovely than their Creator; and her reason, aided by the light of grace, makes her understand that there is nothing more lovely than God, and that he can only be taken away from those who reject him, since to possess him is only to desire him, and to refuse him is to lose him.

Thus she rejoices at having found a good which cannot be wrested from her so long as she shall desire it, and which has nothing above it.

And in these new reflections she enters into sight of the grandeur of her Creator, and into humiliations and profound adorations. She becomes, in consequence, reduced to nothing and being unable to form a base enough idea of herself, or to conceive an exalted enough idea of this

sovereign good, she makes new efforts to abase herself
to the lowest abysses of nothingness, in considering God in
the immensities which she multiplies without ceasing. In
fine, in this conception, which exhausts her strength, she
adores him in silence, she considers herself as his vile and
useless creature, and by her reiterated homage adores and
blesses him, and wishes to bless and to adore him forever.
Then she acknowledges the grace which he has granted
her in manifesting his infinite majesty to so vile a worm;
and after a firm resolution to be eternally grateful for it,
she becomes confused for having preferred so many vanities to this divine master; and in a spirit of compunction
and penitence she has recourse to his pity to arrest his
anger, the effect of which appears terrible to her. In the
sight of these immensities ....

She makes ardent prayers to God to obtain of his mercy
that, as it has pleased him to discover himself to her, it may
please him to conduct her to him, and to show her the
means of arriving there. For as it is to God that she aspires,
she aspires also only to reach him by means that come
from God himself, because she wishes that he himself should
be her path, her object, and her final end. After these
prayers, she begins to act, and seeks among these ....

She begins to know God, and to desire to reach him; but
as she is ignorant of the means of attaining this, if her
desire is sincere and true, she does the same as a person
who, desiring to reach some place, having lost his way,
and knowing his aberration, would have recourse to those
who knew this way perfectly, and ....
....

She resolves to conform to his will during the remainder
of her life; but as her natural weakness, with the habit that
she has of the sins in which she has lived, have reduced
her to the impotence of attaining this felicity, she implores
of his mercy the means of reaching him, of attaching herself to him, of adhering to him eternally................
Thus she perceives that she should adore God as a creature,
render thanks to him as a debtor, satisfy him as a criminal,
and pray to him as one poor and needy.

CONVERSATION OF PASCAL

WITH M. DE SACI

ON EPICTETUS AND MONTAIGNE

" M. PASCAL came, too, at this time, to live at Port-Royal des Champs. I do not stop to tell who this man was, whom not only all France, but all Europe admired; his mind always acute, always active, was of an extent, an elevation, a firmness, a penetration, and a clearness exceeding any thing that can be believed. . . . This admirable man, being finally moved by God, submitted this lofty mind to the yoke of Jesus Christ, and this great and noble heart embraced penitence with humility. He came to Paris to throw himself into the arms of M. Singlin, resolved to do all that he should order him. M. Singlin thought, on seeing this great genius, that he should do well to send him to Port-Royal des Champs, where M. Arnauld would cope with him in the sciences, and where M. de Saci would teach him to despise them. He came therefore to live at Port-Royal. M. de Saci could not courteously avoid seeing him, especially having been urged to it by M. Singlin; but the holy enlightenment which he found in the Scripture and in the Fathers made him hope that he would not be dazzled by all the brilliancy of M. Pascal, which nevertheless charmed and carried away all the world. He found in fact all that he said very just. He acknowledged with pleasure the strength of his mind and conversation. All that M. Pascal said to him that was remarkable he had seen before in St. Augustine, and doing justice to every one, he said: ' M. Pascal is extremely estimable in that, not having read the Fathers of the Church, he has of himself, by the penetration of his mind, found the same truths that they had found. He finds them surprising, he says, because he has not found them in any place; but for us, we are accustomed to see them on every side in our books.' Thus, this wise ecclesiastic, finding that the ancients had not less light than the moderns, held to them, and esteemed M. Pascal greatly because he agreed in all things with St. Augustine.

" The usual way of M. De Saci, in conversing with people, was to adapt his conversation to those with whom he was talking. If he met, for example, M. Champagne, he talked with him of painting. If he met M. Hamon, he talked with him of medicine. If he met the surgeon of the place, he questioned him on surgery. Those who cultivated the vine, or trees, or grain, told him all that was remarkable about them. Every thing served to lead him speedily to God and to lead others there with him. He thought it his duty therefore to put M. Pascal in his province, and to talk with him of the philosophical readings with which he had been most occupied. He led him to this subject in the first conversations that they had together. M. Pascal told him that his two most familiar books had been Epictetus and Montaigne, and highly eulogized these two minds. M. de Saci, who had always thought it a duty to read but little of these two authors, entreated M. Pascal to speak of them to him at length."

" Epictetus," says he, " is among the philosophers of the world who have best understood the duties of man. He requires, before all things, that he should regard God as his principal object; that he should be persuaded that he governs every thing with justice; that he should submit to him cheerfully, and that he should follow him voluntarily in every thing, as doing nothing except with the utmost wisdom: as thus this disposition will check all complaints and murmurs, and will prepare his mind to suffer tranquilly the most vexatious events. Never say, says he, I have lost this; say rather, I have restored it. My son is dead, I have restored him. My wife is dead, I have restored her. So with property and with every thing else. But he who has deprived me of it is a wicked man, you say. Why does it trouble you by whom the one who has lent it to you demands it of you again? While he permits you the use of it, take care of it as property belonging to another, as a man who is travelling would do in an inn. You ought not, says he, to desire that things should be done as you wish, but you ought to wish that they should be done as they are done. Remember, says he elsewhere, that you are here as an actor, and that you play the part in a drama that it pleases the manager to give you. If he gives you a short one, play a short one; if he gives you a long one, play a long one; if he wishes you to feign the beggar, you should do it with all the simplicity possible to you; and so with the rest. It is your business to play well the part that is given you; but to choose it is the business of another. Have every day before your eyes death and the evils which seem the most intolerable; and you will never think of any thing lower and will desire nothing with excess.

"He shows, too, in a thousand ways what man should do. He requires that he should be humble, that he should conceal his good resolutions, especially in the beginning, and that he should accomplish them in secret: nothing destroys them more than to reveal them. He never tires of repeating that the whole study and desire of man should be to perceive the will of God and to pursue it.

"Such sir, said M. Pascal to M. de Saci, was the enlightenment of this great mind that so well understood the duties of man. I dare say that he would have merited to be adored if he had also known his impotence as well, since it is necessary to be a god to teach both to men. Thus as he was clay and ashes, after having so well comprehended what was due, behold how he destroys himself in the presumption of what can be done. He says that God has given to every man the means of acquitting himself of all his obligations; that these means are always in our power; that we must seek felicity through the things that are in our power, since God has given them to us for this end: we must see what there is in us that is free; that wealth, life, esteem, are not in our power, and therefore do not lead to God; but that the mind cannot be forced to believe what it knows to be false, nor the will to love what it knows will render it unhappy; that these two powers are therefore free, and and that it is through them that we can render ourselves perfect; that man can by these powers perfectly know God, love him, obey him, please him, cure himself of all his vices, acquire all the virtues, render himself holy, and thus the companion of God. These principles of a diabolic pride lead him to other errors, as that the soul is a portion of the divine substance; that sorrow and death are not evils; that one may kill himself when he is persecuted to such a degree that he has reason to believe that God calls him, and others.

"As for Montaigne, of whom you wish too, sir, that I should speak to you, being born in a Christian State, he made profession of the Catholic religion, and in this there was nothing peculiar. But as he wished to discover what morals reason would dictate without the light of faith, he based his principles upon this supposition; and thus, considering man as destitute of all revelation, he discourses in this wise. He puts all things in a universal doubt, so general that this doubt bears away itself, that is whether he doubts, and even doubting this latter proposition, his uncertainty revolves upon itself in a perpetual and restless circle, alike opposed to those who affirm that every thing is uncertain and to those who affirm that every thing is not so, because he will affirm nothing. It is in this doubt which doubts itself, and in this ignorance which is ignorant of itself, and which he calls his master-form, that lies the essence of his opinion, which he was unable to express by any positive term. For if he says that he doubts, he betrays himself in affirming at least that he doubts; which being formally against his intention, he could only explain it by interrogation; so that, not wishing to say: "I do not know," he says: "What do I know?" Of this he makes his device, placing it under the scales which, weighing contradictories, are found in perfect equilibrium: that is, it is pure Pyrrhonism. Upon this principle revolve all his discourses and all his essays; and it is the only thing that he pretends really to establish, although he does not always point out his intention. He destroys in them insensibly all that passes for the most certain among men, not indeed to establish the contrary with a certainty to which alone he is the enemy, but merely to show that, appearances being equal on both sides, one knows not where to fix his belief.

"In this spirit he jests at all affirmations; for example, he combats those who have thought to establish in France a great remedy against lawsuits by the multitude and the pretended justice of the laws: as if one could cut off the

root of the doubts whence arise these lawsuits, and as if
there were dikes that could arrest the torrent of uncertainty
and take conjectures captive! Thus it is that, when he
says that he would as soon submit his cause to the first
passer-by as to judges armed with such a number of ordinances, he does not pretend that we should change the
order of the State,—he has not so much ambition; nor
that his advice may be better,—he believes none good. It
is only to prove the vanity of the most received opinions;
showing that the exclusion of all laws would rather diminish the number of disputants whilst the multiplicity of laws
serves only to increase them, since difficulties grow in proportion as they are weighed; since obscurities are multiplied by commentaries; and since the surest way to understand the meaning of a discourse is not to examine it,
and to take it on the first appearance: as soon as it is
scrutinized, all its clearness becomes dissipated. In the
like manner he judges by chance of all the acts of men
and the points of history, sometimes in one way, sometimes
in another, freely following his first impression, and, without constraining his thought by the rules of reason, which
has only false measures, he delights to show, by his example, the contrarieties of the same mind. In this free
genius, it is alike equal to him to get the better or not
in the dispute, having always, by either example, a means
of showing the weakness of opinions; being sustained with
so much advantage in this universal doubt, that he is
strengthened in it alike by his triumph and his defeat.

"It is from this position, floating and wavering as it is,
that he combats with an invincible firmness the heretics
of his times in respect to their affirmation of alone knowing
the true sense of the Scripture; and it is also from this
that he thunders forth most vigorously against the horrible
impiety of those who dare to affirm that God is not. He
attacks them especially in the apology of Raimond de Se-
bonde; and finding them voluntarily destitute of all revelation, and abandoned to their natural intelligence, all faith
set aside, he demands of them upon what authority they
undertake to judge of this sovereign Being who is infinite by his own definition, they who know truly none of

the things of nature! He asks them upon what principles they rest; he presses them to show them. He examines all that they can produce; and penetrates them so deeply, by the talent in which he excels, that he demonstrates the vanity of all those that pass for the firmest and the most natural. He asks whether the soul knows any thing; whether she knows herself; whether she is substance or accident, body or spirit, what is each of these things, and whether there is any thing that does not belong to one of these orders; whether she knows her own body, what is matter and whether she can discern among the innumerable variety of bodies from which it is produced; how she can reason if she is material; and how she can be united to a particular body and feel its passions if she is spiritual: when she commenced to be? with the body or before? and whether she will end with it or not; whether she is never mistaken; whether she knows when she errs, seeing that the essence of contempt consists in not knowing it; whether in her obscurity she does not believe as firmly that two and three make six as she knows afterwards that they make five; whether animals reason, think, talk; and who can determine what is time, what is space or extent, what is motion, what is unity, what are all the things that surround us and are wholly inexplicable to us; what is health, sickness, life, death, good, evil, justice, sin, of which we constantly speak; whether we have within us the principles of truth, and whether those which we believe, and which are called axioms or common notions, because they are common to all men, are in conformity with the essential truth. And since we know but by faith alone that an all-good Being has given them to us truly in creating us to know the truth, who can know without this light whether, being formed by chance, they are not uncertain, or whether, being formed by a lying and malicious being, he has not given them to us falsely in order to lead us astray? Showing by this that God and truth are inseparable, and that if the one is or is not, if it is certain or uncertain, the other is necessarily the same. Who knows then whether the common-sense, that we take for the judge of truth, can be the judge of that which has created it? Besides, who knows what truth is, and how can we be sure of having it without understanding it? Who knows even what is being which it is impossible to define, since there is nothing more general, and since it would be necessary at first, to explain it, to use the word itself: It is being . . . ? And since we know not what is soul, body, time, space, motion, truth, good, nor even being, nor how to explain the idea that we form within ourselves, how can we assure ourselves that it is the same in all men, seeing that we have no other token than the uniformity of consequences, which is not always a sign of that of principles; for they may indeed be very different, and lead nevertheless to the same conclusions, every one knowing that the true is often inferred from the false.

"Lastly, he examines thus profoundly the sciences, both geometry, of which he shows the uncertainty in the axioms and the terms that she does not define, as centre, motion, etc., physics in many more ways, and medicine in an infinity of methods; history, politics, ethics, jurisprudence, and the rest. So that we remain convinced that we think no better at present that in a dream from which we shall wake only at death, and during which we have the principles of truth as little as during natural sleep. It is thus that he reproaches reason divested of faith so strongly and so cruelly that, making her doubt whether she is rational, and whether animals are so or not, or in a greater or less degree, he makes her descend from the excellence which she has attributed to herself, and places her through grace on a level with the brutes, without permitting her to quit this order until she shall have been instructed by her Creator himself in respect to her rank, of which she is ignorant; threatening, if she grumbles, to place her beneath every thing, which is as easy as the opposite, and nevertheless giving her power to act only in order to remark her weakness with sincere humility, instead of exalting herself by a foolish insolence."

"M. de Saci, fancying himself living in a new country, and listening to a new language, repeated to himself the words of St. Augustine: O God of truth! are those who know these subtleties of reasoning therefore more pleasing to thee? He pitied this philosopher who pricked and tore himself on every side with the thorns that he formed, as St. Augustine said of himself when he was in this state. After some meditation, he said to M. Pascal:

"I thank you, sir; I am sure that if I had read Montaigne a long time, I should not know him so well as I do, since the conversation that I have just had with you. This man should wish that he might never be known, except by the recitals that you make of his writings; and he might say with St. Augustine: *Ibi me vide, attende*. I believe assuredly that this man had talent; but I know not whether you do not lend to him a little more than he had, by the logical chain that you make of his principles. You can judge that having passed my life as I have done, I have had little counsel to read this author, the works of whom had nothing of that which we ought chiefly to seek in our reading, according to the rule of St. Augustine, because his works do not appear to proceed from a solid basis of humility and piety. We should forgive those philosophers of former times who styled themselves academicians, for putting every thing in doubt. But what need had Montaigne to divert the mind by reviving a doctrine which passes now in the eyes of Christians for the folly? This is the judgment that St. Augustine passes on these persons. For we can say after him of Montaigne: He sets faith aside in every thing that he says; therefore we, who have faith, should set aside every thing that he says. I do not blame the talent of this author, which was a great gift from God; but he might have used it better, and made a sacrifice of it to God rather than to the devil. What avails a blessing when one uses it so ill? *Quid proderat*, etc., said this holy doctor of him before his conversion. You are fortunate, sir, in having raised yourself above these people, who are called doctors, who are plunged in drunkenness, but whose hearts are void of truth. God has poured out into your heart other sweets and other attractions than those which you find in Montaigne. He has recalled you from that dangerous pleasure, *a jucunditate pestifera*, says St. Augustine, who renders thanks to God that he has forgiven him the sins which he had committed in delighting too much in vanity. St. Augustine is so much the more credible in this that he held formerly the same sentiments; and as you say of Montaigne that it is through universal doubt that he combats the heretics of his times, so through this same doubt of the academicians, St. Augustine forsook the heresy of the Manicheans. As soon as he belonged to God, he renounced these vanities, which he calls sacrileges. He perceived with what wisdom St. Paul warned us not to suffer ourselves to be seduced by these discourses. For he acknowledges that there is in them a certain harmony which fascinates: we sometimes believe things true only because they are narrated eloquently. Those are dangerous viands, says he, that are served up in fine dishes; but these viands, instead of nourishing the heart, starve it. We then resemble men who sleep, and who fancy that they eat while sleeping: these imaginary viands leave them as empty as they were before.

"M. de Saci made several similar remarks to M. Pascal: whereupon M. Pascal said to him, that if he complimented him on thoroughly possessing Montaigne, and of knowing how to construe him well, he could tell him without flattery that he understood St. Augustine much better, and that he knew how to construe him much better, though little to the advantage of poor Montaigne. He expressed himself as being extremely edified by the solidity of all that he had just represented to him; nevertheless, being full of his author, he could not contain himself, and thus continued:

"I acknowledge, sir, that I cannot see without joy in this author proud reason so irresistibly baffled by its own weapons, and that fierce contention of man with man, which, from the companionship with God, to which he had exalted himself by maxims, hurls him down to the nature of brutes; and I should have loved with all my heart the minister of so great a vengeance, if, being a disciple of the Church by faith, he had followed the rules of ethics, in bringing men whom he had so usefully humiliated, not to irritate by new crimes him who alone can draw them from the crimes which he has convicted them of not being able even to know.

"But he acts on the contrary like a heathen in this wise.

On this principle, says he, outside of faith every thing is in uncertainty, and considering how much men seek the true and the good without making any progress towards tranquillity, he concludes that one should leave the care of them to others; and remain nevertheless in repose, skimming lightly over subjects for fear of going beyond one's depth in them; and take the true and the good on first appearances, without dwelling on them, for they are so far from being solid that if one grasps them ever so lightly, they will slip through his fingers and leave them empty. For this reason he follows the evidence of the senses and common-sense, because he would be obliged to do violence to himself to contradict them, and because he knows not whether he would gain by it, ignorant as to where the truth is. So he shuns pain and death, because his instinct impels him to it, and because he will not resist for the same reason, but without concluding thence that these may be the real evils, not confiding too much in these natural emotions of fear, seeing that we feel others of pleasure which are accused of being wrong, although nature speaks to the contrary. Thus there is nothing extravagant in his conduct; he acts like the rest of mankind, and all that they do in the foolish idea that they are pursuing the true good, he does from another principle, which is that probabilities being equal on either side, example and convenience are the counterpoises that decide him.

"He mounts his horse like a man that is not a philosopher, because he suffers it, but without believing that this is his right, not knowing whether this animal has not, on the contrary, the right to make use of him. He also does some violence to himself to avoid certain vices; and he even preserves fidelity to marriage on account of the penalty that follows irregularities; but if the trouble that he takes exceeds that which he avoids, it does not disturb him, the rule of this action being convenience and tranquillity. He utterly rejects therefore that stoical virtue which is depicted with a severe mien, fierce glance, bristling locks, and wrinkled and moist brow, in a painful and distorted posture, far from men, in a gloomy silence, alone upon the summit of a rock: a phantom, he says, fit to frighten children, and which does nothing else with continual effort than to seek the repose which it never attains. His own is simple, familiar, pleasant, playful, and as we may say sportive: she follows whatever charms her, and toys negligently with good and bad accidents, reclining effeminately in the bosom of a tranquil indolence, from which she shows to those who seek felicity with so much toil that it is only there where she is reposing, and that ignorance and incuriosity are soft pillows for a well-balanced head, as he himself has said.

"I cannot conceal from you, sir, that in reading this author and comparing him with Epictetus, I have found that they are assuredly the two greatest defenders of the two most celebrated sects of the world, and the only ones conformable to reason, since we can only follow one of these two roads, namely: either that there is a God, and then we place in him the sovereign good; or that he is uncertain, and that then the true good is also uncertain, since he is incapable of it. I have taken extreme pleasure in remarking in these different reasonings wherein both have reached some conformity with the true wisdom which they have essayed to understand. For if it is pleasing to observe in nature her desire to paint God in all his works, in which we see some traces of him because they are his images, how much more just is it to consider in the productions of minds the efforts which they make to imitate the essential truth, even in shunning it, and to remark wherein they attain it and wherein they wander from it, as I have endeavored to do in this study.

"It is true, sir, that you have just shown me, in an admirable manner, the little utility that Christians can draw from these philosophic studies. I shall not refrain however, with your permission, from telling you still further my thoughts on the subject, ready, however, to renounce all light that does not come from you, in which I shall have the advantage either of having encountered truth by good fortune or of receiving it from you with certainty. It appears to me that the source of the errors of these two sects, is in not having known that the state of man at the present time differs from that of his creation; so that the one, remarking some traces of his first greatness and being ignorant of his corruption, has treated nature as sound and without need of redemption, which leads him to the height of pride; whilst the other, feeling the present wretchedness and being ignorant of the original dignity, treats nature as necessarily infirm and irreparable, which precipitates it into despair of arriving at real good, and thence into extreme laxity. Thus these two states which it is necessary to know together in order to see the whole truth, being known separately, lead necessarily to one of these two vices, pride or indolence, in which all men are invariably before grace, since if they do not remain in their disorders through laxity, they forsake them through vanity, so true is that which you have just repeated to me from St. Augustine, and which I find to a great extent; for in fact homage is rendered to them in many ways.

"It is therefore from this imperfect enlightenment that it happens that the one, knowing the duties of man and being ignorant of his impotence, is lost in presumption, and that the other, knowing the impotence and being ignorant of the duty, falls into laxity; whence it seems that since the one leads to truth, the other to error, there would be formed from their alliance a perfect system of morals. But instead of this peace, nothing but war and a general ruin would result from their union; for the one establishing certainty, the other doubt, the one the greatness of man, the other his weakness, they would destroy the truths as well as the falsehoods of each other. So that they cannot subsist alone because of their defects, nor unite because of their opposition, and thus they break and destroy each other to give place to the truth of the Gospel. This it is that harmonizes the contrarieties by a wholly divine act, and uniting all that is true and expelling all that is false, thus makes of them a truly celestial wisdom in which those opposites accord that were incompatible in human doctrines. And the reason of this is, that these philosophers of the world place contrarieties in the same subject; for the one attributed greatness to nature and the other weakness to this same nature, which could not subsist; whilst faith teaches us to place them in different subjects: all that is infirm belonging to nature, all that is powerful belonging to grace. Such is the marvellous and novel union which God alone could teach, and which he alone could make, and which is only a type and an effect of the ineffable union of two natures in the single person of a Man-God.

"I ask your pardon, sir, said M. Pascal to M. de Saci, for being thus carried away in your presence into theology, instead of remaining in philosophy, which alone was my subject; but I was led to it insensibly; and it is difficult not to enter upon it whatever truth may be discussed, because it is the centre of all the truths; which appears here perfectly, since it so obviously includes all those that are found in these opinions. Thus I do not see how any of them could refuse to follow it. For if they are full of the idea of the greatness of man, what have they imagined that does not yield to the promises of the Gospel, which are nothing else than the worthy price of the death of a God? And if they delighted in viewing the infirmities of nature, their ideas do not equal those of the real weakness of sin, of which the same death has been the remedy. Thus all find in it more than they have desired; and what is marvellous, they who could not harmonize in an infinitely inferior degree, then find themselves in unison!"

"M. de Saci could not refrain from testifying to M. Pascal that he was surprised to see how well he knew how to interpret things; but he acknowledged at the same time that every one had not the secret of making on these readings such wise and elevated reflections. He told him that he was like those skilful physicians, who by an adroit method of preparing the most deadly poisons knew how to extract from them the most efficacious remedies. He added, that though he saw clearly, from what he had just said, that these readings were useful to him, he could not believe however that they would be advantageous to many people of slow intellect, who would not have elevation of mind enough to read these authors and judge of them, and to know how to draw pearls from the midst of the dunghill, *aurum ex stercore*, as said one of the Fathers. This could be much better said of these philosophers, the dunghill of whom, by its black fumes, might obscure the wavering faith of those who read them. For this reason he would always counsel such persons not to expose themselves lightly to these readings, for fear of being destroyed with these philosophers, and of becoming the prey of demons and the food of worms, according to the language of the Scripture, as these philosophers have been."

" As to the utility of these readings, said M. Pascal, I will tell you simply my thought. I find in Epictetus an incomparable art for troubling the repose of those who seek it in external things, and for forcing them to acknowledge that they are veritable slaves and miserable blind men; that it is impossible that they should find any thing else than the error and pain which they fly, unless they give themselves without reserve to God alone. Montaigne is incomparable for confounding the pride of those who, outside of faith, pique themselves in a genuine justice; for disabusing those who cling to their opinions, and who think to find in the sciences impregnable truths; and for so effectually convicting reason of its want of light and its aberrations, that it is difficult, when one makes a good use of its principles, to be tempted to find repugnance in mysteries, for the mind is so overwhelmed by him, that it is far from wishing to judge whether the Incarnation or the mystery of the Eucharist are possible; which the generality of mankind discuss but too often.

" But if Epictetus combats indolence, he leads to pride, so that he may be very injurious to those who are not persuaded of the corruption of the most perfect justice which is not from faith. And Montaigne is absolutely pernicious to those who have any leaning to impiety or vice. For this reason these readings should be regulated with much care, discretion, and regard to the condition and disposition of those to whom they are counselled. It seems to me only that by joining them together they would not succeed ill, since the one is opposed to the evil of the other: not that they could bestow virtue but only disturb vice; the soul finding itself combated by contrarieties, the one of which expels pride and the other indolence, and being unable to be tranquil in any of these vices by their reasonings, or to shun them all."

" It was thus that these two persons of so fine an intellect agreed at last upon the subject of the reading of these philosophers, and met at the same goal, which they reached however by a somewhat different method; M. de Saci arriv-

ing there at once through the clear views of Christianity,
and M. Pascal reaching it only after many turns by clinging
to the principles of these philosophers."

THE ART OF PERSUASION

THE art of persuasion has a necessary relation to the manner in which men are led to consent to that which is proposed to them, and to the conditions of things which it is
sought to make them believe.

No one is ignorant that there are two avenues by which
opinions are received into the soul, which are its two principal powers: the understanding and the will. The more
natural is that of the understanding, for we should never
consent to any but demonstrated truths; but the more common, though the one contrary to nature, is that of the will;
for all men are almost led to believe not of proof, but by
attraction. This way is base, ignoble, and irrelevant: every
one therefore disavows it. Each one professes to believe and
even to love nothing but what he knows to be worthy of belief and love.

I do not speak here of divine truths, which I shall take
care not to comprise under the art of persuasion, because
they are infinitely superior to nature: God alone can place them
in the soul and in such a way as it pleases him. I know that
he has desired that they should enter from the heart into
the mind, and not from the mind into the heart, to humiliate
that proud power of reasoning that pretends to the right to
be the judge of the things that the will chooses; and to
cure this infirm will which is wholly corrupted by its filthy
attachments. And thence it comes that whilst in speaking of
human things, we say that it is necessary to know them
before we can love them, which has passed into a proverb,[1]
the saints on the contrary say in speaking of divine things
that it is necessary to love them in order to know them, and
that we only enter truth through charity, from which they
have made one of their most useful maxims.

From which it appears that God has established this super-

[1] Ignoti nulla cupido—" We do not desire what we do not know."

natural order, which is directly contrary to the order that should be natural to men in natural things. They have nevertheless corrupted this order by making of profane things what they should make of holy things, because in fact we believe scarcely any thing except that which pleases us. And thence comes the aversion which we have to consenting to the truths of the Christian religion that are opposed to our pleasures. "Tell us of pleasant things and we will hearken to you," said the Jews to Moses; as if the agreeableness of a thing should regulate belief! And it is to punish this disorder by an order which is conformed to him, that God only pours out his light into the mind after having subdued the rebellion of the will by an altogether heavenly gentleness which charms and wins it.

I speak therefore only of the truths within our reach; and it is of them that I say that the mind and the heart are as doors by which they are received into the soul, but that very few enter by the mind, whilst they are brought in in crowds by the rash caprices of the will, without the counsel of the reason.

These powers have each their principles and their mainsprings of action.

Those of the mind are truths which are natural and known to all the world, as that the whole is greater than its part, besides several particular maxims that are received by some and not by others, but which as soon as they are admitted are as powerful, although false, in carrying away belief, as those the most true.

Those of the will are certain desires natural and common to all mankind, as the desire of being happy, which no one can avoid having, besides several particular objects which each one follows in order to attain, and which having the power to please us are as powerful, although pernicious in fact, in causing the will to act, as though they made its veritable happiness.

So much for that which regards the powers that lead us to consent.

But as for the qualities of things which should persuade us, they are very different.

Some are drawn, by a necessary consequence, from common principles and admitted truths. These may be infallibly persuasive; for in showing the harmony which they have with acknowledged principles there is an inevitable necessity of conviction, and it is impossible that they shall not be received into the soul as soon as it has been enabled to class them among the principles which it has already admitted.

There are some which have a close connection with the objects of our satisfaction; and these again are received with certainty, for as soon as the soul has been made to perceive that a thing can conduct it to that which it loves supremely, it must inevitably embrace it with joy.

But those which have this double union both with admitted truths and with the desires of the heart, are so sure of their effect that there is nothing that can be more so in nature.

As, on the contrary, that which does not accord either with our belief or with our pleasures is importunate, false, and absolutely alien to us.

In all these positions, there is no room for doubt. But there are some wherein the things which it is sought to make us believe are well established upon truths which are known, but which are at the same time contrary to the pleasures that interest us most. And these are in great danger of showing, by an experience which is only too common, what I said at the beginning—that this imperious soul, which boasted of acting only by reason, follows by a rash and shameful choice the desires of a corrupt will, whatever resistance may be opposed to it by the too enlightened mind.

Then it is that a doubtful balance is made between truth and pleasure, and that the knowledge of the one and the feeling of the other stir up a combat the success of which is very uncertain, since, in order to judge of it, it would be necessary to know all that passes in the innermost spirit of the man, of which the man himself is scarcely ever conscious.

It appears from this, that whatever it may be of which we wish to persuade men, it is necessary to have regard to the person whom we wish to persuade, of whom we must know the mind and the heart, what principles he acknowledges, what things he loves; and then observe in the thing in question what affinity it has with the acknowledged principles, or with the objects so delightful by the pleasure which they give him.

So that the art of persuasion consists as much in that of pleasing as in that of convincing, so much more are men governed by caprice than by reason!

Now, of these two methods, the one of convincing, the other of pleasing, I shall only give here the rules of the first; and this in case we have granted the principles, and remain firm in avowing them: otherwise I do not know whether there could pe an art for adapting proofs to the inconstancy of our caprices.

But the manner of pleasing is incomparably more difficult, more subtle, more useful, and more admirable; therefore, if I do not treat of it, it is because I am not capable of it; and I feel myself so far disproportionate to the task, that I believe the thing absolutely impossible.

Not that I do not believe that there may be as sure rules for pleasing as for demonstrating, and that he who knows perfectly how to comprehend and to practice them will as surely succeed in making himself beloved by princes and by people of all conditions, as in demonstrating the elements of geometry to those who have enough imagination to comprehend its hypotheses. But I consider, and it is, perhaps, my weakness that makes me believe it, that it is impossible to reach this. At least I know that if any are capable of it, they are certain persons whom I know, and that no others have such clear and such abundant light on this matter.

The reason of this extreme difficulty comes from the fact that the principles of pleasure are not firm and stable. They are different in all mankind, and variable in every particular with such a diversity that there is no man more different from another than from himself at different times. A man has other pleasures than a woman; a rich man and a poor man have different enjoyments; a prince, a warrior, a merchant, a citizen, a peasant, the old, the young, the well, the sick, all vary; the least accidents change them.

Now there is an art, and it is that which I give, for showing the connection of truths with their principles, whether of truth or of pleasure, provided that the principles which have once been avowed remain firm, and without being ever contradicted.

But as there are few principles of this kind, and as, apart from geometry, which deals only with very simple figures, there are hardly any truths upon which we always remain agreed, and still fewer objects of pleasure which we do not change every hour, I do not know whether there is a means of giving fixed rules for adapting discourse to the inconstancy of our caprices.

This art, which I call the *art of persuading,* and which, properly speaking, is simply the process of perfect methodical proofs, consists of three essential parts: of defining the terms of which we should avail ourselves by clear definitions; of proposing principles or evident axioms to prove the thing in question; and of always mentally substituting in the demonstrations the definition in the place of the thing defined.

The reason of this method is evident, since it would be useless to propose what it is sought to prove, and to undertake the demonstration of it, if all the terms which are not intelligible had not first been clearly defined; and since it is necessary in the same manner that the demonstration should be preceded by the demand for the evident principles that are necessary to it, for if we do not secure the foundation we cannot secure the edifice; and since, in fine, it is necessary in demonstrating mentally, to substitute the definitions in the place of the things defined, as otherwise there might be an abuse of the different meanings that are encountered in the terms. It is easy to see that, by observing this method, we are sure of convincing, since the terms all being understood, and perfectly exempt from ambiguity by the definitions, and the principles being granted, if in the demonstration we always mentally substitute the definitions for the things defined, the invincible force of the conclusions cannot fail of having its whole effect.

Thus, never can a demonstration in which these conditions have been observed be subject to the slightest doubt; and never can those have force in which they are wanting.

It is, therefore, of great importance to comprehend and to possess them; and hence, to render the thing easier and more practicable, I shall give them all in a few rules which include all that is necessary for the perfection of the definitions, the axioms, and the demonstrations, and consequently of the entire method of the geometrical proofs of the art of persuading.

Rules for Definitions

I. Not to undertake to define any of the things so well known of themselves that clearer terms cannot be had to explain them.

II. Not to leave any terms that are at all obscure or ambiguous without definition.

III. Not to employ in the definition of terms any words but such as are perfectly known or already explained.

Rules for Axioms

I. Not to omit any necessary principle without asking whether it is admitted, however clear and evident it may be.

II. Not to demand, in axioms, any but things that are perfectly evident of themselves.

Rules for Demonstrations

I. Not to undertake to demonstrate any thing that is so evident of itself that nothing can be given that is clearer to prove it.

II. To prove all propositions at all obscure, and to employ in their proof only very evident maxims or propositions already admitted or demonstrated.

III. To always mentally substitute definitions in the place of things defined, in order not to be misled by the ambiguity of terms which have been restricted by definitions.

These eight rules contain all the precepts for solid and immutable proofs, three of which are not absolutely necessary and may be neglected without error; while it is difficult and almost impossible to observe them always exactly, although it is more accurate to do so as far as possible; these are the three first of each of the divisions.

For definitions. Not to define any terms that are perfectly known.

For axioms. Not to omit to require any axioms perfectly evident and simple.

For demonstrations. Not to demonstrate any things well-known of themselves.

For it is unquestionable that it is no great error to define and clearly explain things, although very clear of themselves, nor to omit to require in advance axioms which cannot be refused in the place where they are necessary; nor lastly to prove propositions that would be admitted without proof.

But the five other rules are of absolute necessity, and cannot be dispensed with without essential defect and often without error; and for this reason I shall recapitulate them here in detail.

Rules necessary for definitions. Not to leave any terms at all obscure or ambiguous without definition;

Not to employ in definitions any but terms perfectly known or already explained.

Rule necessary for axioms. Not to demand in axioms any but things perfectly evident.

Rules necessary for demonstrations. To prove all propositions, and to employ nothing for their proof but axioms fully evident of themselves, or propositions already demonstrated or admitted;

Never to take advantage of the ambiguity of terms by failing mentally to substitute definitions that restrict and explain them.

These five rules form all that is necessary to render proofs convincing, immutable, and to say all, geometrical; and the eight rules together render them still more perfect.

I pass now to that of the order in which the propositions should be arranged, to be in a complete geometrical series.

After having established[2].................................
....

This is in what consists the art of persuading, which is comprised in these two principles: to define all the terms of

[2] The rest of the phrase is wanting; and all this second part of the composition, either because it was not redacted by Pascal, or because it has been lost, is found neither in our MS. nor in Father Desmolets.—*Faugère.*

which we make use; to prove them all by mentally substituting definitions in the place of things defined.

And here it seems to me proper to anticipate three principal objections which may be made:

1st, that this method has nothing new; 2d, that it is very easy to learn, it being unnecessary for this to study the elements of geometry, since it consists in these two words that are known at the first reading; and, 3d, that it is of little utility, since its use is almost confined to geometrical subjects alone.

It is necessary therefore to show that there is nothing so little known, nothing more difficult to practise, and nothing more useful or more universal.

As to the first objection, that these rules are common in the world, that it is necessary to define every thing and to prove every thing, and that logicians themselves have placed them among the principles of their art, I would that the thing were true and that it were so well known that I should not have the trouble of tracing with so much care the source of all the defects of reasonings which are truly so common. But so little is this the case, that, geometricians alone excepted, who are so few in number that they are single in a whole nation and long periods of time, we see no others who know it. It will be easy to make this understood by those who have perfectly comprehended the little that I have said; but if they have not fully comprehended this, I confess that they will learn nothing from it.

But if they have entered into the spirit of these rules, and if the rules have made sufficient impression on them to become rooted and established in their minds, they will feel how much difference there is between what is said here and what a few logicians may perhaps have written by chance approximating to it in a few passages of their works.

Those who have the spirit of discernment know how much difference there is between two similar words, according to their position, and the circumstances that accompany them. Will it be maintained, indeed, that two persons who have read the same book, and learned it by heart, have a like acquaintance with it, if the one comprehends it in such a manner that he knows all its principles, the force of its conclusions, the

answers to the objections that may be made to it, and the
whole economy of the work; while to the other these are but
dead letters and seeds, which, although like those which have
produced such fruitful trees, remain dry and unproductive in
the sterile mind that has received them in vain.

All who say the same things do not possess them in the
same manner; and hence the incomparable author of the *Art
of Conversation*[3] pauses with so much care to make it understood that we must not judge of the capacity of a man by the
excellence of a happy remark that we have heard him make;
but instead of extending our admiration of a good speech to
the speaker, let us penetrate, says he, the mind from which it
proceeds; let us try whether he owes it to his memory, or to
a happy chance; let us receive it with coldness and contempt,
in order to see whether he will feel that we do not give to
what he says the esteem which its value deserves: it will
oftenest be seen that he will be made to disavow it on the
spot, and will be drawn very far from this better thought in
which he does not believe, to plunge himself into another
quite base and ridiculous. We must, therefore, sound in what
manner this thought is lodged in its author;[4] how, whence,
to what extent he possesses it; otherwise, the hasty judgment
will be a rash judge.

I would inquire of reasonable persons whether this principle: *Matter is naturally wholly incapable of thought,* and
this other: *I think, therefore I am,* are in fact the same in
the mind of Descartes, and in that of St. Augustine, who said
the same thing twelve hundred years before.[5]

In truth, I am far from affirming that Descartes is not the
real author of it, even though he may have learned it only
in reading this distinguished saint; for I know how much difference there is between writing a word by chance without
making a longer and more extended reflection on it, and
perceiving in this word an admirable series of conclusions,
which prove the distinction between material and spiritual
natures, and making of it a firm and sustained principle of a
complete metaphysical system, as Descartes has pretended to

[3] Montaigne, *Essais,* liv. III, chap. viii.—*Faugère.*
[4] Montaigne's expression is: "Feel on all sides how it is lodged in its author." *Essais,* same chapter.—*Ibid.*
[5] *Civ. Dei,* l. XI, c. xxvi.

do. For without examining whether he has effectively succeeded in his pretension, I assume that he has done so, and it is on this supposition that I say that this expression is as different in his writings from the same saying in others who have said it by chance, as is a man full of life and strength from a corpse.

One man will say a thing of himself without comprehending its excellence, in which another will discern a marvellous series of conclusions, which make us affirm boldly that it is no longer the same expression, and that he is no more indebted for it to the one from whom he has learned it, than a beautiful tree belongs to the one who cast the seed, without thinking of it, or knowing it, into the fruitful soil which caused its growth by its own fertility.

The same thoughts sometimes put forth quite differently in the mind of another than in that of their author: unfruitful in their natural soil, abundant when transplanted. But it much oftener happens that a good mind itself makes its own thoughts produce all the fruit of which they are capable, and that afterwards others, having heard them admired, borrow them, and adorn themselves with them, but without knowing their excellence; and it is then that the difference of the same word in different mouths is the most apparent.

It is in this manner that logic has borrowed, perhaps, the rules of geometry, without comprehending their force; and thus, in placing them by chance among those that belong to it, it does not thence follow that they[6] have entered into the spirit of geometry, and I should be greatly averse if they gave no other evidence of it than that of having mentioned it by chance, to placing them on a level with that science that teaches the true method of directing the reason.

But I should be, on the contrary, strongly disposed to exclude them from it, and almost irrevocably. For to have said it by chance, without having taken care that every thing was included within it, and instead of following this light to wander blindly in useless researches, pursuing what they promise but never can give, is truly showing that they are not very clear-sighted, and much more than if they had failed to follow the light, because they had not perceived it.

[6] Doubtless *the logicians.—Faugère.*

The method of not erring is sought by all the world. The logicians profess to guide to it, the geometricians alone attain it, and apart from their science, and the imitations of it, there are no true demonstrations. The whole art is included in the simple precepts that we have given; they alone are sufficient, they alone afford proofs; all other rules are useless or injurious. This I know by long experience of all kinds of books and persons.

And on this point I pass the same judgment as those who say that geometricians give them nothing new by these rules, because they possessed them in reality, but confounded with a multitude of others, either useless or false, from which they could not discriminate them, as those who seeking a diamond of great price amidst a number of false ones, but from which they know not how to distinguish it, should boast, in holding them all together, of possessing the true one equally with him who without pausing at this mass of rubbish lays his hand upon the costly stone which they are seeking and for which they do not throw away the rest.

The defect of false reasoning is a malady which is cured by these two remedies. Another has been compounded of an infinity of useless herbs in which the good are enveloped and in which they remain without effect through the ill qualities of the compound.

To discover all the sophistries and equivocations of captious reasonings, they have invented barbarous names that astonish those who hear them; and whilst we can only unravel all the tangles of this perplexing knot by drawing out one of the ends in the way proposed by geometricians, they have indicated a strange number of others in which the former are found included without knowing which is the best.

And thus, in showing us a number of paths which they say conduct us whither we tend, although there are but two that lead to it, it is necessary to know how to mark them in particular. It will be pretended that geometry which indicates them with certainty gives only what had already been given by others, because they gave in fact the same thing and more, without heeding that this boon lost its value by abundance, and was diminished by adding to it.

Nothing is more common than good things: the point in

question is only to discriminate them; and it is certain that they are all natural and within our reach and even known to all mankind. But they know not how to distinguish them. This is universal. It is not among extraordinary and fantastic things that excellence is to be found, of whatever kind it may be. We rise to attain it and become removed from it: it is oftenest necessary to stoop for it. The best books are those, which those who read them believe they themselves could have written. Nature, which alone is good, is wholly familiar and common.

I make no doubt therefore that these rules, being the true ones, are simple, artless, and natural, as in fact they are. It is not *Barbara* and *Baralipton* that constitute reasoning. The mind must not be forced; artificial and constrained manners fill it with foolish presumption, through unnatural elevation and vain and ridiculous inflation, instead of solid and vigorous nutriment. And one of the principal reasons that diverts those who are entering upon this knowledge so much from the true path which they should follow, is the fancy that they take at the outset that good things are inaccessible, giving them the name of *great, lofty, elevated, sublime*. This destroys every thing. I would call them *low, common, familiar:* these names suit them better; I hate such inflated expressions.

DISCOURSE

ON THE PASSION OF LOVE[1]

MAN is born for thought; therefore he is not a moment without it; but the pure thoughts that would render him happy, if he could always maintain them, weary and oppress him. They make a uniform life to which he cannot adapt himself; he must have excitement and action, that is, it is necessary that he should sometimes be agitated by those passions the deep and vivid sources of which he feels within his heart.

The passions which are the best suited to man and include many others, are love and ambition: they have little connec-

[1] The authenticity of this fragment is disputed.

tion with each other; nevertheless they are often allied; but they mutually weaken, not to say destroy, each other.

Whatever compass of mind one may have, he is capable of only one great passion; hence, when love and ambition are found together, they are only half as great as they would be if only one of them existed. The time of life determines neither the beginning nor the end of these two passions; they spring up in the earliest years and subsist very often unto the tomb. Nevertheless, as they require much warmth, young persons are best fitted for them, and it seems that they abate with years: this however is very rare.

The life of man is miserably brief. It is usually computed from his first entrance into the world; for my part, I would only compute it from the birth of reason and from the time that man begins to be influenced by it, which does not ordinarily happen before twenty years of age. Before this time, we are children, and a child is not a man

How happy is a life that begins with love and ends with ambition! If I had to choose, this is the one I should take. So long as we have ardor we are amiable; but this ardor dies out, is lost; then what a fine and noble place is left for ambition! A tumultuous life is pleasing to great minds, but those who are mediocre have no pleasure in it; they are machines everywhere. Hence when love and ambition begin and end life, we are in the happiest condition of which human nature is capable.

The more mind we have the greater the passions are, since the passions being only sentiments and thoughts that belong purely to the mind although they are occasioned by the body, it is obvious that they are no longer any thing but the mind itself, and that thus they fill up its entire capacity. I speak here only of the ardent passions, for the others are often mingled together and cause a very annoying confusion; but this is never the case in those who have mind.

In a great soul everything is great.

It is asked whether it is necessary to love? This should not be asked, it should be felt. We do not deliberate upon it, we are forced to it, and take pleasure in deceiving ourselves when we discuss it.

Definiteness of mind causes definiteness of passion; this is why a great and definite mind loves with ardor, and sees distinctly what it loves.

There are two kinds of mind: the one geometrical, and the other what may be called the imaginative (*de finesse*).

The former is slow, rigid, and inflexible in its views, but the latter has a suppleness of thought which fastens at once upon the various pleasing qualities of what it loves. From the eyes it goes to the heart itself, and from the expression without it knows what is passing within.

When we have both kinds of mind combined, how much pleasure is given by love! For we possess at the same time the strength and the flexibility of mind essentially necessary for the eloquence of two persons.

We are born with a disposition to love in our hearts, which is developed in proportion as the mind is perfected, and impels us to love what appears to us beautiful without ever having been told what this is. Who can doubt after this whether we are in the world for anything else than to love? In fact, we conceal in vain, we always love. In the very things from which love seems to have been separated, it is found secretly and under seal, and man could not live a moment without this.

Man does not like to dwell with himself; nevertheless he loves; it is necessary then that he seek elsewhere something to love. He can find it only in beauty; but as he is himself the most beautiful creature that God has ever formed, he must find in himself the model of this beauty which he seeks without. Every one can perceive in himself the first glimmerings of it; and according as we observe that what is without agrees or disagrees with these, we form our ideas of beauty or deformity in all things. Nevertheless, although man seeks wherewith to fill up the great void he makes in going out of himself, he cannot however be satisfied with every kind of object. His heart is too large; it is necessary at least that it should be something that resembles him and approaches him as near as may be. Hence the beauty that can satisfy man consists not only in fitness, but also in resemblance; it is restricted and confined to the difference of sex.

Nature has so well impressed this truth on our souls, that we find a predisposition to all this; neither art nor study is required; it even seems that we have a place to fill in our hearts which is thus filled effectively. But we feel this better than we can express it. It is only those who know how to confuse and contemn their ideas who do not see it.

Although this general idea of beauty may be engraven in the innermost part of our souls with ineffaceable characters, it does not prevent us from being susceptible of great differences in its individual application; but this is only in the manner of regarding what pleases us. For we do not wish for beauty alone, but desire in connection with it a thousand circumstances that depend on the disposition in which it is found, and it is in this sense that it may be said that each one possesses the original of his beauty, the copy of which he is seeking externally. Nevertheless, women often determine this original. As they have an absolute empire over the minds of men, they paint on them either the qualities of the beauties which they possess or those which they esteem, and by this means add what pleases them to this radical beauty. Hence there is one epoch for blondes, another for brunettes, and the division there is among women in respect to esteem for the one or the other makes at the same time the difference among men in this regard.

Fashion even and country often regulate what is called beauty. It is a strange thing that custom should mingle so strongly with our passions. This does not hinder each one from having his idea of beauty by which he judges others and with which he compares them; it is on this principle that a lover finds his mistress the most beautiful and proposes her as a model.

Beauty is divided in a thousand different ways. The most proper object to sustain it is a woman. When she has intellect, she enlivens it and sets it off marvellously. If a woman wishes to please, and possess the advantages of beauty or a portion of them at least, she will succeed; and even though men take ever so little heed of it, although she does not strive for it, she will make herself loved. There is an accessible point in their hearts; she will take up her abode there.

Man is born for pleasure; he feels it; no other proof of it is needed. He therefore follows his reason in giving himself to pleasure. But very often he feels passion in his heart without knowing in what it originated.

A true or false pleasure can equally fill the mind. For what matters it that this pleasure is false, if we are persuaded that it is true?

By force of speaking of love we become enamored. There is nothing so easy. It is the passion most natural to man.

Love has no age; it is always young. So the poets tell us; it is for this that they represent it to us under the figure of a child. But without asking any thing of it, we feel it.

Love gives intellect and is sustained by intellect. Address is needed in order to love. We daily exhaust the methods of pleasing; nevertheless it is necessary to please and we please.

We have a fountain of self-love which represents us to ourselves as being able to fill several places outside of ourselves; this is what makes us happy to be loved. As we desire it with ardor, we quickly remark it and perceive it in the eyes of the person who loves. For the eyes are the interpreters of the heart; but he alone who is interested in them can understand their language.

Man by himself is something imperfect; he must find a second in order to be happy. He oftenest seeks it in equality of condition, because in that the liberty and the opportunity of manifesting his wishes are most easily found. Yet he sometimes rises above this, and feels the kindling flame although he dares not tell it to the one who has caused it.

When we love a woman of unequal condition, ambition may accompany the beginning of the love; but in a little time the latter becomes master. It is a tyrant that will suffer no companion; it wishes to be alone; all the other passions must bend to it and obey it.

An elevated attachment fills the heart of man much better than a common and equal one; and little things float in his capacity; none but great ones lodge and dwell therein.

We often write things which we only prove by obliging every one to reflect upon himself, and find the truth of which we are speaking. In this consists the force of the proofs of what I assert.

When a man is fastidious in any quality of his mind, he is so in love. For as he must be moved by every object that is

outside of himself, if there is any thing that is repugnant to
his ideas, he perceives and shuns it; the rule of this fastidiousness depends on a pure, noble, and sublime reason. Thus
we can believe ourselves fastidious without actually being so,
and others have the right to condemn us; whilst for beauty
each one has his rule, sovereign and independent of that of
others. Yet between being fastidious and not being so at
all, it must be granted that when one desires to be fastidious
he is not far from actually being so. Women like to perceive fastidiousness in men, and this is, it seems to me, the
most vulnerable point whereby to gain them: we are pleased
to see that a thousand others are contemned and that we
alone are esteemed.

Qualities of mind are not acquired by habit; they are only
perfected. Whence it is easy to see that fastidiousness is a
gift of nature and not an acquisition of art.

In proportion as we have more intellect, we find more
original beauties; but this is not necessary in order to be in
love; for when we love, we find but one.

Does it not seem that as often as a woman goes out of herself to impress the hearts of others, she makes a place void
for others in her own? Yet, I know some who affirm that
this is not true. Dare we call this injustice? It is natural
to give back as much as we have taken.

Attachment to the same thought wearies and destroys the
mind of man. Hence for the solidity and permanence of the
pleasure of love, it is sometimes necessary not to know that
we love; and this is not to be guilty of an infidelity, for we
do not therefore love another; it is to regain strength in
order to love the better. This happens without our thinking
of it; the mind is borne hither of itself; nature wills it, commands it. It must however be confessed that this is a miserable consequence of human weakness, and that we should be
happier if we were not forced to change of thought; but there
is no remedy.

The pleasure of loving without daring to tell it, has its
pains, but it has its joys also. What transport do we not feel
in moulding all our actions in view of pleasing the person
whom we infinitely esteem! We study each day to find the
means of revealing ourselves, and thus employ as much

time as if we were holding converse with the one whom we love. The eyes kindle and grow dim at the same moment, and although we do not see plainly that the one who causes this disorder takes heed of it, we still have the satisfaction of feeling all these emotions for a person who deserves them so well. We would gladly have a hundred tongues to make it known; for as we cannot make use of words, we are obliged to confine ourselves to the eloquence of action.

Up to this point we have constant delight and sufficient occupation. Thus we are happy; for the secret of keeping a passion constantly alive is to suffer no void to spring up in the mind, by obliging it to apply itself without ceasing to what moves it so agreeably. But when it is in the state that I have just described, it cannot last long, because being sole actor in a passion in which there must necessarily be two, it is difficult to hinder it from soon exhausting all the emotions by which it is agitated.

Although the passion may be the same, novelty is needed; the mind takes delight in it, and he who knows how to procure it, knows how to make himself loved.

After having gone thus far, this plenitude sometimes diminishes, and receiving no assistance from the side of its source, we decline miserably, and hostile passions take possession of a heart which they rend into a thousand pieces. Yet a ray of hope, however faint it may be, exalts us as high as we were before. This is sometimes a play in which women delight; but sometimes in feigning to have compassion, they have it in reality. How happy we are when this is the case!

A firm and solid love always begins with the eloquence of action; the eyes have the best share in it. Nevertheless it is necessary to conjecture, but to conjecture rightly.

When two persons are of the same sentiments, they do not conjecture, or at least one conjectures what the other means to say without the other understanding it or daring to understand.

When we love, we appear to ourselves quite different from what we were before. Thus we imagine that every one perceives it; yet nothing is more false. But because the perception of reason is bounded by passion, we cannot assure ourselves and are always suspicious.

When we love, we are persuaded that we shall discover the passion of another: thus we are afraid.

The longer the way is in love, the greater is the pleasure that a sensitive mind feels in it.

There are certain minds to which hopes must long be given, and these are minds of refinement. There are others which cannot long resist difficulties, and these are the grossest. The former love longer and with more enjoyment; the latter love quicker, with more freedom, and sooner end.

The first effect of love is to inspire a profound respect; we have veneration for what we love. It is very just; we see nothing in the world so great as this.

Authors cannot tell us much of the love of their heroes; it is necessary that they should have been the heroes themselves.

Wandering in love is as monstrous as injustice in the mind.

In love, silence is of more avail than speech. It is good to be abashed; there is an eloquence in silence that penetrates more deeply than language can. How well a lover persuades his mistress when he is abashed before her, who elsewhere has so much presence of mind! Whatever vivacity we may have, it is well that in certain junctures it should be extinguished. All this takes place without rule or reflection, and when the mind acts, it is without thinking of it beforehand. This happens through necessity.

We often adore one that is unconscious of it, and do not fail to preserve an inviolable fidelity, although its object knows nothing of it. But this love must be very refined or very pure.

We know the minds of men, and consequently their passions, by the comparison that we make between ourselves and others.

I am of the opinion of him who said that in love one forgets his fortune, his relatives, and his friends; the most elevated attachments go as far as this. What causes us to go so far in love is that we do not think we have need of anything else than the object of our love: the mind is full;

there is no longer any room for care or solicitude. Passion cannot exist without excess: thence it comes that we care no longer for what the world says, as we know already that our conduct ought not to be condemned, since it comes from reason. There is fulness of passion, and can be no beginning of reflection.

It is not an effect of custom, it is an obligation of nature, that men make the advances to gain the attachment of women.

This forgetfulness that is caused by love, and this attachment to the object of our love, make qualities spring up that we had not before. We become magnificent, without ever having been so.

The miser himself who loves becomes liberal, and does not remember ever to have had a contrary disposition; we see the reason of this in considering that there are some passions which contract the soul and render it stagnant, and that there are others which expand it and cause it to overflow.

We have unaptly taken away the name of reason from love and have opposed them to each other without good foundation, for love and reason are but the same thing. It is a precipitation of thought which is impelled to a side before fully examining every thing, but it is still a reason, and we should not and cannot wish that it were otherwise, for we would then be very disagreeable machines. Let us not therefore exclude reason from love, since they are inseparable. The poets were not right in painting Love blind; we must take off his bandage and restore to him henceforth the enjoyment of his eyes.

Souls fitted for love demand a life of action which becomes brilliant in new events. The external excitement must correspond with the internal, and this manner of living is a marvellous road to passion. Thence it is that courtiers are more successful in love than citizens, since the former are all fire and the latter lead a life in the uniformity of which there is nothing striking: a tempestuous life surprises, strikes, and penetrates.

It seems as though we had quite another soul when we love than when we do not love; we are exalted by this passion and become all greatness; the rest therefore must have proportion, otherwise this does not harmonize and is consequently disagreeable.

The pleasing and the beautiful are only the same thing; every one has his idea of it. It is of a moral beauty that I mean to speak, which consists in external words and actions. We have a rule indeed for becoming agreeable; yet the disposition of the body is necessary to it, but this cannot be acquired.

Men have taken pleasure in forming for themselves so elevated a standard of the pleasing that no one can attain it. Let us judge of it better, and say that this is simply nature with surprising facility and vivacity of mind. In love these two qualities are necessary. There must be nothing of force, and yet there must be nothing of slowness: habit gives the rest.

Respect and love should be so well proportioned as to sustain each other without love being stifled by respect.

Great souls are not those that love oftenest; it is a violent love of which I speak; an inundation of passion is needed to move them and fill them. But when they begin to love, they love much more strongly.

It is said that there are some nations more amorous than others; this is not speaking rightly, or at least it is not true in every sense.

Love consisting only in an attachment of thought, it is certain that it must be the same over all the earth. It is true that, considering it otherwise than in the thought, the climate may add something, but this is only in the body.

It is with love as with good sense; as one man believes himself to have as much mind as another, he also believes that he loves the same. Yet, they who have the most perception, love even to the most trifling things, which is not possible for others. It is necessary to be very subtle to remark this difference.

One cannot feign to love unless he is very near being a lover, or at least unless he loves in some direction; for the mind and the thoughts of love are requisite for this seeming, and how shall we find means of speaking well without this? The truth of passion is not so easily disguised as serious truth.

We must have ardor, activity, and prompt and natural warmth of mind for the former; the latter we conceal by slowness and pliancy, which it is easier to do.

When we are at a distance from the object of our love, we resolve to do or to say many things; but when we are near, we are irresolute. Whence comes this? It is because when we are at a distance reason is not so much perturbed, but is strangely so in the presence of the object: now for resolution, firmness is needed, which is destroyed by perturbation.

In love we dare not hazard, because we fear to lose every thing; it is necessary, however, to advance, but who can say how far? We tremble constantly until we have found this point. Prudence does nothing towards maintaining it when it is found.

There is nothing so embarrassing as to be a lover, and to see something in our favor without daring to believe it; we are alike opposed by hope and fear. But finally the latter becomes victorious over the other.

When we love ardently, it is always a novelty to see the person beloved. After a moment's absence, he finds a void in his heart. What happiness is it to find her again! he feels at once a cessation of anxiety.

It is necessary, however, that this love should be already far advanced; for when it is budding, and has made no progress, we feel indeed a cessation of anxiety, but others supervene.

Although troubles thus succeed each other, one is not hindered from desiring the presence of his mistress by the hope of suffering less; yet, when he sees her, he fancies that he suffers more than before. Past troubles no longer move him, the present touch him, and it is of those that touch him that he judges.

Is not a lover in this state worthy of compassion?

OF THE GEOMETRICAL SPIRIT

WE may have three principal objects in the study of truth: one to discover it when it is sought; another to demonstrate it when it is possessed; and a third, to discriminate it from the false when it is examined.

I do not speak of the first; I treat particularly of the second, and it includes the third. For if we know the method of proving the truth, we shall have, at the same time, that of discriminating it, since, in examining whether the proof that is given of it is in conformity with the rules that are understood, we shall know whether it is exactly demonstrated.

Geometry, which excels in these three methods, has explained the art of discovering unknown truths; this it is which is called *analysis,* and of which it would be useless to discourse after the many excellent works that have been written on it.

That of demonstrating truths already found, and of elucidating them in such a manner that the proof of them shall be irresistible, is the only one that I wish to give; and for this I have only to explain the method which geometry observes in it; for she teaches it perfectly by her examples, although she may produce no discourse on it. And since this art consists in two principal things, the one in proving each proposition by itself, the other in disposing all the propositions in the best order, I shall make of it two sections, of which the one will contain the rules for the conduct of geometrical, that is, methodical and perfect demonstrations; and the second will comprehend that of geometrical, that is, methodical and complete order: so that the two together will include all that will be necessary to direct reasoning, in proving and discriminating truths, which I design to give entire.

SECTION FIRST—Of the method of geometrical, that is, of methodical and perfect demonstrations.

I cannot better explain the method that should be preserved to render demonstrations convincing, than by explaining that which is observed by geometry.

But it is first necessary that I should give the idea of a method still more eminent and more complete, but which mankind could never attain; for what exceeds geometry surpasses us; and, nevertheless, something must be said of it, although it is impossible to practise it.[1]

This true method, which would form demonstrations in the highest excellence, if it were possible to arrive at it, would consist in two principal things: the one, in employing no term the meaning of which had not first been clearly explained; the other, in never advancing any proposition which could not be demonstrated by truths already known; that is, in a word, in defining every term, and in proving every proposition. But to follow the same order that I am explaining, it is necessary that I should state what I mean by *definition*.

The only definitions recognized in geometry are what the logicians call *definitions of name,* that is, the arbitrary application of names to things which are clearly designated by terms perfectly known; and it is of these alone that I speak.

Their utility and use is to elucidate and abbreviate discourse, in expressing by the single name that has been imposed what could otherwise be only expressed by several terms; so that nevertheless the name imposed remains divested of all other meaning, if it has any, having no longer any than that for which it is alone designed. Here is an example:

If we are under the necessity of discriminating numbers that are divisible equally by two from those which are not, in order to avoid the frequent repetition of this condition, a

---

[1] After this paragraph occur in the MS. the following lines, written in a finer hand, and inclosed in parenthesis:

" . . . is much more to succeed in the one than the other, and I have chosen this science to attain it only because it alone knows the true rules of reasoning, and, without stopping at the rules of syllogisms which are so natural that we cannot be ignorant of them, stops and establishes itself upon the true method of conducting reasoning in all things, which almost every one is ignorant of, and which it is so advantageous to know, that we see by experience that among equal minds and like circumstances, he who possesses geometry bears it away, and acquires a new vigor.

" I wish, therefore, to explain what demonstrations are by the example of those of geometry, which is almost the only one of the human sciences that produces infallible ones, because she alone observes the true method, whilst all the others are, through a natural necessity, in a sort of confusion, which the geometricians alone know exceedingly well how to comprehend."

On the margin of this fragment is in the MS. the following note: "That which is in small characters was hidden under a paper, the edges of which were glued, and upon which was written the article beginning: I cannot better explain, etc."—*Faugère.*

name is given to it in this manner: I call every number divisible equally by two, *an even number*.

This is a geometrical definition; because after having clearly designated a thing, namely, every member divisible equally by two, we give it a name divested of every other meaning, if it has any, in order to give it that of the thing designated.

Hence it appears that definitions are very arbitrary, and that they are never subject to contradiction; for nothing is more permissible than to give to a thing which has been clearly designated, whatever name we choose. It is only necessary to take care not to abuse the liberty that we possess of imposing names, by giving the same to two different things.

Not that this may not be permissible, provided we do not confound the consequences, and do not extend them from the one to the other.

But if we fall into this error, we can oppose to it a sure and infallible remedy: that of mentally substituting the definition in the place of the thing defined, and of having the definition always so present, that every time we speak, for example, of an even number, we mean precisely that which is divisible into two equal parts, and that these two things should be in such a degree joined and inseparable in thought, that as soon as the discourse expresses the one, the mind attaches it immediately to the other. For geometricians, and all those who proceed methodically, only impose names on things to abbreviate discourse, and not to diminish or change the idea of the things of which they are discoursing. And they pretend that the mind always supplies the full definition to the concise terms, which they only employ to avoid the confusion occasioned by the multitude of words.

Nothing more promptly and more effectually removes the captious cavils of sophists than this method, which it is necessary to have always present, and which alone suffices to banish all kinds of difficulties and equivocations.

These things being well understood, I return to the explanation of the true order, which consists, as I have said, in defining every thing and in proving every thing.

This method would certainly be beautiful, but it is abso-

lutely impossible; for it is evident that the first terms that
we wished to define would imply precedents to serve for their
explanation, and that in the same manner, the first propositions that we wished to prove would imply others which
had preceded them; and thus it is clear that we should never
reach the first.

Thus, in pushing our researches further and further, we
arrive necessarily at primitive words which can no longer be
defined, and at principles so clear that we can find no others
that can serve as a proof of them.

Hence it appears that men are naturally and immutably
impotent to treat of any science so that it may be in an absolutely complete order.

But it does not thence follow that we should abandon every
kind of order.

For there is one, and it is that of geometry, which is in
truth inferior in that it is less convincing, but not in that it
is less certain. It does not define every thing and does not
prove every thing, and it is in this that it is inferior; but it
assumes nothing but things clear and constant by natural
enlightenment, and this is why it is perfectly true, nature
sustaining it in default of discourse.

This order, the most perfect of any among men, consists
not at all in defining every thing or in demonstrating every
thing, nor in defining nothing or in demonstrating nothing,
but in adhering to this middle course of not defining things
clear and understood by all mankind, and of defining the
rest; of not proving all the things known to mankind, and
of proving all the rest. Against this order those sin alike
who undertake to define everything and to prove every
thing, and who neglect to do it in those things which are not
evident of themselves.

This is what is perfectly taught by geometry. She does
not define any of these things, *space, time, motion, number,
equality,* and similar things which exist in great number, because these terms so naturally designate the things that they
mean, to those who understand the language, that their eluci-
dation would afford more obscurity than instruction.

For there is nothing more feeble than the discourse of
those who wish to define these primitive words. What neces-

sity is there, for example, of explaining what is understood
by the word *man?* Do we not know well enough what the
thing is that we wish to designate by this term? And what
advantage did Plato think to procure us in saying that he
was a two-legged animal without feathers? As though the
idea that I have of him naturally, and which I cannot express, were not clearer and surer than that which he gives
me by his useless and even ridiculous explanation; since a
man does not lose humanity by losing the two legs, nor
does a capon acquire it by losing his feathers.

There are those who are absurd enough to explain a word
by the word itself. I know some who have defined light in
this wise: *Light is a luminary movement of luminous bodies,*
as though we could understand the words *luminary* and
luminous without the word light.[2]

We cannot undertake to define being without falling into
the same absurdity: for we cannot define a word without beginning with the word *it is,* either expressed or understood.
To define being therefore, it is necessary to say *it is,* and thus
to employ the word defined in the definition.

We see clearly enough from this that there are some words
incapable of being defined; and, if nature had not supplied
this defect by a corresponding idea which she has given to all
mankind, all our expressions would be confused; whilst
we use them with the same assurance and the same certainty
as though they were explained in a manner perfectly exempt
from ambiguities; because nature herself has given us, without words, a clearer knowledge of them than art could acquire by our explanations.

It is not because all men have the same idea of the essence
of the things that I say that it is impossible and useless to
define.

For, for example, time is of this sort. Who can define it?

[2] Pascal alludes here to Father Noël, a Jesuit, with whom he had had a
warm discussion on the subject of his *Expériences touchant le vide.* In a
letter that he wrote to Father Noël in 1647, he said: "The sentence which
precedes your closing compliments defines light in these terms: *Light* is
a *luminous motion of rays composed of lucid, that is, luminous bodies;* upon
which, I have to tell you that it seems to me that you ought first to have
defined what *luminous* is, and what a *lucid* or *luminous body* is, for till
then, I cannot understand what light is. And as we never make use in
definitions of the term of the *thing defined,* I should have difficulty in con-
forming to yours which says: Light is a luminary motion of a luminous
body."—*Faugère.*

And why undertake it, since all men conceive what is meant in speaking of time, without any further definition? Nevertheless there are many different opinions touching the essence of time. Some say that it is the movement of a created thing; others, the measure of the movement, etc. Thus it is not the nature of these things that I say is known to all; it is simply the relation between the name and the thing; so that at the expression *time,* all direct their thoughts towards the same object; which suffices to cause this term to have no need of being defined, though afterwards, in examining what time is, we come to differ in sentiment after having been led to think of it; for definitions are only made to designate the things that are named, and not to show the nature of them.

It is not because it is not permissible to call by the name of *time* the movement of a created thing; for, as I have just said, nothing is more arbitrary than definitions.

But after this definition there will be two things that will be called by the name of *time:* the one is what the whole world understands naturally by this word and what all those who speak our language call by this term; the other will be the movement of a created thing, for this will also be called by this name, according to this new definition.

It is necessary therefore to shun ambiguities and not to confound consequences. For it will not follow from this that the thing that is naturally understood by the word *time* is in fact the movement of a created thing. It has been allowable to name these two things the same; but it will not be to make them agree in nature as well as in name.

Thus, if we advance this proposition—*time is the movement of a created thing,* it is necessary to ask what is meant by this word *time,* that is, whether the usual and generally received meaning is left to it, or whether it is divested of this meaning in order to give to it on this occasion that of the movement of a created thing. For if it be stripped of all other meaning, it cannot be contradicted, and it will become an arbitrary definition, in consequence of which, as I have said, there will be two things that will have the same name. But if its ordinary meaning be left to it, and it be pretended nevertheless that what is meant by this word is the movement of a created thing, it can be contradicted. It is no longer an arbitrary definition, but a proposition that must be proved, if it is not evident of itself; and this will then be a principle or an axiom, but never a definition, since in this enunciation it is not understood that the word *time* signifies the same thing as the *movement of a created thing,* but it is understood that what is conceived by the term *time* is this supposed movement.

If I did not know how necessary it is to understand this perfectly, and how continually occasions like this, of which I give the example, happen both in familiar and scientific discourses, I should not dwell upon it. But it seems to me, by the experience that I have had from the confusion of controversies, that we cannot too fully enter into this spirit of precision, for the sake of which I write this treatise rather than the subject of which I treat in it.

For how many persons are there who fancy that they have defined time, when they have said that it is the measure of movement, leaving it, however, its ordinary meaning! And nevertheless they have made a proposition and not a definition. How many are there, in the like manner, who fancy that they have defined movement, when they have said: *Motus nec simpliciter motus, non mera potentia est, sed actus entis in potentia!* And nevertheless, if they leave to the word *movement* its ordinary meaning as they do, it is not a definition but a proposition; and confounding thus the definitions which they call *definitions of name,* which are the true arbitrary definitions permissible and geometrical, with those which they call *definitions of thing,* which, properly speaking, are not at all arbitrary definitions, but are subject to contradiction, they hold themselves at liberty to make these as well as others: and each defining the same things in his own way, by a liberty which is as unjustifiable in this kind of definitions as it is permissible in the former, they perplex every thing, and losing all order and all light, become lost themselves and wander into inextricable embarrassments.

We shall never fall into such in following the order of geometry. This judicious science is far from defining such primitive words as *space, time, motion, equality, majority, diminution, whole,* and others which every one understands.

But apart from these, the rest of the terms that this science employs are to such a degree elucidated and defined that we have no need of a dictionary to understand any of them; so that in a word all these terms are perfectly intelligible, either by natural enlightenment or by the definitions that it gives of them.

This is the manner in which it avoids all the errors that may be encountered upon the first point, which consists in defining only the things that have need of it. It makes use of it in the same manner in respect to the other point, which consists in proving the propositions that are not evident.

For, when it has arrived at the first known truths, it pauses there and asks whether they are admitted, having nothing clearer whereby to prove them; so that all that is proposed by geometry is perfectly demonstrated, either by natural enlightenment or by proofs.

Hence it comes that if this science does not define and demonstrate every thing, it is for the simple reason that this is impossible.[3]

It will perhaps be found strange that geometry does not define any of the things that it has for its principal objects: for it can neither define motion, numbers, nor space; and nevertheless these three things are those of which it treats in particular, and according to the investigation of which it takes the three different names of *mechanics, arithmetic,* and *geometry,* this last name belonging to the genus and species.

But this will not surprise us if we remark that, this admirable science only attaching itself to the simplest things, this same quality which renders them worthy of being its objects renders them incapable of being defined; so that the lack of definition is a perfection rather than a defect, since it does not come from their obscurity, but on the contrary from their extreme obviousness, which is such that though it may not have the conviction of demonstrations, it has all their certainty. It supposes therefore that we know what is the thing that is understood by the words *motion, number, space;* and

[3] Here the MS. adds in parenthesis: " (But as nature punishes all that science does not bestow, its order in truth does not give a superhuman perfection, but it has all that man can attain. It has seemed to me proper to give from the beginning of this discourse this, etc.)."—*Faugère.*

without stopping to define them to no purpose, it penetrates their nature and discovers their marvellous properties.

These three things which comprehend the whole universe, according to the words: *Deus fecit omnia in pondere, in numero, et mensura,*[4] have a reciprocal and necessary connection. For we cannot imagine motion without something that moves; and this thing being one, this unity is the origin of all numbers; and lastly, motion not being able to exist without space, we see these three things included within the first.

Time even is also comprehended in it; for motion and time are relative to each other; speed and slowness, which are the differences of motion, having a necessary relation to time.

Thus there are properties common to all these things, the knowledge of which opens the mind to the greatest marvels of nature.

The chief of these comprehends the two infinitudes which are combined in every thing: the one of greatness the other of littleness.

For however quick a movement may be, we can conceive of one still more so; and so on *ad infinitum,* without ever reaching one that would be swift to such a degree that nothing more could be added to it. And, on the contrary, however slow a movement may be, it can be retarded still more; and thus *ad infinitum,* without ever reaching such a degree of slowness that we could not thence descend into an infinite number of others, without falling into rest.

In the same manner, however great a number may be, we can conceive of a greater; and thus *ad infinitum,* without ever reaching one that can no longer be increased. And on the contrary, however small a number may be, as the hundredth or ten thousandth part, we can still conceive of a less; and so on *ad infinitum,* without ever arriving at zero or nothingness.

However great a space may be, we can conceive of a greater; and thus *ad infinitum,* without ever arriving at one which can no longer be increased. And, on the contrary, however small a space may be, we can still imagine a smaller; and so on *ad infinitum,* without ever arriving at one indivisible, which has no longer any extent.

[4] " God has made all things in weight, number and proportion."

It is the same with time. We can always conceive of a greater without an ultimate, and of a less without arriving at a point and a pure nothingness of duration.

That is, in a word, whatever movement, whatever number, whatever space, whatever time there may be, there is always a greater and a less than these: so that they all stand betwixt nothingness and the infinite, being always infinitely distant from these extremes.

All these truths cannot be demonstrated; and yet they are the foundations and principles of geometry. But as the cause that renders them incapable of demonstration is not their obscurity, but on the contrary their extreme obviousness, this lack of proof is not a defect, but rather a perfection.

From which we see that geometry can neither define objects nor prove principles; but for this single and advantageous reason that both are in an extreme natural clearness, which convinces reason more powerfully than discourse.

For what is more evident than this truth, that a number whatever it may be, can be increased—can be doubled? Again, may not the speed of a movement be doubled, and may not a space be doubled in the same manner?

And who too can doubt that a number, whatever it may be, may not be divided into a half, and its half again into another half? For would this half be a nothingness? And would these two halves, which would be two zeros, compose a number?

In the same manner, may not a movement, however slow it may be, be reduced in speed by a half, so that it will pass over the same space in double the time, and this last movement again? For would this be a perfect rest? And would these two halves of velocity, which would be two rests, compose again the first velocity?

Lastly, may not a space, however small it may be, be divided into two, and these halves again? And how could these two halves become indivisible without extent, which joined together made the former extent?

There is no natural knowledge in mankind that precedes this, and surpasses it in clearness. Nevertheless, in order that there may be examples for every thing, we find minds

excellent in all things else, that are shocked by these infinities and can in no wise assent to them.

I have never known any person who thought that a space
could not be increased. But I have seen some, very capable
in other respects, who affirmed that a space could be divided
into two indivisible parts, however absurd the idea may
seem.

I have applied myself to investigating what could be the
cause of this obscurity, and have found that it chiefly consisted in this, that they could not conceive of a continuity
divisible *ad infinitum,* whence they concluded that it was
not divisible.

It is an infirmity natural to man to believe that he possesses truth directly; and thence it comes that he is always
disposed to deny every thing that is incomprehensible to
him; whilst in fact he knows naturally nothing but falsehood, and whilst he ought to receive as true only those things
the contrary of which appear to him as false.

And hence, whenever a proposition is inconceivable, it is
necessary to suspend the judgment on it and not to deny it
from this indication, but to examine its opposite; and if this
is found to be manifestly false, we can boldly affirm the
former, however incomprehensible it may be. Let us apply
this rule to our subject.

There is no geometrician that does not believe space divisible *ad infinitum.* He can no more be such without this principle than man can exist without a soul. And nevertheless
there is none who comprehends an infinite division; and he
only assures himself of this truth by this one, but certainly
sufficient reason, that he perfectly comprehends that it is
false that by dividing a space we can reach an indivisible
part, that, is, one that has no extent.

For what is there more absurd than to pretend that by
continually dividing a space, we shall finally arrive at such
a division that on dividing it into two, each of the halves
shall remain indivisible and without any extent, and that thus
these two negations of extensions will together compose an
extent? For I would ask those who hold this idea, whether
they conceive clearly two indivisibles being brought into
contact; if this is throughout, they are only the same thing,

and consequently the two together are indivisible; and if it is not throughout, it is then but in a part; then they have parts, therefore they are not indivisible.

If they confess, as in fact they admit when pressed, that their proposition is as inconceivable as the other, they acknowledge that it is not by our capacity for conceiving these things that we should judge of their truth, since these two contraries being both inconceivable, it is nevertheless necessarily certain that one of the two is true.

But as to these chimerical difficulties, which have relation only to our weakness, they oppose this natural clearness and these solid truths: if it were true that space was composed of a certain finite number of indivisibles, it would follow that two spaces, each of which should be square, that is, equal and similar on every side, being the one the double of the other, the one would contain a number of these indivisibles double the number of the indivisibles of the other. Let them bear this consequence well in mind, and let them then apply themselves to ranging points in squares until they shall have formed two, the one of which shall have double the points of the other; and then I will make every geometrician in the world yield to them. But if the thing is naturally impossible, that is, if it is an insuperable impossibility to range squares of points, the one of which shall have double the number of the other, as I would demonstrate on the spot did the thing merit that we should dwell on it, let them draw therefrom the consequence.

And to console them for the trouble they would have in certain junctures, as in conceiving that a space may have an infinity of divisibles, seeing that these are run over in so little time during which this infinity of divisibles would be run over, we must admonish them that they should not compare things so disproportionate as is the infinity of divisibles with the little time in which they are run over: but let them compare the entire space with the entire time, and the infinite divisibles of the space with the infinite moments of the time; and thus they will find that we pass over an infinity of divisibles in an infinity of moments, and a little space in a little time; in which there is no longer the disproportion that astonished them.

Lastly, if they find it surprising that a small space has as many parts as a great one, let them understand also that they are smaller in measure, and let them look at the firmament through a diminishing glass, to familiarize themselves with this knowledge, by seeing every part of the sky in every part of the glass.

But if they cannot comprehend that parts so small that to us they are imperceptible, can be divided as often as the firmament, there is no better remedy than to make them look through glasses that magnify this delicate point to a prodigious mass; whence they will easily conceive that by the aid of another glass still more artistically cut, they could be magnified so as to equal that firmament the extent of which they admire. And thus these objects appearing to them now easily divisible, let them remember that nature can do infinitely more than art.

For, in fine, who has assured them that these glasses change the natural magnitude of these objects, instead of re-establishing, on the contrary, the true magnitude which the shape of our eye may change and contract like glasses that diminish?

It is annoying to dwell upon such trifles; but there are times for trifling.

It suffices to say to minds clear on this matter that two negations of extension cannot make an extension. But as there are some who pretend to elude this light by this marvellous answer, that two negations of extension can as well make an extension as two units, neither of which is a number, can make a number by their combination; it is necessary to reply to them that they might in the same manner deny that twenty thousand men make an army, although no single one of them is an army; that a thousand houses make a town, although no single one is a town; or that the parts make the whole, although no single one is the whole; or, to remain in the comparison of numbers, that two binaries make a quaternary, and ten tens a hundred, although no single one is such.

But it is not to have an accurate mind to confound by such unequal comparisons the immutable nature of things with their arbitrary and voluntary names, names dependent upon the caprice of the men who invented them. For it is clear that to facilitate discourse the name of *army* has been given to twenty thousand men, that of *town* to several houses, that of *ten* to ten units; and that from this liberty spring the names of *unity, binary, quaternary, ten, hundred,* different through our caprices, although these things may be in fact of the same kind by their unchangeable nature, and are all proportionate to each other and differ only in being greater or less, and although, as a result of these names, binary may not be a quaternary, nor the house a town, any more than the town is a house. But again, although a house is not a town, it is not however a negation of a town; there is a great difference between not being a thing, and being a negation of it.

For, in order to understand the thing to the bottom, it is necessary to know that the only reason why unity is not in the ranks of numbers, is that Euclid and the earliest authors who treated of arithmetic, having several properties to give that were applicable to all the numbers except unity, in order to avoid often repeating that *in all numbers except unity this condition is found,* have excluded unity from the signification of the word *number,* by the liberty which we have already said can be taken at will with definitions. Thus, if they had wished, they could in the same manner have excluded the binary and ternary, and all else that it pleased them; for we are master of these terms, provided we give notice of it; as on the contrary we may place unity when we like in the rank of numbers, and fractions in the same manner. And, in fact, we are obliged to do it in general propositions, to avoid saying constantly, that *in all numbers, as well as in unity and in fractions, such a property is found;* and it is in this indefinite sense that I have taken it in all that I have written on it.

But the same Euclid who has taken away from unity the name of number, which it was permissible for him to do, in order to make it understood nevertheless that it is not a negation, but is on the contrary of the same species, thus defines homogeneous magnitudes: *Magnitudes are said to be of the same kind, when one being multiplied several times may exceed the other;* and consequently, since unity can, being multiplied several times, exceed any number whatsoever, it is precisely of the same kind with numbers through its essence and its immutable nature, in the meaning of the same Euclid who would not have it called a number.

It is not the same thing with an indivisible in respect to an extension. For it not only differs in name, which is voluntary, but it differs in kind, by the same definition; since an indivisible, multiplied as many times as we like, is so far from being able to exceed an extension, that it can never form any thing else than a single and exclusive indivisible; which is natural and necessary, as has been already shown. And as this last proof is founded upon the definition of these two things, indivisible and extension, we will proceed to finish and perfect the demonstration.

An indivisible is that which has no part, and extension is that which has divers separate parts.

According to these definitions, I affirm that two indivisibles united do not make an extension.

For when they are united, they touch each other in some part; and thus the parts whereby they come in contact are not separate, since otherwise they would not touch each other. Now, by their definition, they have no other parts; therefore they have no separate parts; therefore they are not an extension by the definition of extension which involves the separation of parts.

The same thing will be shown of all the other indivisibles that may be brought into junction, for the same reason. And consequently an indivisible, multiplied as many times as we like, will not make an extension. Therefore it is not of the same kind as extension, by the definition of things of the same kind.

It is in this manner that we demonstrate that indivisibles are not of the same species as numbers. Hence it arises that two units may indeed make a number, because they are of the same kind; and that two indivisibles do not make an extension, because they are not of the same kind.

Hence we see how little reason there is in comparing the relation that exists between unity and numbers with that which exists between indivisibles and extension.

But if we wish to take in numbers a comparison that represents with accuracy what we are considering in extension, this must be the relation of zero to numbers; for zero is not of the same kind as numbers, since, being multiplied, it cannot exceed them: so that it is the true indivisibility of number, as indivisibility is the true zero of extension. And a like one will be found between rest and motion, and between an instant and time; for all these things are heterogeneous in their magnitudes, since being infinitely multiplied, they can never make any thing else than indivisibles, any more than the indivisibles of extension, and for the same reason. And then we shall find a perfect correspondence between these things; for all these magnitudes are divisible *ad infinitum,* without ever falling into their indivisibles, so that they all hold a middle place between infinity and nothingness.

Such is the admirable relation that nature has established between these things, and the two marvellous infinities which she has proposed to mankind, not to comprehend, but to admire; and to finish the consideration of this by a last remark, I will add that these two infinites, although infinitely different, are notwithstanding relative to each other, in such a manner that the knowledge of the one leads necessarily to the knowledge of the other.

For in numbers, inasmuch as they can be continually augmented, it absolutely follows that they can be continually diminished, and this clearly; for if a number can be multiplied to 100,000, for example, 100,000th part can also be taken from it, by dividing it by the same number by which it is multiplied; and thus every term of augmentation will become a term of division, by changing the whole into a fraction. So that infinite augmentation also includes necessarily infinite division.

And in space the same relation is seen between these two contrary infinites; that is, that inasmuch as a space can be infinitely prolonged, it follows that it may be infinitely diminished, as appears in this example: If we look through a glass at a vessel that recedes continually in a straight line. it is evident that any point of the vessel observed will continually advance by a perpetual flow in proportion as the ship recedes. Therefore if the course of the vessel is extended *ad infinitum,* this point will continually recede; and yet it will never reach that point in which the horizontal ray carried from the eye to the glass shall fall, so that it will constantly approach it without ever reaching it, unceasingly dividing the space which will remain under this horizontal point without ever arriving at it. From which is seen the necessary conclusion that is drawn from the infinity of the extension of the course of the vessel to the infinite and infinitely minute division of this little space remaining beneath this horizontal point.

Those who will not be satisfied with these reasons, and will persist in the belief that space is not divisible *ad infinitum,* can make no pretensions to geometrical demonstrations, and although they may be enlightened in other things, they will be very little in this; for one can easily be a very capable man and a bad geometrician.

But those who clearly perceive these truths will be able to admire the grandeur and power of nature in this double infinity that surrounds us on all sides, and to learn by this marvellous consideration to know themselves, in regarding themselves thus placed between infinitude and a negation of extension, between an infinitude and a negation of number, between an infinitude and a negation of movement, between an infinitude and a negation of time. From which we may learn to estimate ourselves at our true value, and to form reflections which will be worth more than all the rest of geometry itself.

I have thought myself obliged to enter into this long discussion for the benefit of those who, not comprehending at first this double infinity, are capable of being persuaded of it. And although there may be many who have sufficient enlightenment to dispense with it, it may nevertheless happen that this discourse which will be necessary to the one will not be entirely useless to the other.

PREFACE TO THE TREATISE ON VACUUM

THE respect that we bear to antiquity is at the present day carried to such a point on subjects in which it ought to have less weight, that oracles are made of all its thoughts and mysteries, even of its obscurities; that novelties can no longer be advanced without peril, and that the text of an author suffices to destroy the strongest reasons...................

Not that it is my intention to correct one error by another, and not to esteem the ancients at all because others have esteemed them too much.

I do not pretend to banish their authority in order to exalt reasoning alone, although others have sought to establish their authority alone to the prejudice of reasoning...........

To make this important distinction with care, it is necessary to consider that the former depend solely on memory and are purely historical, having nothing for their object except to know what the authors have written; the latter depend solely on reasoning and are entirely dogmatic, having for their object to seek and discover concealed truths.

Those of the former kind are limited, inasmuch as the books in which they are contained......................

It is according to this distinction that we must regulate differently the extent of this respect. The respect that we should have for ....

In matters in which we only seek to know what the authors have written, as in history, geography, jurisprudence, languages, and especially in theology; and in fine in all those which have for their principle either simple facts or divine or human institutions, we must necessarily have recourse to their books, since all that we can know of them is therein contained; hence it is evident that we can have full knowledge of them, and that it is not possible to add any thing thereto.

If it is in question to know who was the first king of the French; in what spot geographers place the first meridian; what words are used in a dead language, and all things of this nature; what other means than books can guide us to them? And who can add any thing new to what they teach us, since we wish only to know what they contain?

Authority alone can enlighten us on these. But the subject in which authority has the principal weight is theology, because there she is inseparable from truth, and we know it only through her: so that to give full certainty to matters incomprehensible to reason, it suffices to show them in the sacred books; as to show the uncertainty of the most probable things, it is only necessary to show that they are not included therein; since its principles are superior to nature and reason, and since, the mind of man being too weak to attain them by its own efforts, he cannot reach these lofty conceptions if he be not carried thither by an omnipotent and superhuman power.

It is not the same with subjects that fall under the senses and under reasoning; authority here is useless; it belongs to reason alone to know them. They have their separate rights: there the one has all the advantage, here the other reigns in turn. But as subjects of this kind are proportioned to the grasp of the mind, it finds full liberty to extend them; its inexhaustible fertility produces continually, and its inventions may be multiplied altogether without limit and without interruption....................................

It is thus that geometry, arithmetic, music, physics, medicine, architecture, and all the sciences that are subject to experiment and reasoning, should be augmented in order to become perfect. The ancients found them merely outlined by those who preceded them; and we shall leave them to those who will come after us in a more finished state than we received them.

As their perfection depends on time and pains, it is evident that although our pains and time may have acquired less than their labors separate from ours, both joined together must nevertheless have more effect than each one alone.

The clearing up of this difference should make us pity the blindness of those who bring authority alone as proof in physical matters, instead of reasoning or experiments; and inspire us with horror for the wickedness of others who make use of reasoning alone in theology, instead of the authority of the Scripture and the Fathers. We must raise the courage of those timid people who dare invent nothing in physics, and confound the insolence of those rash persons who produce novelties in theology. Nevertheless the misfortune of the age is such, that we see many new opinions in theology, unknown to all antiquity, maintained with obstinacy and received with applause; whilst those that are produced in physics, though small in number, should, it seems, be convicted of falsehood as soon as they shock already received opinions in the slightest degree; as if the respect that we have for the ancient philosophers were a duty, and that which we bear to the most ancient of the Fathers solely a matter of courtesy! I leave it to judicious persons to remark the importance of this abuse which perverts the order of the sciences with so much injustice; and I think that there will be few who will not wish that this *liberty*[1] might be applied to other matters, since new inventions are infallible errors in the matters[2] which we profane with impunity; and since they are absolutely necessary for the perfection of so many other subjects incomparably lower, which nevertheless we dare not approach.

Let us divide our credulity and suspicion with more justice, and limit this respect we have for the ancients. As reason gives it birth, she ought also to measure it; and let us consider that if they had continued in this restraint of not daring to add any thing to the knowledge which they had received, or if those of their times had made the like difficulty in receiving the novelties which they offered them, they would have deprived themselves and their posterity of the fruit of their inventions.

As they only made use of that which had been bequeathed to them as a means whereby to gain more, and as this happy daring opened to them the way to great things, we should take that which they acquired in the same manner, and by their example, make of it the means and not the end of our study, and thus strive while imitating to surpass them.

For what is more unjust than to treat our ancestors with more deference than they showed to those who preceded them, and to have for them that inviolable respect which they have only merited from us because they had not the like for those who possessed the same advantage over them? ....

The secrets of nature are concealed; although she is continually working, we do not always discover her effects: time reveals them from age to age, and although always alike in herself she is not always alike known.

[1] The word here underlined, which we restore by conjecture, is blank in the MS.—*Faugère.*
[2] Here seems to be needed *theological matters.*—*Ibid.*

The experiments that give us the knowledge of these secrets are multiplied continually; and as they are the sole principles of physics, the consequences are multiplied in proportion.

It is in this manner that we may at the present day adopt different sentiments and new opinions, without despising *the ancients and*[3] without ingratitude, since the first knowledge which they have given us has served as a stepping-stone to our own, and since in these advantages we are indebted to them for our ascendency over them; because being raised by their aid to a certain degree, the slightest effort causes us to mount still higher, and with less pains and less glory we find ourselves above them. Thence it is that we are enabled to discover things which it was impossible for them to perceive. Our view is more extended, and although they knew as well as we all that they could observe in nature, they did not, nevertheless, know it so well, and we see more than they.

Yet it is marvellous in what manner their sentiments are revered. It is made a crime to contradict them and an act of treason to add to them, as though they had left no more truths to be known.

Is not this to treat unworthily the reason of man and to put it on a level with the instinct of animals, since we take away the principal difference between them, which is that the effects of reason accumulate without ceasing, whilst instinct remains always in the same state? The cells of the bees were as correctly measured a thousand years ago as to-day, and each formed a hexagon as exactly the first time as the last. It is the same with all that the animals produce by this occult impulse. Nature instructs them in proportion as necessity impels them; but this fragile science is lost with the wants which give it birth: as they received it without study, they have not the happiness of preserving it; and every time it is given them it is new to them, since the . . . nature having for her object nothing but the maintenance of animals in a limited order of perfection, she inspires them with this necessary science . . . always

---

[3] Break of two or three words in the MS. We supply them by the words *italicized.—Faugère.*

the same, lest they may fall into decay, and does not permit them to add to it, lest they should exceed the limits that she has prescribed to them. It is not the same with man, who is formed only for infinity. He is ignorant at the earliest age of his life; but he is instructed unceasingly in his progress; for he derives advantage, not only from his own experience, but also from that of his predecessors; since he always retains in his memory the knowledge which he himself has once acquired, and since he has that of the ancients ever present in the books which they have bequeathed to him. And as he preserves this knowledge, he can also add to it easily; so that men are at the present day in some sort in the same condition in which those ancient philosophers would have been found, could they have survived till the present time, adding to the knowledge which they possessed that which their studies would have acquired by the aid of so many centuries. Thence it is that by an especial prerogative, not only does each man advance from day to day in the sciences, but all mankind together make continual progress in proportion as the world grows older, since the same thing happens in the succession of men as in the different ages of single individuals. So that the whole succession of men, during the course of many ages, should be considered as a single man who subsists forever and learns continually, whence we see with what injustice we respect antiquity in philosophers; for as old age is that period of life most remote from infancy, who does not see that old age in this universal man ought not to be sought in the times nearest his birth, but in those the most remote from it? Those whom we call ancient were really new in all things, and properly constituted the infancy of mankind; and as we have joined to their knowledge the experience of the centuries which have followed them, it is in ourselves that we should find this antiquity that we revere in others.

They should be admired for the results which they derived from the very few principles they possessed, and they should be excused for those in which they failed rather from the lack of the advantage of experience than the strength of reasoning.

For were they not excusable in the idea that they enter-

tained of the *milky way*, when, the weakness of their vision
not having yet received the assistance of art, they attributed
this color to a greater density in that part of the heavens
which reflected the light more strongly? But would we not
be inexcusable for remaining in the same opinion, now that,
by the aid of the advantages procured us by the telescope,
we have discovered in it an infinite number of small stars,
whose more abundant splendor has revealed to us the true
cause of this whiteness!

Had they not also cause for saying that all corruptible
bodies were inclosed within the orbit of the moon, when,
during the course of so many ages they had not yet re-
marked either corruption or generation outside of this space?

But ought we not to be assured of the contrary, when the
whole world has manifestly beheld comets kindle and disappear far beyond the limits of that sphere?

In the same way, in respect to vacuum, they had a right to
say that nature would not suffer it, since all their experiments
had always made them remark that she abhorred, and could
not suffer it.

But if the modern experiments had been known to them,
perhaps they would have found cause for affirming what
they found cause for denying, for the reason that vacuum
had not yet appeared. Thus, in the judgment they formed
that nature would not suffer vacuum, they only heard nature
spoken of in the condition in which they knew her; since, to
speak in general terms, it would not have been sufficient to
have seen it constantly in a hundred cases, a thousand, or any
other number, however great it may have been; since, if a
single case remained unexamined, this alone would suffice
to prevent the general definition, and if a single one was
contrary, this alone......................................
For in all matters the proof of which consists in experiments,
and not in demonstrations, we can make no universal assertion, except by the general enumeration of all the parts and
all the different cases. Thus it is that when we say that the
diamond is the hardest of all bodies, we mean of all the
bodies with which we are acquainted, and we neither can nor
ought to comprehend in this assertion those with which we
are not acquainted; and when we say that gold is the heaviest

of all bodies, we should be presumptuous to comprehend in this general proposition those which have not yet come to our knowledge, although it is not impossible that they may exist in nature.

In the same manner, when the ancients affirmed that nature would not suffer a vacuum, they meant that she would not suffer it in any of the experiments they had seen, and they could not, without temerity, comprehend in it those which had not come to their knowledge. Had they done so, they would doubtless have drawn from them the same conclusions, and would, by their acknowledgment, have sanctioned them by this antiquity which it is sought at present to make the sole principle of the sciences.

Thus it is that, without contradicting them, we can affirm the contrary of what they say; and, whatever authority, in fine, this antiquity may have, truth should always have more, although newly discovered, since she is always older than all the opinions that we have had of her, and it would be showing ourselves ignorant of her nature to imagine that she may have begun to be at the time when she began to be known.

NEW FRAGMENT OF THE TREATISE ON VACUUM

WHAT is there more absurd than to say that inanimate bodies have passions, fears, horrors; that insensible bodies, without life, and even incapable of it, may have passions which presuppose a soul at least sensitive to experience them? Besides, if the object of this horror were a vacuum, what is there in a vacuum that could make them afraid? What is there meaner and more ridiculous?

This is not all; if they have in themselves a principle of motion to shun a vacuum, have they arms, legs, muscles, nerves?